Data Analytics for Organisational Development

Data Analytics for Organisational Development

Unleashing the Potential of Your Data

Uwe H. Kaufmann
Amy B.C. Tan

WILEY

Library of Congress Cataloging-in-Publication Data:

Names: Kaufmann, Uwe H., author. | Tan, Amy B. C., author.
Title: Data analytics for organisational development : unleashing the
    potential of your data / Uwe H. Kaufmann, Amy BC Tan.
Description: Chichester, West Sussex, United Kingdom : Wiley, 2021. |
    Includes index.
Identifiers: LCCN 2021012021 (print) | LCCN 2021012022 (ebook) | ISBN
    9781119758334 (hardback) | ISBN 9781119758310 (adobe pdf) | ISBN
    9781119758372 (epub) | ISBN 9781119758327 (obook)
Subjects: LCSH: Business enterprises—Data processing. | Organizational
    change.
Classification: LCC HF5351 .K3237 2021 (print) | LCC HF5351 (ebook) | DDC
    658/.0557—dc23
LC record available at https://lccn.loc.gov/2021012021
LC ebook record available at https://lccn.loc.gov/2021012022

SKY7DC90ED7-E248-4F32-9CDF-F499A6D52020_062221

To our beloved children, Nicole and Christopher, Priscilla and Pearl.

Contents

Foreword

Managerial decisions are still often based on 'gut feelings' instead of clear facts. While this can be helpful depending on your intuition, more often than not, for most of us this doesn't yield the most optimal results. In today's world, tools that enable leaders and other change agents to make evidence-based decisions are increasingly available. Yet many do not have the knowledge to implement these cutting-edge tools in order to be able to put forward necessary organisational changes. If you are among these people, who wish to turn raw data into beneficial information for change management and organisational development, then this book is for you.

We met the authors Amy Tan and Dr Uwe Kaufmann the first time at a conference in the Singapore University of Technology and Design (SUTD). Due to our common interest in helping organisations and their members excel, we connected easily. In particular, we noted a clear match between their consulting fields on organisational effectiveness and our previous consulting experience and research on understanding the enablers of effective organisational change. Subsequently, Amy came to pursue her (part-time) PhD with our Change Management & Organizational Behaviour (CMOB) research group at the University of Twente, where she's applying what this book is about, which is using data for understanding the drivers for effective employee behaviours. Dr Uwe Kaufmann brings abundant, international experience in applying data – for instance, through Lean Six Sigma – to advance customer experience and work processes.

This book provides hands-on tips on how to harness and unleash the potential of data to support managers and leaders in decision-making, change management and organisational development. The authors have captured this essence by providing in this book real-life cases that they have personally experienced from working in various private and public organisations. They guide you through these cases step-by-step, following a plausible data analytics cycle that is applicable in any situation where a business question needs to be answered using data. This book is also filled with practical short assignments for learners to test their understanding after studying a chapter.

Organisational transformation requires agile and unconventional thinking, including by its architects. Using 'hard' data to support 'soft' change processes may be considered as such. We regard Amy and Uwe as the most versatile and professional change consulting duo around the globe – they will help you learn very many things of importance to your daily life at work.

Prof. Dr Celeste Wilderom

Dr Desirée van Dun

University of Twente, the Netherlands

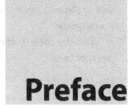

Preface

Do you like statistics?

If you feel like affirming this question, you belong to a minority, in our opinion. In this case, you will hopefully recognise many familiar tools and methods in this book. You may discover some new insights into their application and our point of view from the perspective of organisational development.

If you feel like answering our question in the negative, you may not want to put away our book too fast. We know how you feel, because we were in a similar situation to you, before we had to learn to deal with data as part of our work. Our job was then, and still is, organisational development in very different organisations with manifold cultural backgrounds.

Here is more about that:

After my study of engineering and passing all exams with nice results, I had put away statistics as a part of my life that was over and done with. Even though I always feel quite comfortable when it comes to dealing with numbers, the importance and usefulness of statistics has not been too clear to me during my studies. While I could easily make use of Gauss' normal distribution in control charts for the benefit of customers of a production line in a modern German engineering plant, it was only after joining General Electric (GE), that I was taught, explained to, and coached how an ANOVA could add value to a typical banking environment.

At GE, data analytics has been used for improving the organisation, better serving customers and employees, and hence increasing efficiency and profitability. General statements like "With this new method we will be able to increase our profitability," were no longer accepted. "How much increase of productivity can we safely assume? What is the risk for this investment going to waste?" were questions that could only be answered with data-based, statistically proven answers.

> During my hard and application-oriented education at GE, I learned that the use of data without the support of the appropriate statistical tools is usually inadequate.
>
> With the case studies shown and explained in this book, I wish to pass on this perspective.
>
> Uwe H. Kaufmann

> I have been in Human Resources the longest time of my professional life. At first as the director of HR for an insurance company, then as director of people matters for a ministry and lastly in the same position with the Organising Committee of the first Youth Olympic Games. I grew up with the understanding that data analytics for people in HR means calculating averages and percentages.
>
> Only in 2002, when I was tasked by my CEO to take up the role of a Black Belt for some insurance-related and some HR projects, I got in touch with serious data analytics. To be honest, at the beginning I was not really excited to take up this role. Only after a very tough training by Uwe H. Kaufmann and his persistent coaching, was I able to appreciate that the new methods and tools would not only benefit my HR function but also improve processes in many other functions of our organisation.
>
> And of course, an HR director who can roll up her sleeves to study activities and increase efficiency in any part of the organisation does really gain acceptance throughout the firm.
>
> Our organisational development activities have been data-driven and supported with statistical methods ever since.
>
> Therefore, I have really benefitted from the training to become a Black Belt – a Lean Six Sigma Black Belt is a first-class data scientist – and changed my perspective on and approach to my work within and outside HR.
>
> Organisational development without data analytics will not work.
>
> Amy B.C. Tan

Together we have written this book because of our career and its close connection between organisational development and data science. This comprehensive perspective is the key to your success in your organisation, as it was and still is for us.

You as leader or manager or supervisor in any function have the non-delegable side-job – often even the main job – as organisational developer, because you have responsibility for business results, for resource utilisation, for customer satisfaction and for engaging your staff. Nowadays, you have more data accessible at your fingertips about all activities and matters of daily business life than ever before. And you have enormously powerful hard- and software available for acquiring, converting, cleaning, and analysing this data to transform it into information beneficial for your organisation.

Use this opportunity!

If you acquire the necessary knowledge and skills, it will not only give your organisation an edge in the fast-changing market but also yourself. With our cases it should be possible for you to follow through typical applications of data analytics in many different organisational development situations and to translate the learned steps into your own environment.

We wish you all the best on the journey to unleash the potential in your data and to be a step ahead of the competition.

Amy B.C. Tan   Uwe H. Kaufmann

About the Authors

Uwe H. Kaufmann

Dr Uwe H. Kaufmann is the founder of the Centre for Organisational Effectiveness. As consultant and coach with many years of experience, his passion lies in supporting organisations to improve their effectiveness. Not only does he apply modern operations management techniques like Business Process Reengineering, Lean, Six Sigma, Data Science or Innovation in his work with clients but he also knows that processes do not run without the right people who are trained, skilled, motivated and engaged.

His clients include many multinational organisations in various industries. Trained as an engineer and experienced in service organisations like GE Capital, Aon and TÜV Rheinland, Uwe is able to work in very diverse industries effectively. Since 2002, he has spent about half of his professional life working with government ministries and agencies in Singapore and Asia.

Uwe is a German national who speaks English and Russian. He is a permanent resident of Singapore, with four children and nine grandchildren . . . and counting.

Email: Uwe@COE-Partners.com
LinkedIn: https://www.linkedin.com/in/uwe-h-kaufmann-a0657a5/
Website: www.COE-Partners.com

Amy B.C. Tan

Amy has more than 20 years of experience in human resource management and organisational development in various industries. She has held senior leadership positions with Nokia, Aon, Ministry of Manpower and the Singapore 2010 Youth Olympic Games Organising Committee. She has led the transformation of the HR functions and several organisational development initiatives for these organisations.

Amy is also a certified Lean Six Sigma Black Belt, and an accredited practitioner in executive coaching and psychological instruments such as MBTI (Myers Briggs Type Indicator®), DiSC, Harrison Assessment and Belbin Team Roles.

Amy Tan is partner and director at the Centre for Organisational Effectiveness, a business advisory firm operating out of Singapore with clients in private and public organisations in South-East-Asia and beyond.

Email: Amy@COE-Partners.com
LinkedIn: https://www.linkedin.com/in/amy-bc-tan-4375991/
Website: www.COE-Partners.com

Introduction: Why Data Analytics is Important

"In God we trust, all others bring data."
W. Edwards Deming (Ratcliffe, 2018)

Everyone remembers the troublesome process of raising a request with IT or the vendor for a small data analysis task and waiting days or even weeks before getting the result. More often than not, the result was not presented in the most useful way or just raised a follow-up question which required new data to answer, new requests for IT or the vendor. For decades, managers have relied on this kind of process because they had no choice. This process has a fundamental flaw: if you want to make timely decisions, lagging and outdated information cannot be used. Hence, timely decisions had to be done without having the foundation of real-time data and sometimes based on gut feeling.

Times have changed. The quantity of available data in all functions of any organisation is growing daily. The access to this data gets easier and easier. Nearly everyone can acquire the data necessary to run their own analyses. And almost everyone has a formidable computer with powerful analytics tools immediately available. The question now is, how to turn the data into business-relevant information for making the right decisions when needed (Data Never Sleeps, 2020).

Hence, it is time to ensure that the right data are collected in an appropriate way, screened, transformed, and analysed using valid methods in a manner that delivers business-relevant information that is turned into intelligence for making appropriate decisions for business success.

Data analytics is the process of collecting, processing, and analysing data with the objective of discovering useful information, suggesting conclusions, and supporting problem solving as well as decision making (Wikipedia, n.d.; Payne, 1976).

 "Data Analytics is a business practice every Manager should be familiar with".

Data analytics encompasses the main components: **descriptive analytics** (post-mortem analysis), **predictive analytics**, and **prescriptive analytics**.

Big Data is characterised by its three Vs, Volume, Velocity, Variety (Russom, 2011). It is too voluminous and complex for conventional hard- and software to handle. At the beginning of the 2000s, the volume of available data went up exponentially and handling such data was reserved to a few companies and organisations who were relying on the analysis of data to stay in business.

Nowadays however, computers with huge data storage and handling capacity are available to nearly any organisation, be it by installing hardware and software inhouse or by renting external capacity. Two trends seem to be the result of this change in the IT environment. Firstly, more and more organisations have the means and see the need to collect data about their operational environment. Secondly, these organisations are widening the scope of their data analytics activities to include all functions.

Not only is there a move from Big Data analytics to analytics of any kind of data, there is also a healthy trend towards involving all levels of management and even junior staff into this, not so new, field of information management. Progressive managers are familiar with the types of data available and with the trends, shifts, or other patterns in their data and can use them for decision making.

The former speciality data analytics is gaining popularity amongst all managers of an organisation. Hence, it is time to ensure that the right data are collected in an appropriate way, screened, transformed, and analysed using valid methods in a manner that delivers business-relevant information that is turned into intelligence that prepares appropriate decisions for business success.

 "The ability to take data – to be able to understand it, to process it, to extract value from it, to visualize it, to communicate it – that is going to be a hugely important skill in the next decades."

Google's Chief Economist Dr Hal R. Varian (2009)

Why This Book Has Been Written

To be very honest, I did not like statistics very much. After I covered statistics during my engineering study, I made sure I passed all the tests and exams and phew . . . never again.

After joining General Electric (GE) in the 1990s, I had to relearn statistics. At GE, acquiring knowledge in statistics was purpose driven, i.e., it was real business problems at hand I had to solve using numbers. Consequentially, I started to gain some degree of interest for maths and stats.

As the following examples testify, having the numbers is good but not enough. In addition, we need to ensure the data are properly collected, cleaned, and analysed before making any decision.

> *Some years ago, the director of a blood bank came back from a meeting with other blood bank heads. She was not happy because she had the chance to compare certain blood bank performance indicators with others and recognised that her own blood bank was obviously wasting more blood products than some other blood banks. She was talking about bags with platelets that were taken from blood donors, tested, and then disposed of because they did not meet the quality standards. By her criteria, this kind of situation was not acceptable.*

> *A team was set up to investigate the root causes for the wastage of the most precious blood products. After data collection and some basic analysis, it became clear that the blood products were not of lower quality than in other countries. The root cause was in the process of evaluating the quality of blood bags – the data collection.*

> *This case example is explained later in this book.*

 "Having wrong data is worse than having no data at all".

This case alone generated some life-long learning that we wish to turn into recommendations:

> *Firstly, **do not trust numbers blindly**. Even numbers that are produced by a computer can be wrong, biased, or otherwise made useless. Check how these numbers were generated and how they got into the computer in the first place.*

> *Secondly, before you perform any data analytics, ensure that the **data are collected following a proper procedure**. Therefore, this book does not start with data analysis. It starts where the collection of the data is thought about and designed.*

> *Thirdly, like the head of the blood bank with her very **powerful business case**, confirm that your data analytics serves a purpose, a need the people with whom you work know, understand, and share. Only with this need, business case, can your data analytics be more than playing with numbers.*

The following chapters elaborate the use of data analytics to solve business problems, to make critical decisions, and to drive organisational strategy. We will identify some typical pitfalls and remedies in the process.

At the moment, there are numerous Data Analytics courses available. Interestingly, many of them have similar titles to Data Analytics for HR Professionals or for Customer Relationship Management. This book takes a wider scope and shows the application of data analytics in any organisational situation, where the proper use of data is critical. Therefore, we call it "Data Analytics for Organisational Development: Unleashing the Potential of Your Data".

This book is written with the intention to close a well-known gap mentioned by Amy Gallo (Gallo, 2018). Every manager should know four powerful analytics concepts in order to be informed about his organisation and to make data-based decisions. These concepts are in no way new. However, they gain more importance with the increased amount of data available and the apparent need – and the chance – to turn this data into business-relevant information. This is supported by the availability of a multitude of easy-to-handle tools for data analysis and data visualisation.

These tools can only be used by managers if these managers understand the basics of data analytics from data acquisition to data analysis. Therefore, as identified by Gallo (2018), managers need to know the basic concepts.

These concepts are randomised controlled experiments, hypothesis testing, regression analysis, and statistical significance.

Randomised controlled experiments include data collection techniques such as any kind of surveys, pilot studies, field experiments, and lab research. Instead of outsourcing such services to specialists and relying on them analysing the results and developing recommendations, it would be beneficial for managers to understand data analytics. This knowledge would certainly help draw customised conclusions for the organisation; conclusions an outsider cannot easily draw. Experiments also comprise testing new routines or products on their performance. Experimenting with processes is a powerful way of improving the output whilst observing and changing settings at the same time in a controlled way.

Hypothesis testing contains statistical tools that compare stratified business-relevant data and answer the question for the "better one" including the inherent risk of this decision being wrong. Hypothesis tests find their application in all units of any organisation. Analysing survey results uses hypothesis tests to answer questions like "Is there a difference between last year's and this year's rating?" or "Did Department A perform better than Department B?" The result of a hypothesis test can be much more than just "Yes" or "No". Hypothesis tests always inform about a risk that comes with making a decision; a risk for making a wrong decision. Many hypothesis tests even give an indication as to what the minimum difference or minimum improvement is, which leads to much better decisions based on the impact of a change or improvement. "What is the minimum improvement if we buy our supplies from Supplier B compared to Supplier A?" can be answered with hypothesis tests.

Regression analysis comprises statistical tools that are used for similar tasks as hypothesis tests. Whilst hypothesis testing usually answers questions about the relationship between two variables, regression models may include a large number of variables at the same time. With this, the interaction between multiple drivers (independent variables) for the same result (dependent variable) can be analysed, which is less effective with hypothesis tests. Hence, regression models help explain complex relationships between many variables at the same time. Additionally, these tools are often applied in predictive statistics, i.e., to use existing data for forecasting the behaviour of machines, devices, organisational units, and even the workforce.

The aforementioned groups of methods are based on one important concept: **statistical significance**. This often-misunderstood concept is the backbone of all statistics, the backbone of all data analytics. Statistical significance informs about the risk one is to take when making a business decision based on data analytics.

In statistics, "never" and "always" do not exist; "0% probability" and "100% probability" are usually not the results of randomised, controlled experiments, hypothesis tests, or regression. Most likely, the result of an analysis lies somewhere in between. Then, it is up to the manager to make a smart, informed, and data-based choice. Understanding the concept of significance is key on the way to a quality decision.

How This Book Is Structured

As this book is about application of data analytics for organisational design, the cases discussed later discuss different data analytics situations in any domain of the value chain of an organisation (Figure 0.1).

Under the **Customer** domain, we cover collection, processing, and analysis of customer-related data. This includes survey data from different customer environments and data measuring the "moment of truth", the moment when the customer experiences the product or service offered.

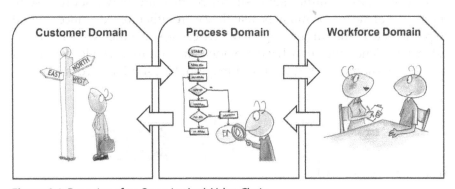

Figure 0.1 Domains of an Organisation's Value Chain

The **Process domain (Operations domain)** includes gathering data from many different operational processes and turning the data into critical information for decision making.

The **Workforce** domain offers ideas for handling organisational data that are used to draw conclusions about different workforce related aspects, be it workforce planning, recruitment, engagement, development, or attrition amongst others.

For each case, we follow through all steps from the questions, hypotheses, or business cases through all stages of data analytics to reach the right decision. The steps mentioned in the following chapters are (Figure 0.2) Formulating a Business Question, Performing Data Acquisition, Conducting Data Preparation, Executing Data Analysis, and Making a Business Decision.

Business Question

In this first step, the business-related issue has to be clearly identified. And, it has to be translated into an indicator, a Key Performance Indicator (KPI) that makes the issue measurable. Better still, this indicator is known to and is being observed by management members, i.e., it is important to someone.

Data Acquisition

There is a multitude of ways to collect data to answer the Business Question. It is usually necessary to validate the method of data collection to ensure useful data for analysis, i.e., data that is representative, reproducible, and accurate enough to provide sufficient information for answering the Business Question. There are statistical tools that help identify potential problems within the data collection process.

Data Preparation

Even if the method of data collection is proven and the instrument is statistically accepted, it can still be that data is not useful.

In surveys, for example, some survey participants may not give useful input. Part of the reason might be that they were either forced or incentivised to participate in the survey. In general, we can assume they were not interested in it. Hence, they may have provided valid input to a well-established survey questionnaire, but the input may not be useful. Or worse yet, the

Figure 0.2 Steps of a Data Analytics Case

input could spoil the subsequent analysis. Such input could be random rating numbers or the same rating numbers for all questions or statements.

Therefore, data preparation is necessary to find and omit such input to feed only data into the analysis that is really value added.

Data preparation also includes formatting the data so that it can be used by the preferred analysis software. More often than not, downloaded data from a system is not in the right format to be fed into the analysis software, Excel for example. However, in most cases data can be reorganised, reformatted, or transformed so that the software can handle it.

Analysis software will not always stop working because of wrongly formatted data. In worst cases, it might just work and produce invalid results.

Data Analysis

Generally, data analysis is carried out in a graphical and statistical way. Usually, both are necessary to ensure proper conclusions. Additionally, graphical analysis may be needed for visualising data and storytelling.

However, graphical analysis without statistical support may lead to poor decisions. This is the same when running statistical analysis without graphical support.

Hence, all data analyses should be done in a two-step approach. Firstly, one or more graphs should be plotted to visualise the data. This visualisation alone may have the power to drive the decision. Secondly, however, it is a good practice to support the graphical analysis with statistics.

For the analysis of data, a variety of tools is available. The selection of the appropriate tool depends on the business question that needs to be answered, the type of data collected and their characteristics. The stratifying factor that drives a decision is usually called "X". The resulting outcome is usually called "Y".

When, for example, the rejection rate of a product is compared between suppliers A and B, then supplier signifies the independent variable X whereas rejection rate denotes the dependent variable Y. Almost all data analytics tasks fit this structure. The application of tools depends on the data type found in X and Y.

Whilst the application of appropriate graphical (Table 0.1) and statistical tools (Table 0.2) will be demonstrated, the tools will not be explained in detail. Supplier, for example, is a discrete X and rejection rate is a discrete Y that is generated by counting satisfied customers and dissatisfied customers. Hence, the upper left field in Table 0.2 is applied. Since we have only two categories, Supplier A and Supplier B in X, the appropriate statistical tool would be a Two-Proportion-Test.

These tables will be referred to in the following cases to select the applicable graphical and statistical tools.

Table 0.1 Graphical Analysis Tools for Various Data Type Situations

		X	
		Discrete	**Continuous**
	Discrete	Bar Charts, Pie Charts,	Probability Plots Reversed Stratified Frequency Plots
Y	**Continuous**	Stratified Frequency Plots	Scatter Plots

Table 0.2 Statistical Analysis Tools for Various Data Type Situations

		X	
		Discrete	**Continuous**
	Discrete	Proportion-Tests	Logistic Regression
Y	**Continuous**	Parametric and Non-Parametric Tests for Central Tendency and Variance	Linear and Non-Linear Regression
		Hypothesis Tests	**Regression**

Business Decision

Very often, data analysis produces results that are hard for staff, who are not trained in data science, to understand. A "p-value", for example, is a key output of many statistical tools but may not be easily understood.

However, the translation of an analysis output like "p-value = 0.03" into a result like "The risk of wasting our money by buying from the more expensive Supplier A is only 3%" changes the conversation about data science.

It is no longer the case of relying on the Data Analyst or Data Scientist to make this translation. Management should understand the basics of data science in order to turn data into information and to draw appropriate conclusions.

Every case presented in this book is based on a real client case. However, to protect our clients, we have taken out names and have amended all data.

What Tools Are Used

Our intention was to provide a reference book that learners can follow step by step. In order to do this popular software is used. In our work with our clients we realised their requirements for the software they wished to use:

> ***Software must be easily available.*** *Nearly everyone in the world has a version of Microsoft Office on the computer. An integral part of this is MS Excel. MS Excel includes many functions that help conduct most of the data acquisition, data preparation, and data analysis tasks described in this book. Some users are not aware of the add-in "**Analysis ToolPak**" that adds even more tools into the MS Excel environment. We will fix that.*

MS Power BI extends the MS Office environment with potent and interactive visualisation and business intelligence facilities. MS Power BI offers data warehouse, data preparation and data discovery capabilities for building dynamic collaborative dashboards. It is available for many MS Office users for free.

R is a programming language for statistical computing and graphics. R Studio offers a user interface and development environment for R. Both software packages are available for free.

Software must be easy to use. *MS Excel is a software package that many people have used before. This means analysts can work with a familiar environment, just adding some new tools. Nearly the same applies to MS Power BI. It might be new to many analysts, but then again it has Microsoft's user interface and many functions that are adapted from MS Excel. The learning curve for MS Power BI should be very steep but short.*

R is a programming language and free software environment for statistical computing and graphics. R is widely used by statisticians and data miners for developing software for wrangling and analysis of data (Wikipedia, 2020). Learning R (via R Studio) is easier for people with a light programming background. The learning curve for R might be longer for many, but the benefits are excellent. R has an endless collection of readymade functions that grows every day. R can even be integrated to MS Power BI so that special functions and graphs can be produced in R and displayed in the familiar and more presentable MS environment.

Software must be compatible *with other commonly used software. The integration of MS Excel tables and graphs into any MS PowerPoint presentation is as seamless as it can be. There is even the possibility of dynamically linking MS Excel or MS Power BI with the data source on any server or any website and inserting the analysis output into MS PowerPoint. This enables the analyst to have the usual impressive PowerPoint pitch or Power BI dashboard with the actual data whenever it is used.*

Each time we introduced other software such as Minitab, SigmaXL, SAS, or SPSS the limited availability of these software packages was an obstacle to implementing the newly learned tools into the organisation.

Therefore, if you want to be successful in your change effort, ensure you consider the above-mentioned points. If I was a business owner or manager responsible for the profit and loss, I would consider carefully, whether I needed to buy a number of licences with an annual licence fee of a new software if MS Excel and R or Python can do the job and are available for free, or within my current Microsoft Office licence fee.

Hence, the cases in this book show analyses done using MS Excel, MS Power BI, and R Studio. In order to follow through, you need to activate an MS Excel Add-In and install the other software. Here are the step-by-step instructions.

Activating and Using MS Excel's Analysis ToolPak

Many MS Excel users are not aware of the tools loaded into this familiar office package. MS Excel not only has functions for nearly every possible data manipulation and analysis task built in but it also comes with an Analysis tool pack that is hardly used.

And, it just needs to be activated to make it show up as a collection of macros that have the potential of making your analysis work much easier.

After loading MS Excel, press File – Options – Add-ins – Go and check the Analysis ToolPak checkbox (Figure 0.3). This is all you need to do in order to add a collection of commonly needed analysis tools to your Excel (Table 0.3). These tools can be found under Data – Data Analysis (Figure 0.4).

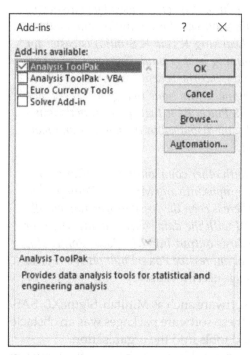

Figure 0.3 Activating MS Excel's Analysis ToolPak

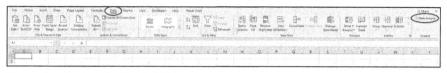

Figure 0.4 Analysis ToolPak in MS Excel

After activating the Analysis ToolPak, the functions shown in Table 0.3 are available.

Table 0.3 Tools Available in MS Excel Analysis ToolPak

■ Anova	■ Fourier Analysis	■ Rank and Percentile
■ Correlation	■ Histogram	■ Regression
■ Covariance	■ Moving Average	■ Sampling
■ Descriptive Statistics	■ Exponential Smoothing	■ t-Test
■ Random Number Generation	■ F-Test Two-Sample for Variances	■ z-Test

Let us get more familiar with the newly discovered set of tools.

TASK 0.1   GENERATE RANDOM DATA

1. Open a new Excel Sheet.

2. Name column A Group and column B Data.

3. Select Data – Data Analysis – Random Number Generation.

4. Select 1 for Number of Variables, 1000 for Number of Random Numbers, Normal for Distribution, 100 for Mean and 5 for Standard Deviation and place the cursor in B2 after selecting Output Range (Figure 0.5).

5. Select Data – Data Analysis – Random Number Generation.

6. Select 1 for Number of Variables, 1000 for Number of Random Numbers, Patterned for Distribution, from 1 to 2 in Steps of 1, repeating each number 5 times, repeating the sequence 100 times and place the cursor in A2 after selecting Output Range (Figure 0.5).

7. Select Column Group, Home – Find & Select – Replace. Find what: 1, Replace with: Group 1, Replace All. Find what: 2, Replace with: Group 2, Replace All.

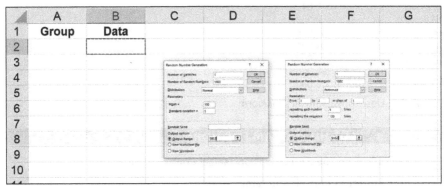

Figure 0.5 Generating Two Columns with Random Data

After you generate the data (Figure 0.6), you will have a different result on your worksheet.

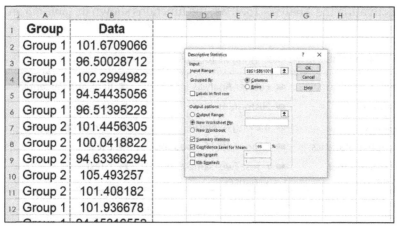

Figure 0.6 Determining Descriptive Statistics for Norm

TASK 0.2   ANALYSE DESCRIPTIVE STATISTICS OF NORM

1. Select Data – Data Analysis – Descriptive Statistics.

2. Select $B$1:$B$1001 for Input Range. Or, just select B1 with your cursor and then select Control + Shift + ⇩ to mark the whole data range.

3. Select New Worksheet Ply and check Summary Statistics and Confidence Level for Mean at 95% (Figure 0.6).

As a result, the descriptive statistics with a list of most basic indicators for your data in Data (Figure 0.7, your descriptive statistics will be different). The descriptive statistics will be explained later in this book.

Data	
Mean	99.6988
Standard Error	0.1570
Median	99.8703
Mode	94.1532
Standard Deviation	4.9662
Sample Variance	24.6635
Kurtosis	-0.0133
Skewness	0.0037
Range	31.0480
Minimum	84.9213
Maximum	115.9693
Sum	99,698.8065
Count	1,000.0000

Figure 0.7 Descriptive Statistics for Norm

TASK 0.3   PLOT HISTOGRAM FOR NORM

1. Select Data on Sheet1 (Mark B1 and select Control + Shift + ⇩).

2. Select Insert – Chart – Histogram.

3. Save your work with the name Norm.xlsx on the desktop or in a folder of your choice.

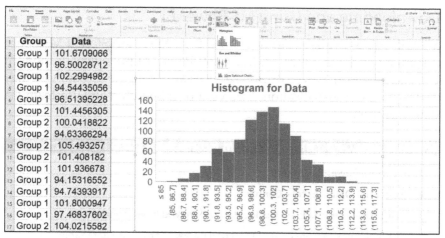

Figure 0.8 Histogram for Norm

The histogram for Data will be created (Figure 0.8). This histogram has been improved by amending the X axis in Bin Width and Tick Marks and by adding a Chart Title. This histogram is ready for insertion into a PowerPoint presentation, Word Document, or even Email or Chat.

TASK 0.4   SHOW BOXPLOT FOR NORM BY GROUP

1. **Select Data and Group on Sheet1 (Mark A1:B1 and select Control + Shift + ⇩).**
2. **Select Insert – Chart – Box and Whisker.**

This command results in the box plot seen in Figure 0.9.

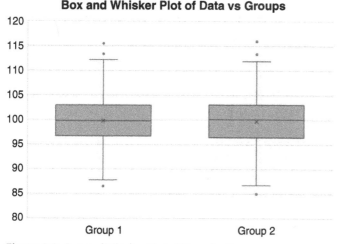

Figure 0.9 Box and Whisker Plot of Norm by Group

Downloading and Using MS Power BI

MS Power BI is available for download from Microsoft Store if MS Office is running on your computer. Microsoft Power BI puts visualisations at your fingertips. If Power BI web services are available to you, you may even share your visualisations, i.e., your dashboards with your team via Power BI server.

TASK 0.5   LOAD THE DATA FROM NORM.XLSX INTO POWER BI

1. Open MS Power BI Desktop.

2. Select Get Data – Excel – Connect.

3. Select Open Norm.xlsx in the location where you have saved it.

4. Check the box in front of Sheet1 – Load (Sheet1 carries the data table).

Unlike Excel, data will not appear in a table on the screen. Data tables and columns are listed under Fields on the right.

TASK 0.6   LOAD A VISUAL FOR A HISTOGRAM FROM THE POWER BI REPOSITORY

1. Select "..." under Visualisations – Get more visuals

2. Search for histogram

3. Add Histogram Chart (or any other histogram of your choice)

4. Select the newly imported histogram icon

5. Increase the size of the plot area to your liking

6. Ensure the histogram plot area is selected.

7. Pull the field Norm from the right into the Values box under Visualisations.

8. Amend the format of Title, Axes, etc. (Figure 0.10)

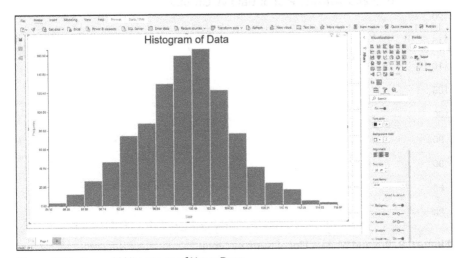

Figure 0.10 Power BI Histogram of Norm Data

Power BI exists for desktop and mobile devices. All versions are available from the Microsoft Store.

Downloading and Using R and R Studio

Firstly, install R and R Studio from any server provided on the websites:

- Download R from `https://www.r-project.org/`.
- Download R Studio from `https://www.rstudio.com/`.
- Start R Studio.

R programming offers a large and ever-growing set of libraries that help programming routines, analyse data, and plot visualisations with minimal code and great flexibility. Most of these libraries need to be loaded before functions can be used. We will elaborate this in detail during our case applications in this book.

TASK 0.7   LOAD THE DATA FROM NORM.XLSX INTO R STUDIO AND LOAD BASIC ANALYSIS AND GRAPHIC PACK "PASTECS" (FIGURE 0.11).

1. Open R Studio.

2. Select File – Import Dataset – From Excel.

3. Select Browse – Norm.xlsx from the location where you have saved it.

4. Select Sheet: Data – Import.

5. Data table Norm is shown in Tab Norm and in Environment.

6. In Tab Packages, Search for "pastecs", if found, check it.

7. If not found, select Install.

8. Install Packages – Packages: pastecs – Install.

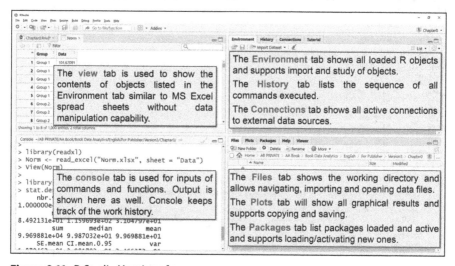

Figure 0.11   R-Studio User Interface

TASK 0.8   ANALYSE DESCRIPTIVE STATISTICS OF NORM.

Type the following in the Console:

```
# See all packages installed and available in Tab Packages
library()     # If package pastecs is part of the list, do
install.packages("pastecs")
# Show packages currently loaded
search()      # If package pastecs is not loaded, do
library(pastecs)
# Show descriptive statistics for all columns at data frame
(table) Norm
stat.desc(Norm)
# Show descriptive statistics for column Data at data frame
(table) Norm
stat.desc(Norm$Data)
```

Output:

1. All columns in table Norm are included in descriptive statistics (Figure 0.12).

2. Only column Data in table Norm is included in descriptive statistics (Figure 0.12).

The output of the descriptive statistics gives an overview of parameters that describe the dataset. It is the most basic analysis for drawing conclusions about central tendency, variation, and shape of the distribution of the dataset.

TASK 0.9   PERFORM NORMALITY TEST (SHAPIRO–WILK TEST) FOR NORM

```
# Performing test on normality of column Data at data frame Norm
shapiro.test(Norm$Data)
```

```
Console
> library(pastecs)
>
> # Show descriptive statistics for all columns at data frame (table) Norm
> stat.desc(Norm)
          Group     Data
nbr.val      NA  1000.00
nbr.null     NA     0.00
nbr.na       NA     0.00
min          NA    84.92
max          NA   115.97
range        NA    31.05
sum          NA 99698.81
median       NA    99.87
mean         NA    99.70
SE.mean      NA     0.16
CI.mean      NA     0.31
var          NA    24.66
std.dev      NA     4.97
coef.var     NA     0.05
>
> # Show descriptive statistics for column Data at data frame (table) Norm
> stat.desc(Norm$Data)
     nbr.val    nbr.null     nbr.na       min       max      range
     1000.00        0.00       0.00     84.92    115.97      31.05
         sum      median       mean   SE.mean CI.mean.0.95      var
     99698.81       99.87      99.70      0.16        0.31      24.66
     std.dev    coef.var
        4.97        0.05
>
```

Figure 0.12 Descriptive Statistics for Norm in R Console

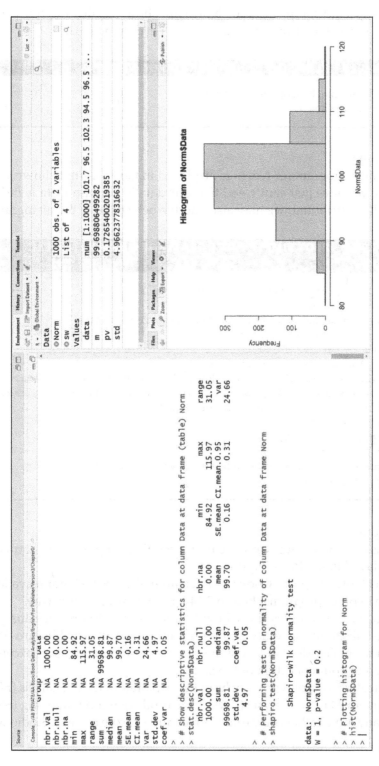

Figure 0.13 Descriptive Statistics, Normality Test and Histogram for Norm

Output:

The normality indicators for Norm are shown indicating that Norm follows normal distribution (Figure 0.13), i.e. p-value > 0.05.

TASK 0.10   PLOT SIMPLE HISTOGRAM FOR NORM

```
# Plotting histogram for Norm
hist(Norm$Data)
```

Output:

A basic histogram for Norm is displayed in tab Plots (not shown).

Since we have just confirmed that our data in column Data is indeed normally distributed, we may also add the bell shape to the histogram.

TASK 0.11   PLOT SIMPLE HISTOGRAM FOR NORM WITH BELL SHAPE

```
# Moving column Data into variable Data
data <- Norm$Data
# Calculating mean and standard deviation of data
m <- mean(data)
std <- sqrt(var(data))
# Plotting histogram for Norm
hist(data, density=20, breaks=20, xlab="Norm", main="Normal
  Curve over Histogram", cex.main=2.00, col="lightblue", cex.
  lab=1.50, cex.axis=1.50, prob=TRUE,)
# Set margin
par(mar = c(5, 5, 5, 5))
# Plot bell shape
curve(dnorm(x, mean=m, sd=std), lwd=2, add=TRUE, yaxt="n",
col="darkblue")
```

Output:

A basic histogram for Norm including bell shape representing normality is displayed in tab Plots (Figure 0.14).

Select Plots – Export – Copy to Clipboard makes the histogram available for use in other programs. Figure 0.14 has been inserted this way.

These basic examples show how R Studio can help produce analyses and visualisations speedily and with minimal input. The Shapiro–Wilk test on normality does not exist in MS Excel and therefore is an excellent addition to your collection of tools.

Particularly complex data analyses like exploratory factor analysis (EFA), confirmatory factor analysis (CFA), structural equation modelling (SEM) and many more rather complicated procedures can be run in R Studio with

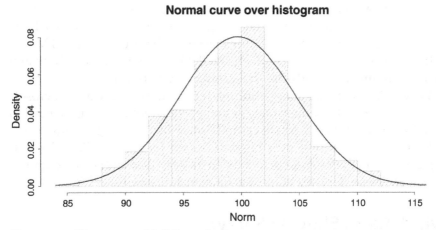

Figure 0.14 Histogram and Bell Shape for Norm

minimal effort. It might be that additional packages need to be loaded to make other tools available. All these packages are accessible for download and installation.

The Help tab offers information for available functions and the packages they are in.

The abovementioned functions do not exist in MS Excel and would be very hard to program in Visual Basic. R Studio fills this gap and enriches your toolbox enormously.

What Is Provided

In addition to this book, a comprehensive set of aids is provided to the reader. These comprise:

- All data used in case studies in this book are provided in the Microsoft Excel format.

- All data analyses have been prepared using Microsoft Excel, partially with the built-in macro collections "Data Analysis Tools" and R Studio.

- All graphical analyses have been conducted using either Microsoft Excel, Microsoft Power BI, or R Studio.

The respective data sets as well as graphical and analytical results are provided, too. To download the files, please visit www.wiley.com and enter "9781119758334" in the search box at the top of the homepage to locate the webpage for this book. Click on "downloads" on the left side of the book's webpage or scroll all the way down to the bottom of the page to see the list of downloadable materials.

There are a multitude of analytics software packages and most of the cases in the book can be analysed using any of these. However, we have not met many people who have fully mastered Microsoft Excel and Microsoft Power BI, which are most likely available for all readers without any investment into new software or learning a new user interface.

We would like to encourage our readers to make full use of Microsoft Excel and Power BI for data analysis and presentation. There is no need to rush for other software if MS Excel and Power BI meet your requirements.

With this, it should be possible for you, the reader, to follow through typical data analytics cases step by step as described in the book, and to customise these steps for your own data analytics cases.

Which Cases Should I Study?

Case studies introduced and analysed in this book make use of different tools for data science tasks. If you wish to start your journey through data analytics with powerful **Microsoft Excel** functions, the following cases might be of interest to you:

1. Which Supplier has the Better Product Quality? (Chapter 3)
2. Why Does Finance Pay Our Vendors Late? (Chapter 3)
3. Do We Have Enough People to Run Our Organisation? (Chapter 4)

In the above-mentioned chapters, only MS Excel tools are employed for data preparation and analysis tasks making use of Excel's Analysis ToolPak.

If you wish to add **Microsoft Power BI** for displaying your data and creating informative and interesting dashboards to your tools backpack, we recommend studying the following cases:

4. What Makes Our Staff Innovate? (Chapter 4)
5. How to Create a Patient Satisfaction Dashboard? (Chapter 2)

After you have mastered the basic steps of data analytics with the previously mentioned tools, you may want to extend your toolset by using a very powerful instrument for data wrangling, data visualisation, and data analysis. The **analytics language R** has become an easy to use and extraordinarily powerful software environment for all tasks data scientists are faced with.

Do not worry. There is no need to learn a programming language. In our case studies we have prepared all the commands that will open the magic of R for you. As you have already seen previously in the chapter, it needs one line of function code to perform a normality test, one line to draw a histogram and one line to give a comprehensive set of descriptive statistics. Whilst learning R we concluded that we were usually much faster working in R than doing a similar task in other software. The following cases will help you dive into R:

6. Great, We Have Improved . . . Or Not? (Chapter 2)
7. What Drives our Patient Satisfaction? (Chapter 2)

8. How to Create a Patient Satisfaction Dashboard? (with R in Power BI) (Chapter 2)

9. Why are We Wasting Blood? (Chapter 3)

10. What Does our Engagement Survey Result Mean? (Chapter 4)

11. What Drives our Staff Out? (Chapter 4)

The final case in particular is filled to the brim with R code to support a rather complex logistic regression analysis task. If you wish to start with R, you may want to begin your journey with the first examples on the list.

We wish you success and fun studying and following our cases. After that it should not be too difficult to apply these tools to your own cases for organisational development.

References

Data Never Sleeps 7.0. (2020). Retrieved from www.domo.com: https://www.domo.com/learn/data-never-sleeps-7#/

Gallo, A. (2018, Oct. 31). 4 Analytics Concepts Every Manager Should Understand. Retrieved from *Harvard Business Review:* https://hbr.org/2018/10/4-analytics-concepts-every-manager-should-understand

Payne, J. W. (1976). Task Complexity and Contingent Processing in Decision Making: An Information Search and Protocol Analysis. *Organizational Behavior and Human Performance*, 366–387.

Ratcliffe, S. (ed.) (2018). W. Edwards Deming. *Oxford Essential Quotations* (6th edn). Oxford: Oxford University Press. Current Online Version: ISBN: 9780191866692.

Russom, P. (2011, Q4). Big Data Analytics. *TDWI Best Practices Report*, 4–10.

Varian, H. R. (2009, Jan. 1). Hal Varian on How the Web Challenges Managers. Retrieved from *McKinsey & Company, Commentary* https://www.mckinsey.com/industries/technology-media-and-telecommunications/our-insights/hal-varian-on-how-the-web-challenges-managers

Wikipedia. (2020). *R.* Retrieved from Wikipedia - The Free Encyclopedia: https://en.wikipedia.org/wiki/R_ (programming_language)

Wikipedia. (n.d.). *Data analysis.* Retrieved from Wikipedia: https://en.wikipedia.org/wiki/Data_analysis

List of Figures and Tables

Introduction to Data Analytics and Data Science

Data science is a "concept to unify statistics, data analysis, machine learning and their related methods" in order to "understand and analyse actual phenomena" with data.

(Hayashi, 1998)

Data science is not a new field of research. It is an old science that we have to rediscover, refresh, and use to turn the ever-increasing amount of data in all facets of professional and personal life into useful information for organisations, their customers, and members.

In this chapter, we will introduce different components of data science and its phases: from organisational questions to value-added information, to data-based conclusions. We will introduce the commonly used graphical and statistical tools for different data type constellations. Additionally, we will discuss the necessary competencies a data scientist should acquire in order to keep up with the fast-moving development in analytics disciplines and related fields.

CONTENTS

- ➤ Components of Data Analytics
- ➤ Big Data and its Relationship to Data Analytics
- ➤ Data Analytics – The Foundation for Data Science and Artificial Intelligence
- ➤ Phases of Data Analytics
- ➤ Competencies of a Data Analyst

SECTION	TOOLS USED
Data Preparation	Ex, R
Data Analysis	Ex, R
Analytical Story Telling	Ex
Analytics Tools Used: Ex . . . MS Excel, R . . . R and R Studio	

Highlights

After completing this chapter, you will be able to . . .

- Relate to Big Data and data science and how to bridge to data analytics.
- Comprehend the importance of starting a data-analytics task with a business-relevant question or hypothesis.
- Understand the significance of preparing, transforming, and cleaning all sets of data before analysing them and drawing conclusions.
- Realise the value of translating data analyst "jargon" into business stories to support the appropriate use of data for the benefit of your organisation.
- Recommend competencies your data scientists need to acquire and strengthen to be prepared for the job.

Components of Data Analytics

Data analytics is an overarching discipline that encompasses the complete management of data including collecting, validating, cleaning, organising, storing, and analysing data. Data analysis is a process of examining in close detail the components of a given set of data, separating them out and studying the parts individually and their relationship between one another. Data analysis as such is a phase of data analytics. Both data analytics and data analysis are used to uncover patterns, trends, and anomalies lying within data, and thereby deliver the insights organisations need to enable evidence-based decision making. Put simply, data analysis looks at the past, while data analytics tries to predict the future (Xia, 2015).

Data analytics comprises the following main components:

1. **Descriptive Analytics** (post-mortem analysis): provides a summary of historical data to generate useful information for organisation-relevant conclusions. It provides cause and effect interconnections for past events.

2. **Predictive Analytics:** provides a summary of historical figures in order to understand patterns in data with the objective to generate predictions about future events. Predictive analytics is based on descriptive analytics.

3. **Prescriptive Analytics** is based on these predictions and the underlying root causes. Prescriptive analytics helps to suggest actions

and evaluate their potential benefits. Prescriptive analytics is often covered as an integral part of predictive analytics.

4. **Text Analytics** uses statistical and non-statistical methods to extract useful information and conclusions out of unstructured data from textual sources.

This book covers all these components in different depths, and they are illustrated in case studies.

⋎Not only is there a move from so-called Big Data analytics to analytics of any kind of data. There is also a healthy trend towards involving all levels of management and the organisation's staff into this not so new field of information management. Progressive managers are familiar with the data available and with trends, shifts, or other patterns in their data and use them in decision-making. Hence, it is about time to ensure that the right data are collected in an appropriate way, screened, organised, and analysed with suitable tools to deliver the insights organisations need to make decisions.

Big Data and its Relationship to Data Analytics

Big Data describes sets of data that are so voluminous and complex that traditional data-processing applications cannot handle them. Big Data is defined by its three Vs, Volume, Velocity, Variety (Russom, 2011).

At the beginning of the 2000s, Big Data posed a serious problem to organisations. On the one hand, the volume of available data went up exponentially. On the other hand, CPU speed and storage capacity could not keep up with the data amount at hand. At that time, handling big data was reserved to a few companies and organisations who relied on the analysis of data to stay in business.

How big is Big Data? Here are some examples of data **created or used every minute** (Data Never Sleeps 7.0, 2020):

- 511,000 tweets sent on Twitter,
- 694,444 hours of video watched via Netflix,
- 4,500,000 videos watched by users on YouTube,
- 4,500,000 searches conducted on Google,
- 18,100,000 messages sent.

In total, it is estimated that the information stored worldwide will exceed 40 Zeta bytes in 2020 (NodeGraph, 2020). That is 40 times $1,000^7$ bytes or 40 x 10^{21} bytes. It is quite hard to imagine this kind of number. In 2010, Google estimated the total number of books ever published as over 129 million (Parr, 2010). Under certain assumptions, these books would fit comfortably on a hard drive with a capacity of about 60 Tera bytes. This would include all books, including Plato's philosophy teachings we still benefit from, those scientific books by Albert Einstein that changed physics, speeches by John F Kennedy the world still remembers and all the rubbish self-portraying autobiographies, mankind certainly does not need. And that is a storage space, some of us have at home and undoubtedly in the company.

> The amount of information stored world-wide in 2020 is about 670 Million times the information of all books ever published.

This sounds really huge and like a great technological achievement of mankind. In order to store all this data, vast server farms have been built all over the world. These servers need to be powered. It is estimated that the internet alone uses more than 10% of the world's energy (McKenzie, 2021). And all these numbers are increasing fast. Considering, that only about 20% of all energy consumed by data centres is produced by renewable sources – 80% of the energy needed still drains our natural resources massively – this achievement must be seen in a different light.

NATURE CAN DO MUCH BETTER

Let us have a look at how Mother Nature handles the task of storing data.

The information that organises all kind of life on earth is the DNA, the blueprint for any form of life from the smallest virus to the human body. The human DNA is copied and stored in every single cell of our body, from a hair cell to a blood cell. A complete human DNA is quite complex and consists of about 1.6 Giga bytes of information. The DNA of a virus has with some Kilo bytes drastically less information since it does not need to store the design of a nose, a leg, or the colour of the eyes.

An adult human body has in average about 30 trillion cells (healthline. Falck, 2018). The size of the body does not necessarily drive the number of cells. Dany de Vito may not have fewer than Arnold Schwarzenegger. We will never know.

Having in mind that every single cell in the body carries the complete blueprint, the complete DNA for the whole body, we can just multiply our 1.6 Giga byte (1.6×10^9) with 30 trillion (30×10^{12}) cells to arrive at a total capacity of the data storage facility of the human body with 48×10^{21} bytes.

As shown earlier, this is roughly the aggregated information ever created by mankind and stored on hundreds of servers worldwide. Yet, Mother Nature can theoretically store all this in one adult human body.

The energy needed to keep this small data storage facility with this huge capacity running is extracted out of three decent meals per day that are completely made from renewable resources.

Beyond storage, the human body has extremely good sensors for data acquisition, is equipped with superb data-processing capabilities, and can perform activities like walking and running.

Considering all this, we should be humble. What we call Big Data, Mother Nature has been able to handle for millions of years very successfully and with much higher efficiency than our best current solution.

The available information partially contains important details about our customers and their buying behaviours, or our competitors and their offerings, potential new hires and their social media profiles, and many other aspects of personal and business life. A large portion of this information is available for us to access – for free or for reasonable fees.

It is a question of time whether this information falls under the category "Big Data". If it does so today, it may not tomorrow, and it will certainly not the day after tomorrow. Today, businesses and even homes can access computers with huge data storage and handling capacity, be it by installing hardware and software inhouse or be it by connecting to external capacity. Consequently, more organisations have the means and see the need to collect data about their customers and competitors, about their operational environment, and about all aspects of their workforce. These organisations widen the scope of their data analytics activities and build the skills to do so.

Some researchers used to suggest that data analytics is mainly describing the handling of user data that is produced by CRM and similar systems and turned into customer intelligence. Today, the scope of data analytics opens up to include all functions of an organisation. Using Big Data analytics can help businesses build customer profiles for creating personalised services and improve customer satisfaction.

Although Big Data has some specific characteristics that may need some special equipment to acquire, clean, and transform the data, the rules and tools for Data Analytics will apply equally.

Data Analytics – The Foundation for Data Science and Artificial Intelligence

There are many terms that turn up when it comes to handling data. In addition to "Big Data", there are terms like "data science", "data analytics", "data mining", "artificial intelligence", "machine learning", "deep learning", "pattern recognition", "neural networks", etc. Here are some attempts towards disambiguation:

If data science is a home for all the methods and tools, then data analytics is a room in that house. Data analytics is more specific and concentrated than data science (Springboard India, 2019). Data analysts examine large data sets to identify trends, develop charts, and create visual presentations to help businesses make more data-driven decisions. Data scientists, on the other hand, design and construct new processes for data modelling, and production using prototypes, algorithms, predictive models, and custom analysis (Burnham, 2019). Therefore, data analytics is the foundation for data science.

Artificial intelligence (AI) is driven by machine learning and deep learning and many other fields. AI is based on many disciplines that are part of data science, and as such, data analytics (Figure 1.1).

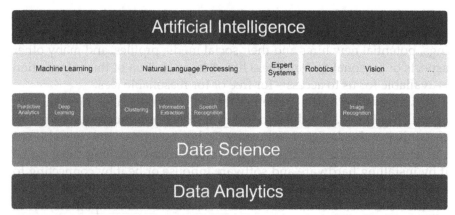

Figure 1.1 Building Blocks of Artificial Intelligence

AMAZON'S ALEXA – AN INTRODUCTION TO ARTIFICIAL INTELLIGENCE

The apparently simplest AI solution is your Alexa at home. In order to get this little device doing what it does, it needs to be connected to the so-called Big Data, the internet. When Alexa needs to answer a standard question asked by a voice known to Alexa, it will be very fast, because the translation of the received soundwaves into useful information follows a pattern Alexa has learned before. And the answer to a standard question is available for download very fast because Amazon's search engines already know this question and make the answer available easily.

When Alexa needs to answer a question that no one has asked before, Alexa takes some seconds to comb through all available sources that could have an answer to that question. Before any search can start, Alexa needs to receive sound waves and converts these sound waves into useful information. If Alexa is exposed to a human speaker with an unusual dialect, it may not work – at first. Alexa needs to learn the new dialect over time. And you will recognise that it gets better and faster.

Somewhere in Amazon's data centres, the new question gets recognised and stored with the answer that was accepted by the listener. Since this question was asked only once, it may not get a high priority. However, the machines will learn that there is interest in a new topic. This alone will trigger further actions.

The activities you actuate by popping a question to your Alexa are part of the domain of AI that includes learning from the data received and improving the algorithms over time. Activities for acquiring voice data and translating it into digits may fall into the domain of data science whereas all analysis done on the way is covered by data analytics tools.

Whilst it is hard to finely distinguish between data science and data analytics, it is safe to say that acquiring data analytics skills prepares for all other related fields. Without data analytics, they will not work.

Practice

- What are the main components of Data Analytics?
- What are the characteristics of Big Data? What are the three V?
- What is the relationship between Artificial Intelligence, Data Science, and Data Analytics?

Phases of Data Analytics

During our time at university, we would most likely have dealt with data analytics. Unfortunately, the Professor often spent his time explaining the derivation and details of the data analysis tools. For example, many of us learned everything about the t-Test including its t-distribution, the p-value, etc. The most interesting fact seemed to be its origin from the Guinness brewery and the student William Gossett who developed it, which was the reason for him not being allowed to publish under his real name but under the pseudonym student. Therefore, the test has been called student test ever since. In our experience, the application examples had been quite weak, so that many of us left university with the mindset to avoid statistics in future because there was obviously not much practical application. We would like to emphasise that only knowing the tool and its background is a competency that will not take the data analyst very far. A good statistician is not necessarily a good data analyst. On the contrary, of the five phases of any data analytics case (Figure 1.2), the data analysis step, i.e., the application of the tool is very often the easier one. In the following, the five phases for data analytics are explained. These phases are considered – in different degrees of depth – in the application cases in this book.

Business Question

Analytics does not produce insights from data. To be worthwhile, analytics must be directed by deliberately chosen and strategically important business questions. For example, *"Why are we discarding more of our precious collected blood than many other blood banks?"* Not only is this question related to an issue that is derived from process efficiency. It also conveys the message of spending more resources than probably necessary. This is always of interest for the management.

Figure 1.2 Phases of Data Analytics

In this first step, the business-related issue should be clearly identified. And it must be translated into a key performance indicator (KPI) or performance criteria that make the issue measurable. This way, we will have control over the performance results, and over time we can monitor the changes of these performance results. Also, having it defined clearly and measurable, allows us to identify the right context for comparison between the current performance result and what it should be. All in all, it is important to first answer the question "Do we have control over the performance results?" before it makes sense to answer any other questions through analytics. Without control, improvement efforts arrived from the analysis may become a complete waste.

Table 1.1 shows some examples of translating business issues into data-related questions or hypotheses.

Table 1.1 Translation of Business Issues into Data Analytics Questions

BUSINESS ISSUES	DATA ANALYTICS QUESTIONS
■ Why are we wasting precious blood products? ■ How can we cut down such wastage?	■ Are we really discarding more blood products than other blood banks? What is the significant difference? ■ What are the drivers for high wastage? ■ Can we change the underlying root causes to reduce the wastage?
■ Has the employee engagement score improved after our investments last year?	■ Is there a significant difference between the employee engagement score this year compared to last year?
■ Why do we take so long to decide about innovation ideas?	■ What is the turnaround time for deciding about our innovation ideas? ■ What is the percentage of ideas accepted or rejected after target time? ■ What are the drivers for long turnaround time?

Data Acquisition

There is a multitude of ways to collect data to answer the Business Question. And, it does not need sophisticated tools or expensive hardware and software to get this data on your computer for analysis. MS Excel and MS Power BI alone have potent data acquisition interfaces that reach into publicly available data sources as well as into servers of multiple designs. An interface for your organisation's server is amongst them.

As Figure 1.4 illustrates, MS Excel and MS Power BI enable us to load data from multiple file types such as from Text/CSV files, from R and Python Scrips etc. Additionally, data can be taken from internal and external databases, be it MS Access, SQL, or MySQL or from IBM, SAP, MS Azure, Salesforce, Google. This includes Big Data files on computer networks in Hadoop format and others. Moreover, data can be downloaded from nearly any website such as Wikipedia, Facebook, LinkedIn, Department of Statistics, and many others. There are practically no limitations.

MS Excel and MS Power BI enable us not only to download data from these and many more sources. They also enable the link to be "hot", i.e., as soon as the destination file on MS Excel or MS Power BI is refreshed, the updated data are re-downloaded from the source. This ensures that the data on the computer are always the latest (Microsoft, 2020).

Task 1.1 will show an example for downloading data from a URL directly into Excel and linking the data to the table available on the URL.

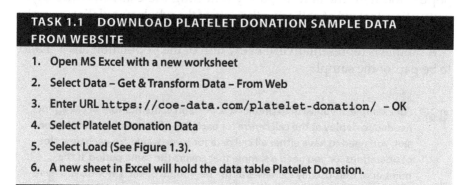

TASK 1.1   DOWNLOAD PLATELET DONATION SAMPLE DATA FROM WEBSITE

1. Open MS Excel with a new worksheet
2. Select Data – Get & Transform Data – From Web
3. Enter URL `https://coe-data.com/platelet-donation/` – OK
4. Select Platelet Donation Data
5. Select Load (See Figure 1.3).
6. A new sheet in Excel will hold the data table Platelet Donation.

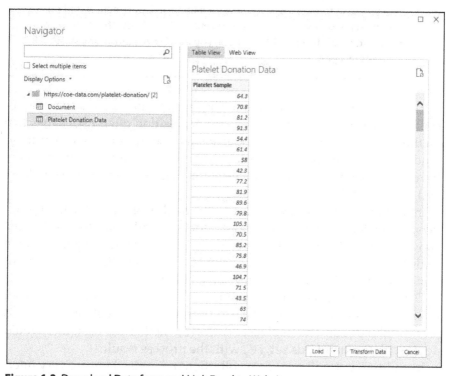

Figure 1.3 Download Data from and Link Excel to Website
Source: Used with permission from Microsoft.

If the data on the website are updated, data in your MS Excel will be renewed as well after refreshing the worksheet.

However, having actual data does not automatically mean the data is correct. All data sources need to be checked regarding their trustworthiness.

It is usually necessary to validate the method of data collection to ensure useful data for analysis, i.e., data that is representative, reproducible, and accurate enough to provide sufficient information for answering the business question. There are statistical tools that help identifying potential problems within the data collection process.

A data sample is a subset of data, that is chosen out of a larger data population with the aim of closely reflecting the characteristics of the population. Instead of gathering the data of the whole population, samples are often taken to reduce time and effort for data collection.

A sample is representative, if every unit of the population has a chance to be part of the sample.

 For example, if you wish to predict the workforce, the number of call agents needed to deploy at the call centre for each day of the week and each time slot, you need to have either all call data for some weeks for each time slot of operations, or you need a sample that covers the same period. If the number of calls usually increases at the beginning of each month, you need to ensure you have historical data for some months. Generally, a representative sample embodies all known variation with data.

If you wish to plan the workforce for a finance department based on volume data for invoices, bills, reports etc. and you know that their busy period starts at the end of November, you need to ensure your dataset includes this period.

The data acquisition method must be reproducible. Not only but especially in the service environment, data acquisition often uses subjective methods. Data are generated through evaluation by operators. In order to render meaningful analysis results, we have to ensure that all operators have the same understanding of the operational definition, of what is "Ok" and what is "defective".

In the blood bank, the evaluation of the quality of one of the final products, the platelet bag, is done by operators after all laboratory tests have shown favourable results. It is necessary that all operators have the same understanding of the operational definition to ensure they deliver reproducible results when assessing the same blood bag.

Data acquisition needs to deliver accurate results, i.e. not only must all operators agree on the result. They also must comply with all standards and thresholds set. The final test is always whether the customer would agree with the standards set, i.e., with the process result.

In addition to traditional data collection methods, there are very interesting new ways of tapping on available data (See list of interfaces on

Figure 1.4 MS Excel and MS Power BI Offer Powerful Interfaces for Data Acquisition
Source: Used with permission from Microsoft.

Figure 1.4) with very little effort, as shown earlier. MS Excel, MS Power BI, and R enable you to link your computer to any dataset (HTML data table) on Wikipedia, Facebook, LinkedIn etc. You can choose to make this link dynamic, it means, to update the data on your computer whenever the online dataset is updated.

However, keep in mind, if data is available on even so-called credible data sources, it is not a guarantee that the data itself is representative, reproducible, and accurate, i.e., helpful for what you wish to analyse.

 If data is published on the internet, it does not automatically mean you can trust this data. Validate this data or validate the source before using it.

Data Preparation

Converting Stacked in Unstacked Data

When servers scrape customer inputs from a survey website, they most likely download the data in a stacked format, i.e., each input makes a row in the resulting table.

Some analysis tools, like ANOVA and other hypothesis tests, need stacked data, some other tools, like regression, work with unstacked data, some tools, like descriptive statistics, work with both arrangements.

Stacking or unstacking data might be a necessary step in any data analysis.

Unstacked data is also called "short data" because the information for different variables is organised in columns next to each other. Stacked data is also called "long data" because the information for different variables is organised in the same column (in Table 1.2, it is called Rating), whereas the name of the variable is placed in a column next to it (in Table 1.2, it is called Step).

Using patient satisfaction data of a case discussed later shows an unstacked data table for rating for steps with 514 rows (514 patients), whereas the stacked version takes 5 x 514 = 2570 rows (5 steps x 514 patients), hence the reason for the name "long data".

Doing this transformation or conversion in Excel is possible:

TASK 1.2   CONVERSION OF STACKED DATA INTO UNSTACKED DATA

1. Open MS Excel.

2. Open the data in ClinicSurveyStacked.xlsx in sheet Stacked.

3. If this table is not formatted as Excel table yet, perform the following steps:

    a. Select the whole table with cursor in A1 and Shift + Ctrl + ⇨ and Shift + Ctrl + ⇩.

    b. Home – Format as Table. The style selected does not make a difference.

    c. Since you have included the header row in your selection, ensure to check the box "My table has headers".

4. With the cursor in the table, select Insert – PivotTable – OK. A Pivot Table is created on a new worksheet.

5. In this new worksheet with the cursor in the template of the PivotTable, select ID from the PivotTable Fields and drag it into Rows, Step into Columns and Rating into Values.

6. If Rating is not switched to Average of Rating, select Sum of Rating or Count of Rating and switch Value Field Settings to Average of Rating.

7. In the same step, you might want to change the Number Format.

8. With the cursor in the Pivot Table, right click PivotTable Options and perform some formatting. For example, in tab Totals & Filters, uncheck both grand totals.

Table 1.2 Comparing Stacked and Unstacked Data

STACKED DATA FOR STEPS – LONG DATA		
ID	**STEP**	**RATING**
190000084	Step1	3.33
190000084	Step2	2.67
190000084	Step3	2.25
190000084	Step4	2.75
190000084	Step5	2.33
190003578	Step1	3.33
190003578	Step2	3.00
190003578	Step3	2.75
190003578	Step4	3.00
190003578	Step5	3.33

UNSTACKED DATA FOR STEPS – SHORT DATA					
ID	**STEP1**	**STEP2**	**STEP3**	**STEP4**	**STEP5**
190000084	3.33	2.67	2.25	2.75	2.33
190003578	3.33	3.00	2.75	3.00	3.33

As a result, a PivotTable has been built that looks like Unstacked Data in Table 1.2. In our case examples later in this book, we will perform this conversion using R.

Cleaning Data

Even if the method of data collection is proven and the instrument is statistically validated, it can still be that data is not useful.

In surveys, for example, some survey participants may not give useful input. Part of the reason might be that they were either forced or incentivised to participate in the survey. Then, we can assume that some of the participants were not interested in our survey. They may have provided valid input to a well-established survey questionnaire, but the input may not be useful. Or worse yet, the input could spoil the following analysis steps. Such input could be random rating or the same rating for all questions or statements.

Therefore, data preparation is necessary to find and omit such input to feed only data that is value-added into the analysis.

Data preparation also includes formatting the data so that it can be used by the preferred analysis software. More often than not, downloaded data from a system is not in the right format to be fed into the analysis software, Excel, for example (Figure 1.5). However, in most cases data can be reorganised, reformatted, or transformed so that the software can handle it. A perfectly formatted data table is shown in Figure 1.6.

Not always will the analysis software stop working because of the wrongly formatted data. In the worst case, it might just work and present incorrect results.

Converting data and transforming data will be shown in case examples later in the book. We will be using software widely available such as MS Excel and R Studio.

ID	Y	Demographics				
Blood Bag ID	Result	IC	Name	Date	DOW	Centrifuge Type
64988	ok	S123...	Amy Z	14 Nov 2019	Thu	G9
64989	ok	S234...	Benny Y	14 Nov 2019	Thu	G9
64990	ok	S345...	Cordula X	14 Nov 2019	Thu	H10
64991	ok	S456...	Dora W	14 Nov 2019	Thu	G9
64992	ok	S567...	Emma V	14 Nov 2019	Thu	G9
64993	ok	S678...	Fong U	14 Nov 2019	Thu	H10
64994	ok	S789...	Gong T	14 Nov 2019	Thu	H10
64995	ok	S900...	Han S	14 Nov 2019	Thu	H10

X				
1st Spin Time - Start	Resting Time Before Pro	Resting Time - Start	Resting Time - End	Resting Time After Pro
14:35	264	16:30	18:00	90
14:35	256	16:30	18:00	90
14:40	218	16:30	18:00	90
14:35	204	16:30	18:00	90
14:35	201	16:30	18:00	90
14:40	220	16:30	18:00	90
14:40	222	16:30	18:00	90
14:40	195	16:30	18:00	90

Figure 1.5 Data Table Before Re-formatting

Source: Used with permission from Microsoft.

Variables

Records Data Sets

BloodBagID	Result	Date	DOW	CentrifugeType	Spin1Start	RestingBeforePro	RestingStart	RestingEnd	RestingAfterPro
64988	ok	14 Nov 2019	Thu	G9	14:35	264	16:30	18:00	90
64989	ok	14 Nov 2019	Thu	G9	14:35	256	16:30	18:00	90
64990	ok	14 Nov 2019	Thu	H10	14:40	218	16:30	18:00	90
64991	ok	14 Nov 2019	Thu	G9	14:35	204	16:30	18:00	90
64992	ok	14 Nov 2019	Thu	G9	14:35	201	16:30	18:00	90
64993	ok	14 Nov 2019	Thu	H10	14:40	220	16:30	18:00	90
64994	ok	14 Nov 2019	Thu	H10	14:40	222	16:30	18:00	90
64995	ok	14 Nov 2019	Thu	H10	14:40	195	16:30	18:00	90

Figure 1.6 Data Table After Re-formatting

Source: Used with permission from Microsoft.

Data Analysis

Descriptive Statistics

The objective of most of our data-analysis procedures is to recognise patterns in data. These patterns are made by variation. Explaining this variation, its root causes, and its meaning for the organisation are key tasks for any data analyst.

The first step in any data analysis should be to determine descriptive statistics. Figure 1.7 shows the descriptive statistics of the platelet extraction process in a blood donation facility. On average, it takes about 73 minutes to complete a cycle of platelet donation.

Why is it important to know descriptive statistics? It is, in this case, the foundation for any scheduling of donors or for planning of nurses, etc. Many decisions are made based on this number. For example, after the nurse has setup the donor and the process has begun running, she knows that there is not much to do for this donor for more than one hour.

Table 1.3 Rules for Formatting Data Tables

RULES FOR FORMATTING DATA TABLES
1. Avoid aggregated data. If possible, acquire raw data in a simple table, sometimes called data frame.
2. This table usually shows variables organised in table columns whereas table rows display datasets, i.e. records of data that belong to the same unit. In the table shown in Figure 1.5, Blood Bag ID marks the row with all data that were collected for this blood bag.
3. Ensure your data has an ID number for each unit. This enables lookup links to other tables. Additionally, it helps when anonymising the data.
4. Data tables for analysis should not carry personal data. Firstly, this is required by law in many countries. Secondly, showing names to the analyser could cause a bias during analysis. Anonymise your data.
5. Make sure your data table has only one header row. Most software would auto select the complete table, even with multiple header rows (Figure 1.5) by default. If it does not allow multiple header rows (Figure 1.5), the software will show error messages during the analysis.
6. Use simple, short headers, i.e. names for variables. Analysis software may cut off long variable names after a certain number of characters. It might be hard to distinguish between them in the analysis result.
7. It could be advantageous to have no spaces in the variable names, i.e. in the headers. That way, some analysis software delivers output that is easier to read.
8. Ensure all data entries in the same column have the same format. For example, MS Excel allows the Date "14 Nov 2019" in our table to be stored as date or as text. Both formats may look exactly the same. However, an analysis involving this column will not work. It pays to be very careful from the beginning of the data collection. This kind of failure is not easy to find.
9. Standardise all names. Especially text fields like "CentrifugeType" must show the same name for the same type. "H10" and "H 10" would mark different types and would split your dataset in smaller samples per type.

Platelet Donation Time in min	
Mean	73.05394737
Standard Error	1.085590784
Median	74
Mode	81.2
Standard Deviation	16.39206137
Minimum	28
Maximum	119.7
Sum	16656.3
Count	228
Confidence Level (95.0%)	2.139123544

Figure 1.7 Descriptive Statistics for Duration of Platelet Donation in min

How good is this conclusion? Conclusions based on averages, on means, are rarely good. More often than not, these conclusions can be quite misleading. It might never happen that the cycle takes 73.05 minutes. It has taken as little as 28 minutes and as much as 119 minutes.

 Do not trust means. Means are often lies. Determine the variation.

The better indicators to describe what is really happening in business situations are indicators that explain the variation such as Minimum, Maximum, Range, and Standard Deviation. Whereas Minimum and Maximum, i.e. Range = Maximum – Minimum, can be calculated for any set of data with always the same meaning, the meaning of Standard Deviation depends on the distribution of the data, on the shape of the histogram.

"A picture is worth a thousand words" applies here as well. The histogram of our platelet donation data, shown in Figure 1.8, tells you much more than the descriptive statistics ever can. It informs you that most of

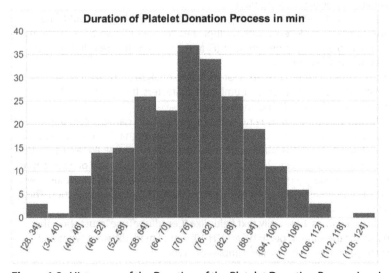

Figure 1.8 Histogram of the Duration of the Platelet Donation Process in min

the time, the platelet donation takes around 74 minutes. Sometimes, the process can make it in around one hour. Sometimes, this process can take towards one and a half hours. The more we deviate from the mean, the 73.05 minutes, the less likely the duration is to happen.

Normal Distribution

This pattern was first discovered and described by Carl Friedrich Gauss, the "greatest mathematician since antiquity" (Dunnington, 2004), more than 200 years ago. Gauss found after observing the variation of errors and several other phenomena in astronomy, physics, and nature, that many of them show a distinct pattern. This pattern is very similar to our Platelet Donation processing time. One of his greatest achievements was the creation of a mathematical function that approximates this very typical pattern.

Applying this mathematical function, the normal distribution curve, the bell shape, has been added to our histogram of the platelet donation processing time (Figure 1.9).

This bell shape is the foundation of almost any data analysis you will ever do. Even if there is no bell shape in your process of interest, due to Gauss' central limit theorem (Lane, n.d.), all other distributions turn into a normal distribution under certain circumstances.

As Figure 1.9 suggests, the histogram does not perfectly follow the model, the bell shape. It nearly never does. However, it is very often close enough to allow us to conduct calculations and prepare decisions using the bell shape instead of the histogram. The bell shape is completely defined by the mean of 73.05 and the standard deviation of 16.39 (See Figure 1.7).

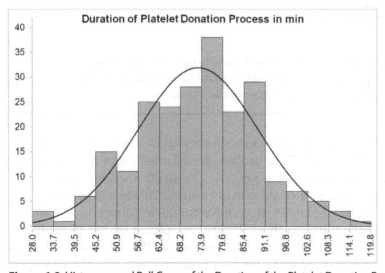

Figure 1.9 Histogram and Bell Curve of the Duration of the Platelet Donation Process in min

It is not difficult to distinguish whether a set of data is significantly different to the bell shape. R can help:

TASK 1.3   PERFORM NORMALITY TEST (SHAPIRO–WILK TEST) FOR PLATELET DONATION TIME

```
# Loading PlateletDonation.xlsx into data frame PlateletDonation
library(readxl)
PlateletDonation <- read_excel("~/PlateletDonation.xlsx")
View(PlateletDonation)
# Loading data from column Data at PlateletDonation into vector
Data
Data <- PlateletDonation$Data
# Performing test on normality of data in vector Data
shapiro.test(Data)
```

OUTPUT:

```
Shapiro-Wilk normality test
data: Data
W = 0.99615, p-value = 0.8463
```

The Shapiro–Wilk normality test statistics for Data indicate that Data follows normal distribution, because p-value > 0.05 (see Table 1.6).

Why is it better to use the bell shape to describe our process or situation rather than the histogram? The bell shape comes with a very distinct characteristic, several indicators the histogram does not have. These indicators can help us make decisions. A prerequisite is, that our bell shape closely enough represents the histogram. The degree of the match between bell shape and histogram can be tested with a normality test. We have completed this test already and can conclude that our dataset can be considered "normal", which means bell-shaped.

 The bell shape does never exactly describe the data set at hand. It is often close enough to allow us using it as model for the data. All models are wrong, but some are useful. (George Box, 1976)

Figure 1.10 gives an introduction. In every bell shape, the mean $\bar{x}$, the average, is in the centre. For our process, the mean is 73.05min. The standard deviation is at 16.39min. When projecting these numbers into Figure 1.10, we can calculate the related percentage ranges. This means, for example, that about 68% of all platelet procedures complete between about 57min and about 89min, whereas about 95% are completed within about 40min and about 106min. Finally, nearly all procedures (99.73%) are completed within about 24min to about 122min. Only about 0.13% would take longer. This is good to know for scheduling the next donors, the workforce, and the apheresis equipment.

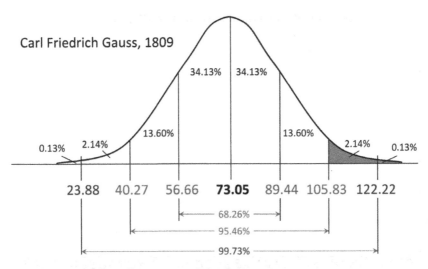

Figure 1.10 Bell Shape for Duration of Platelet Donation

Let us say, the nurse has started a platelet donation process and wanted to know whether there is time to catch a bus to pick up a son from childcare centre. When starting the donation process, the nurse took responsibility for this donor. The bus is arriving in one hour and 45 minutes (105min). Can this donor's cycle be completed in time? How likely is it that this donor is done before the nurse needs to leave?

The graph shows that 105.83min is located at the end of the 95.46% range. This means, there is 4.54% / 2 = 2.27% chance (shaded area) that this process takes longer than 105.83min. The nurse would probably decide that this risk is so low that it is most likely that the donor's cycle will be completed. The nurse does not need to "transfer" the donor to a colleague. Moreover, the nurse would very likely ignore our calculation and draw the same conclusion based on experience after being on the job for years. The shape of the distribution together with the parameters mean and standard deviation represent the experience of the nurse gathered over years, although the nurse would probably never do the maths.

This quite simple example displays the fundamental mechanism of the working of numerous statistical tools.

Many data sets do not show a bell shape from the outset. This sounds bad since our powerful statistical tool does not seem to apply. Still, this is very often an indication for something that is changing the process. Figure 1.11 displays a non-bell-shaped histogram. In many data analysis cases, this might be the start for the analysis.

The task of the data analyst is to identify the reasons for this pattern. In our case, we have plotted a histogram of all blood donation types together. It includes donations of whole blood, of plasma, of platelets, and the donations coming from blood mobile drives. The characteristics of these donation types are quite different, they show up as multi-modal patterns. This in itself is a discovery that typically drives the next analysis steps.

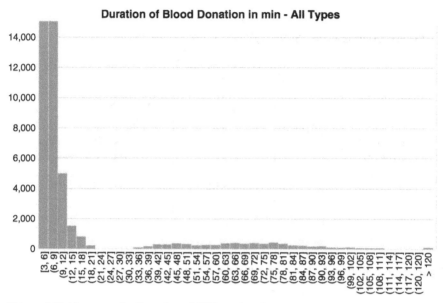

Figure 1.11 Histogram for Duration of All Donation Types

Types of Data

A variety of tools is available for the analysis of data. Table 1.4 shows a small range of the most used tools in data-analysis cases. Nearly all the tools presented in this table are based on a normal distribution. Without understanding the basics of normal distribution, understanding these tools is quite challenging.

Table 1.4 Graphical and Statistical Tools for Different Data Types

	DISCRETE X		CONTINUOUS X
	2 Groups	2 or more Groups	Reverse box plot, reverse dot plot.
Discrete Y	Bar chart, pie chart	Bar chart, pie chart	
			Probability plot
	Two-Proportions-Test	Chi² Test	Logistic Regression,
			Design of Experiments
Continuous Y	Stratified frequency plots like box plot, dot plot, violin plot	Stratified frequency plots like box plot, dot plot, violin plot	Scatter plots
			Scatter matrix plots
	t-Tests	ANOVA	Linear Regression
	Tests for Equal Variances	Tests for Equal Variances	Non-linear Regression,
			Design of Experiments
	Non-parametric Tests	Non-parametric Tests	
	Hypothesis Tests		**Regression Analyses**

The selection of the appropriate tool depends on the business question that needs to be answered, the type of data collected, and their characteristics. The factor, the independent variable that drives a decision is usually called "X". The resulting outcome, the dependant variable is usually called "Y".

Generally, data analysis is done in a graphical and in a statistical way. Usually, both are necessary to ensure proper conclusions. Additionally, graphical analysis may be needed for visualising data and storytelling. Remember, a picture is worth a thousand words.

However, graphical analysis without statistical support may lead to wrong decisions; similarly for running statistical analysis without graphical support.

Therefore, all data analyses should be done in a two-step approach. Firstly, one or more graphs should be plotted to visualise the data. This visualisation alone may have the power to drive the decision. Secondly, yet, it is a good practice to support the graphical analysis with statistics.

When, for example, the rejection rate of a product is compared between months, January and April, then month signifies the independent variable X whereas rejection rate denotes the dependent variable Y. Many data analytics tasks fit in this X-Y-structure.

The application of tools depends on the data type found in X and Y. There are two major types of data, continuous and discrete. Table 1.5 shows these types including subcategories for discrete data.

Depending on the type of data in X and Y, only appropriate tools are to be selected for analysis. Otherwise, the analysis will not work. Or, much worse, the analysis will work and will give misleading results.

It is generally possible to transform continuous data into discrete data. In Figure 1.12, the performance from CHL Orange is shown in two different ways. On the left, every single data point of the delivery time is plotted over time. By inserting the customer requirement, the limit of 5 minutes, the number of on-time deliveries and late deliveries is established. On the right, this percentage

Table 1.5 Discrete versus Continuous Data

DATA TYPE	POSSIBLE VALUES	EXAMPLES
Continuous	Any value.	Temperature, distance, size,…
Discrete Count	Any non-negative integer	0, 1, 2, 3, 4, 5…
Discrete Ordinal	Distinct number of categories	Job Level 1, 2, 3, 4…
	Ranking of categories.	Hierarchy level Executive, Manager, Head…
	Likert Scale.	Rating Poor, Fair, Satisfactory, Good, Excellent
Discrete Categorical	Distinct number of categories	Groups like CHL Green, CHL Red
	No basic sequence.	Team A, team B, team C
		Operator Tan, operator Lee

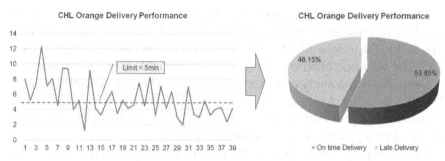

Figure 1.12 Comparison between Continuous Data and Discrete Data

is shown as a pie chart. The graph on the left can be considered showing continuous data, whereas the graph on the right displays discrete data.

By transforming continuous data into discrete, by aggregating data, the following disadvantages arise:

1. There is no information about the performance over time.
2. There is no information about how good is "good" and how bad is "bad", i.e. how close the data points are to the limit.
3. There is no information about the variation in the data.
4. There are many fewer tools for analysis to deal with discrete data versus continuous data.
5. Tools for continuous data are more powerful than those for discrete data.

Therefore, it is a very bad idea to transform continuous into discrete data. Keep the raw data. Aggregated data are much less useful for data analysis. Nevertheless, discrete data will always be an important part of the analysis.

Tools for Data Analysis

Analysing Discrete X & Discrete Y Relationship

Supplier, for example, is a discrete X and the rejection rate is a discrete Y that is generated by counting good units and rejected units (Figure 1.13). Hence, the upper left field in Table 1.4 is applied.

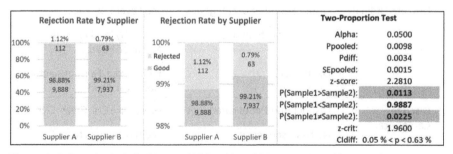

Figure 1.13 Data Analysis for Discrete X (Month) and Discrete Y (Good/Rejected Units)

Since we have only two categories, Supplier A and Supplier B in X, the appropriate statistical tool would be a Two-Proportions-Test. The first graph (Figure 1.13) does not suggest any difference because of a wrong scale. The second graph (Figure 1.13) might suggest that there is a difference in the rejection rate between Supplier A with 1.12% and Supplier B with 0.79%. The assumption of a difference can only be confirmed with the appropriate statistical tool, the two-proportion test.

Figure 1.13 reveals that the probability (p-value) for being wrong with the hypothesis "Rejection Rate of Supplier A (Sample1) is higher than Rejection Rate of Supplier B (Sample2)" is only 1.12%, i.e., P(Sample1>Sample2): 0.0113 = 1.13%. A strong contributor to the statistical decision is the sample size of 10,000 for Sample A and 8000 for Sample B. This fact makes the difference between the graph and the statistics. The graph would look the same for a sample size of 1000 and 800, respectively. However, the statistics becomes much stronger with growing sample size.

 A larger sample is always better for the analysis. Smaller samples reduce the chance to find what you are looking for.

We can argue that a rejection rate of 1.12% versus 0.79% might be a small difference. However, if this leads to many more customers complaining about the refrigerator or any home appliances because of a faulty part, we need to rethink our decision.

 The Power of Graphical Illustration
The graph used for presenting data often leads to a certain conclusion. Differences in the graphs may propose different conclusions, even for the same data.

For the same combination of discrete X and discrete Y and more than two groups, the graphical tool can be similarly a column chart (or series of pie charts) and the statistical tool of choice would be a Chi^2 Test.

 "I only believe in statistics that I doctored myself."

(Churchill, n.d.)

Analysing Discrete X & Continuous Y Relationship Using Means

If there is a discrete X (CHL Group) and a continuous Y (Delivery Time), the graphical tool of choice is usually a stratified frequency plot like a stratified histogram, dot plot, box plot, or a variant like a violin plot (see Table 1.4). If there are only two group averages to compare, the statistical tool of choice would be a two-sample t-test or a paired t-test depending on the circumstances (see Table 1.4).

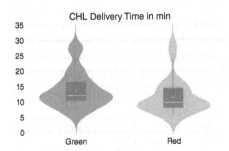

t-Test: Two-Sample Assuming Unequal Variances		
	CHL Green	*CHL Red*
Mean	10.4103	7.4447
Variance	7.0195	2.4323
Observations	29	38
Hypothesized Mean Difference	0	
df	43	
t Stat	5.3606	
P(T<=t) one-tail	0.0000	
t Critical one-tail	1.6811	
P(T<=t) two-tail	0.0000	
t Critical two-tail	2.0167	

Figure 1.14 Data Analysis for Discrete X (CHL Group) and Continuous Y (Delivery Time)

Figure 1.14 shows this combination. The graph gives a weak indication that the delivery time for CHL Red is lower than for CHL Green. There is a large portion of overlap between the datasets for Red and Green. Only the statistical tool, the two-sample t-test gives the truth. The "P(T<=t) two-tail" delivers the p-value of 0.000, i.e., 0% risk to assume that CHL Red performs its delivery significantly faster than CHL Green (see also DeliveryTime.xlsx). There is practically zero chance that these sets of data for CHL Red and CHL Green show like that only by chance, that both teams perform in the same way.

If there are more group averages to compare, the graphs to show are the same, i.e. stratified frequency plots such as stratified histogram, dot plot, box plot, or violin plot. The statistical tool of choice would be ANOVA (Analysis of Variance) as mentioned in Table 1.4 provided the data are normally distributed.

Analysing Discrete X & Continuous Y Relationship Using Variances

If the task at hand is to compare variances, a different set of tools needs to be deployed. For example, if you wish to find out whether different processes, procedures, or even operators produce different variation, test for equal variance can help. Let's say if you know that your supplier CHL Green always takes longer time than CHL Red, you can get prepared for that fact. To the contrary, if supplier CHL Blue performs with a larger variation, this could be much worse for any customer of this team because the outcome would be unpredictable (Figure 1.15).

If you want to test the relationship of groups of non-normal data, you need to consider non-parametric tests. We will illustrate this in subsequent cases.

Analysing Continuous X & Continuous Y Relationship

On the right-hand side of Table 1.4, a number of regression tools is shown. The most commonly used regression tool is linear regression.

CHL Delivery Time in min

▪ Green ▪ Orange ▪ Red ▪ Yellow ▪ Blue

Anova: Single Factor

Groups	Count	Sum	Average	Variance
Green	29	301.9	10.4103	7.0195
Red	38	282.9	7.4447	2.4323
Orange	39	210.6	5.4000	5.7542
Yellow	32	263.3	8.2281	6.2356
Blue	100	1322.289083	13.2229	39.3957

ANOVA

Source of Variation	SS	df	MS	F	P-value	F crit
Between Groups	2217.40	4	554.3507	28.0871	0.0000	2.4104
Within Groups	4598.68	233	19.7368			
Total	6816.09	237				

Figure 1.15 Data Analysis of Groups with Different Variances

Understanding this tool sets the foundation for many forecasting models. This tool can analyse the relationship between many drivers (Xs), and one Y. These Xs can be continuous and discrete. Regression analysis is widely used for analysing survey data and helps to find relationships between survey indicators.

A typical task for regression would be the analysis of drivers for employee engagement or customer satisfaction. Cronbach Alpha calculation, exploratory and confirmatory factor analysis as well as structural equation modelling are special applications of regression analysis.

Figure 1.16 shows a simple linear regression example. First, we can confirm that there is a significant relationship between both variables since Significance F, the p-value for the implicit ANOVA is less than 0.05. Next, the quality of the relationship can be drawn from the R^2 with 49.17% (R Square = 0.4917). In this case the coding time accounts for about half of the variation in the delivery time. And, there might be other Xs that explain part of the 50.83% residual variation. For a service process, an R^2 of 0.4917 for only one X can be considered a good rate.

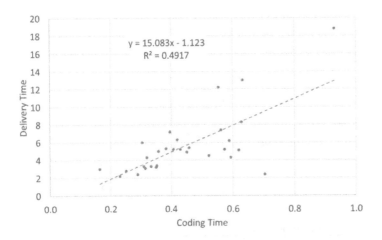

Regression Statistics	
Multiple R	0.7012
R Square	0.4917
Adjusted R Square	0.4540
Standard Error	2.6286
Observations	30

ANOVA

	df	SS	MS	F	Significance F
Regression	2	180.4523	90.2262	13.0587	0.0001
Residual	27	186.5507	6.9093		
Total	29	367.0030			

	Coefficients	Standard Error	t Stat	P-value
Intercept	-1.1209	3.2968	-0.3400	0.7365
Coding Time	15.0826	2.9526	5.1082	0.0000
Packaging Time	-0.0203	29.0779	-0.0007	0.9994

Figure 1.16 Data Analysis for Continuous X (Coding Time) and Continuous Y (Delivery Time)

Analysing Continuous X & Discrete Y Relationship

Logistic regression is a tool that fills a gap. Since regression analysis needs a continuous Y – or a quasi-continuous Y such as a Likert scale – regression cannot be used when the Y has only two levels.

Say, you wish to analyse the drivers for employees leaving your organisation. There is a long list of potential factors like age, tenure, salary, workload, engagement score, satisfaction with supervisor, job level, time since last promotion, etc. The only Y is whether this employee leaves or not. This Y cannot be considered as continuous. It is discrete with only two levels, a worst-case scenario for data analysis. For this kind of situation, logistic regression has been developed with the effect that the yes/no Y is turned into a probability for yes and no, the probability for an employee leaving the organisation. This probability behaves like a continuous Y, and the analysis becomes much more powerful. Please, read more about this in Chapter 4 of this book.

All tools discussed here are covered in case discussions as part of this book. Table 1.4 will be referred to in these cases to select the applicable graphical and statistical tools.

Whilst the application of appropriate graphical and statistical tools will be demonstrated, the tools will not be explained in detail.

Business Decision

Very often, data analysis produces results that are hard to comprehend by management or staff who are not trained in data analytics. A "p-value", for example, is a key output of many statistical tools but is not easily understood by the majority.

However, the translation of an analysis output like "p-value = 0.03" into a result like "The risk of wasting our money by buying from this more expensive vendor is only 3%" changes the conversation about data analytics.

It is no longer the case of relying on the Data Analyst or Data Scientist to make this translation. Management should understand the basics of data analytics in order to turn data into information and draw appropriate conclusions (Gallo, 2018).

Analytical Story Telling

Today, there is much enthusiasm in organisations about Big Data and data analytics. However, unless decision makers understand analytics and its implications, they may not change their behaviours to adopt analytical approaches for drawing conclusions and making decisions based on data. Data analysts or data scientists who care whether their work is implemented, i.e. whether it changes decisions and influences others, care about this issue and devote a great deal of time and effort to it. They are even concerned about communicating the results of their analyses.

Communicating about analytics has not traditionally been viewed as a subject for the education of quantitative analysts. Typically, those with a strong analytical orientation focus heavily on analytical methods and not too much on how to communicate effectively about analytics. Therefore, the job of the data analyst is not only to collect and validate representative data, clean, transform, and analyse that, but also to translate the statistical message in a way that is understandable, compelling, and interesting enough to be taken into account when planning strategy and making decisions.

People hardly remember numbers. They remember pictures, and stories that are created and inspired by these pictures. Picturesque storytelling has become an important skill in organisations. If you can pack your message in a good story, you have a better chance of "selling" it, of convincing your audience.

Telling a good story means considering at least the following questions.

Who is the Audience?

A certain story may work very well for one audience but not for another one. An average group of middle management in a healthcare setting, for instance, has a limited appetite for statistics. A group of scientists from a blood lab, to the contrary, expect details. They need statistics and will be disappointed if you cannot explain them. They will most likely challenge you. Know about your audience and think what is important to them, what concerns them, and what is their educational background.

How to show the Data?

These days, there are new tools to communicate the results of analytics and you should be aware of the possibilities. Of course, the appropriate communication tool depends on the situation and your audience. The data type helps you decide the tool to use. Not everything can and must be shown with bar charts or line graphs. We can do better than that. A bar chart is a last resort.

Figure 1.17 shows the different story you can tell with a box plot versus a bar chart. The bar chart only illustrates the mean of your data sets. After you have mentioned that CHL Blue takes on average longer than all other teams and CHL Orange is the fastest team, your story ends. The box plot, however, reveals that the Blue team not only is the slowest but also shows a huge variation. Yet, the fastest performance for Blue is with 1 minute faster than any other team's best performance. The longest delivery time for Blue is at 31 minutes. Unfortunately, 50% of all Blue deliveries take longer than the slowest delivery of team Orange and team Red.

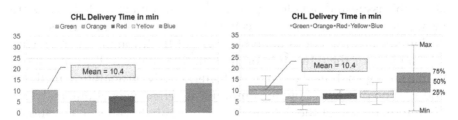

Figure 1.17 Bar Chart (Column Chart) versus Box Plot for Presenting Data

Figure 1.18 adds more information about the distribution of the data in an easy and attractive way with a violin plot.

For continuous data, replace your bar charts and column charts with box plots or other alternatives.
Your audience will highly appreciate it.

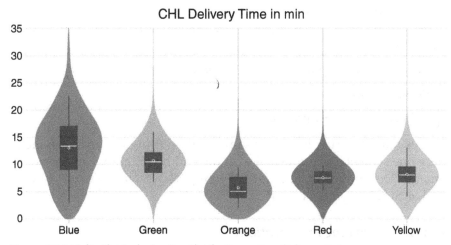

Figure 1.18 Violin Plot Inclusive Box Plot for Presenting Delivery Data

What is the Purpose of the Presentation?

Consider the intention for your presentation. What do you want the audience to do with your data? Is it only for information or does the dataset need to be seen as important enough to drive a business decision? Ensure your audience "gets your message".

Let us assume your presentation needs to highlight a change, a before-after-situation, or advantages and disadvantages, etc. that leads to an important decision like buying the better equipment or amending a process. Then thumbs-up or thumbs-down for your investment suggestion depends on your presentation. Make the message understood and stick.

Leaving it to the audience to read from the data what is the "good news" is most likely not the best strategy. Ensuring the message gets across usually means, presenting in an interesting way. Add graphics and pictures that help make the point (Figure 1.19).

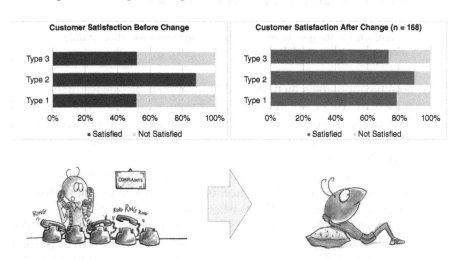

Figure 1.19 Illustrating your Presentation

And, ensure you repeat the key message.

Will Smith once quipped about making a convincing presentation in three steps:

First, tell them what you are going to tell them.

Second, tell them.

Third, tell them what you told them.

This remark certainly carries some truth. Putting the key message in only one sentence as a conclusion at the end of your story might not be enough. Depending on the length of your pitch, you might have lost your audience before you get there.

How to simplify the Presentation?

You are probably very proud having mastered the data analytics task and all the new tools and you wish to show your audience your achievements. Stop. Consider what is important to them.

Let us take a look at this message presented to the senior management:

"Last year, the satisfaction score of our loan customers was at 67%. After stratifying the data into loan type, we found that the score was especially low for type 1 and type 3 customers with 52%. Type 2 customers were more satisfied with 88%. After changing the process of loan application with focus on type 1 and type 3 loans, our average satisfaction score is now at 80% with type 1 at 79%, type 2 at 90% and type 3 at 73%.

We wanted to find out whether this change is significant and applied a two-proportion-test because we have discrete data in X and Y. The test gave us a p-value of 0.0141. This means there is a significant difference between last year's customer satisfaction and the sample taken this year after implementing the pilot process.

Therefore, we suggest to roll-out the change since we will certainly increase customer satisfaction".

Although your management undoubtedly appreciates the result that leads to increased customer satisfaction, they may not welcome the "statistics talk". Part of the reason might be, that some of them will not know what you are talking about, but they will not show that, and hence they will not ask you for clarification.

What they might think is this: Does this increase in customer satisfaction likely turn into increased customer retention and customer loyalty and consequently growth of the market share?

A statement like "Last year's market research has shown that a 10% increase in customer satisfaction might lead to a 3% growth in market share, hence we should be able to increase our market share by about 7% if we implement our solution" will hit the nerves of the management.

No one needs to know about the tools used and the p-value as a result. The p-value usually stands for a risk: "The risk for investing in the new process and not getting any return is quite marginal at 1.4%. Hence, I suggest we do that" is a much clearer message. Risk is management talk!

If someone in your audience is interested in the tools you have learned and applied, have this information on back-up slides. This shows that you are prepared. Show what you have learned if they ask. After all, they probably sent you to a data analytics course for that purpose.

Storytelling is probably as old as mankind itself. We know that strong leaders tell stories to convey information and motivate listeners. Analytical storytelling or data journalism, when mapped to the audience attributes, can help anyone or any organisation clarify their thinking, improve their decision quality, and inspire action.

 The success of your presentation depends more on the "How" than on the "What".
Good contents cannot compensate for a bad pitch.

Deploying Analytics Tools

Many data analysis tools mentioned in this book need normal data, i.e. data with a distribution that comes close to a normal distribution. Without the help of some statistics, it is not easy to determine whether normal distribution can be assumed.

For large sample sizes – more than 100 – the histogram of the data can give some indication whether the data could be normal. However, for smaller samples, histograms are a bad way of judging.

When using Descriptive Statistics under Data – Data Analysis – Descriptive Statistics in MS Excel, Kurtosis and Skewness are generated. As a rule of thumb, normality might be assumed if both assumptions, $-2 \leq Kurtosis \leq 2$ and $-2 \leq Skewness \leq 2$ are valid.

The best way is still to perform a normality test on your data. A very powerful test for normality is the **Shapiro–Wilk** test. If for some reason this test is not available, use another one from the R code listed in Table 1.6.

Practice

- What are the typical phases one has to follow when working on Data Analytics cases?
- What are potential sources for data acquisition?
- What are the characteristics of Gauss's bell-shaped curve? How to construct it? What are areas of interest under the curve?
- What are graphical and statistical tools used for any X-Y-combination?
- What are characteristics of discrete and continuous data? Why is it important to distinguish? Name three examples for each category!

Table 1.6 Normality Tests

NORMALITY TESTS	
Data:	Continuous Data.
	Discrete Ordinal Data.
Null Hypothesis H_0:	There is no significant difference between Data and the Gauss' normal distribution. Data is normal.
Alternative Hypothesis H_A:	There is a significant difference between Data and the Gauss' normal distribution. Data is not normal.
Decision:	If p-value < 0.05, reject H_0 and accept H_A.
	I.e. if p-value $\geq$ 0.05, Data can be considered normally distributed.
Assumptions:	None
R code:	```

```
# Loading Data in vector Data
Data <- yourDataFrame$yourColumn
# Loading necessary packages for
Shapiro-Wilk
install.packages("stats")
library(stats)
# Performing Shapiro-Wilk test
shapiro.test(Data)
# Loading necessary packages for
Anderson-Darling
install.packages("nortest")
library(nortest)
# Performing Anderson-Darling test
ad.test(Data)
# Performing Lilliefors (Kolmogorov-
Smirnov) test
lillie.test(Data)
# Performing Pearson chi-square test
pearson.test(Data)
# Performing Cramer-von Mises test
cvm.test(Data)
```

Please complete the following steps:

- Download the introduction data for data analysis from Data Analysis.xlsx.
- Perform data plots for each X-Y-combination.
- Perform statistical analysis for each X-Y-combination.
- Prepare a short presentation to explain why you have chosen which tool set for analysis.
- Prepare a story to tell your findings.

Competencies of a Data Scientist

"Data Scientist: The Sexiest Job of the 21st Century."
(Davenport, 2012/10)

The competencies of a data analytics professional and a data scientist are largely similar and depend on the source. The data analytics professional has been around for decades whereas the name of the data scientist was created not long ago (Hayashi, 1998). Even for the data analytics professional, the job has evolved over time.

- In the past, Big Data was non-existent and out of reach. It is in reach now. The professional should be able to deal with it.

- In the past, the data analytics professionals mainly focused on statistics. Nowadays, we suggest that these professionals should have a good portion of IT background in their rucksacks, too.

- In the past, these professionals, even if they existed in an organisation, were not people who would sit in the board room or present to the bosses. Today, the data analyst has a chance to develop into the **trusted advisor** to the management. The analyst might become the one who is asked for data-driven insights before important decisions are made.

Competencies Needed in Data Analytics Phases

Figure 1.20 highlights the competency domains needed in different phases of data analytics case work.

For the **first phase** of formulating a business question and translating it into a data analytics question, the data analyst is required to have a good **business acumen**. This business acumen uplifts the data analyst from someone who is seen as the "data guy" to the "trusted advisor" who understands business and can handle data.

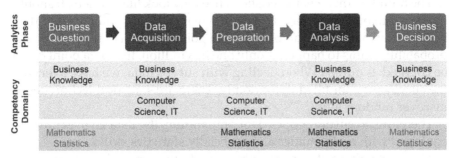

Figure 1.20 Steps of a Data Analytics Case and Related Competency Domains

The **second phase**, the data acquisition phase, needs the data analyst to know how to get data. In the past, we wrote a request to IT to ask them to download the data. This IT request usually took time to get implemented, was very often not implemented the way we wanted it to be done, and had to be repeated multiple times until the data we needed were available.

Asking IT to download the data for analysis usually meant, when we got the data, it was already outdated. Almost never did we obtain a link into the database that allowed us to acquire up-to-date information. Today, we have the hardware that can handle a large amount of data even on a notebook. And, we have software that allows us to establish links to virtually any data source that keeps us always up to date. Some **computer science and IT knowledge** come in handy for the data analyst to do most of this himself. For that purpose, he might want to equip himself with **basic skills in SQL** (Structured Query Language) to be able to tap into internal and external databases for data acquisition. Do not underestimate **MS Excel**. This comes with impressive data acquisition power for even quite large data sets and the huge benefit of familiarity.

The **third phase** deals with data preparation which includes cleaning, transforming, and validating data sets before any analysis can be done. This phase is often seen as the most time-consuming phase in data analytics. Similar to data acquisition, this might need skills and experience in **computer science and IT** because it often requires using **MS Excel** for "usual data sets" and additional software like **R, Python, Hadoop and others** for Big Data.

What is considered a usual data set? This is hard to answer. The latest hardware on your computer, the latest version of MS Excel and superb experience in using them pushes the boundary quite far out. When the computer takes too long to open the MS Excel table with some hundred thousand data sets or the VLOOKUP between some such tables gives up, then it is time to consider R or Python – before buying a new computer.

Since cleaning and validating the data is a job the data analyst cannot delegate to someone else, some statistical knowledge is of great advantage. Often, data sets have typo errors or misleading input. Some of these errors can be found by their characteristics since they look like outliers. It should not be up to our gut feeling to decide whether a data point is an outlier. Statistics can help. For example, if a data point is far out of the rest and the probability of this to happen is only one in a million, that data point could be counted as outlier. When dealing with survey data, we have to ensure the survey was not filled in randomly. There are statistical techniques to discover random input.

Therefore, to ensure proper data preparation, the data analyst must be equipped with **mathematics** and especially **statistics skills**.

The **fourth phase**, the analyse phase marks the core of the data analytics case work. Although, it is most likely less time-consuming than the previous phase, it generates the important output and is therefore critical. This phase often needs some **computer science and IT** skills for the same reason as before. The analysis is done on software like MS Excel, R, Python, SPSS, SigmaXL, Minitab, SAS etc. This software needs to be handled properly before it can be of use.

Of course, **mathematics and statistics** is here more needed than in any other phase. Whilst it is not necessary to have a full statistics background, it is crucial to know its application.

Data analysis is almost never straight forward. Since it is the process of gaining insights into the organisation, it is the process of continuously learning about it and adapting the methodology on the way. And it is the phase of surprises. Almost always, our analysis generates an "Aha!" or a "Really?". Then the data scientist needs to either go back to the business asking questions like "Can this really be?". Or she can answer most of this kind of question herself if she is equipped with a good portion of **business acumen**.

Figure 1.11 illustrates this type of situation. A newly hired statistician who does not know much about blood donation processes might generate this plot and conclude that blood donation is not normally distributed – which eliminates many analysis tools from use. If a blood bank experienced staff does this analysis, she concludes immediately that there are different donation types mixed. Analysing them one by one will be much more appropriate than running the tests for all of them together. Knowing the organisation avoids wrong conclusions.

The **fifth phase** necessitates the data scientist to translate the analysis result into business language to suggest a certain course of action or to prepare a decision. **Business knowledge** is obviously a prerequisite for this work. However, this phase cannot be done by someone who does not understand the analysis result. Hence, a good grasp of **statistics** is vital here as well.

In conclusion, we strongly suggest having a data scientist being equipped with knowledge, skills, and experience in the following competency domains: Business Acumen, Computer Science, and IT as well as Mathematics and Statistics (Figure 1.21).

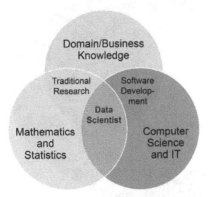

Figure 1.21 Essential Competency Domains of a Data Scientist

Key Roles of Today's Managers and Leaders

Today's managers are confronted with an ever-changing business environment. And the speed of change increases steadily. These changes affect customers' and suppliers' behaviours, competitors' offerings, and characteristics of their own staff. In order to keep pace with these changes, managers' antennas need to be out constantly, and the frequency of getting data from these antennas needs to increase as well.

 "If all you have is a hammer, everything looks like a nail."
(Maslow, 1966)

Therefore, data-driven companies like Google, Amazon, Microsoft, Walmart, eBay, LinkedIn, and Twitter (Davenport, 2012/10) have built their own data science teams who are even capable of customising and extending the available toolkit for their purpose.

Is it necessary for companies and organisations who are not like Google to have a data analytics team? Certainly not. Do we ask every manager to understand the organisation's financials? Yes, we do. Financials are based on **lagging indicators**, Hence, when we see them, there is little chance to influence them. Most data about customers, processes, and staff are based on **leading indicators**. If we understand them, we can still influence the results – the financials. This makes some of them at least as important as the financials themselves.

Therefore, in our opinion, today's managers should play a key role in understanding patterns in data and draw conclusions out of them. They should have a chance and the will to extend their set of competencies to grow into the role of a data scientist (Gallo, 2018).

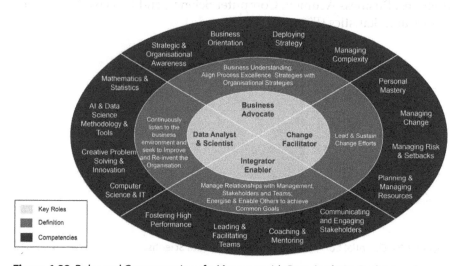

Figure 1.22 Roles and Competencies of a Manager with Data Analytics Background

Figure 1.22 summarises the competencies that might be expected of today's manager. Of course, the depth of acquiring the competencies depends on the business situation, the manager's role in the organisation, and many other factors. Still, just ignoring the role of the data scientist is not an option in the near future.

FROM MANAGER TO DATA ANALYSING MANAGER

Jeremy is deputy department head in a medium size educational institution. We met Jeremy when we went through a series of Lean Six Sigma projects together with the objective to make their operations lean.

Whenever we start this kind of journey with any organisation, the chances are high that participants introduce themselves with the usual apology like "I don't like statistics and I may not do very well in this discipline". They say this because they know that a proper Lean Six Sigma comes with a good portion of statistics. And they say this because their exposure to statistics has been the mandatory lessons in university – which can be quite challenging and often very dry.

Jeremy did not introduce this statement. Instead, he said, "I need to brush up on my statistics". During our Lean Six Sigma projects together, Jeremy was a keen learner and a terrific challenger. We knew that when Jeremy asked a question, it was usually beneficial for the whole class. His focus was on learning and understanding what was taught.

His department head, let us call her Amanda, turned out to be an exceptional support for Jeremy and for their Lean Six Sigma projects. She made sure that Jeremy had access to all data necessary. After each Lean Six Sigma session, all participants had to apply on their own data what they had learned. Amanda asked Jeremy for update presentations during his project work. They, together with their department, applied learnings on how to analyse and visualise information and to draw conclusions.

And they did. Very soon after the kick-off, the first change in their process was triggered by the lack of some necessary information. Amanda and Jeremy took note of that and amended the way the data were recorded. Many more suggestions and finally changes were driven by learnings out of the data.

Years later, when the whole organisation went through a Strategic Workforce Planning project, Jeremy turned out to be the best internal resource to have when preparing and running this project. Not only was he able to help us with his institutional knowledge to find the most suitable way for data collection, analysis etc. He also led this effort for a number of departments in an excellent way.

In the meantime, we met Jeremy attending one of our Data Analytics workshops. "I just wanted to hone my skills in statistics since it has proved to be a very important and advantageous discipline for modern managers", he answered when asked for the reason to attend.

Jeremy is an example of a manager who is open to learn and apply an essential skill, data analytics, in the data-driven world of today.

References

Box, G. E. P. (1976). Science and Statistics. *Journal of the American Statistical Association*, 71 (356): 791–799.

Burnham, K. (2019, Aug. 18). *Data Analytics vs Data Science: A Breakdown*. Retrieved from Northeastern University: `https://www.northeastern.edu/graduate/blog/data-analytics-vs-data-science/`

Churchill, W. S. (n.d.) Winston Churchill Quotes. Retrieved from `https://slife.org/winston-churchill-quotes/`

Data Never Sleeps 7.0. (2020). Retrieved from `www.domo.com`: `https://www.domo.com/learn/data-never-sleeps-7#/`

Davenport, T. H. (2012/10). Data Scientist: The Sexiest Job of the 21st Century. *Harvard Business Review*, 70–76.

Dunnington, G. W. (2004). *Gauss: Titan of Science*. Washington, DC: The Mathematical Association of America.

Gallo, A. (2018, Oct 31). 4 Analytics Concepts Every Manager Should Understand. Retrieved from *Harvard Business Review*: `https://hbr.org/2018/10/4-analytics-concepts-every-manager-should-understand`

Hayashi, C. (1998). *What is Data Science? Fundamental Concepts and a Heuristic Example*. Tokyo: Springer Japan.

healthline. Falck, S. (2018, Jul. 16). How Many Cells Are in the Human Body? Fast Facts. Retrieved from healthline: `https://www.healthline.com/health/number-of-cells-in-body`

Lane, D. M. (n.d.). Normal Distributions. Retrieved from Online Statistics Education: An Interactive Multimedia Course of Study: `http://onlinestatbook.com/2/normal_distribution/normal_distribution.html`

Maslow, A. (1966). *The Psychology of Science*. New York: Harper & Row.

McKenzie, J. (2021, Jan. 13). Powering the Beast: Why We Shouldn't Worry about the Internet's Rising Electricity Consumption. *Physics World*. Retrieved from `https://physicsworld.com/a/powering-the-beast-why-we-shouldnt-worry-about-the-internets-rising-electricity-consumption/`

Microsoft. (2020, Sep. 22). Data Sources in Power BI Desktop. Retrieved from `docs.microsoft.com`: `https://docs.microsoft.com/en-us/power-bi/connect-data/desktop-data-sources`

NodeGraph. (2020). How Much Data is on the Internet? *The Big Data Facts Update 2020*. Retrieved from NodeGraph: `https://www.nodegraph.se/how-much-data-is-on-the-internet/`

Parr, B. (2010, Aug. 5). There Are 129,864,880 Books in the Entire World. Mashable. Retrieved from: `https://mashable.com/2010/08/05/number-of-books-in-the-world/`

Russom, P. (2011, Q4). Big Data Analytics. *TDWI Best Practices Report*, pp. 04-10.

Springboard India. (2019, Aug. 12). Data Science vs Data Analytics – How to Decide which one is Right for You? Retrieved from Springboard India: `https://medium.com/@springboard_ind/data-science-vs-data-analytics-how-to-decide-which-one-is-right-for-you-41e7bdec080e`

Xia, B. S. (2015). Review of business intelligence through data analysis. *Benchmarking*, 300–311.

List of Figures and Tables

Customer Domain – Customer Analytics

Customer analytics is a branch of data science that deals with data from and about customers, especially data about the behaviour of customers before, during, or after product and service delivery. Analysing this data might lead to extracting important information for the purpose of market segmentation, developing marketing strategies, and consequently growing the market share.

CONTENTS

- ➤ Why Customer Analytics
- ➤ Listen to the Voice of your Existing Customers
- ➤ Understanding Customer Expectations
- ➤ Studying the Complete Customer Experience
- ➤ Designing Customer Surveys
- ➤ Conclusion

CASE	CASE TITLE	TOOLS USED
1	Great, We Have Improved . . . or Not?	Ex, R
2	What Drives our Patient Satisfaction?	Ex, R
3	How to Create a Patient Satisfaction Dashboard	Ex, BI, R

Tools Used: Ex . . . MS Excel, BI . . . MS Power BI, R . . . R and R Studio

Highlights
After completing this chapter, you will be able to . . .

- ■ Understand the importance of customer analytics.
- ■ Comprehend the complexity of customer data analytics.

- Set up systems and channels to listen to your customers.
- Implement customer analytics in your organisation.

Why Customer Analytics?

Customer analytics is linked to the **Customer** domain (Figure 2.1). It covers the collection, processing, and analysis of customer-related data. This includes survey data from different customer environments and data measuring the "moment of truth", the moment when the customer experiences the product or service offered.

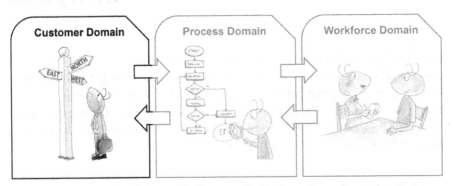

Figure 2.1 Customer Analytics and its Focus on the Customer Domain

This data might lead to information for the purposes of market segmentation, developing marketing strategies, and consequently growing the market share.

The underlying principle of customer analytics is predicting future customer behaviour based on the understanding of past behaviour. It is necessary to get to know your customers, existing and potential.

What are the benefits of knowing your customers?

1. **Building trust and loyalty**. Regularly **listening to the voice of existing customers** is vital to retain and build lasting relationship with the customers. Keeping our promises and always meeting customers' expectations is the foundation of our relationship with the customers. If the customers trust us, they come back and buy from us again. Disappointed customers do not do that. They look for alternatives.

2. **Creating growth opportunities. Knowing our customers** gives us a deeper sense of customer understanding which in turn provides the business with information about consumers' buying behaviour, interests, and engagements. It helps businesses to locate opportunities to initiate new products or services.

3. **Having a business model based on customer knowledge**. Today, more than 50 billion devices are connected to the internet globally,

with mobile being the primary internet device for most individuals. Using this connectivity for **studying their experience** helps businesses to transit from existing products and traditional distribution models to those that deliver what the customers want.

Establishing our company in Singapore in 2006 was quite easy. Even then, everything worked online. After some minutes on the respective government website, the company was set up. The next step was attaching a business banking account to that company. This could not be done online.

After phoning some multinational banks and recognising that SME business was not something they wanted to have, we ended up following a friend's recommendation calling a local bank. The banker we were talking with, let us call him Hui Jun, listened to our requirements, and recommended their new business banking account that was tailored especially for an SME. We felt some relief since our banking problem was settled.

Stop, not yet!

Hui Jun asked us to visit him in the branch for verification purpose and to get the necessary signatures. Unfortunately, we were scheduled to leave for China for a couple of weeks and had no chance to sign our papers. This would have meant that we could not raise any invoice for weeks or even months.

Hui Jun must have felt our dilemma and asked whether we were at home in the evening. After a split second of irritation, we answered that we were. He asked whether he could visit us at home with all banking paperwork.

Said and done. Hui Jun came to our house having all account opening papers well prepared. We signed after getting his explanation and had our business banking account.

Even today we still talk about this banking experience – and the banker who went the extra mile. We are still with this bank and recommend it whenever we can.

This outstanding employee has turned us into very loyal customers.

Listen to the Voice of Your Existing Customers

When customers send you a signal, take it very seriously.

"Oh, this is just a complaint from one customer" was uttered by someone working in a financial institution. If you have thousands of customers, you might be tempted to react like that if one of them complains about a certain experience. This reaction will breed a mindset that is completely wrong.

A study in German financial institutions revealed that what you see or hear from customers is only a fraction of the truth (Bonn, 2006). This study uncovered that behind each complaint you receive, there is a multitude of customers who may have a similar reason for complaint (Figure 2.2). However, they do not complain. They just walk. They found that the factor might be around 25.

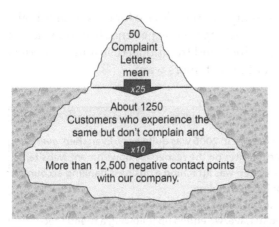

Figure 2.2 The Iceberg – Hidden Complaints in Banking

Furthermore, this study exposed another hidden truth. Not everything leads to complaints. There are small annoyances or irritations that are not worth complaining about. Still, if they remain annoying, this customer might walk as well. The factor here is found to be about 10.

HOW TO TURN YOUR CUSTOMERS AWAY

Since my trusted German bank did not operate private customer business in Singapore, I needed to look out for another bank after my relocation to Asia. I signed up with Bank A, one of the multinational banks with global reach, so that I could serve my studying kids in Germany whenever there was a need. Setting up accounts was smooth and fast.

When I asked them for supplementary cards for my grown-up kids in Germany, it seemed to be another routine banking experience. I filed the application, received the cards, and send them to my kids near Cologne.

My son tried to use the card for topping up petrol – and failed because he did not receive the necessary One Time Password (OTP) on his German mobile phone. After trying three times, he paid cash and left the petrol station that was full of customers on a weekday morning – with a humiliated feeling.

Of course, I personally showed up in the premier lounge of my bank to settle this problem. Most important for me was not that the card did not work. The most crucial issue was the result of that, the embarrassment of my son in front of many customers, some of them were certainly his neighbours.

After receiving a set of convincing apologies from my trusted relationship manager and the promise, that this would be fixed immediately, I told my son and asked him to try again.

Two weeks later, he did. No OTP was sent to his hand phone. Again! There was no change.

After wasting time by going back to the bank and expressing my anger, I had the chance to talk to a manager who had recently flown in from the UK. He understood, apologised, and promised.

Another two weeks later, my son tried the card again and got rejected.

This was enough for me to leave the bank. I did not bother to tell them. I left.

This study should concern us very much. One complaint certainly does not represent one frustrated customer, but about 25 customers who are more or less ready to look for another service provider. And this one complaint hints that there might be around 250 slightly annoyed customers who could be on the way out sooner or later.

These studies are not new. However, we are of the opinion that the conclusions of this and many other studies must not be forgotten. Data analytics is not just for Big Data. Taking care of your existing customers is your first responsibility.

HOW TO DISAPPOINT YOUR CUSTOMERS – AND TURN THEM AWAY

Bank B did never impress me with their service. Therefore, I stopped using their services years ago. I went into the bank to close my account, since I do not have a lot of trust in them. Although I requested closure of all accounts, for some reason, there was still a balance on my credit card account. Unfortunately, this amount was negative, i.e. my credit card shows a small amount of savings. For 18 months, I received monthly statements showing this negative amount. They even included a form and envelope with payment instructions. I am tempted to send them a negative cheque trying to stop this. I guess this will not work. In the meantime, we have wasted a considerable amount of wood for printing this, for nothing.

This is not worth sending a complaint. But this is something I let everyone know. For sure.

Understanding Customer Expectations

For understanding customer expectations, different tools can be used. A very simple yet powerful tool is the Kano Analysis (Revelle, 2004).

Kano Analysis is a tool that can greatly help to structure customer needs based on feedback given. It divides customer needs in four categories (Kaufmann, 2018b):

- **Musts**: Customer expects this characteristic to be fulfilled, even without talking about it. However, fulfilling this need does not result in customer satisfaction, it just avoids dissatisfaction. Example: Your new car comes with an aircon (Figure 2.3). You will probably not even ask whether your new car has aircon onboard since this is standard. You certainly do not ask for brakes. However, if they do not provide something you consider a must, you become extremely disappointed.

- **Satisfiers** (The More the Better): Not meeting this need results in dissatisfaction. Delivering on this requirement generates satisfaction – the more the better. Example: Fuel efficiency of a car is of great interest for most customers. They will ask for it or check the specifications.

- **Delighters**: Customer does not expect the service provider meeting this characteristic; hence it does not result in dissatisfaction if not

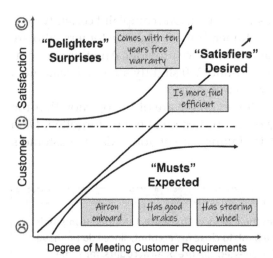

Figure 2.3 Kano Diagram for Buying a Car

present. However, this characteristic can be used to differentiate your product or service in the market, to form a unique selling point. Example: Receiving your new car with ten years free warranty would be far beyond your expectations.

- **Indifferent**: Customer does not perceive this characteristic as necessary nor does it cause satisfaction if present. Example: Car manual shows an additional feature – a foreign language.

Customer expectations are not stagnant in Figure 2.3. Over time, they usually move from delighters to satisfiers and finally musts. Example: At the beginning of the 1980s, the availability of airbags in a car was not something we would worry about. This changed over the years. From one airbag to two airbags was a big step and certainly a characteristic buyers would check out. Nowadays, we assume our car has enough airbags to keep us safe. Do we ask for the number? I have not done this for a long time. It is a must.

WHEN A MUST CRITERION IS NOT MET

I recently bought a new notebook computer. I have been working on first-class notebooks for the last 30 years. I ordered my notebook with the usual accessories as I always do.

After receiving my notebook from my favourite and trusted brand, I unpacked it, docked it in, synchronised it, did some settings, and started using it. Everything was extremely smooth as expected.

Some hours later my new notebook told me that I needed to charge the battery. I was incredibly surprised to receive this signal since my notebook was connected to the docking station. For me this meant and still means, the charging is taken care of. After checking all connections without finding any loose ones, I contacted the service hotline for my notebook.

> After checking of my order, they told me that my new docking station does not charge the computer. They recommended connecting a power adapter to the computer, whilst another one was busy powering my docking station.
>
> It took me a while until I realised that Mr Kano has caught up to me. They asked me whether I checked the charging function of the docking station when I placed my order. Of course, I did not. A major function of a docking station is to charge the computer. I have been used to this for at least 20 years and I expect this. Hence, I see this as a must the same way a car comes with brakes.
>
> Sure, my computer vendor was right. I did not ask for it. But this did not stop me from being extremely disappointed. In the meantime, they replaced everything, and the whole thing is running as clockwork.
>
> Did I consider changing my computer vendor whom I have trusted for 12 years? I sure did. And, I have not made up my mind until the next order needs to be placed.

Analysing our customer feedback regarding these categories of customer perception for our product or service will be of huge value for improving performance and gaining market share. How can we use our customer-satisfaction data to establish a Kano analysis? There are data analysis tools that will help.

Studying the Complete Customer Experience

When studying customer satisfaction, the customer experience, we usually focus on key features of our products or service delivery, on those features we know they value most. Many organisations have mapped a service blueprint and concentrate on the touch points, the "moments of truth" identified (Eyung, 2019).

Very often, these are the themes that end up as questions in customer satisfaction surveys. These surveys are essential and give a large portion of feedback about how the organisation is doing. However, in an ever-changing environment and frequently fluctuating customer expectations, these surveys ought to change as well. A survey that was developed years ago, might not be fit for today. Part of the reason is that the so-called touchpoints might have shifted, and delighters do not have the power to delight any longer. As shown before, delighters and satisfiers become musts over time.

Whilst analysing all data about your existing and potential customers, it is critical to value the "old methods" of interacting with your customers.

According to Hennessy (2019), some of the ways of interfacing with customers are:

- **Spending time with end users**. Even if you have a rather business-to-business relationship, someone uses your products or services at the end, the end-consumer. Talking to end-consumers instead of relying on the distributor or channel or implementer adds value to your business. Your direct customer, the other business, tries to help you getting information about your end-consumers' needs.

However, they very likely may have another perspective on your products and your services.

Let us assume you buy from Amazon or Lazada. Neither Amazon nor Lazada make any products, the logistics provider does neither. However, they deal with millions of different products, hence they are not able to care about the characteristics of each product. Waiting for the feedback from end consumers on the Amazon or Lazada platform is mostly not fruitful because people usually do not take the time to give feedback. On many occasions, the maker of the products I bought via Lazada contacted me for comments. And, if they do this, I almost certainly give my opinion. This is a powerful way of getting feedback from end-consumers who are so far away from them.

- **Watch Consumers Buying your Product.** Analysing the shopping behaviour of buyers might lead to many ideas of how to improve their experience and increase your revenue. There are two ways of doing so. Firstly, you can dive into the data that shows shoppers' behaviour. For example, it tells you what people buy at a DIY shop when they have a certain project. And you will find that for some projects, they appear multiple times. Can you help them avoiding multiple trips? Secondly, you might just watch them making their rounds in the shop. Some DIY shops are huge. By watching them selecting and trying, you might learn something about your shop layout and improve it. And you might learn about their needs and help them better.

- **Go to Gemba and watch Consumers Using your Product or Experiencing your Service.** Apart from all data that is available today, observing customers experiencing your service is still an unbeatable way of getting information about your service delivery processes (Tan, 2017).

  After completing a day of project work at the blood bank, we left the building. On the way, we took the lift down. In the lift, we met a young man who obviously came from the blood donation. We asked him for his experience. "Oh, all nurses and doctors are very friendly and highly professional. It is a very nice environment. Good job", he said. And we could see that he meant what he stated. Only after we insisted on learning one thing we could improve in the process, he mentioned – almost ashamed to say it – "They are a bit slow."

  After getting this feedback, we went back and checked his timing and the evaluation he gave. His evaluation was perfect with compliments. The timing was at the average.

  Since the blood bank always gets outstanding evaluations, the conclusion of "slow process" was not their top priority. Only a few wrote this down.

 A sincere conversation with some of your customers can never be replaced by electronic means of data collection.

Designing Customer Surveys

After having highlighted multiple times that talking to the customer is never out of fashion and we must not disregard this channel of getting feedback, we acknowledge the necessity of getting additional information from hundreds or even thousands of people via a survey.

When you design, deliver, and install a gas turbine at a customer's power plant, you are in continuous touch with several representatives of your customer. And the information flow is quite smooth. A survey might not even be necessary.

When you offer banking products to consumers, you have a customer base of thousands or millions. You cannot reach all customers personally on the phone to ask for feedback. In this case, a survey might be a good addition to other means like observing customers and collecting data about their behaviour. For this kind of organisation, running surveys is a must.

An additional reason for conducting surveys might be the fact that only one out of 25 customers who receive a bad service will really complain (Bonn, 2006). There is a chance that some of the others are willing to give feedback if we provide the channel of the survey for them.

Since surveys cost a considerable amount of money especially when they are done by market research companies, it might be a good idea to design, conduct, and analyse your own survey. For this purpose, we have povided some hints in the following sections:

Determine the Purpose of your Survey

Firstly, a survey could be focusing on receiving a **high-level feedback** about your performance as an organisation. The Net Promoter Score (NPS) is usually derived out of one single question: "How likely are you to recommend our product or service to a friend or colleague?"

This question is usually followed by an open question that ask for explanation for the rating. The greatest advantage of NPS is its simplicity for the surveyed person. The NPS is more likely to receive an answer.

The disadvantage is that it gives very little information if the surveyed people do not provide an explanation for their rating.

Secondly, a survey could check whether the result, the **outcome of your service delivery** meets the customer's expectations. The design could be similar to that of the NPS.

Thirdly, a survey could question the **customer experience at critical touchpoints**. This survey is usually more detailed and has very specific questions. This is at the same time the advantage of this kind of survey because it delivers much more information by virtually guiding the customers through the process again and asking them to rate or compare their experience at these touchpoints. The obvious disadvantage is that fewer customers will take it because it takes much more time than the other two survey types.

You may even combine these and other surveys to ask the same customers at different point in time different questions. This depends very much on your organisation, your offerings and your customer base.

Use Proven Questionnaires

Designing a questionnaire is not trivial. If possible, use questions from credible sources that are reliable, tested, and validated. There are questions for nearly all purposes available. Use them.

Designing your own questions should be a last resort. If one is not trained in this kind of undertaking, it can even lead to an embarrassment for your organisation. Sending out an unprofessionally developed questionnaire to thousands of consumers would not be supporting your brand.

A questionnaire should have a mix of different kinds of questions.

A survey should be able to be completed within five minutes. The longer it takes, the more likely it is to lose the respondent on the way.

It might be a good idea to incentivise participation.

Use Proven Scales

Most survey questions or statements are answered using Likert scale variants. They use intensity, frequency, probability, quality, or agreement qualifiers (Rohrmann, 2007). Whilst NPS typically has a ten-point scale, most satisfaction ratings are shorter. A four-point scale is quite short, a seven-point scale is quite long. Rohrmann (2007) recommends using a five-point scale and offers names for each level for different purposes.

Test Your Survey Questionnaire

As always, run a test survey with your questionnaire. Then invite your pilot group for feedback – if this is not already asked for during the survey. Rework your questionnaire and test again if necessary.

If your questionnaire is new, it might be inevitable to test the internal consistency of the questionnaire. One of the commonly used indicators of internal consistency is Cronbach's alpha coefficient. Additionally, it is needed to check for validity of the questionnaire by having the mentioned pilot run. This way you can test how well the questionnaire measures what it is purported to measure.

Test whether your survey works on all platforms. For example, a survey that is designed on Google Chrome looks different on Microsoft Edge. Test whether it works on different screen sizes. If it looks good on notebook and tablet, it could still be necessary to scroll left–right on mobile phones. This will deter some users.

Decide on the Distribution of the Questionnaire

Ensure that your survey has a chance to reach every consumer group. If you have consumers who are not online, but they make a significant customer base, you cannot leave them out. Make sure you reach them.

Select an Appropriate Timing for your Survey

Surveys are most effective when the customer has a recent experience of using your product or services. If the survey is sent out once a year, customers may not even remember what happened the last time they used your bank. If you conduct a short survey every time the customer finishes using your product, you may get feedback. If there is anything to say about the service delivery, customers will most likely state it.

Begin with the End in Mind

It is a good practice to design your survey having in mind the analysis you want to run after the survey. This includes considering the sample size you need in order to have a useful information at the end.

For example, if 1000 customers answer your survey, your margin of error is usually around +/−2% to +/−3%. This means, your satisfaction score can only be given with a confidence interval of 4% to 6%. This might be OK. However, if these 1000 responses come from three different regions, your sample size per region melts away and your results become merely useless. This means, it is necessary to have a certain number of responses from all demographics. If 80% use normal giro accounts and 20% use multi-currency accounts, you may want to have a similar percentage of responses in your survey, unless you decide to focus only on one of these groups.

If you wish to run correlation analysis with the survey data to identify what drives overall satisfaction or loyalty rating, make sure the questions for these indicators are built in.

Some More Considerations

Don't force your customers to fill in certain questions. They might have a reason for not doing so. By forcing them, you might lose the whole response, or you might just receive useless data.

Be careful when asking personal questions. Your customers might not trust your anonymity statement.

If you wish to compare survey results over time in so called longitudinal studies, you can only do so if you do not change anything. Keep the questions untouched. Send out your survey the same way at the same time of the year or time of the month etc. Keep the style and the format. Any change might render your survey as different. The result might be incomparable.

Conclusion

Today, all organisations have more data than ever before. Analysing this data will teach important lessons and will generate great opportunities. However, do not get too isolated from your customers by focussing too much on data. Data only carries part of the truth. The other part comes from interacting with your customers.

Customer expectations change over time. And the speed of these adjustments increases. Therefore, it is not enough to measure customer satisfaction frequently. We have to adjust the way we measure and what we measure and analyse along with the changing customer expectations.

Large organisations are experiencing the disadvantage of being detached from the customer. They detect trends but are much less agile to implement changes than smaller players who are closer to the customers and flexible enough to change fast or customise their offerings for certain customer groups.

Practice

- What are different kinds of customer need? What does the Kano diagram say?
- What are ways to study customer experience?
- What do you need to consider if you wish to design your own customer survey?

Case 1: Great, We Have Improved . . . or Not?

Many companies spend a considerable amount of money on customer surveys every year. Customer survey results are being used to amend strategies, design new products and/or services, focus improvement activities, and celebrate success. Since the impact of customer survey results can be quite hefty the data driving important decisions should be trustworthy. The question is: Can we always rely on what we see?

A life insurance company – let us call them MyInsurance – with worldwide market reach, was celebrating their success of improving their customers' satisfaction in 2019. They proudly presented the results: "In Thailand we have achieved 58% (57.86%) satisfied customers as compared to year 2018 when it was only 54% (53.93%)." This sounds good, right? In a market with millions of consumers, an increase in satisfaction of 4% would mean, the number of customers who would happily buy from MyInsurance again has increased by some ten thousand.

What is Sampling?

A very simple experiment will help you understand what sampling means: Buy one 200g package of chocolate M&Ms. Open your package and count the number of M&Ms in your package. This number – the population – was 233 in our case.

Your task is to find out the proportion of yellow M&Ms in this package, by sampling.

Sampling means taking a small number of M&Ms out of the population in a representative way. We took a bowl and filled in our M&Ms. After some shaking and stirring, we turned around and counted a sample of 20 M&Ms out of the bowl – blindly. The first sample gave us no yellow at all. We put our sample back into the population and counted a new sample with 20. The second sample revealed 4 yellow M&Ms. Eight more samples gave us 2, 3, 3, 6, 3, 5, 4 and 3 yellow M&Ms, respectively.

Doing the math, our samples suggested that our population had 0%, 20%, 10%, 15%, 15%, 30%, 15%, 25% and 15% yellow, respectively. Which sample was correct? None was. All of the samples give only an indication for the real percentage of yellow in the population.

Now, please count the total number of yellow M&Ms. In our experiment this number was 43. It means we had 18.5% (43/233) yellow in our population. None of the samples was able to show this exact percentage.

Sampling results vary even though the population is untouched. Drawing conclusions based on this variation may result in expensive mistakes.

This kind of conclusion could be too fast. Why? For obvious reasons, MyInsurance did not really ask millions of customers for their opinion. They only managed to gather the opinion from 280 customers. And this is called sampling. Such approach is being applied in every kind of organisation in every sector many times a day.

The Problem with Sampling

Sampling is based on a comparatively small number of customers, called "Sample", and it is used to draw conclusions about the "Population". Population in this case refers to the entire pool of customers whose opinion we are interested in. Sampling has a huge advantage: it saves money and time and is especially used when it is nearly impossible to collect data from the whole population or when the process of testing can destroy the object like drop testing of mobile phones. This advantage is paid for with a disadvantage: the "Margin of Error" or "Confidence Interval".

Understanding Confidence Intervals

Confidence Interval is the range in which we expect the population value to be. Since we do sampling, we can only guess what the "real" value is. In sampling, we never know. This confidence interval cannot be avoided, even with a perfectly representative sample under "ideal conditions". However, this interval can be reduced by increasing the sample size or by decreasing the variance in the population. The latter is usually not possible. Hence the only choice one has is to determine the minimum sample size for the confidence interval one is expecting.

What does this mean in the case of MyInsurance? With some simple statistics (Figure 2.5) we can calculate the Confidence Interval for our samples based on the sample size we have got:

In 2018, the "real" customer satisfaction level was between 48% and 60%. In 2019, it was between 52% and 64%. So, can we still conclude that we have improved?

Obviously, we cannot!

If MyInsurance wishes to distinguish between a customer satisfaction level of 54% and 58%, they need to have confidence intervals for 54% and 58% that do not overlap. If they would overlap, we could not distinguish between both. Hence, we need confidence intervals of +/−2% or less for both.

The estimation of the sample size for this requirement tells us that we would need to involve nearly 2500 customers in our satisfaction survey each year. Again, based on the sample of 280 customers we have taken it can easily be that there has been no change at all or even worse a decrease in customer satisfaction. We will never know until we have more data to give us a better result.

Unfortunately, in our example, MyInsurance has no reason to celebrate success due to increase in customer satisfaction. Assuming an increase in customer satisfaction could be totally wrong.

Means Are Lies

Very often important decisions are based on means coming from small samples of data. Sometimes these small samples of data are poorly collected or have a large variation. We usually do not care a lot about variation in

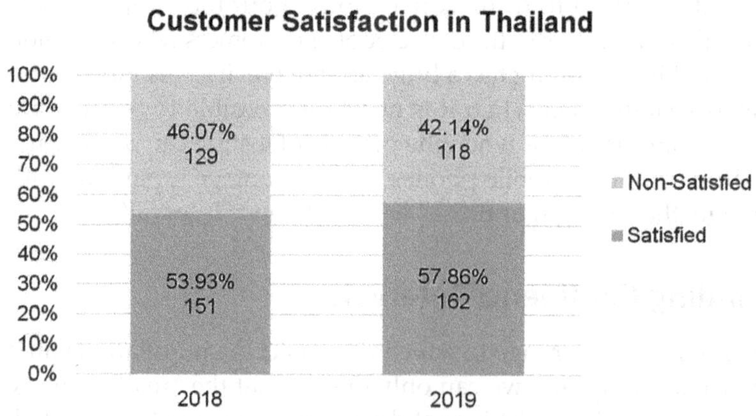

Figure 2.4 Customer Satisfaction in Thailand in 2018 and 2019

our daily professional or personal life. The thing that matters most is the average, the mean. This mean is easy to calculate, and everyone understands what it stands for . . . at least we tend to think we understand. However, every mean coming out of a sample is only correct for that sample, it is "wrong" for the whole we are trying to make a decision about.

 Management would take a great leap in decision making by changing the way they look at data: Do not trust the yield you have got for your production line, ask for the confidence interval for that. Do not make an investment decision based on a small sample of data, ask for the minimum improvement this investment will give you.

Business Question

This case is posing the question "Is there a significant improvement from customer satisfaction level in 2018 to that in 2019?"

Why is this question important to get an answer for? There are some reasons:

- Firstly, you wish to know whether the efforts in improvements you have invested in have paid off.

- Secondly, you might be interested in what improvement you could count on, having in mind that simply comparing the satisfaction level is not good enough.

- Thirdly, you may want to make sure that the bonus you pay out for improved customer satisfaction is well grounded.

Data Collection

In our situation, the data are already collected, and it is hard to get additional data without paying more money to the market research company doing this job. Therefore, we use the data at hand collected by customer surveys in 2018 and 2019 in Thailand (Table 2.1).

It is a good practice by market research companies to protect the anonymity of survey participants by not revealing the raw data. For data analytics, this poses a challenge since there is usually no way to find out what the survey results are made of.

Table 2.1 Customer Satisfaction Data for MyInsurance in Thailand in 2018 and 2019

	2018	2019
Satisfied Customers	151	162
Non-Satisfied Customers	129	118
Total	280	280

Figure 2.4 shows a column chart to represent customer satisfaction data for 2018 and 2019. Since the raw data are not available, this column chart or a pie chart are the only data plots available in this kind of situation.

Data Processing

Our data is available as a combination of sample size and percentage satisfaction for 2018 and 2019 respectively. Percentage satisfaction shows the share of customers who have marked our service delivery overall with eight, nine or ten on a ten-point scale. The data analysis is possible with this kind of data. Since we only use two levels of satisfaction, i.e. "satisfied" (rating eight, nine or ten) or "not satisfied" (rating one to seven), our customer satisfaction is to be treated as discrete data.

Data Analysis

Whenever data are collected through sampling, a certain degree of sampling error needs to be taken into consideration. This sampling error, the so-called confidence interval – can be calculated and depends on the following parameters

- The data type used to describe the operationally important variable. This data type can be discrete or continuous. Discrete data is often gathered by counting characteristics. Continuous data is often gathered by measuring dimensions.
- The variation in the data.
- The confidence level for the estimation needed. Usually, we assume a confidence level of 95%.
- The size of the data in the sample and its relationship to the size of the population. If the sample size is less than 5% of the population, the population size is of less importance for the estimation of the confidence interval.

The calculation of the confidence interval for discrete data can be done using Excel (TwoProportionTest.xlsx, Figure 2.5).

As shown, in 2018 (Sample 1) our customer satisfaction level has been between 48.1% and 59.8%. Due to the small sample, we cannot give more precise results.

Similarly, the satisfaction level in 2019 (Sample 2) was between 52.1% and 63.6%. With the current data, there is no way to distinguish between the 2018 and 2019 satisfaction levels. Even worse, there is a small risk, that the satisfaction level in 2019 was lower than in 2018.

In this case, a two-proportion test (Figure 2.5) can be performed to identify the risk of assuming a difference, i.e. an improvement. For this test, the raw data are needed. This means, we need the number of satisfied and non-satisfied customers for 2018 and 2019, respectively.

Two-Proportion Test and 95% Confidence Interval for Discrete Sampling					
	Sample1	**Sample2**		**Two-Proportion Test**	
Enter **Population Size** Here	100,000	100,000		Alpha:	0.0500
Enter **Sample Size** Here	280	280		Ppooled:	0.5589
Enter **Number of Events** Here	151	162		Pdiff:	-0.0393
				SEpooled:	0.0420
Proportion	53.93%	57.86%		z-score:	-0.9362
				P(Sample1>Sample2):	**0.8254**
Precision	5.83%	5.78%		P(Sample1<Sample2):	**0.1746**
				P(Sample1≠Sample2):	**0.3492**
				z-crit:	1.9600
Result	48.10% < p < 59.76%	52.08% < p < 63.63%		CIdiff:	-12.15 % < p < 4.30 %

Confidence Intervals of Two Discrete Samples							
Sample 2							
Sample 1							
0.0%	10.0%	20.0%	30.0%	40.0%	50.0%	60.0%	70.0%

Figure 2.5 Two-Proportion Test for Survey Results in 2018 and 2019

Figure 2.5 shows the results of the two-proportion test for comparing the customer satisfaction level for 2018 and 2019. The risk of assuming that there is a difference between the customer satisfaction in 2018 and 2019 is 34.92% (P(Sample1≠Sample2)).

Another useful indicator for decision making is the confidence interval for the difference between the samples (CIdiff). If this confidence interval includes 0, it means that the difference can be 0. In our case, the difference can be anything from –12.15% to 4.30%, i.e. the difference can be positive or negative. Hence, there is even a chance for the customer satisfaction in 2019 being lower than in 2018.

This calculation can be done very comfortably with R as well.

TASK 2.1   PERFORM TWO-SAMPLE Z-TEST:

Open R Studio.

```
# Loading necessary packages
install.packages("stats")
library(stats)
# Compute the two-proportion z-test, two-sided
prop.test(x = c(151, 162), n = c(280, 280))
```

THE OUTPUT OF THIS TWO-PROPORTION Z-TEST:

```
2-sample test for equality of proportions with continuity
correction

data: c(151, 162) out of c(280, 280)
X-squared = 0.72435, df = 1, p-value = 0.3947
alternative hypothesis: two.sided
95 percent confidence interval:
 -0.12503912 … 0.04646769
sample estimates:
  prop 1    prop 2
0.5392857 0.5785714
```

This simple calculation confirms what we know already. Proportion 1 is at 53.93% and proportion 2 is at 57.86%. The p-value for this test is 0.3947 (39.47%). Hence, there is not enough evidence to say that there is a change. This p-value is different to the one generated with Excel due to a slightly dissimilar algorithm.

The confidence interval for the difference between both proportions reaches from −12.50% to 4.65%. This again says, there is even a chance that the rating has dropped.

The R calculation confirms that there is no improvement from 2018 to 2019.

Business Decision

From the analysis, p-value, 0.3492 (see Figure 2.5), can be directly translated into the risk for the assumption that there is a difference between both proportions.

Once again, the assumption that MyInsurance was successful in improving customer satisfaction in Thailand bears a risk of about 35%. If there is a bonus paid for a good job, then there is a 35% risk that this bonus is paid without justification.

Even worse, the customer satisfaction level for 2018 lies somewhere between 48% and 60% and for 2019 between 52% and 64%, respectively. There is a chance that the satisfaction was towards 58% in 2018 and around 52% in 2019. This means, there is a chance that there was a reduction of customer satisfaction from 2018 to 2019.

The only valid conclusion in this kind of situation is, that we do not have enough data to confirm an improvement in customer satisfaction.

So, how much data would be enough?

This depends on the difference we want to detect. Let us assume, we would like to be able to show an improvement of 2% or more. This means the precision d for both samples together must not exceed 2%. To simplify the case, we just calculate the sample size for both samples with a d of 1% (in the formulae it is 0.01). The formula for the sample size is directly drawn from the formula for the confidence interval. With the formula for sample size of discrete data

Equation 2.1: Sample Size for Estimating Proportions (Discrete Data)

$$n = \left(\frac{2}{d}\right)^2 p(1-p),$$

the calculations for 2018 and 2019 look like this:

$$n_{2018} = \left(\frac{2}{0.01}\right)^2 0.5393(1-0.5393) = 9,938$$

$$n_{2019} = \left(\frac{2}{0.01}\right)^2 0.5786\left(1-0.5786\right) = 9753$$

This means, nearly 10,000 survey responses are needed for each year in order to be able to detect an improvement in customer satisfaction of 2% or more.

 Equation 2.1 means, that for reducing the precision, i.e. the confidence interval to 50%, the sample size needs to be increased to about 4 times.

Analytical Storytelling

The assumption that MyInsurance was successful in improving customer satisfaction in Thailand bears a risk of about 35%. If there is a bonus paid for a good job, then there is a risk of 35% that this bonus is paid for nothing.

Even worse, the real customer satisfaction level for 2018 might be even better than 2019, hence there could be a drop in customer satisfaction in Thailand from 2018 to 2019.

Again, everyone who says there is a higher degree of customer satisfaction in Thailand in 2019 is an optimist.

What If We Had All The Data?

The above business decision and story is all we could deliver if we had subcontracted our survey to a market research agency to conduct this study for us every year.

This approach has some clear advantages:

- *Our customers know that a third party is conducting this survey. Hence, they most likely give more truthful answers if the market research company waves an "anonymity promise".*
- *There is no need to build a market research team which we only need once a year. This saves us costs.*
- *The external party is specialised in this survey. We can trust the survey being conducted and analysed in the utmost professional manner.*

There is one major caveat of this approach:

You will probably never see the raw data since this is most likely a contractual agreement. Hence you cannot do your own "deeper analysis".

Let us assume, we do have the raw data for customer satisfaction in Thailand for 2018 and 2019. Then we know how our data is distributed. As Figure 2.6 suggests, there is a concentration of ratings around 7, 8, and 9. Since the percentage is calculated as a proportion of rating 8, 9, and 10 overall ratings, the real distribution below 8 does not matter and is not visible in the percentage rating.

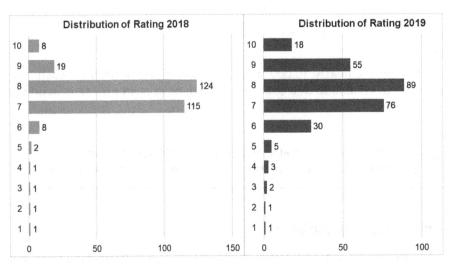

Figure 2.6 Distribution of Ratings in 2018 and 2019

Simulating a potential rating distribution for the 2019 rating results in Figure 2.7 and shows, that there is an infinite number of patterns hidden behind exactly the same rating of 57.9%.

👉 **Evaluating survey results on percentages only is an awfully bad idea.**

Fortunately, most of the patterns have their root causes. Without having the raw data, a root cause analysis is impossible. However, by giving potential root causes for these patterns to the market research organisation, you enable them to do this job.

Root causes for patterns in data are stratifying factors, that you want your data to be divided by. These stratifying factors are often demographics like division, department, group, location, gender, age, employer, sector like public or private, and many more.

For example, if you think there could be a different rating coming from different territories, you need to ensure that your survey participants are either given to your market research company including their location. It means, you give all demographics together with the names of your customers to your market research vendor so that they can link the survey results to these demographics and do all analysis you wish to have.

Or you let the respondents self-declare the location by providing this option in the survey. Be careful: not everyone will answer. And not all who answer will declare correctly.

The learning here is: if you prepare your market research vendor with all the necessary information, they can analyse your data in many different directions. If they receive raw data for Thailand as shown in Figure 2.7, they are able to analyse whether the demographics that makes the difference

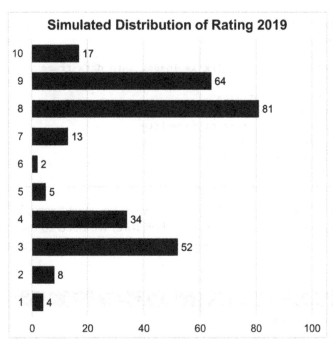

Figure 2.7 Simulated Rating Distribution for 2019

between these two clusters is location or something else. This makes your customer satisfaction data much more powerful and certainly more actionable.

Since this simulated rating distribution (Figure 2.7) would turn out exactly the same rating score of 57.9% (rating of 8, 9 or 10), it would not raise any suspicion.

But nothing beats plotting the data. Comparing the plot "Simulated Rating Distribution for 2019" with "Distribution of Rating in 2019" reveals the truth.

 Without any doubt, one of the best learnings I had during my education at General Electric was this message:
Three rules for data analysis: Plot the data, plot the data, plot the data.

In the following, we compare two sets of non-normal data with each other.

TASK 2.2   LOAD THE DATA FROM GREAT.XLSX INTO R STUDIO AND CHECK FOR NORMALITY

1. Open R Studio.

2. In the Files window, navigate to your directory and select Great.xlsx.

3. Select Import Dataset.

4. Select Sheet Great.

5. Select Range A1:D281.

```
# Loading library for inserting Excel file loads automatically
library(readxl)
library(stats)
# Uploading Excel file Great.xlsx is loaded into data frame
Great
Great <- read_excel("Great.xlsx",
  sheet = "Raw", range = "A1:D281")
# Performing Shapiro-Wilk test of normality
shapiro.test(Great$Sample2018)
shapiro.test(Great$Sample2019)
shapiro.test(Great$Sim2019)
```

All p-values of these three normality tests show to be nearly zero, i.e. our data in all three columns is not normal. Therefore, we need to use a non-parametric test to compare these samples with each other. We suggest the Wilcoxon test.

TASK 2.3   PERFORM WILCOXON TEST:

```
# Loading library rstatix
library(rstatix)
library(utils)
# Stack data in GreatStacked and ignore column ID
GreatStacked <- stack(Great, select = -ID)
# Perform Wilcoxon test on GreatStacked
wilcox_test(GreatStacked, values ~ ind)
```

TEST OUTPUT:

	group1	group2	n1	n2	statistic	p	p.adj	
1	Sample2018	Sample2019	280	280	36219	0.101	0.202	ns
2	Sample2018	Sim2019	280	280	40200	0.589	0.589	ns
3	Sample2019	Sim2019	280	280	44124	0.009	0.026	*

This Wilcoxon test is a substitute for the two-sample t-test for non-normal data. The output illustrates the pairwise comparisons for all pairing combinations.

Line 1 shows an adjusted p-value – adjusted for multiple comparisons – of 0.202. This means, there is not enough evidence that there is a difference between the rating shown in Sample2018 and Sample2019.

Line 2 indicates an adjusted p-value of 0.589. This means, there is not enough evidence that there is a difference between the rating shown in Sample2018 and Sim2019.

However, line 3 reveals an adjusted p-value of 0.026. Assuming, our acceptable risk for making decisions (alpha risk) is at 0.05 or 5%, we can conclude that the ratings in Sample2019 and Sim2019 are significantly different.

Keep in mind, the rating for Sample2019 and Sim2019 are both 57.9%.

If we plot the data, we get an indication for a different rating. If we apply suitable statistics, we confirm this indication.

Having an assumption based on a plot is a good start. Confirming this assumption with proper statistics makes you a Data Analyst.

Deploying Analytics Tools

This case illustrates how customer satisfaction scores are often reported. Since the rating data usually comes in Likert scales, it would statistically be perfect to be treated as discrete ordinal.

If there are only two proportions to be compared and we know only sample sizes and successes, the two-proportion z-test can be applied. Sample sizes are both 280 with success in 2018 at 151 and in 2019 at 162.

This requires the presence of at least count five in both groups for successes and non-successes. Our data complies with this requirement.

Analysing discrete ordinal data offers a limited set of tools that are generally less powerful than tools that deal with continuous data.

If means need to be compared but data is non-normal non-parametric tests can be considered. These tests do not compare means but medians, i.e. the sequence and counts of the data in the samples. They are based on the assumption that both samples show a similar distribution, i.e. a similarly wide pattern.

Table 2.2 Two-Proportion z-Test

TWO-PROPORTION Z-TEST	
Data in X :	Discrete X – Groups (1 and 2)
Data in Y :	Discrete Y – Counts
Null Hypothesis H_0 :	$P_1 = P_2$
Alternative Hypothesis H_A :	$P_1 \neq P_2$
Decision:	If p-value is < 0.05, reject H_0 and accept H_A.
Assumptions:	Counts in all four cells must be at least 5, i.e. x_1, n_1-x_1, x_2, n_2-x_2 must be at least 5
| **R code:** | ```
# Loading necessary packages
install.packages("stats")
library(stats)
# Compute the two-proportion z-test
result
prop.test(x = c(x1, x2), n = c(n1, n2))
# x1 … number of successes for group 1
# n1 … number of trials for group 1
# x2 … number of successes for group 2
# n2 … number of trials for group 2
``` |
```

Table 2.3 Two-Sample Wilcoxon Test

TWO-SAMPLE WILCOXON TEST (KAUFMANN, 2020)	
Data in X :	Discrete X – Groups (variable)
Data in Y :	Continuous Y, Discrete ordinal (value), non-normal
Null Hypothesis H_0 :	$median_1 = median_2$
Alternative Hypothesis H_A :	$median_1 \neq median_2$
Decision:	If p-value is < 0.05 ($\alpha = 0.05$), reject H_0 and accept H_A.
Assumptions:	Sample sizes must be at least 6.
	Samples must have similar distribution.

R code:	```# Loading necessary packages```
	```library(rstatix)```
	```# Performing non-parametric Wilcox test```
	```wilcox_test(GreatStacked, values ~ ind)```

Source: Based on Kaufmann, U. H. 2020

Practice

- What is sampling and what is the consequence of sampling?
- What is a confidence interval?
- How do you need to change the sample size if you wish to reduce the confidence interval to 50%?
- Please, complete the following steps:

  - Download the data for this case from www.wiley.com.
  - Perform plots for the data for 2018 and 2019 using R.
  - Perform statistical analysis for the difference between 2018 and 2019 using R.
  - Prepare a short presentation to report the result and your recommendation to the management.

Case 2: What Drives our Patient Satisfaction?

For many service organisations, conducting patient surveys to assess the satisfaction level of their patients is a must. Running a survey once or twice a year is one option. This however is less powerful because some of your patients may have forgotten about the experience and cannot really give helpful feedback even if they take the time to do so. Useless survey responses are the outcome.

The closer the survey follows the process, the better is the impression about the service just received. And the result of the survey is more useful,

Figure 2.8 Simple Six-Point Rating at Singapore Government Website

Source: Ministry of Manpower

too. Many companies have implemented a quite simple survey after the job is completed.

1. After we receive our deliveries from online shopping services, we get an SMS asking us to rate the service of the logistics provider. Conveniently, they ask for two inputs. Firstly, they offer rating from one star to five stars. Secondly, they allow comments.

2. A similar five-star rating is requested after a taxi ride.

3. When leaving a public toilet, we can indicate our satisfaction regarding the cleanliness of the toilet by selecting one of five or six different emoticons.

4. Most mobile apps offer a similar style rating whenever we try to close or leave the app (Figure 2.8). Users who wish to elaborate more about their experience with the Online Services can use the "Tell Us More" option. It is a good bet that this option is more often used for complaints or hints for improvement than compliments. And that is perfectly ok.

These simple ratings generate some feedback for the service provider. Yet, the simplicity is bought with a lack of detail. When you as the service provider receive five stars, you do not need to worry too much. However, when you receive one or two stars, someone is not happy. In order to close the loop and start analysis whenever the rating is low, you should call back and ask for the reason. The call back is often possible because the above-mentioned surveys are usually linked to a person's ID. Consumers will very likely appreciate the call and explain in detail what exactly happened.

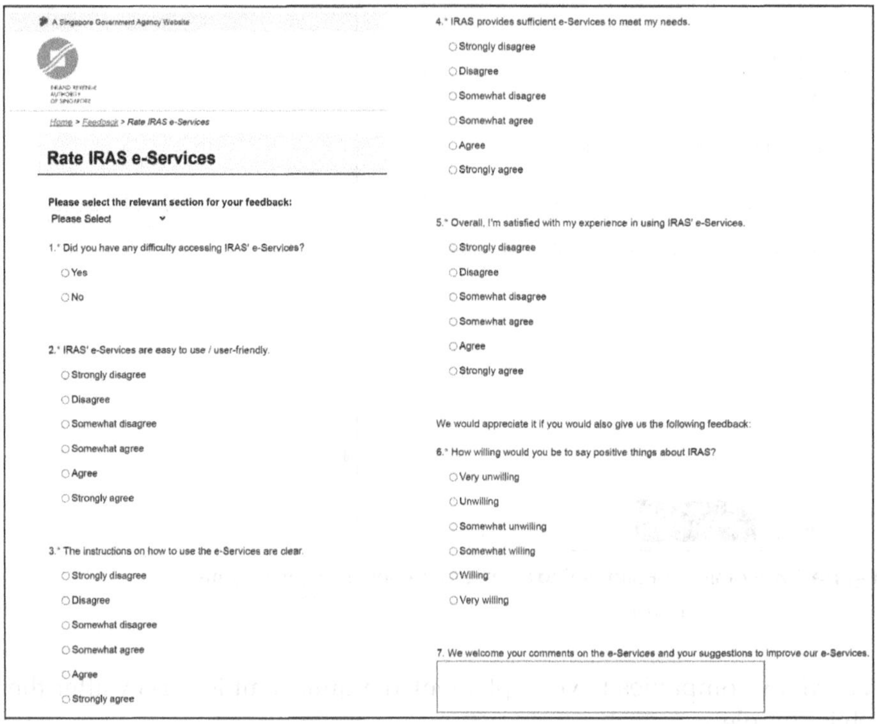

A Singapore Government Agency Website

Home > Feedback > Rate IRAS e-Services

Rate IRAS e-Services

Please select the relevant section for your feedback:
Please Select

1.* Did you have any difficulty accessing IRAS' e-Services?
- ○ Yes
- ○ No

2.* IRAS' e-Services are easy to use / user-friendly.
- ○ Strongly disagree
- ○ Disagree
- ○ Somewhat disagree
- ○ Somewhat agree
- ○ Agree
- ○ Strongly agree

3.* The instructions on how to use the e-Services are clear.
- ○ Strongly disagree
- ○ Disagree
- ○ Somewhat disagree
- ○ Somewhat agree
- ○ Agree
- ○ Strongly agree

4.* IRAS provides sufficient e-Services to meet my needs.
- ○ Strongly disagree
- ○ Disagree
- ○ Somewhat disagree
- ○ Somewhat agree
- ○ Agree
- ○ Strongly agree

5.* Overall, I'm satisfied with my experience in using IRAS' e-Services.
- ○ Strongly disagree
- ○ Disagree
- ○ Somewhat disagree
- ○ Somewhat agree
- ○ Agree
- ○ Strongly agree

We would appreciate it if you would also give us the following feedback:

6.* How willing would you be to say positive things about IRAS?
- ○ Very unwilling
- ○ Unwilling
- ○ Somewhat unwilling
- ○ Somewhat willing
- ○ Willing
- ○ Very willing

7. We welcome your comments on the e-Services and your suggestions to improve our e-Services.

Figure 2.9 More Elaborate Rating at Singapore Government Website
Source: Ministry of Finance

If the only feedback you receive is a star rating or smiley and sometimes a comment, the opportunities for analysis are quite limited. However, longitudinal studies are always possible, i.e. studies of the feedback over time. This does not give any details about reasons for increase or decrease. Still, it may highlight the first signal that something is going on. And that is a good start.

The patient survey can give more feedback if you ask more questions. And, if there is a structure built into the questions, the survey analysis can provide very valuable output. Such an example is shown in Figure 2.9. The first question for "any difficulty accessing IRAS' e-Services" gives only two answers as options. Questions 2 to 4 are questions for other details whereas Questions 5 and 6 ask for an overall rating. Question 6 has a similar meaning as the Net Promoter Score but uses six levels instead of ten.

There is plenty of room for applying data analytics procedures on the data collected this way.

Since the government agency should know who has used their service and has rated it, they should be able to link the survey rating to all available demographics. These demographics give opportunities for stratifying the data and hoping there is a pattern.

Let us see this in more detail in the following example.

Patient Satisfaction in an Outpatient Clinic

Almost everyone has the experience of visiting the neighbourhood clinic for general medical consultation such as a cold or another minor illness with our family doctors.

One of our neighbourhood clinics continually runs patient satisfaction surveys. They used to give every patient a survey form, in hard copy, upon leaving the clinic. Nowadays, they push the survey via our mobile phones to elicit feedback on our way home from the clinic. Paper and digital form carry the same information; hence the information goes into the same database.

The typical steps (Table 2.4) a patient goes through are

- Step 1: Registration,
- Step 2: Pre-consultation screening with check of temperature, blood pressure, weight,
- Step 3: Consultation by the doctor,
- Step 4: Dispensing medicine,
- Step 5: Receiving payment for medicine and treatment (and survey).

These steps are considered as touch points by the clinic. For each of these touch points, multiple questions are asked (Figure 2.10) and a rating on a scale from 1 to 5 is offered. The rating follows a Likert scale design with the levels

1. .. Poor.
2. .. Fair.
3. .. Satisfactory.
4. .. Good.
5. .. Excellent.

Why does the clinic collect this kind of data? They want to find out how they are doing and where they can do better.

Figure 2.10 Service Delivery Touchpoints with Indicators for Customer Satisfaction

Table 2.4 Steps in Clinic and Rating Criteria

PROCESS STEP	DESCRIPTION/STAFF	INDICATORS
Step 1	Registration by Clerk or Nurse	Friendly & Courteous Prompt & Attentive Helpful
Step 2	Screening by Nurse	Friendly & Courteous Prompt & Attentive Helpful
Step 3	Consultation by Doctor	Friendly & Courteous Prompt & Attentive Communicates Clearly Competent
Step 4	Dispensing Medicine by Pharmacist or Nurse	Friendly & Courteous Prompt & Attentive Communicates Clearly Competent
Step 5	Receiving Payment by Clerk or Nurse	Friendly & Courteous Prompt & Attentive Helpful

Business Question

Whenever this kind of survey is conducted, at least the following questions, might be of interest:

1. How does the patient feedback compare for all process steps?
2. Which indicators show room for improvement?
3. Which steps/indicators are most important to our patients?
4. How are we doing over time?

Translating these questions into hypotheses will yield the following:

Hypothesis 1: There is a significant difference between the ratings for steps – At least one step is rated differently

The general intend of hypothesis testing is always to find a significant difference, i.e. a measurable difference between the groups for which the probability of obtaining this difference by chance is very small (usually less than 5%). Most statistical tools are designed for exactly this purpose. In our case, we assume that at least one of the steps receives a significantly higher or lower rating. We are especially interested in the bad news, since this might call for action.

Hypothesis 2: There is a significant difference between the ratings for indicators – At least one indicator is rated differently

Finding out the steps with significantly different rating is not enough. In order to plan for actions, it is of advantage to see which indicator is rated lower. I.e., it would be of great interest to know if the potentially different rating for the Doctor is caused by competency or by communication style, etc.

Hypothesis 3: There is a significant relationship between the rating for a process step and the overall rating

Knowing which process steps or indicators contribute most to the overall rating helps to prioritise potential actions. A significantly lower rating on a step that does not seem too important to the patient is less critical than the one on a strong driver for overall satisfaction.

Hypothesis 4: There is a pattern over time

Often, rating changes over time. This is not only true from week to week or month to month. This could also be true for rating over the day or rating over the week. In some industries, Monday is a "bad day". Other service providers experience afternoon fatigue. Analysing this could help us further when redesigning the process or organising and developing the workforce for this kind of situation.

Data Acquisition

Data have been provided by the clerk of the clinic whose job is to collate all data weekly. His job includes handing out the feedback form or getting the patients to scan the QR code to complete the form online before the patients leave. The collation of the rating results is done by only one clerk so that there is less room for clerk-driven errors.

When designing the survey, the clinic wanted to have a comprehensive survey that is easy to answer. Therefore, they did not formulate questions or statements, but instead listed only the name of the step, and the indicators with checkboxes for the rating. It appeared to be less time consuming to fill in this survey.

It can be believed that this was one reason why people took the survey.

The name of the data file is ClinicSurveyStacked.xlsx.

Data Preparation

It is a good practice to format the data table as a table, so that MS Excel treats it as such. This can be achieved by the following steps.

TASK 2.4 LOAD THE DATA AND FORMAT IT AS A TABLE (FIGURE 2.11):

Open MS Excel.

Open the data in ClinicSurvey.xlsx in sheet Survey.

Select the whole table with cursor in A1 and Shift + Ctrl + ⇨ and Shift + Ctrl + ⇩.

Select Home – Format as Table. The style selected does not make a difference.

Since you have included the header row in your selection, ensure to check the box "My table has headers".

Name the newly created table by setting Table Design – Table Name: UnStacked.

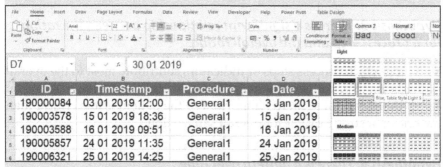

Figure 2.11 Format Unstacked Data Table as Excel Table

Source: Used with permission from Microsoft.

Transforming Data

Data transformation includes activities of converting data from one format to another, from one structure to another. Converting numbers into text (string) or aggregating raw data to create a new variable are applications of data transformation. Transferring a data set with a certain distribution into another one for the purpose of applying specific tools marks a more complex application of data transformation.

Our data is unstacked, i.e. we have the so-called short data format with each row representing all ratings by one patient identified by ID, the patient ID.

This data shows ratings for all indicators and for the overall impression. It does not carry overall rating for each step. Hence, we need to transform the indicators for each step into an average rating for the step for each patient.

TASK 2.5 TRANSFORM INDICATOR RATING INTO AVERAGE RATING FOR EACH STEP:

1. **In the first row at the first free column after the data table, most likely in cell Z1 write Step1. This adds a column to the newly created table.**

   In cell Z2, write = AVERAGE(Unstacked[@[Step1friendly]:[Step1helpful]]).

   This will automatically populate the Step1 ratings for all patients.

Step4comp	Step5friendly	Step5prompt	Step5helpful	Step1	Step2	Step3	Step4	Step5	StdDev
4	4	4	4	4.00	4.00	4.00	4.00	4.00	-
3	3	3	3	3.00	3.00	3.25	2.75	3.00	0.34
4	4	4	4	4.00	4.00	4.00	4.00	4.00	0.34
3	3	3	3	3.00	2.67	3.25	3.00	3.00	0.34
3	3	3	3	3.00	3.33	3.00	2.75	3.00	0.34
4	4	4	4	4.00	4.33	3.75	4.00	4.00	0.34
4	4	4	4	4.33	3.67	4.00	4.00	4.00	0.34

Figure 2.12 Calculating Standard Deviation to Identify Unhelpful Ratings

Source: Used with permission from Microsoft.

Applying this task for all five steps gives the average rating for each step by each rater.

Dealing with Unhelpful Input

There was some cleaning necessary after receiving the data file. For instance, there were some ratings of people who obviously were not in the mood or did not have time to give serious feedback. They evaluated all indicators with the same rating, i.e. all indicators for all steps received a 3. Others did this with a 5.

This kind of input is not helpful but will slightly change the information analysed from the data. By adding a column with the formula for standard deviation

StdDev = STDEV.S(UnStacked[@[Overall]:[Step5helpful]]),

rows with rating without variation can be detected. After inputting this formula, the table might be sorted by column StdDev, so that rows with 0 standard deviation turn to the top of the table. These rows have been eliminated (row 1 in Figure 2.12).

Dealing with Missing Input

Missing entries happen in all kind of surveys, if the input is not enforced. Enforcing the input to avoid empty cells, i.e. not allowing to submit the survey before all boxes are ticked could spoil the input since some raters might just give up. Others might give arbitrary input just to be able to submit. Therefore, it was decided to allow patients to leave ratings open. There might be reasons for them doing so.

In order to detect empty cells especially in very large worksheets, another column gets added that counts the number of blanks with this function

Blanks = COUNTIF((UnStacked[@[Overall]:[Step5helpful]]),"")

Range "UnStacked[@[Overall]:[Step5helpful]]" covers all rating data columns from "Overall" to "Step5helpful" at table "UnStacked". Again, by sorting column Blanks in a descending order, all rows with Blanks will be on top (row 1 in Figure 2.13).

Some analytical tools tolerate empty cells, i.e., these tools can be applied without any problem. Descriptive statistics and hypothesis tests usually work with columns that carry empty cells.

Step5friendly	Step5prompt	Step5helpful	Step1	Step2	Step3	Step4	Step5	StdDev	Blank
3	3	3	3.00	3.00	3.25	2.50	3.00	0.44	2.00
4	4	4	4.00	4.00	4.00	4.00	4.00	-	-
3	3	3	3.00	3.00	3.25	2.75	3.00	0.34	-
4	4	4	4.00	4.00	4.00	4.00	4.00	0.34	-
3	3	3	3.00	2.67	3.25	3.00	3.00	0.34	-
3	3	3	3.00	3.33	3.00	2.75	3.00	0.34	-

Figure 2.13 Detecting Blank Cells in Data Table

Source: Used with permission from Microsoft.

Some other analytical tools however – regression analysis is one of them – do not work with empty cells. They need a full set of all x-y combinations without any blanks.

What do we do with the Blanks if we wish to run a regression analysis?

Strategy 1:   Delete the whole record (the whole row) containing empty cells. This strategy might be applied, whenever a large dataset has only a few records with empty cells. Then, the sample size does not change drastically.

Strategy 2:   Replace the empty cell with either mean, median or the most frequent value of this column. This strategy keeps the sample size, i.e., it is the way to go when the sample size is small.

In our data file, we experienced only one data set with empty cells out of 516 rows of data. Thus, we have decided to eliminate the respective row leaving us with 515 complete datasets.

Sometimes, missing input is coded with "0" or "NA" or similar. Whereas "NA" or any other text will usually render an error and stop the respective operation, "0" will not. Since "0" is a number just like "1", "2" etc. it will be treated as a valid input. This will result in misleading or wrong conclusions and must be avoided. Therefore, we extend our formula for Blanks to

Blanks = SUM (COUNTIFS((UnStacked[@[Overall] : [Step5helpful]]), {"0","","NA"})).

This formula counts how many entries are found with "0", "" or "NA" and sums these counts up to a total number. If your data shows other code for missing input, you may want to include that code in the {}. This will greatly help to clean the data easily. We save the amended data in sheet "Cleaned".

Data Analysis

Before any analysis for confirming our hypotheses, it is a good practice to calculate descriptive statistics for indicators, variables, and overall.

Descriptive Statistics

There are many ways for calculating descriptive statistics. Excel offers comprehensive descriptive statistics in its Data Analysis ToolPak:

Data – Data Analysis – Descriptive Statistics.

Parameter	Overall	Step1friendly	Step1prompt	Step1helpful	Step2friendly	Step2prompt	Step2helpful	Step3friendly	Step3prompt	Step3comm
Rating 1	9	1	9	8	8	8	8	8	8	8
Rating 2	35	43	72	42	114	124	4	117	131	97
Rating 3	184	200	214	167	193	169	190	179	203	223
Rating 4	258	225	186	248	173	198	312	191	122	157
Rating 5	28	45	33	49	26	15	0	19	50	29
% Rating 4/5	55.6%	52.5%	42.6%	57.8%	38.7%	41.4%	60.7%	40.9%	33.5%	36.2%
Mean	3.51	3.53	3.32	3.56	3.18	3.17	3.57	3.19	3.15	3.20
StdDev	0.78	0.78	0.85	0.83	0.89	0.88	0.60	0.88	0.96	0.86
n	514	514	514	514	514	514	514	514	514	514

Figure 2.14 Descriptive Statistics for Indicators (Extract)

Source: Used with permission from Microsoft.

Figure 2.15 Customer Satisfaction Rating for each Indicator as 4/5%

For our purpose, we calculate the descriptive statistics using Excel functions. For instance, for the indicator Step1friendly, the calculation looks like:

In B2= COUNTIF(Cleaned[Overall],"=1") and similarly for all other rows.

In B7 =SUM(B5:B6)/SUM(B2:B6), i.e. the number of rating 4 and 5 over the total number of ratings for Overall.

In B8=AVERAGE(Cleaned[Overall]), i.e. the average of all ratings for indicator Overall.

In B9=STDEV.S(Cleaned[Overall]), i.e. the standard deviation of all ratings for indicator Overall.

Extend/copy your formulae to the right up to Step5helpful.

Similarly, descriptive statistics for each step have been computed using the data created during transformation (Figure 2.14). There are multiple ways of analysing survey data. Assuming patient satisfaction is achieved if patient rates 4 or 5, a percentage of this rating, the desirable rating, is a very common way of showing survey results. Figure 2.15 illustrates the rating results per indicator. For purposes of comparison, we display another bar/column chart demonstrating the rating average for the same indicators (Figure 2.16).

Whilst the pictures generated by %4/5 and by averages show a similar pattern, they do not bear the same message or the same emphasis on the message. For example, Step2helpful is rated 81% with 4 or 5 and shows an average of 3.8. Step3competent is rated 71% with 4 or 5 but shows an average of 3.9. This hints that the distribution for both indicators might be different

Figure 2.16 shown below.

Figure 2.16 Customer Satisfaction Rating for each Indicator as Averages

Figure 2.17 Box Plot for Rating per Step

as seen in the standard deviation of 0.41 versus 0.79. In the case of indicators, bar and column charts cannot be replaced by box plots because they can only take five distinct values, i.e. the box plot will not look very telling.

However, since the rating for each rater per step is an average, it will show better as a box plot (Figure 2.17).

Hypothesis 1: There is a significant difference between the ratings for steps

Whilst this box plot is a clearer illustration and has certainly more potential for storytelling, it cannot be used for decision making, i.e. for answering the question whether we are performing better or worse in any of the Steps in the eyes of the patient.

For this purpose, an ANOVA is a better tool. The analysis of variance (ANOVA) is designed to check whether seemingly different averages are created by different datasets. This means, it answers the question whether there is a significant difference between the average ratings for process steps. ANOVA can be executed in Excel by this function:

Data – Data Analysis – Anova: Single Factor, where Input Range is $Z$1:$AD$515 and Alpha is 0.05.

Anova: Single Factor				
SUMMARY				
Groups	*Count*	*Sum*	*Average*	*Variance*
Step1	514	1,782.0000	3.4669	0.5357
Step2	514	1,700.3333	3.3080	0.4531
Step3	514	1,728.5000	3.3628	0.5779
Step4	514	1,652.2500	3.2145	0.5378
Step5	514	1,739.6667	3.3846	0.2960

ANOVA					
Source of Variation	*SS*	*df*	*MS*	*F*	*P-value*	*F crit*
Between Groups	18.0513	4	4.5128	9.3993	0.0000	2.3754
Within Groups	1,231.5185	2565	0.4801			
Total	1,249.5698	2569				

Figure 2.18 Result of ANOVA for Steps 1 to 5

The name ANOVA is misleading. It is designed to find significant differences between averages. It does that by comparing the averaged variance within the groups (Step1, ..., Step5) with the overall variance.

The result of the ANOVA for Step1 to Step5 is shown in Figure 2.18. The single most important output of the ANOVA is the p-value. In this case, ANOVA tells us that there is a significant difference between the averages of each step. Unfortunately, Excel's ANOVA does not tell us where the difference lies. This can be found by calculating the confidence intervals (95% confidence level for an alpha of 0.05) of the averages for Step1 to Step5. Rule of thumb is, if confidence intervals of two steps overlap, the assumption of a significant difference between these two steps cannot be accepted.

As Table 2.5 shows, ANOVA requires continuous data that are normally distributed. Unfortunately, testing data on normality in Excel is not straightforward. This is where R can help.

TASK 2.6   LOAD DATA FROM CLINICSURVEY.XLSX INTO R STUDIO:

1. **Open R Studio.**

2. **In the Files window, navigate to your directory and select ClinicSurvey.xlsx**

3. **Select Import Dataset**

4. **Select Sheet Cleaned**

5. **Select Range A1:AD515**

```
# Library for inserting Excel file loads automatically
library(readxl)
# Excel file ClinicSurvey.xlsx is loaded into data frame
    ClinicSurvey
ClinicSurvey <- read_excel("ClinicSurvey.xlsx", sheet =
    "Cleaned", range = "A1:AD515")
# Install graphic pack Pastecs
install.packages("pastecs")
```

```
library(pastecs)
# Test Step1 to Step5 on normality using Shapiro-Wilk normality
test
shapiro.test(ClinicSurvey$Step1) # Repeat for Step2 to Step5
```

All p-values for the normality test result in practically zero (p-value = 5.639×10^{-10}, 3.281×10^{-14}, 2.547×10^{-08}, 8.031×10^{-10}, 6.095×10^{-16}). This means there is no doubt at all, that data of all steps are non-normal. Hence, ANOVA is not the right tool to compare the rating of Steps1 to 5 with each other.

Alternatives for ANOVA for non-normal data are non-parametric tests such as Kruskal–Wallis test or pairwise Wilcox test. In order to run these tests, data need to be stacked.

TASK 2.7   STACK DATA FOR ALL STEPS AND INDICATORS:

```
# Stack indicator data
stackedInd <- stack(ClinicSurvey, select = c("Overall",
    "Step1friendly", "Step1prompt", "Step1helpful",
    "Step2friendly","Step2prompt", "Step2helpful",
    "Step3friendly", "Step3prompt", "Step3comm", "Step3comp",
    "Step4friendly", "Step4prompt", "Step4comm",
    "Step4comp","Step5friendly", "Step5prompt", "Step5helpful"))
# View stacked indicator data
View(stackedInd)
# Stack step data
stackedStep <- stack(ClinicSurvey, select = c("Step1","Step2",
    "Step3","Step4","Step5"))
# View stacked step data
View(stackedStep)
```

In the next step, we perform descriptive statistics for steps.

TASK 2.8   PERFORM SUMMARY STATISTICS FOR STEPS:

```
# Load required packages
install.packages("ggpubr")
library(ggpubr)
install.packages("dplyr")
library(dplyr)

# Compute summary statistics by groups: count, mean, sd
group_by(stackedStep, ind) %>%
 summarise(
 count = n(),
 mean = mean(values, na.rm = TRUE),
 sd = sd(values, na.rm = TRUE)
 )
```

```
SUMMARY STATISTICS FOR GROUPS STEP1 TO STEP5 ARE SHOWN:

    ind count mean   sd
1 Step1  514   3.47 0.732
2 Step2  514   3.31 0.673
3 Step3  514   3.36 0.760
4 Step4  514   3.21 0.733
5 Step5  514   3.38 0.544
```

From this result, we could assume that Step4 might receive a slightly lower rating than all other steps. We need to confirm this assumption with statistics. In the next task, we perform non-parametric tests.

TASK 2.9   PERFORM KRUSKAL–WALLIS TEST

```
# Perform Kruskal-Wallis test
kruskal.test(values ~ ind, data = stackedStep)
```

TASK 2.10   PERFORM PAIRWISE WILCOX TEST

```
# Perform Pairwise Wilcox test
pairwise.wilcox.test(stackedStep$values, stackedStep$ind,
    p.adjust.method = "BH")
```

KRUSKAL–WALLIS OUTPUT READS:

```
Kruskal-Wallis rank sum test
data: values by ind
Kruskal-Wallis chi-squared = 34.929, df = 4, p-value = 4.803e-07
```

This means, there is a significant difference between the rating for steps. Unfortunately, this test does not show the significantly different step. Therefore, pairwise comparison using Wilcox was performed.

PAIRWISE WILCOX OUTPUT READS:

```
Pairwise comparisons using Wilcoxon rank sum test with continuity correction
data: stackedStep$values and stackedStep$ind
        Step1    Step2    Step3    Step4
Step2 0.00079 -        -        -
Step3 0.03375 0.30304  -        -
Step4 3.6e-07 0.05381  0.00436  -
Step5 0.03375 0.12236  0.48200  0.00077
```

The p-values displayed for every possible combination bring some interesting insights:

1. Step1 is rated significantly different to all other steps.

2. Step4 is rated significantly different to Step3.

3. Step5 is rated significantly different to Step4.

This output does not reveal whether Step1 is rated better or worse than Step2, Step1 is rated better or worse than Step3 etc. This could be found out by checking the descriptive statistics of Task 2.8.

However, it would be easier if we had a graphical answer to the aforementioned questions. A plot would illustrate exactly the rating of all steps against each other. And, for presentation purpose the table above is not suitable anyway. Although, a confidence interval for means is not the best way of presenting the results because of non-normal data, it still is a plot that can be explained.

TASK 2.11   PLOT CONFIDENCE INTERVALS FOR ALL STEPS:

```
# Plot confidence intervals for steps
ggline(stackedStep, x = "ind", y = "values", add = c("mean_ci"),
    ylab = "Rating", xlab = "", main = "Confidence Intervals
    for Step Rating") + theme(text = element_text(size = 16),
    plot.margin = margin(t=1, r=2, b=1, l=2, unit = "cm")) +
    grids(linetype = "dashed")
```

The resulting plot is illustrating what the numbers told already: Step1 is rated higher than all other steps. Step4 is rated significantly lower than Step3. Step5 is rated significantly higher than Step4. Hence, it is clear that Step4, "Dispensing Medicine", deserves some attention because of its low rating (Figure 2.19).

In fact, it is not advisable and, statistically speaking, wrong to talk about Step2 receiving a lower rating than Step3. Any such comparison is not supported by statistics. If you talk about the difference between Step2 and Step3, you run a risk of 30.3% that you are wrong (see Task 2.10 output). This is what we would call "Fake News".

A Data Analyst or Data Scientist does not talk about a difference seen between the rating for Step2 and Step3 for example. There is not enough evidence for that conclusion.

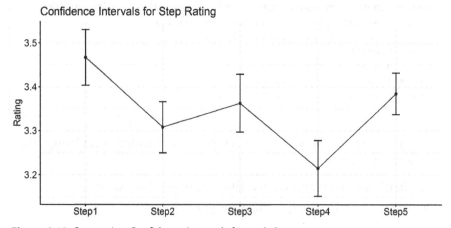

Figure 2.19 Comparing Confidence Intervals for each Step

There are many ways to do analysis with R. This statistics package is comparable to SPSS in its functions, but with its open architecture, it grows faster than SPSS and offers more flexibility to satisfy all your statistics, graphical, and programming needs.

There are sources available online to vary any parameter of each plot for any of the hundreds of plots. This (Community, 2020) is one of the sources to learn about R functions for statistics, plots, and programming.

Hypothesis 2: There is a significant difference between the ratings for indicators

As seen in Figures 2.15 and 2.16, there seems to be a difference between indicators. Since we have 17 indicators, the pairwise comparison of all together might not be a smart way of analysing them.

Practically, the five steps are mostly run by five different people or teams. Giving all of them hints for improvement within their step could be the clever decision.

TASK 2.12   STACK INDICATOR DATA FOR EACH STEP TOGETHER IN ONE DATASET:

```
# Stack indicator data for step1
stackedInd1 <- stack(ClinicSurvey, select = c("Step1friendly",
    "Step1prompt", "Step1helpful"))
# Stack indicator data for step2
stackedInd2 <- stack(ClinicSurvey, select = c("Step2friendly","S
    tep2prompt", "Step2helpful"))
# Stack indicator data for step3
stackedInd3 <- stack(ClinicSurvey, select = c("Step3friendly",
    "Step3prompt", "Step3comm", "Step3comp"))
# Stack indicator data for step4
stackedInd4 <- stack(ClinicSurvey, select = c("Step4friendly",
    "Step4prompt", "Step4comm", "Step4comp"))
# Stack indicator data for step5
stackedInd5 <- stack(ClinicSurvey, select = c("Step5friendly",
    "Step5prompt", "Step5helpful"))
```

If you wish to see the results of these operations, use the View function to display the resulting table in the data frame pane in R Studio.

TASK 2.13   PERFORM PAIRWISE WILCOX TEST FOR INDICATORS AT STEP1:

```
# Perform Pairwise Wilcox test
pairwise.wilcox.test(stackedInd1$values, stackedInd1$ind,
    p.adjust.method = "BH")
```

PAIRWISE WILCOX TEST OUTPUT:

```
Pairwise comparisons using Wilcoxon rank sum test with continuity
  correction
data: stackedInd1$values and stackedInd1$ind
            Step1friendly  Step1prompt
 Step1prompt    0.00017 -
 Step1helpful   0.22056        2.7e-06
```

This output means, there are significant differences between Step-
1friendly and Step1prompt as well as between Step1prompt and
Step1helpful. And following the numbers at Figure 2.14, we can conclude for Step1 that the characteristic "Prompt & Attentive" receives
the lowest rating (Figure 2.20).

**TASK 2.14   PLOT CONFIDENCE INTERVALS FOR ALL
INDICATORS AT STEP1:**

```
# Plot confidence intervals for indicators at step1
ggline(stackedInd1, x = "ind", y = "values", add = c("mean_ci"),
    ylab = "Rating", xlab = "", main = "Confidence Intervals for
    Indicator Rating at Step1")
 + theme(text = element_text(size = 16))
 + grids(linetype = "dashed")
```

The output confirms the conclusion. It seems that the team at Step1 lacks
in attending to patients promptly. It could be that patients experience
waiting at the registration counter (Figure 2.20).

We wish to generate statistics and plots for all other steps as well. Hence,
we use the commands as shown previously and replace the step number
in the "stackedInd1" to represent Step2 to Step5.

As a result, we learn that the rating for all characteristics for each step
shows variation and partially significant differences. In order to demonstrate what to focus on when planning interventions, we can use either of
the five plots to draw conclusions step by step. Or, in order to simplify the
procedure, we plot all data together in one plot (Figure 2.21).

**TASK 2.15   PLOT CONFIDENCE INTERVALS FOR ALL
INDICATORS AT ALL STEPS:**

```
# Plot confidence intervals for all indicators. Turn X labels by
    45 degrees
plot <- ggline(stackedInd, x = "ind", y = "values", add
    = c("mean_ci"),
ylab = "Rating", xlab = "", remove = "Overall", main="Mean Plot
    with 95% CI", adj = 0)
plot + grids(linetype = "dashed") + rotate_x_text(45)
```

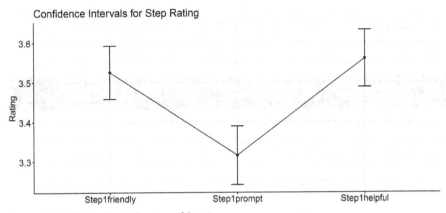

Figure 2.20 Rating for Indicators of Step1

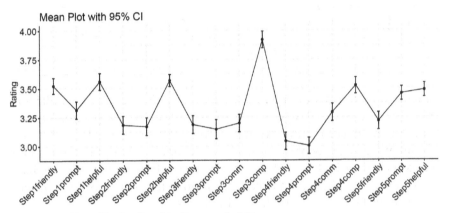

Figure 2.21 Plot of Rating for all Indicators of all Steps

From this plot, it is obvious that the staff at the clinic is very helpful. Doctor and pharmacist receive a high rating for their competency but could be more friendly and prompt. The clerks at the payment counter come across as prompt and helpful.

This rating gives some input for the story to tell the management. This is certainly information that can trigger some actions.

Hypothesis 3: There is a significant relationship between the rating for a process step and the overall rating

This analysis will help to prioritise activities. A significantly lower rating on a step that does not seem too important to the patient is less critical than one on a strong driver for overall satisfaction.

The tool of choice for this task is regression analysis. Usually, the work starts with linear models. Before we analyse anything, we plot our data. For multiple X and one Y a scatter matrix plot is the tool of choice.

TASK 2.16   SHOW SCATTER MATRIX PLOT OF ALL STEPS VS OVERALL

```
# Loading necessary packages if not loaded yet
library(graphics)
# Generating upper panel to show Pearson's correlation
    coefficient
cor.panel <- function(x, y, ...)
{
   par(usr = c(0, 1, 0, 1))
   txt <- as.character(format(cor(x, y), digits=2))
   text(0.5, 0.5, txt, cex = 4* abs(cor(x, y)))
}
# Plotting scatter matrix plot (put overall last so that it is
    in last row
pairs(~ Step1+Step2+Step3+Step4+Step5+Overall, upper.panel =
    cor.panel, data = ClinicSurvey, main = "Correlation Matrix
    of Steps versus Overall")
```

Figure 2.22 shows the scatter matrix plot for all Xs, i.e. rating for all Steps against each other and against the Y, Overall rating. By putting Overall last in the pairs () function, we have the scatter plots of all Steps versus Overall in the last row of the plot. Since we replace the upper panel of the matrix with the display of all respective correlation coefficients, we have the correlation coefficient matrix in addition to the plots. Correlation coefficients have been generated following Pearson.

This plot offers some first insights into our dataset ClinicSurvey:

1. Step5 seems to be the weakest driver for Overall with r = 0.53. This means, patients' overall rating is little driven by patients' rating of Step5. The scatter plot for Step5 versus Overall on the lower right shows a very soft pattern.

2. All other steps seem to be influencing Overall much stronger with Step2 being the strongest (r = 0.87). This is represented by larger r values corresponding to more distinct patterns.

3. Strong correlation seems to exist between all steps with the highest between Step1 and Step4 (r = 0.92). Hence the scatter plot between Step1 and Step4 is the one with the clearest pattern (third from the bottom on the left column). This will most likely pose a problem in our regression model with variance inflation factors (VIF) turning out too high.

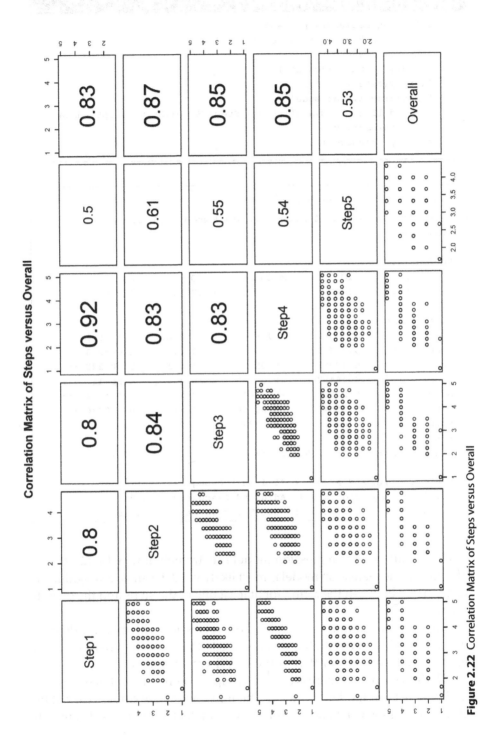

Figure 2.22 Correlation Matrix of Steps versus Overall

> **TASK 2.17   BUILD LINEAR MODEL AND SHOW REGRESSION RESULT OF ALL STEPS VS OVERALL:**
>
> ```
> # Loading necessary packages
> install.packages("tidyverse")
> library(tidyverse)
> install.packages("caret")
> library(caret)
> # Building linear model
> stepModel1 <- lm(Overall~Step1+Step2+Step3+Step4+Step5, data =
>     ClinicSurvey)
> summary(stepModel1)
> ```

> **LINEAR REGRESSION OUTPUT:**
>
> ```
> lm(formula = Overall ~ Step1 + Step2 + Step3 + Step4 + Step5, data =
> ClinicSurvey)
>
> Residuals:
>     Min        1Q       Median      3Q         Max
>  -1.73901   -0.15879   0.02412    0.17679    1.45156
>
> Coefficients:
>               Estimate    Std. Error   t value    Pr(>|t|)
> (Intercept)   0.04782     0.09324      0.513      0.608273
> Step1         0.18983     0.05115      3.711      0.000229  ***
> Step2         0.46457     0.04465     10.406      < 2e-16   ***
> Step3         0.27582     0.03810      7.239      1.68e-12  ***
> Step4         0.14647     0.05660      2.588      0.009936  **
> Step5        -0.03939     0.03276     -1.203      0.229717
> ---
> Signif. codes:  0 '***' 0.001 '**' 0.01 '*' 0.05 '.' 0.1 ' ' 1
>
> Residual standard error: 0.3174 on 508 degrees of freedom
> Multiple R-squared: 0.8341, Adjusted R-squared: 0.8324
> F-statistic: 510.7 on 5 and 508 DF, p-value: < 2.2e-16
> ```

The p-value for the regression model is extremely low with $<2.2 \times 10^{-16}$. This means the regression model is most likely valid, i.e. there is a significant relationship between the rating for at least one of the steps and the overall rating.

However, for a multiple regression, i.e. a regression with multiple drivers, the relationship between the drivers needs to be checked before a final verdict can be given. For that purpose, VIFs are calculated.

VIF shows whether there is a relationship, a collinearity between drivers in the regression model. If there is, the influence of the drivers cannot be clearly distinguished, hence the model parameters might be misleading. If

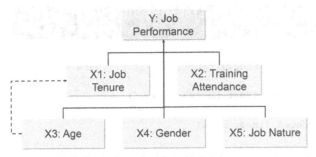

Figure 2.23 Model with Potential Collinearity

this model is supposed to be used for prediction purpose, the prediction might be off.

Figure 2.23 shows a regression model with likely collinearity. All five Xs are potentially driving the Y. Furthermore, there is a high likelihood that X3 drives X1, because job tenure goes up with progressing age. It means the influence of age on job performance exists directly and via job tenure. With this relationship between two or more X, the model will be overloaded and p-values, R^2, as well as coefficients will be erroneous. The resulting model is not useful for any purpose.

Usually, two or more Xs have an elevated VIF since this concept involves more than one X. The way out is to eliminate one of the X hoping that this fixes the problem. The X to remove is not necessarily the one with the highest VIF. It is recommended to remove the X that is harder to determine, to control, or less practical in other ways.

TASK 2.18   DETERMINE VIF FOR ALL DRIVERS, I.E. FOR STEP1, STEP2 . . . STEP5:

```
# Opening necessary package
library(car)
# Determining VIF values (Must be less than 5)
vif(stepModel1)
```

VIF OUTPUT:

Step1	Step2	Step3	Step4	Step5
7.136180	4.598660	4.271018	8.773096	1.617276

The VIF output shows Step1 and Step4 with VIF values that are higher than five. It is very likely that the ratings for these two steps are related. This could be because the staff who usually run Medicine Dispensing often double up to do the Registration. If this is true, removing Step1 from the model should bring the VIF of Step4 down.

TASK 2.19   ELIMINATE STEP1 AND DETERMINE VIF FOR STEP2 . . . STEP5:

```
# Building linear model
stepModel2 <- lm(Overall~Step2+Step3+Step4+Step5, data =
    ClinicSurvey)
# Determining VIF values (Must be less than 5)
vif(stepModel2)
# Applying the reduced linear model
summary(stepModel2)
```

VIF OUTPUT:

Step2	Step3	Step4	Step5
4.563095	4.229270	4.077891	1.615399

This confirms our assumption. Now, our model is good for analysis.

REGRESSION OUTPUT:

```
lm(formula = Overall ~ Step2 + Step3 + Step4 + Step5, data =
ClinicSurvey)

Residuals:
   Min        1Q      Median      3Q        Max
-1.72261   -0.16042   0.03315    0.18250    1.40928

Coefficients:
               Estimate    Std. Error   t value    Pr(>|t|)
(Intercept)    0.13076     0.09165      1.427      0.154
Step2          0.47914     0.04503      10.641     < 2e-16   ***
Step3          0.28980     0.03839      7.550      2.03e-13  ***
Step4          0.30014     0.03907      7.682      8.09e-14  ***
Step5         -0.04353     0.03314      -1.313     0.190
---
Signif. codes:  0 '***' 0.001 '**' 0.01 '*' 0.05 '.' 0.1 ' ' 1

Residual standard error: 0.3214 on 509 degrees of freedom
Multiple R-squared:  0.8296,        Adjusted R-squared:  0.8282
F-statistic: 619.4 on 4 and 509 DF,   p-value: < 2.2e-16
```

The analysis of a regression model usually needs the following steps:

1. Analysis of VIF if multiple X are in the model. VIF must be < 5. This has been achieved already.

2. Analysis of model p-value. Model p-value must be < 0.05. As shown, the model p-value is $< 2.2 \times 10^{-16}$, i.e. practically zero.

3. All p-values for X (Pr(>|t|)) must be < 0.05. The p-value of Step5 is 0.19, this means this factor is not related to the overall rating. The overall rating is not driven by the impression, patients have at Step5. Hence, we need to remove this step from the model and rerun it.

4. The residuals must meet certain conditions for the model to be valid.

TASK 2.20   ELIMINATE STEP5 AND DETERMINE REGRESSION MODEL FOR STEP2 . . . STEP4 WITH OVERALL:

```
# Building linear model
stepModel3 <- lm(Overall~Step2+Step3+Step4, data = ClinicSurvey)
# Applying the reduced linear model
summary(stepModel3)
```

Now, all p-values for X (Pr(>|t|)) are < 0.05. The model seems valid and the factors Step2, Step3, and Step4 are drivers for the overall evaluation. In order to find out, which is the strongest driver, we use the Estimates. Step2, the screening by the nurse, has the largest impact on the overall assessment by patients with a coefficient of 0.46 (0.46154). Step4 shows a coefficient of 0.30 (0.29855) and Step2 is the least impactful driver with 0.29 (0.28709).

With this model we are able to explain 82.8% of overall variation by the three mentioned steps. This shows a considerably high $R^2_{adjusted}$, because only about 17% of the variation in overall rating is not due to the three steps.

In order to ensure, this model is really valid, we need to check the residuals. Residuals are the differences between the points calculated by the regression equation out of the Xs and the dependent variable Y. The equation is

$$Overall = -0.06 + 0.46 * Step2 + 0.29 * Step3 + 0.30 * Step4.$$

If this equation is applied to all combinations of Step2, Step3, Step4, the result of the equation will result in Fits. The difference between Overall and Fit is called Residual, i.e. leftover variation. These residuals need to be studied to confirm the model.

When analysing survey data, i.e. data that has been collected using a Likert scale, the residual plots may not turn out to be "perfect". The requirements are:

- Residuals are normally distributed.
- Residuals over all Xs do not show a pattern.
- Residuals over time do not show a pattern.
- Residuals over fits do not show a pattern.

Residuals that look "perfect" do not show any pattern. Though, this is not possible to see in Likert scale generated data since the input is very structured and has only five levels. The above-mentioned plots (Figure 2.24) show some irregularities.

This will output the 4 in 1 residual plot as shown in Figure 2.24:

TASK 2.21   PERFORM RESIDUAL PLOTS:

```
# Plotting residuals
par(mfrow = c(2, 2)) # Switching to 2 x 2 plot
plot(stepModel3, cex.lab=1.5, cex.axis=1.2)
par(mfrow = c(1, 1)) # Return to single section plot
```

For finding out when these irregularities occur, we apply the residual plot over time (Figure 2.25).

TASK 2.22   PLOT STANDARDISED RESIDUALS OVER DATE:

```
# Sorting ClinicSurvey by date
ClinicSurvey <- ClinicSurvey[order(ClinicSurvey$Date),]
# Installing and opening necessary package
install.packages("olsrr")
library(olsrr)
# Plotting residuals
ols_plot_resid_stand(stepModel3)
```

Standardised residuals are supposed to be within –2 and +2. Since we observe much larger standardised residuals, we list them out for easier reference:

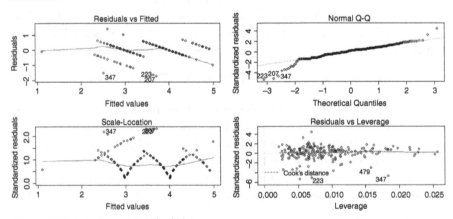

Figure 2.24 Four-in-one Residual Plot

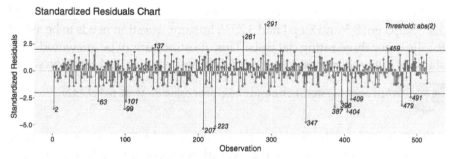
Figure 2.25 Standardised Residual Plot of stepModel3 over Time

TASK 2.23   LIST OUTLIERS WITH LARGE STANDARDISED RESIDUAL:

```
# Installing and opening necessary package
install.packages("car")
library(car)
# Listing outliers, i.e. large standardised residuals
outlierTest(stepModel3)
```

THE OUTPUT OF THIS OUTLIER TEST SHOWS 4 RATINGS WITH LARGE RESIDUALS:

	rstudent	unadjusted p-value	Bonferroni p
207	-5.510359	5.6964e-08	2.9279e-05
223	-5.272353	1.9942e-07	1.0250e-04
347	-4.848660	1.6539e-06	8.5008e-04
291	4.433928	1.1344e-05	5.8306e-03

Column 1 indicates which observations are concerned.

TASK 2.24   LIST ROWS WITH OUTLIERS AS REGISTERED ABOVE FROM CLINICSURVEY IN COLUMNS 1 (ID), 2 (TIMESTAMP), 8 (OVERALL), 27 (STEP2), 28 (STEP3), 29 (STEP4):

```
# Listing rows for outliers, i.e. large standardised residuals
ClinicSurvey[c(207, 223, 347, 291), c(1, 2, 8, 27, 28, 29)]
```

THE OUTPUT LOOKS LIKE THIS:

	ID	TimeStamp	Overall	Step2	Step3	Step4
1	190036293	2019-06-06 18:45:00	2	3.33	3.5	3.75
2	190036733	2019-06-11 17:47:00	2	3.33	3.25	3.75
3	190049592	2019-09-12 20:06:00	1	2	3	2.25
4	190046778	2019-08-26 09:15:00	4	2.67	2.25	2.25

The question is, how can the evaluation for Overall be 2 if Step2 received 3.33, Step3 got 3.5 and Step4 had 3.75? The same question needs to be asked for the other three rating datasets. This question cannot be answered with statistics but with process knowledge, business acumen and common sense.

 "When applying statistics, always keep your common sense switched on."

Further study of the circumstances of these evaluations needs to be done to answer the question why the overall assessment is so low whilst the individual steps received a high rating. For statistical analysis purpose, these points might be taken out of the model since they may falsify the result and lead to wrong conclusions. This study can be done based on the output of Task 2.24 in combination with Figure 2.25.

This information, we can take to a management presentation.

Hypothesis 4: There is a pattern over time

Analysing all kind of data over time is a good habit. Time itself does not influence anything. But over time there are usually changes. Staff change over time, the number of patients depends on the time of day or day of the week, etc. Therefore, we analyse our satisfaction data over time. Our data contain three indicators representing time.

- Firstly, we have the date of the treatment.
- Secondly, we can use day of the week (DOW).
- Thirdly, we can study whether patient satisfaction depends on the time of day (TimeSlot).

There are multiple ways of doing this analysis. We begin with a graphical representation of DOW.

TASK 2.26   PLOT OVERALL SATISFACTION BY DOW:

```
# Saving the plot of Overall by DOW in order of weekdays
plot <- ggline(ClinicSurvey, x = "DOW", y = "Overall",  order =
    c("Mon", "Tue", "Wed", "Thu", "Fri", "Sat"), add = c
    ("mean_ci"),  ylab = "Overall Rating", xlab = "", main="Mean
    Plot with 95% CI by DOW")
# Adding gridlines and plotting
plot + grids(linetype = "dashed")
```

The output of this plot shows a trend of growing customer satisfaction over the course of a week (Figure 2.26).

It seems that there is a difference between the first four days and the last two days of the week. This needs to be checked as before.

As mentioned earlier, a day of the week does not change anything itself. It needs to be studied what factors change over the week. For this purpose, it would be beneficial to identify which of the steps contributes most to

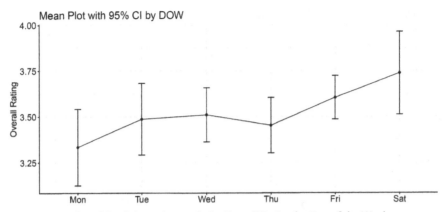

Figure 2.26 Plot of Confidence Intervals for Overall Rating by Day of the Week

this presumed trend. Then, the underlying root causes could probably be identified.

Is it that at the beginning of the week, visiting doctors, trainee doctors from local universities do the job whilst the experienced doctors come in on Fridays and Saturdays? Or is it that the number of patients towards end of week goes down so that on the one hand the waiting time goes down and on the other hand the stress for all staff goes down, which results in higher satisfaction? More analysis needs to be done.

TASK 2.27   PLOT OVERALL SATISFACTION BY TIMESLOT (TIME OF DAY):

```
# Saving the plot of Overall by TimeSlot in order of time of day
plot <- ggline(ClinicSurvey, x = "TimeSlot", y = "Overall",
   order = c("09-11", "11-13", "13-15", "15-17", "17-19"),
   add = c("mean_ci"), ylab = "Overall Rating", xlab = "",
   main="Mean Plot with 95% CI by TimeSlot")
# Adding gridlines and plotting
plot + grids(linetype = "dashed")
```

The output of this plot shows a drop of patient satisfaction at the end of the day. The necessary hypothesis test to confirm this trend will likely find that it is safe to talk about low patient satisfaction at the end of the day (Figure 2.27).

It needs to be studied which process step creates this change in patient satisfaction and whether this is due to the number of patients who visit their doctor after work at the end of the day, i.e. due to increased patient numbers.

This study can only be done with business acumen and process understanding.

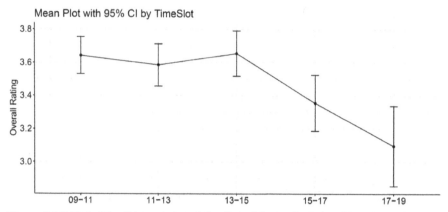

Mean Plot with 95% CI by TimeSlot

Figure 2.27 Plot of Confidence Intervals for Overall Rating by Time of Day (TimeSlot)

Business Decision

Based on data from 514 patients evaluating our services between Jan to Dec 2019, the following conclusions can be presented:

1. Patients have rated our services in steps Registration, Screening, Consultation, Dispensation of Medicine, and Payment. Whilst the average rating for Screening, Consultation, and Payment receives a similar evaluation overall, the step to Hand Out Medicine is significantly rated lower and Registration is rated significantly higher than all other steps.

2. Patients have rated our service characteristics quite differently. Whilst doctor's and pharmacist's competency are rated quite highly, their behavioural traits such as "friendly & courteous", "prompt & attentive", and "clear communication" are not seen as good. "Friendly & courteous" as well as "Prompt & attentive" of the Screeners leave some room for improvement as well.

3. There is a clear indication that patient satisfaction is higher at the end of each week and lower at the end of each day.

Analytical Storytelling

After analysing our patient satisfaction score, we need to conclude that we reach only 56% overall satisfaction out of 514 patients who have participated in the survey. This means, about 226 patients did not leave our clinic satisfied or very satisfied. In fact, nine out of the 514 gave a poor rating (rating 1), whereas 35 rated us fair. From 184 patients, we received an overall satisfactory rating. 258 patients rated us overall good and 28 excellent.

Issuing medicine marks the process step with the lowest rating (Figure 2.27). Is seems that patients have to wait at steps Screening, Consultation, and Medicine Dispensing which undermines the rating for "Prompt & Attentive". The apparent bottleneck most likely brings down the rating

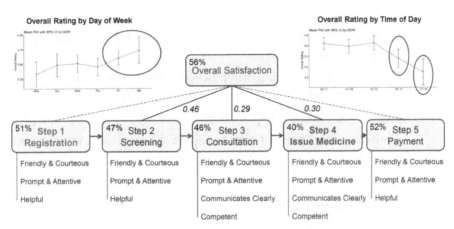

Figure 2.28 Summary of Findings of Analysis of Patient Satisfaction Data

for "Friendly & Courteous" for our staff because they are under pressure to work through the jam. However, the assumption of a bottleneck is just based on patients' feedback and needs further study.

Our staff is seen as helpful and competent (Figure 2.28).

Additionally, we have found that the patient satisfaction rating depends on the time of the day and the day of the week. On Fridays and especially Saturdays, patient satisfaction gets significantly higher than earlier in the week. We still need to study whether this has to do with the fact that less patients visit us on those days.

It does not come as a surprise that patients are less satisfied when they are treated after 17:00h. These patients most likely had to wait longer and got frustrated over time.

The overall satisfaction is very much driven by the impression patients gather in the Screening, Consultation, and Medicine Dispensing steps. The treatment during Registration and Payment seems to be less important for patients.

Further study needs to be done to check the assumptions mentioned about patient traffic over time and its relationship with patient satisfaction. For that, the data collection will be amended.

There is some room for improvement. Let us work on that.

Practice

- What tools are available for comparing averages of multiple groups for normal and non-normal data?
- What tools are available for testing the relationship between multiple continuous variables?
- What is multi-collinearity, how does it affect the result of a regression analysis and how do we deal with this kind of situation?
- Please, complete the following steps:

  – Download the data for this case from www.wiley.com.

- Study the Scatter Matrix Plot for Overall and Step1 to Step5 (Figure 2.29) and explain it. What is the correlation coefficient between Step3 and Step5?
- Check whether there is a difference for patient satisfaction for Step1 over DOW and over TimeSlot. Perform the appropriate plot.
- Repeat the same for Step2 to Step 5. Perform the appropriate plot.
- Prepare a short presentation to report the result and your recommendation to the management of the clinic.

Deploying Analytics Tools

Analysing customer satisfaction scores is usually a compromise. Since the rating generally comes in when a respondent inputs his or her "satisfaction level" on Likert scales, it would statistically be more appropriate to treat this data as discrete ordinal. Analysing discrete ordinal data offers a limited set of tools that are generally less powerful than tools that deal with continuous data.

Therefore, most analyses of survey data involve tools that assume Likert scale results are continuous. The caveat is that some of the prerequisites of these tools are violated. For example, in the previous case we could have used ANOVA (Table 2.5) to compare the rating coming from patients who have undergone different parts of our service delivery chain, different touch points.

ANOVA is based on two assumptions:

Firstly, ANOVA assumes the data in comparison is continuous and normally distributed. However, Likert scale data are hardly normally distributed. We have tested normality, found a deviation from normality and deployed non-parametric tests.

Secondly, ANOVA assumes the data in comparison having non-significantly different variance (standard deviation). This can be checked.

The **Kruskal–Wallis test** (Table 2.6) was conducted to find whether there is a difference between groups. Since this test does not show which group or groups are different, we performed a **Pairwise Wilcox test** (Table 2.7) to locate the difference indicated by Kruskal–Wallis. This pairwise comparison can even be performed without running Kruskal–Wallis first.

Regression (Table 2.8) does not need normally distributed data in neither dependent variable nor in independent variables. Yet, regression is based on the assumption, that the residuals as a result of the regression are normally distributed. For the same reason as above, this might not be the case. Residuals coming from highly structured data – only showing levels 1 to 5 in all ratings – will have a distinct pattern.

However, the alternatives are limited. If we would treat discrete data as such, we would involve much less powerful tools, tools that deal with discrete Xs and discrete Y. These tools deliver much less information out of the analysis. And there are only limited ways for doing prediction, what regression does very nicely.

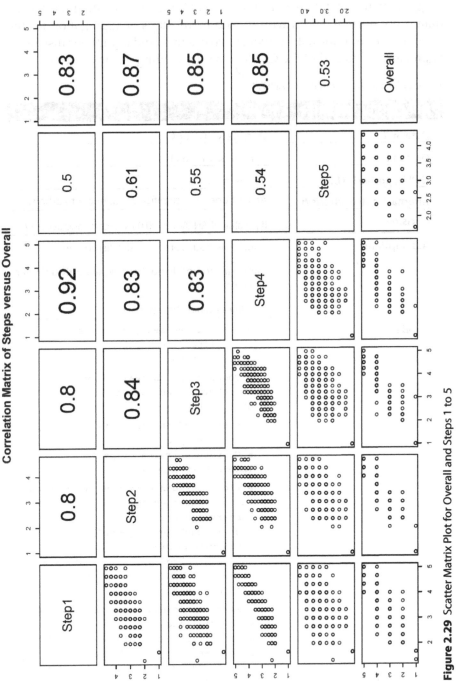

Figure 2.29 Scatter Matrix Plot for Overall and Steps 1 to 5

Plotting non-normal data, as shown in Figures 2.17, 2.19 and others, is done using average rating for different categories like Step, Indicators etc., including the **Confidence Interval for the Mean (CI Mean)**. This approach suggests that our data is nearly normal. Unfortunately, the Likert scale data is not normal, and it would need many steps of aggregation for the result to turn out normal. However, we use this kind of plot because other aggregations instead of the CI Mean are less telling, i.e. less useful.

Table 2.5 Analysis of Variance – ANOVA

ANALYSIS OF VARIANCE – ANOVA	
Data in X:	Discrete X – Groups
Data in Y:	Continuous, normal
Null Hypothesis H_0:	$\mu_1 = \mu_2 = \ldots = \mu_n$
Alternative Hypothesis H_A:	At least one μ_i is significantly different to others.
Decision:	If p-value of ANOVA is < 0.05, reject H_0 and accept H_A.
Assumptions:	Data in all groups are normally distributed.
	Data in all groups do not have significantly different variance.
	Residuals do not show pattern.
R code:	

```
# Loading necessary packages
install.packages("stats")
library(stats)

# Compute the analysis of variance
stepANOVA <- aov(values ~ ind, data =
stackedStep)

# Summary of the analysis
summary(stepANOVA)
# Compute pairwise comparison
TukeyHSD(stepANOVA)

# Plot confidence intervals for steps
install.packages("gplots")
library("gplots")
install.packages("ggpubr")
library("ggpubr")
ggline(stackedStep, x = "ind", y =
"values",  add = c("mean_ci"),  ylab =
"Rating", xlab = "")

# Plot confidence intervals for steps
with gridlines
plot <- plotmeans(values ~ ind, data =
stackedStep, p=0.95, barwidth=2,
 xlab = "", ylab = "Rating", ylim =
c(2.9, 3.5),
 error.bars = c("conf.int"),
level=0.95,
 main = "Mean Plot with 95% CI")
plot + grids(linetype = "dashed") +
rotate_x_text(45)
```

Table 2.6 Kruskal–Wallis test

KRUSKAL–WALLIS TEST	
Data in X :	Discrete X – multiple Groups
Data in Y :	Continuous. Not normal.
Null Hypothesis H_0 :	$median_1 = median_2 = \ldots = median_n$
Alternative Hypothesis H_A :	At least one $median$ is significantly different.
Decision:	If p-value is < 0.05, reject H_0 and accept H_A .
Assumptions:	Shape of distribution in groups is similar.
R code:	```# Loading necessary packages\ninstall.packages("stats")\nlibrary(stats)\n# Perform Kruskal-Wallis test for\nvalues by groups in ind\nkruskal.test(values ~ ind, data =\nstackedStep)```

Table 2.7 Pairwise Wilcox Test

PAIRWISE WILCOX TEST	
Data in X :	Discrete X – multiple Groups tested in pairs
Data in Y :	Continuous Y, discrete ordinal (values), non-normal
Null Hypothesis H_0 :	$median_1 = median_2$
Alternative Hypothesis H_A :	$median_1 \neq median_2$
Decision:	If p-value is < 0.05 ($\alpha = 0.05$), reject H_0 and accept H_A .
Assumptions:	Sample sizes must be at least 6.
	Samples must have similar distribution.
R code:	```# Loading necessary packages\nlibrary(rstatix)\n# Perform Pairwise Wilcox test\npairwise.wilcox.test(stackedStep$values,\nstackedStep$ind, p.adjust.method = "BH")```

Table 2.8 Multiple Linear Regression

MULTIPLE LINEAR REGRESSION	
Data in X :	Continuous, no normality required.
	Can be applied for discrete ordinal data.
	Discrete X (groups) can be used as factors.
Data in Y :	Continuous, no normality required.
	Can be applied for discrete ordinal data.
Null Hypothesis H_0 :	No significant relationship between any X and Y
Alternative Hypothesis H_A :	At least one X influences Y significantly
Decision:	1. All VIF must be < 5. Consider removing X with high VIF. 2. If p-value of ANOVA is < 0.05, reject H_0 and accept H_A. 3. X has significant influence if p-value of X < 0.05. Remove non-significant Xs and rerun model.
Assumptions:	Residuals are normally distributed.
	Residuals over all Xs do not show pattern.
	Residuals over time do not show pattern.
	Residuals over fits do not show pattern.
	No unusual observations (outliers). Consider removing.
	No points with influential observations (high leverage points). Consider removing.
R code:	```# Loading necessary packages
install.packages("tidyverse")
library(tidyverse)
install.packages("car")
library(car)
install.packages("olsrr")
library(olsrr)

# Building linear model
stepModel <- lm(Overall~Step1+Step2
+Step3+Step4+Step5, data = ClinicSurvey)
summary(stepModel)

Determining VIF values (Must be less
than 5)
VIF(stepModel)

# Plotting residuals
par(mfrow = c(2, 2))
plot(stepModel)
ols_plot_resid_stud_fit(stepModel)
ols_plot_resid_stand(stepModel)

Listing outliers
outlierTest(stepModel)``` |

Case 3: How to Create a Patient Satisfaction Dashboard

Once the analysis of the patient satisfaction data has been done, there is no need to run another analysis very soon, right?

Wrong!

Nowadays, the environment is changing at an increased rate. This has an impact on customers of organisations and therefore, on the organisations as well. It is critical to know about these changes as they happen. This needs building data analytics systems that constantly acquire the newest data, analyse them, and present information and conclusions in a useful, comprehensive, and appealing way.

This is what dashboards are for. Dashboards used to be the whiteboards carrying A4 papers with slightly outdated information presented in tables and graphs. With the availability of new technology – a large HD screen costs as much as a family dinner – it is timely to rethink the concept of dashboards.

A dashboard is a visual display of a core set of metrics that provide management with a quick summary of performance, not unlike the dashboard used in your car (Kaufmann, 2003).

Deciding about Metrics to Illustrate our Clinic Performance

Before building a dashboard, we need to decide which indicators, i.e. metrics we want to show. A dashboard usually has multiple functions and the indicators should help to fulfil these functions.

Like the dashboard in the car, it must inform timely about the current performance at that moment, such as speed. For this purpose, the dash needs leading indicators, that is metrics that lead to our action before our erroneous performance causes us to pay a fine. These leading indicators are mostly complemented by lagging indicators, such as metrics that analyse the performance over time and lead to non-immediate actions. In the car, this would be measuring the consumption of petrol and the remaining petrol in the tank that makes us stop at a petrol station.

In our clinic case, we have analysed the patient satisfaction data. This analysis has led to priorities in terms of improvement activities which we want to measure regarding their effectiveness.

The dashboard should be able to answer the following questions:

1. How have we been doing today and this week?
2. Which steps and indicators are rated significantly lower?
3. Is there a long-term trend, i.e., are we getting better or worse in important indicators?

Building a Clinic Dashboard with MS Power BI and R

On the one hand, there are plenty of tools around that offer platforms for building dashboards. On the other hand, we could easily build a dashboard with MS Excel since we have this software already sitting on our computers and we are very familiar with it.

Microsoft's Power BI is a package that belongs to MS Office but is usually not installed. The desktop version is available for download from the Microsoft Store. A great advantage of Power BI is its similarity with the MS Office package. It beats MS Excel in visualisations, its purpose and strength, but it does not have the analytics power of its sibling.

MS Power BI makes up for the lack of analytics tools by allowing the inclusion of customised R and Python modules for analysis and display. This makes Power BI a very comprehensive package for building your own dashboards.

Let us get familiar with Power BI (see also other sources like Microsoft, 2020). It does not matter whether you opt for Power BI desktop or Power BI. The functionality is about the same.

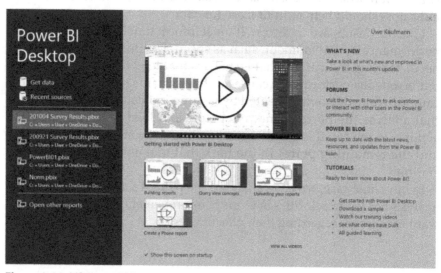

Figure 2.30 MS Power BI Start-up Screen

Source: Used with permission from Microsoft.

TASK 2.28   LOAD DATA FROM CLINICSURVEY.XLSX INTO POWER BI:

1. Open Microsoft Power BI. This will show the start-up screen (Figure 2.30).

2. If this is your first time using Power BI, you may want to create an account. Please, take a minute and do so. You can use your existing Microsoft credentials.

3. In the Startup Screen, select Get data.

4. In the Get Data window, select Excel.

5. Navigate to the folder with your data and select ClinicSurveyStacked.xlsx.

6. In the Navigator window, check the table Cleaned. Select Load.

7. Now your data is loaded into Power BI. It is a good habit to start creating a report file for your dashboard by saving your report under File – Save As – ClinicSurvey.pbix.

8. On the right hand panel, select Cleaned and Rename it to Stacked.

Now we have loaded our data into Power BI. Before we create visuals on our report to design our dashboard, we want to work on the data table. Assuming, the cleaning of data has been done before, we just need to enhance our data table by creating additional columns showing aggregations of data. For example, it would be good to have a column that indicates Step and Indicator together. We create the column StepInd.

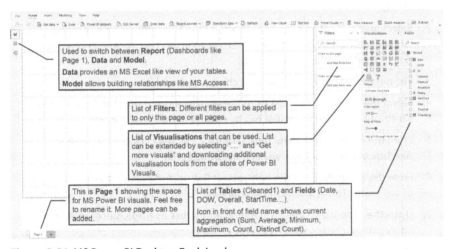

Figure 2.31 MS Power BI Desktop Explained

Source: Used with permission from Microsoft.

TASK 2.29   BUILD ADDITIONAL COLUMNS FOR AGGREGATED DATA:

1. Navigate to the icon for Data on the left-hand panel (Figure 2.31).

2. Select Stacked on the right. The table with our Stacked data is displayed.

3. On top select Calculations – New column.

4. Insert StepInd = Stacked[Step] & " " & Stacked[Indicator], hit Enter. Column StepInd is created.

5. On top select Calculations – New column.

6. Insert Weekday = weekday(Stacked[Date],2) & " " & format(Stacked[Date],"ddd"), hit Enter. Column Weekday is created.

You can generate more columns at any time.

Generally, it is not necessary to type the whole command in Power BI. For example, if you wish to insert Stacked[Step1friendly], you just need to type Step1 and PowerBI offers a list of options to choose from.

In the next step, we will be designing some visuals to show our patient satisfaction performance.

Studying Patient Satisfaction Score over Time:

TASK 2.30   INSERT REPORT TITLE AND LINE CHART (TIME SERIES PLOT) VISUAL:

1. Navigate to the icon for Report on the left-hand panel. Our dashboard is empty.

2. Select Insert – Text box from the Insert menu. This adds a text box somewhere on the empty dashboard. Feel free to insert text, format and reposition it. This works like PowerPoint.

3. The next step inserts a simple Line chart onto our dash.

4. Select the icon for Line chart from the visualisations pane (1 in Figure 2.32). An empty frame for the visual has been built in the report space.

5. From the Fields Pane on the right (Figure 2.33), select Date and pull it into the Axis box of our visual. The visual must be selected.

6. From the Fields Pane on the right, select Rating and pull it into the Values box of our visual. The visual must be selected.

7. Open the drop-down menu on Rating and select Average, since we wish to aggregate our rating data by average.

8. Open the drop-down menu on Date and select Date instead of Date Hierarchy.

9. You may want to add a trendline to your Line chart. Open the Analytics icon next to the brush and select the trendline.

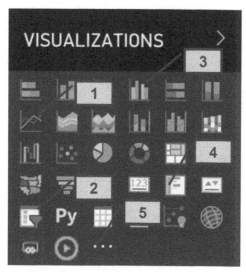

Figure 2.32 Power BI Visualisations Pane
Source: Used with permission from Microsoft.

The result does not look too impressive yet and we could have done this in MS Excel as well. Let us add some more visuals to make our dashboard answer the questions we raised before.

TASK 2.31   INSERT SLICER TO CHANGE REPORT SCOPE:

1. Unselect all visuals by clicking with the cursor outside.

2. Select the icon for slicer from the visualisations pane (2 in Figure 2.32). An empty frame for the visual has been built on the report space.

3. This slicer acts as a filter. We want to define the timeframe which is covered by the report. Therefore, we pull the Date into this visual. The date gets applied immediately and we see a time slider with a beginning and an end date. There are different ways to use the slicer. Selecting the start date or end date box opens a calendar. These calendars can be used to set the timeframe for the report. Of course, the slider does a similar job.

4. With the slicer still selected, we open the drop-down menu for Date underneath the visualisations pane and select Date Hierarchy. This results in the slider changing to an extendable item "2019". By selecting the show more arrows, Quarters, Months and finally Days open. By selecting what you want to show in your report, you can easily zoom into details within a certain timeframe. The slicer scope gets applied to the report immediately.

Our dashboard gets better. But it does not look the way it should. Now, this is where the question of personal taste comes in. The final settings for the layout and the cosmetics of your dashboard are up to you. If you want to amend the format, follow the next Task.

Figure 2.33 Power BI Fields Pane

Source: Used with permission from Microsoft.

TASK 2.32   FORMAT VISUALS ON THE REPORT:

1. Select the Line chart on your report and open its Format by selecting the brush under the visualisations pane. Now, all the formatting options are accessible underneath.

2. Open X Axis, navigate to Title and switch it off. It is quite obvious that the date is shown. We do not need to waste space for that.

3. Open Y Axis, navigate to Value Decimal Places and set it to 1, so that we are able to even see smaller differences later. Feel free to switch off this Title as well.

4. Keep the Gridlines switched on since this is a nice help for reading the chart.

5. Open Data colors. You may want to change the colour of your data line.

6. Open Title and amend it if you feel like that. The Title text is usually not so nice since it is automatically generated. "Patient Satisfaction over Time" seems to be better. We change the Alignment of the new Title to Center and increase the Text size to 16. A Background colour of white, 10% darker high-lights the title nicely.

7. Select the slicer on your report and open its Format by selecting the brush under the visualisations pane.

8. Open Title after switching it on. Input "Reporting Period" in Title text. Change the Alignment of the new Title to Center and increase the Text size to 16, with the Background color of white, 10% darker.

The major purpose of a line chart is to show the data over time to identify potential trends and extreme points.

Our dataset in ClinicSurveyStacked.xlsx shows two days with rather low ratings. By selecting these low points, it becomes obvious that on 31 Jan 2019, the average rating was only 2.17 whereas on 07 Dec 2019 it was 2.28.

This line chart demonstrates aggregated data – average of all data points for the same date and time. It means all indicators on that day are averaged. This might not be our intention because we do have 17 metrics over all five process steps Registration, Screening, Consultation, Dispensation of Medicine, and Payment. And in addition, we do have an "Overall" assessment from patients. Is it better to treat this overall assessment differently, since we calculate an overall assessment by averaging all 17 metrics anyway?

TASK 2.33   APPLY FILTER TO A VISUAL:

1. Select the Line chart on your report.

2. Open the Filters pane on the right.

3. Pull field "Indicator" into the Filters pane under Filters in this visual where it says "Add data fields here".

4. Select all indicators and unselect "Overall". Now, the filter is applied.

The result is shown in Figure 2.34. Whilst this dashboard is able to highlight whether there are trends and extreme data points over time, this dashboard does not show the satisfaction per process step and indicator (see Table 2.4).

Studying Patient Satisfaction Score by Indicator

It would not be very practical to show all 17 metrics, i.e. the lines for all 17 indicators in the same line chart. Thus, we decide applying a column chart with one column per indicator so that comparing the performance is pretty easy.

TASK 2.34   INSERT COLUMN CHART VISUAL:

1. Select the icon for Column Chart from the visualisations pane (3 in Figure 2.32). An empty frame for the visual has been built on the report space.

2. From the Fields Pane on the right (Figure 2.33), select StepInd and pull it into the Axis box of our visual. The visual must be selected.

3. From the Fields Pane on the right, select Rating and pull it into the Values box of our visual. The visual must be selected.

4. Open the drop-down menu on Rating and select Average.

5. Open field "Indicator" in the Filters pane under Filters in this visual.

6. Select all indicators and unselect "Overall". Now, we do not have the bar for the overall rating. You may want to switch this back on if necessary.

7. Feel free to perform the necessary formatting to this visual as described before.

Figure 2.34 Patient Satisfaction Dashboard with Line Chart and Slicer

Additionally, we suggest making this column chart a bit more interesting.

TASK 2.35   CHANGE Y AXIS. CHANGE BAR COLOUR DEPENDING ON VALUE:

1. Select the Column Chart on your report and open its Format by selecting the brush under the visualisations pane.

2. Open Y Axis, navigate to Value Decimal Places and set it to 1, so that we are able to see even smaller differences later. Feel free to switch off this Title as well. Set Start to 1 and End to 5.

3. Open Data colors, select the f(x) button under Default color. Default color opens.

4. Set Format by to Color scale, Based on field to Average of Rating, Summarization to Average, Minimum to Lowest value and red, Maximum to Highest value and green, select Diverging and set Center to Middle value and amber.

Now we have a dashboard which is easy to understand and easy to be presented (Figure 2.35). The last amendment has made our bar chart change colour according to the value in the bar. We have just set the longest bars to be shown in green and the shortest in red, whilst all bars in between get a different shade of amber.

MS Power BI is not MS PowerPoint. And this is a good thing because MS Power BI makes it easy to present information in an interactive way. By default, all visuals are connected, and the slicers alter all visuals in the same way.

For example, if we change the timeframe on the slicer, all connected visuals show only the information for this timeframe. Try it out and amend the slicer and you will see the visuals changing simultaneously.

Even better, if one element on a visual is selected, only the information for this element is shown on the other visuals. That is, if a metric, an indicator is selected, only the time series data for this indicator is shown above. And if the low datapoint on 07 Dec is selected in the line chart, only the information for exactly that day is shown for all metrics. Except, this is not immediately visible on the report. We may need to add some more information.

TASK 2.36   ADD INFORMATION ABOUT REPORT SCOPE AND NUMBER OF DATA POINTS:

1. Select the icon for Multi-row card from the visualisations pane (4 in Figure 2.32). An empty frame for the visual has been built on the report space.

2. The information we want to show is: Start of Reporting, End of Reporting, Number of Data Points. This information needs to be determined first. For this purpose, we use Measures.

Figure 2.35 Power BI Dashboard for Patient Satisfaction

3. On top in menu Calculations, select New measure. An Excel-like formula bar opens. Input the following after opening a New measure each time:

4. DateMin = format(MIN(Stacked[Date]),"dd mmm yyyy"). Enter.

5. DateMax = format(MAX(Stacked[Date]),"dd mmm yyyy"). Enter.

6. DateNum = sumX(relatedtable(Stacked),if(Stacked[Measure] = "Step-1friendly", 1, 0)). Enter.

7. From the Fields Pane on the right (Figure 2.33), select the newly created measures DateMin, DateMax, and DateNum and pull them into the Fields box of our new visual. The average rating of all selected data points can be included as well by pulling Rating into the same box. The visual must be selected.

8. Select the new Multi-row card and complete the formatting as described before.

Now, this card informs about the real scope of reporting. For example, when selecting the last high rating point in the line chart, the Report Scope window shows that this rating average of 4.38 consists of two data points, i.e. two patients who have rated the service on 11 Dec. 2019.

Figure 2.36 illustrates this situation with only one day in the scope of the report. On that 11 Dec. 2019, two patients submitted their rating giving us a minimum a 3.5 and a maximum of 5. The column chart displays in wide bars the rating for the whole year, since no item in the slicer has been selected. The thin bars overlaying the wide bars demonstrate the rating for exactly the 11 Dec. 2019.

The indicator "Friendly and Courteous" at "Step1", for instance, received an average rating of 3.5 over the year. On the 11 Dec., however, the rating went up to 4.50. This way, it is quite easy to comb through the data and look for interesting insights. And the follow up question should always be something like "Why did we receive this outstanding rating on that day and not on other days?"

This is when organisational knowledge comes in with an answer like "I have checked. On 11 Dec., the volume was quite low. On that day, not many patients have visited our clinic and those who visited were treated with little Christmas gifts that were left over after our Christmas dinner and dance."

We know already that weekday (DOW) and TimeSlot make a difference as well. How do we show it in our dashboard?

TASK 2.37   ADD NEW VISUALS FROM POWER BI REPOSITORY AND USE IT FOR DOW AND TIMESLOT:

1. Duplicate Page 1

2. Select the icon . . . Get more visuals at the end of the visualisations pane (5 in Figure 2.32). This opens the Power BI Visuals window.

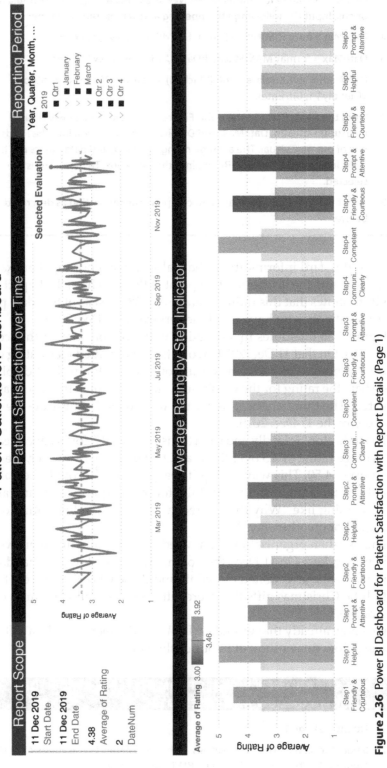

Figure 2.36 Power BI Dashboard for Patient Satisfaction with Report Details (Page 1)

3. Since we would like to add box and whisker charts (box plots) to this dashboard, we search for "box".

4. Add the Box and Whisker chart. After that, it is available at the Visualisations pane.

5. Select the newly created icon for Box and Whisker chart. An empty frame for the visual has been built on the report space.

6. The information we want to show is: TimeSlot as Category, Date as Sampling and Rating as Values.

7. Date needs to be set to Date under the drop-down menu. It means, we average the data per day and add them into the chart. Therefore, this chart will not generate any output when only one day is selected as mentioned before.

8. Do the same operations for another Box and Whisker chart showing the customer satisfaction over the day of week.

9. Before this is done, an additional column is needed to make it look nicer. Add column Weekday = weekday(Stacked[Date],2) & " " & format(Stacked[Date],"ddd"). Enter.

10. The information we want to show is: Weekday as Category, Date as Sampling and Rating as Values.

11. Use the brush to beautify both visuals as discussed before.

The resulting dashboard bears a lot of information (Figure 2.37). Sometimes the box plots are not straightforward to read and understand. In this case, it is amazingly easy to switch the visual to a bar chart or another one. This needs minimal adjustments since Power BI tries to fit the new chart to the available data.

There is another consideration. Why not add some statistical analytics to the dashboard?

Adding Statistical Analysis to your Dashboard

There are some statistical analysis tools available in Power BI. For example, after downloading a Control Chart visual (for instance by Nova Silva BV) from the repository, you may just select your Line chart and click the icon for Control Chart. The line chart turns into a control chart immediately. If Automatic recalculation under Chart settings is set to on, the control chart applies some simple rules to identify whether there could have been changes in the process that justify a recalculation of the control limits. These are statistical aids that help in studying and understanding our datasets.

 "A control chart uses existing variation in the data and analyses whether something unexpected happens, i.e. something that is not within the 99.73% probability range."

As shown before, R has much more powerful tools available. Visuals created by customised R code can be added to the dashboard effortlessly.

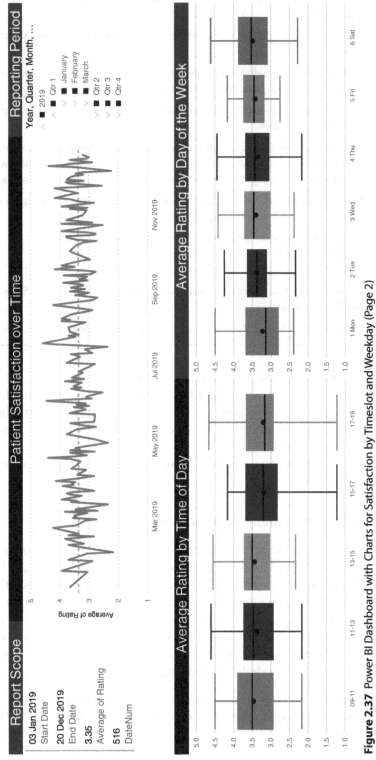

Figure 2.37 Power BI Dashboard with Charts for Satisfaction by Timeslot and Weekday (Page 2)

TASK 2.38   ADD NEW VISUAL BASED ON R CODE:

1. Open File – Options and settings – Options – R scripting and ensure that Power BI has Detected R home directories and Detected R IDEs.

2. Select the icon R for R script visual from the Visualisations pane. This opens an R visual on your dashboard. If you do not have any empty space, create another page at the bottom and do it at page 2. You can copy or move your visual from one page to another one at any time.

3. For showing the rating difference between different weekdays – similar to the box plot – select DOW from the Fields pane and pull it into the new R visual. Do the same for Rating. Ensure Rating in Values is set to Don't summarize.

4. There is a caveat: When PowerBI passes data to R, it groups the data already, even if is set to Don't summarize. You can avoid this by adding a field that is unique per row of the table, such as an ID. In our case, please pull TimeStamp into the R visual as well, although we don't need it. It avoids Power BI grouping the data by DOW. Make sure, TimeStamp is **not set** to Hierarchy.

5. A filter for Rating can be added by pulling Indicator to Filters on visual and set to Overall, for example.

6. Open the R script editor on the bottom of the screen. It shows that a data. frame with three columns, TimeStamp, DOW and Rating, has been created. It means this set of data is now available for R.

```
# The following code to create a dataframe and remove duplicated
rows is always executed and acts as a preamble for your script:

# dataset <- data.frame(TimeStamp, DOW, Rating)
# dataset <- unique(dataset)


# Paste or type your script code here:

# Installing and opening necessary package
library(ggpubr)
# Saving the plot of Overall by DOW in order of weekdays
plot <- ggline(dataset, x = "DOW", y = "Rating",  order = c("Mon",
    "Tue", "Wed", "Thu", "Fri", "Sat"),  add = c("mean_ci"),
    size = 1, point.color = "blue", color = "blue",  ylab = "Rating",
    xlab = "") # , main="Mean Plot with 95% CI by Weekday"
# Adding gridlines and plotting
plot + grids(linetype = "dashed") + theme(text = element_text(size
    = 16))
```

Feel free to add another R script visual, for example for TimeSlot. The result will be a Dashboard with visualisations and even a touch of statistics by adding the confidence interval plots for weekday and time of day (Figure 2.38).

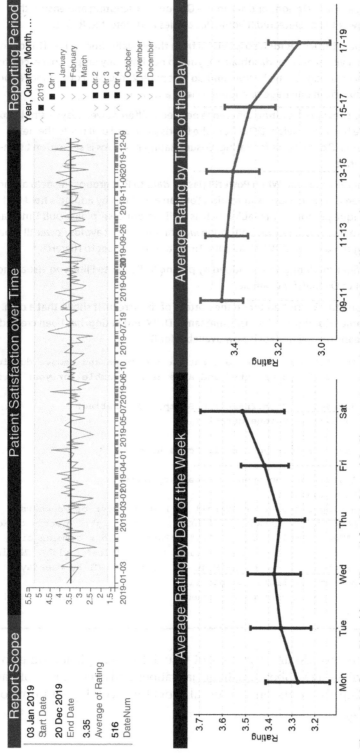

Figure 2.38 Power BI Dashboard (Page 3) for Q2, Q3, and Q4 Showing Patient Satisfaction Control Chart, Indicator Score, and R Visuals Showing CI Plots for Patient Satisfaction by Timeslot and Weekday

The benefit of having these plots in Power BI instead of a separate R Studio session is that the dashboard becomes dynamic. Change the reporting period with the slicer and all plots get adjusted.

The integration of R into Power BI provides a very powerful package for acquiring, transforming, and analysing data and presenting it for analytical storytelling and decision making. Since R has a large user community who is continuously working on developing new solutions, the extensions R can bring to Power BI are virtually unlimited. Even if you are less experienced with R, you may find it well worth the effort to try out these advanced and easy-to-use Power BI components.

Using MS Power BI for Analytical Storytelling

Having a well-designed dashboard is a good prerequisite for an impressive and convincing presentation. Adding a good story line is even better. If the story line would help to provoke exactly the questions for which you have the answers for – may be even by "playing" with the Power BI dashboard – that would be marvellous.

Start with an interesting question

If we assume, that the only "interest" in our patient satisfaction data was epitomised in the question "So, how did we do yesterday? Any complaints?", then there is a lot of news we can bring to the audience in our monthly presentation.

"Why is our patient satisfaction going down?" is a powerful statement to start with. No one wants that. How do you show it? The best way is using part of your dashboard. Since you can have multiple report pages in your Power BI dashboard, you may want to build your story from page to page. The first page – we call it Time Plot – shows the details. You have added a trendline to reveal the bad news in data.

If someone asks for the days with especially low rating, you point at them and get the date and average rating for that day. You will highlight that the lowest rating is given by one patient on the 07 Dec. with 2.24. You may get the question like that "Which points should we actually study? It cannot be that we go back and check all points that are lower than three. Then we waste time on data analytics instead of serving our patients!"

Build up your chart as you present

This is when you may want to switch the line chart to become a control chart. This needs only selecting the line chart and then clicking the icon for control chart. A control chart is made for exactly the purpose of answering this very question. You highlight that all data points that are outside the control range are signalling that something is different in our processes. So, for a start, deal with all data points that are out of the control range

(Figure 2.38). At the same time, you want to bring the attention to the metrics, i.e. the satisfaction indicators, patients are asked to evaluate. For instance, selecting the second low rating point reveals, that on 31 Jan. one patient rated the clinic service with 2.18. To everyone's surprise, the competency of the doctor was rated at only two.

"We must have had a visiting doctor on that day. The patient got angry and filled in our questionnaire with all low scores. Not true, the ladies in Payment probably spotted that this patient was not in good shape and saved the image of our clinic. Probably".

By clicking on the bar showing the satisfaction for competency of doctors, the control chart or line chart will only show exactly this indicator's data over time. This will help to reply to the previous comment.

Finally, you wish to highlight that there is a non-significant increase of satisfaction towards the end of the week. More importantly yet, the satisfaction goes down significantly for patients who visit the clinic at the end of the day. It might be a good idea to check number of patients and staff strengths over the day.

Bring up your recommendations

In closing your presentation, and after summarising what was said, you may want to offer recommendations that read:

1. Further analysing customer satisfaction data together with patient volume per time slot and per weekday to find out whether there is a correlation.

2. Studying all special data points to find out what happened on those days with exceptionally low and high rating.

3. Fully implementing the mobile app for patient satisfaction ratings. This will help to get more patients to participate in the rating.

4. Innovating the incentives for participating in the survey. Since only a small percentage of patients participate – on some days there are none – we may overlook some important information.

With this, you should have given an impactful presentation to your management team. Most importantly, everything is data-driven and trustworthy. And, with new data in the excel sheet, you do not need to create a new presentation. The new data will automatically update all information on your Power BI dashboard.

Conclusion

Using data to drive customer centricity should always start with using the voice of our existing customers. This way, we avoid treating all customers

Ear

King

Ten Eyes:
Full Attention

One Heart:
Wholeheartedly,
Sincerely

Figure 2.39 Ting – The Art of Listening

the same or trying to get the highest net promoter score across all customers. We would rather use data to customise the way we service our target customers. To achieve this, organisations need to transform and gear their teams to not only understand what their target and most valuable customers want but also use available first- and third-party data to understand their near term and future needs.

A data-driven culture for customer centricity is a journey for organisations. It starts with better data rather than big data. Collecting more data does not necessarily lead to greater business intelligence – and in many ways can expose the brand to issues that impact customer trust.

Did you never wonder what will happen to your data when you agree to participate in surveys or other means of data collection? And, if you do this using your hand phone or computer, you are certain they can link the input you gave to your person via login or location data, IP address or other means. Do you always trust when the organisation asking you for your input claims that they will not use your personal details for any other purpose than stated on the app? Keep in mind that your customers and prospects share your sentiments when you try to collect data from them. The moment of truth is not how you use the statistics to analyse the data. It is the short moment when you can either gain their trust or lose it.

Collecting data from and about your customers and prospects via electronic means seems the way to go. Yet do not forget to really listen to your customers. Listening is an art. Listening (in Chinese "Ting") used to be written in Chinese as shown in Figure 2.39. This Chinese word reminds us that listening has more to do with the ear – than the mouth. It suggests treating the speaker, our customer, like the King. It further says that we should do listening by paying full attention (Ten Eyes) and do this sincerely (One Heart means wholeheartedly). If you do this face-to-face, you will sure learn something because your customers will feel taken seriously. And go to Gemba, when you do this.

Practice

- What kinds of indicator should be part of a dashboard?
- What tools do you use to show performance over time?
- What is a control chart and how do you use it?
- What is a box and whisker plot and how do you interpret it?
- Why do we use R within Power BI? What do we gain?

Please, complete the following steps:

- Download the dashboard ClinicSurvey.pbix for this case from www.wiley.com.
- Insert a new visual Key Influencers into a new report page. Analyse the key influencers for Rating by adding StepInd into Explain by.
- Elaborate the Key Influencers for Increase and Decrease in Rating. Prepare a short report.

References

Bonn, J. (2006). *Qualität im Privatkundengeschäft von Kreditinstituten. In: Simultan hybride Qualitätsstrategie im Privatkundengeschäft von Kreditinstituten.* Wiesbaden: Deutscher Universitäts-Verlag.

Community. (2020). A Comprehensive Index of R Packages and Documentation from CRAN, Bioconductor, GitHub and R-Forge. Retrieved from R Package Documentation: https://rdrr.io/

Eyung, L. (2019, Aug. 1). How to build a service blueprint and what you can achieve with it. Retrieved from Govtech Singapore: https://www.tech.gov.sg/media/technews/how-to-build-service-blueprint-and-what-you-can-achieve-with-it

Hennessy, J. L. (2019, May 1). 5 Ways to Know Your Customer Better Than Your Competitors Do. Retrieved from KelloggInsight: https://insight.kellogg.northwestern.edu/article/5-ways-to-know-your-customer-better-than-your-competitors-do

Kaufmann, U. H. (2018, Mar. 17). Make Use of Your Survey Data – Kano It. Retrieved from COE: https://coe-partners.com/make-use-of-your-survey-data-kano-it/

Kaufmann, U. H. (2020, Jun. 13). Making Sence of the Wilkoxon Test. Retrieved from COE: https://coe-partners.com/making-sense-of-the-wilcoxon-test/

Kaufmann, U. H. (2003). Managing with Dashboards. In A. M. Consulting, *Six Sigma Leadership Handbook* (pp. 265–275). Hoboken, NJ: John Wiley & Sons, Inc.

Microsoft. (2020). Microsoft Power BI Guided Learning. Retrieved from Microsoft: `https://docs.microsoft.com/en-us/power-bi/guided-learning/`

Revelle, J. B. (2004). Quality Essentials: A Reference Guide from A to Z. ASQ Quality Press. Retrieved from ASQ Quality Press: `https://asq.org/quality-resources/kano-model`

Rohrmann, B. (2007, Jan.). Verbal Qualifiers for Rating Scales: Socio-linguistic Considerations and Psychometric Data. Melbourne, Australia. Retrieved from: `http://rohrmannresearch.net/pdfs/rohrmann-vqs-report.pdf`.

Tan, E. (2017, Apr. 24). Gemba? I Was There. Retrieved from COE: `https://coe-partners.com/gemba-i-was-there/`

List of Figures and Tables

Process Domain – Operations Analytics

"Think analytically, rigorously, and systematically about a business problem and come up with a solution that leverages the available data".

(Woods, 2012).

For a long period, businesses have relied on experience, trial, and error to make decisions. Data analytics has added a new aspect to the decision-making process, giving business leaders access to new and previously unavailable insights. In many cases, there is too much information available for one to thoroughly digest, analyse, and interpret.

In this chapter, we will discuss Data Analytics in the Process Domain. We will present different methods for Operations Analytics through case studies.

CONTENTS

➤ Why Operations Analytics?

➤ Dimensions of Operations Analytics

➤ Roles and Deployment of Operations Analytics

➤ Conclusion

CASE	CASE DESCRIPTION	TOOLS USED
4	Which Supplier has the Better Product Quality?	Ex
5	Why Does Finance Pay Our Vendors Late?	Ex
6	Why are We Wasting Blood?	Ex, R

Tools Used: Ex . . . MS Excel, BI . . . MS Power BI, R . . . R and R Studio

Highlights
After completing this chapter, you will be able to . . .

- Understand the importance of operations analytics.

- Determine the dimensions of operations analytics.

- Define and validate measures for operations analytics.

- Establish the model for operations analytics.

- Implement operations analytics in your organisation.

Why Operations Analytics?

Given that digitisation had such a transformative effect on customer behaviour and relationships, it is perhaps not surprising that many organisations focus their digital transformation efforts on the entire customer journey. However, in the race to focus on the customer, it was all too easy to ignore operations (Capgemini, 2017). As data show, focusing on the customer would generate considerably less benefits for average organisations compared to benefits from usage of data in operational improvement (Figure 3.1).

Figure 3.1 Benefits of Usage of Data in Operations Improvement (Technet, 2014/Capgemini)

For organisations to stay competitive, the need for emphasising data-driven analysis and decision-making in operations rather than just customer-focused processes is becoming a strategic priority. Operations analytics is important as organisations ride on the digitisation landscape.

We have discussed the application of analytics in customer-facing activities in the previous chapter. Now, it is time to talk about analytics in operations (Figure 3.2). This includes operations in manufacturing and in non-manufacturing environments.

Using data for controlling manufacturing processes is not new. For many years, the best cars in the world are made on fully automated processes with little manual intervention. These processes are full of sensors to get thousands of data in real time through leading indicators. This data is used automatically to adjust what needs to be adjusted in order to produce high quality products. Machines and robots that perform this kind of automated processes have analytics and decision-making processes built in. The underlying principles applied by these machines and robots are very similar to what is discussed in this book. The principles are known to process owners and process operators.

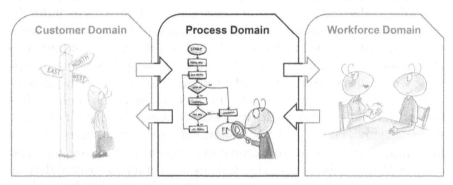

Figure 3.2 Operations Analytics and its Focus on the Process Domain

However, making use of data for decision-making in service operations is still lagging behind. Part of the reasons might be that service processes are often less transactional than manufacturing processes. Many service processes are mostly driven by human intervention which thus increases variation, and sometimes seems to limit controllability. Yet, this argument is often used as an excuse for not rethinking the way service operations are performed.

The impact of operations analytics is measurable far beyond improving the productivity of operational processes.

Tesco, for example, used sophisticated analysis to comb through supply chain data, identify opportunities to reduce waste and to match stock to demand fluctuations (Tesco saves millions with supply chain analytics, 2013). Apart from the financial gain, the biggest win for the company was a model built by their supply chain analytics team that is able to predict the customer buying behaviour driven by the weather. Using weather forecast data, Tesco is now able to adjust the stock level to what people want in different weather situations. Another big win was achieved by analysing discounts and promotions. With thousands of promotions running every day, each shop's stock controller was not able to do a proper forecast, resulting in some products being stocked too high and some products running out of stock.

Their supply chain analytics team built a sophisticated predictive model based on historical data available about past promotions and discounts. This model was made available to the stock controllers with the effect of saving 50-million-pounds worth of stock. Not only has the stock been reduced. At the same time, they have ensured that there is a 97% chance to have the goods available a customer asks for. They are able to use the data to speak facts.

However, a study by Capgemini Consulting (Capgemini, 2017) shows a sobering fact that only 18% of the 446 organisations studied had widely deployed operations analytics and achieved the desired results.

There are two major prerequisites that need to be in place for operations analytics to be successful:

Firstly, organisations who aim to implement operations analytics successfully need to have a clear and robust data strategy. This includes the integration of all datasets across the organisation. This means the same up-to-date datasets are available to all functions at any point in time. This also means that data from external sources, i.e., suppliers, vendors, customers, or partners are collected and integrated into the operations datasets.

Secondly, operations analytics is for business decision-making. It is important to note that analytics is based on models. In using it as a tool, we need to understand the basic assumptions and limitations of employing a model and use our intuition and experience to fill the gaps and enhance the analysis process. The study by Capgemini uncovered that not all organisations who build a data analytics environment and infrastructure in operations are able to reap the benefits because of a lack of usage of analysis results for business management purposes.

Dimensions of Operations Analytics

Operations analytics focuses on the process domain (Figure 3.2) and as such includes process design, process improvement, and process management. Process design is an activity each process undergoes only rarely, when there is a new customer need or a strategic change that cannot be supported with the existing process. Process redesign can also happen, when there is new technology that might enable drastic changes to the existing process with a major benefit for process customers, the organisation, and/or process stakeholders. Innovative solutions often drive the design of new processes or redesign of existing processes.

For example, the newly available ways to make payments from/to private and corporate accounts have drastically reshaped payment processes. Whilst the payment was done via cheque or on a website not so long ago, now it can be handled on any handphone easily. This is much less resource intensive, much faster, and similarly safe.

Process Design Using Analytics

The foundation for process analytics needs to be established during process design (Figure 3.3). This includes considerations about historical data that help build a model for process management and process improvement (Aon, 2003, pp. 219–244). This also incorporates in-process and external sensors to acquire necessary data for process management and process

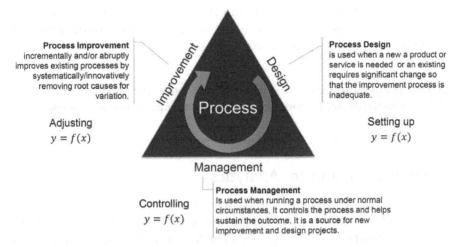

Figure 3.3 Dimensions of Process/Operations Analytics

improvement. Data sources and sensors are usually located within an organisation's own operations and at suppliers' or customers' operations.

The result of operations design is one or a set of operations models. This can be put in the model formula (Kaufmann, 2018, pp. 74–91)

$$Y = f\left(X_1, X_2, X_3, \ldots, X_n\right)$$

With

$Y\ldots$ process output measures (dependent variables) and

$X_1, X_2, X_3, \ldots, X \ldots$ input and process measures (independent variables).

This formula means that output measures, i.e. the process results, depend on a series of measures within the process and on the inputs. If the process is not new and a certain minimum amount of historical data exists, this relationship can be established in a more or less complex formula. This formula can be used to model the process. A process model helps when the output of the process needs to be corrected. Good models let the operator simulate a process change whilst observing the process results. Without even touching the process, the best input and process variable settings for the process change can be calculated and tested with a high statistical probability – if the model has a good fit.

One of the most powerful ways to establish the relationship between potential drivers X and the process results Y – to establish a model for a process – is Design of Experiments (DOE) (Aon, 2003, p. 206).

The use of statistical thinking was identified by western researchers as a key differentiator that made Japanese products, especially Japanese cars, much more reliable and the underlying operations much more effective (Aon, 2003, pp. 219–220) in the last century. The importance of statistical thinking has even increased with the availability of much more data about basically all elements of the process and the supply chain. Establishing the model that best describes the process requires more than basic statistical thinking. And so does process management.

 During Process Design, the model for operations analytics is set up including all measures for input, process, and output as well as their relationship.

Defining Measures for Analytics

Since data analytics needs a sufficient supply of accurate, representative, and reproducible data, establishing the measures for all X and Y is an important step (Aon, 2003, pp. 265–275). Measures for leading indicators are better for process management and the necessary analytics than those for lagging indicators.

 Operations Analytics Needs Leading Indicators
Since the purpose of operations analytics for process management is to automatically or manually make adjustments to a process in response to change of process parameters before the process result turns bad, operations analytics needs to be based on measures for leading indicators rather than lagging indicators.

For example, a bank loan application process might have many indicators. One of them, the survey result data collected a few times a year shows the process quality using a lagging indicator, because when the survey is conducted and the result is available, the loan application process for the customers surveyed is long done. There is no chance to correct anything in the process before the customer receives the result, the good or poor service. Another one, the backlog of loan applications in the inbox of people processing the loans, to the contrary, shows whether there is additional manpower needed in order to deliver to the promised turnaround time. This kind of indicator is leading because there are chances to make adjustments to process parameters before the result gets affected.

Y measures are output measures. Their relevance is decided by the process customer, i.e. an internal or external customer.

Internal customers are often colleagues who receive the unit of interest after other colleagues have completed their activity on the mentioned unit.

In the example of a bank loan, applications are first screened on completeness and correctness. After the screeners have done their part, the credit check is done, after that the loan approval. The output measures Y for screeners are completeness and correctness. Both measures become input measures X for the credit check. The completed credit check delivers additional output measures to the final step, the loan approval decision.

External customers do not know and do not care about these internal steps and their measures. For them, the most important output measures are the result of the credit decision (rejected or approved) and the turn-around time from application to decision.

Additionally, other departments may have an interest in the result of the loan approval. The Risk Department for example needs to ensure that the bank does not underwrite loans that have a low chance of being paid back. Hence, they receive data for their related checks and actions, too.

X measures are input and process measures. Their relevance is decided by their relationship to the output measures. Input measures are used to assess the quality of process inputs from internal or external suppliers. For our bank loan approval process, typical inputs are the loan application from the applicant as well as the credit information about the applicant delivered by the credit bureau. The loan application is checked on correctness and completeness. Both are input measures because the process to generate the application is outside our control, i.e., done by the applicant. The credit information supplied by the credit bureau is checked on certain considerations before the credit decision is made. Since turnaround time is an output measure, i.e. important for the applicant, the processing time for each process step must be a process measure. Other process measures could be the correctness of the credit decision and the competency – knowledge, skills, attitude – of the staff working in the process.

For each potential input and process measure, its relevance is decided by its importance for the output measures. In our loan application process, for instance, potential process measures could also be the age of the staff running the process or whether they have a dog at home or not. However, it is highly unlikely that these measures would be considered relevant because they do not drive the output in any way. The system of input, process, and output measures and their statistically proven relationship between each other builds the model for the process.

This will be shown in later parts of the book.

 What makes a good Measure?

1. A good measure is relevant for the organisation and aligned with strategic goals.

2. A good measure is quantitative, i.e. it can be applied to assess a characteristic using a number.

3. A good measure is easily understood by process stakeholders.

4. For a good measure, data are available or can be obtained.

5. A good measure supports accuracy, representability, and reproducibility of data.

Process Management Using Analytics

Process management includes all activities required to ensure a process delivers output according to specification, customer needs, and organisational requirements.

A vital input for process management is the model designed to manage the process. This model is either developed during the design of the process. Or it is derived afterwards. After this model is established, it is fed by data from internal or external data sources to generate measures for the $X_1, X_2, X_3, ..., X_n$ in the model. These measures will naturally have some variation. With the help of the model, the Y can be calculated, and the process settings adjusted before any product or service is delivered.

This process adjustment might be done automatically via actuators in closed, fully automated production systems. In less automated production systems, and in supply chain or service environments, the information about process measures might be delivered to a dashboard for the management to draw conclusions and make decisions. These decisions can be as diverse as illustrated below:

1. Adjusting pressure settings in a paint shop if the characteristics of the supplied paint vary beyond a threshold.

2. Changing supplier for parts because of change of quality characteristics outside a certain limit.

3. Moving nurses from lab to donation room if number of blood donors waiting and/or waiting time exceeds a maximum.

4. Increasing the number of call agents if number of incoming calls surpasses a ceiling.

5. Ordering barbeque goods if its stock level in supermarket falls below a re-order point and outside temperature grows beyond a certain level.

Some time-critical decisions should be automated in order to affect the output in a timely manner. Others can be left to the management for making the decision. All of them are made after understanding the relationship between critical process drivers $(X_1, X_2, X_3, ..., X_n)$ and the process result (Y) (Figure 3.4).

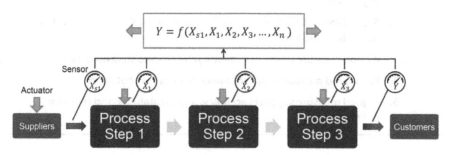

Figure 3.4 Process with Measures for X and Y

Data analytics is the foundation for building a robust, reliable model for process management.

 "All models are wrong. But some are useful."

(George Box, 1976)

Process Improvement Using Analytics – The Power of DMAIC

Almost all process improvement methods require data collection and analysis to solve quality or process problems. Although many traditional data analysis techniques can be used to develop the quality of products and processes, massive data collected by industry 4.0 technologies should be mined with powerful data analysis methods that produce meaningful results from the dataset. It is possible to make effective decisions by utilising the analysis methods that are part of each step of a Lean Six Sigma cycle.

 Process Design or Process Improvement – Process Experience Counts
For operations analytics, process experience is key. Even for redesigning an outdated process, the experience, i.e. the typical X and Y relationships, the model, the process parameters should be considered. They can be of great help. At least, they may show what did not work.

The best process improvement and process reengineering approach we have ever learnt follows the Lean Six Sigma methodology (Kaufmann, 2018). This methodology is deployed on projects for solving specific business problems and follows five powerful and rigid phases, Define, Measure, Analyse, Improve, and Control (DMAIC).

While DMAIC builds on earlier approaches to problem solving such as Plan-Do-Check-Act (PDCA), Business Process Reengineering (BPR), and Total Quality Management (TQM), the rigour required throughout DMAIC projects is one of the elements that differentiates it from other approaches (Aon, 2003, pp. 196–218). DMAIC projects demand a no-shortcut approach that requires discipline to execute and is fully data driven.

At the same time as Ford's Q101 was developed as a powerful toolset to use analytics in automotive companies and their suppliers, Motorola brought statistics into operations and into the board room with its Six Sigma initiative to save their bleeding TV business (Pierce, 2011). With the comprehensive and modern tools that are part of each Six Sigma project – now most likely Lean Six Sigma project – DMAIC takes care of many tasks required by operations analytics (Table 3.1).

Table 3.1 Operations Analytics Tasks Covered by DMAIC Phase

DMAIC PHASE	CONTRIBUTION TO OPERATIONS ANALYTICS
Define	- Collecting the requirements of the process customer and related problems.
	- Identifying output measures Y.
Measure	- Identifying potential drivers for output measures Y, i.e. input measures X and process measures X.
	- Setting up data collection procedures.
	- Validating data collection procedures.
	- Determining descriptive statistics for X and Y.
	- Visualising X and Y data.
Analyse	- Visualising $X - Y$ relationships.
	- Testing significance of $X - Y$ relationships.
	- Establishing/testing $X - Y$ model: $Y = f\left(X_1, X_2, X_3, \ldots, X_n\right)$.
Improve	- Piloting improved process and its settings on X.
	- Instituting process management procedures for use of model.
	- Standardising new process operations.
Control	- Applying process management procedures.
	- Automatically adjusting process or signalling deviation to process owners if deviation is detected.

The use of data analysis at every stage, especially in the measure (M) and analyse (A) stages, has critical importance to making correct, data-driven, business-relevant, and reproducible decisions.

 During process improvement, the model for operations analytics might be altered after making amendments to the process.

Roles and Deployment of Operations Analytics

As with any initiative, the implementation of Operations Analytics requires resources and an infrastructure to be effective (Aon, 2003, pp. 57–83). When Motorola established their award-winning Six Sigma initiative, they built it on a strong foundation of infrastructure and deployment steps. Many of the factors that made Motorola successful will apply to any other organisation on their journey to implement operations analytics.

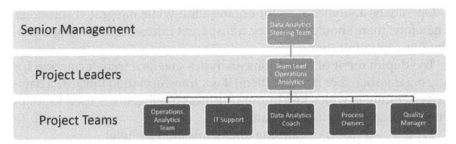

Figure 3.5 Example for Operations Analytics Deployment Infrastructure

As operations analytics is driven from the top, it is appropriate to have a **Operations Analytics steering team** consisting of the management team to drive this initiative (see Figure 3.5). A steering team is the primary driver for the deployment of operations analytics. The **Data Analytics Steering Team** carries out the following tasks:

1. Aligning operations analytics to business strategy and objectives.

2. Setting priorities for the roll-out, i.e. deciding about opportunities for analytics application, the return for the investment, and the sequence of test and implementation.

3. Establishing goals for operations analytics projects.

4. Appointing project team members and leaders.

5. Monitoring team and project progress.

6. Supervising implementation of operation analytics routines.

The steering team should have a good understanding of the newest technology available for operations analytics, potential data sources, and data analytics techniques including statistics. And, of course, they must know the business requirements.

Similarly, the **operations analytics team lead** is required to have good business acumen. A requirement of the role is excellent knowledge about the opportunities given by modern technology and a solid grasp of complex statistical tools for building functioning business models. For a team lead, soft skills such as influencing skills for communicating and engaging stakeholders, managing change, etc. are critical.

The **operations analytics project team** consists of process stakeholders who ensure proper representation of their processes as well as their process customers. Since operations analytics most likely involves setting up or upgrading IT infrastructure, knowledge about the newest developments of data acquisition techniques, artificial intelligence tools, robotic process automation (RPA) solutions, etc. must be brought into the team. Additionally, knowledge and expertise about data cleaning, data transformation, data analysis and visualisation solutions must be available to the team. Finally, the customer perspective must be represented, most likely by the quality manager. Depending on the specifics of the project, other departments might need to be invited into the team as well.

Operations analytics aims for organisation-wide, integrated solutions. Therefore, there should be a very transparent infrastructure using a continuous communication.

The deployment of operations analytics means a transformation for any organisation. For many of them, it is a transformation towards a data-driven culture in which just-in-time business intelligence is used to adapt operations and with it, the organisation.

Typical steps for transforming an organisation include:

- *Setting the tone, i.e. the executive owning the transformation must set the tone early, formulate the data strategy and stick to it. The message can be something like "When you make a decision, show me the data!" or "Our objective is to automate 30% of our recurring activities!"*
- *Aligning the Rewards and Recognition system to support operations analytics, namely the use of data and the education of all staff to do so.*
- *Deciding about the necessary training in disciplines such as data analytics and science, Artificial Intelligence, etc. and who has to be trained.*
- *Ensuring data analytics becomes part of career development discussions.*
- *Determining organisational priorities for the roll-out.*

Good leadership is possibly the most important prerequisite to implement operations analytics in an organisation.

Conclusion

Operations analytics is not new. With the accessibility of a multitude of data about nearly every facet of organisational processes and with the availability of powerful hard- and software, it is easier than ever to build effective operations analytics systems. These systems help to understand the relationship between different parts of an organisation as well as their effect on the outcome. Most importantly, this understanding can be used to set up a model for ongoing management and improvement of the organisation, an operations analytics model. With this knowledge, increase in customer satisfaction, organisational efficiency and productivity as well as staff approval can be modelled, pursued, and achieved.

Since many of the operations analytics concepts are similar with those used in Lean Six Sigma, organisations with experience in that methodology have an advantage. Experienced Lean Six Sigma Black Belts or Green Belts with successful projects under their belts might be considered to be a part or to lead the data analytics team after upgrading them with the necessary modern data analytics skills.

In the following cases, we will show ways to use operations analytics at different operational situations. The focus is not so much on the automation of the underlying processes but on the method to gather, transform, clean and model data for decision making, the foundation of operations analytics.

KEY SUCCESS FACTORS FOR OPERATIONS ANALYTICS DEPLOYMENT

1. Operations analytics deployment must be driven from the top. It cannot be delegated to IT people who know all the newest tools, or to data analysts who appreciate the statistics. Management must own it and must make use of IT support and data analysts' coaching.

2. Operations analytics must start with a proper organisation-wide education about the topic of analytics. Asking management to read about analytics is not good enough (Gallo, 2018).

3. Operations analytics must be focused on improving organisational performance, i.e. it must be relevant for the business to be accepted and adopted.

4. Operations analytics needs a proper infrastructure with dedicated and educated resources to support this initiative. They must be measured on the effect of operations analytics.

5. Operations analytics can be used for staff development. For example, if each manager is measured on his contribution to operations analytics, there will be a good chance for making it happen.

Practice Questions

- What are benefits of operations analytics?
- What are the three dimensions of operations analytics?
- What are X and Y in operations analytics?
- What are characteristics of good measures?
- What is the relationship between DMAIC and operations analytics?
- How does our organisation deploy operations analytics?

Case 4: Which Supplier has the Better Product Quality?

Generally, procurement departments are tasked to make important buying decisions. They are usually squeezed between three different requirements. Firstly, the products must meet or exceed the specifications reliably. Secondly, the price should be competitive. And thirdly, delivery must be done on time. This applies to manufacturing and service organisations, equally.

The following case focuses on ensuring that vendors meet the stated requirements long-term. Data available are only a set of units and measurements for initial sample inspection.

For this case, samples of parts and their data from three suppliers for a critical component in our refrigerator production are studied. Based on only 58, 45, and 60 parts, respectively, the presumably best possible supplier to support our production long-term is identified. The decision is possible after stepwise plotting the data in different ways and applying some functions of MS Excel's Analysis ToolPak. Examining only descriptive statistics would have been insufficient, potentially leading to a wrong purchasing conclusion.

Business Question

The obvious question each procurement team needs to answer is: What is the best supplier in terms of product quality. After answering this question, price negotiations are easier. And the delivery terms will be settled at the same time.

It does not matter whether a blood bank buys blood bags from different suppliers or a fridge maker buys parts for fridges. It is a usual practice to order a sample of goods to do detailed inspection on them. Although, there will always be a bias involved – who sends bad parts for first article inspection to a potential customer – a thorough inspection usually pays off.

Data Acquisition

It is nearly impossible for the customer to draw a random sample of the goods on his own. Usually, the sample is provided by the supplier.

In our case, three suppliers have delivered 45, 58, and 60 Spacer parts to our FridgeMaker for first article inspection, respectively. These Spacer parts have been measured according to the specification agreed upon with the suppliers. The lower specification limit is LSL = 10.2mm, whereas the upper specification limit is USL = 10.8mm.

Data Analysis

As shown in Table 3.2, all suppliers meet the required specification with all parts, to no surprise. Now, procurement could make their decision based on price. If the quality is the same, the cheapest will get the contract. Right?

Table 3.2 Parameters of Spacer Data from Three Suppliers

PARAMETER	SUPPLIER A	SUPPLIER B	SUPPLIER C
Sample Size	58	45	60
Mean	10.45	10.44	10.51
Standard deviation	0.14	0.16	0.16
Yield	100%	100%	100%

Stop. This could be a mistake.

Although, we do not have a lot of data, we certainly can get more information out of what we have. After all, our decision will have an impact on our production line of refrigerators for the next year at least.

TASK 3.1   LOAD DATA AND GET AN OVERVIEW

1. Open the data in file FridgeMaker.xlsx in worksheet Spacer.

2. Ensure table is formatted as Excel Table by pointing inside table Home – Format as Table – Select Format – Check My Table as Header.

3. Name the table by pointing inside table Table Design – Name Table "Stacked" for stacked data and "Unstacked" for unstacked Data. Ensure Header Row and Filter Button are checked.

4. Select Data – Data Analysis – Descriptive Statistics.

5. Select $B$1:$D$61 for Input Range. Check Labels in First Row.

6. Select New Worksheet Ply and check Summary Statistics and Confidence Level for Means at 95%.

Minimum and **maximum** of the descriptive statistics seen in Table 3.3 show that all Suppliers meet the specifications. This is not a surprise. To the contrary, it would be a big blow if they did not since they want to sell their spacers to FridgeMaker.

If their processes are capable, they have not only all datapoints within specifications but also shaped following **normal** distribution since there is no reason why the process would not produce normal data. If the process shows Gauss' bell shape and is capable, it would be expected to have

Table 3.3 Descriptive Statistics for Spacer

PARAMETER	SUPPLIER A	SUPPLIER B	SUPPLIER C
Mean	10.4488	10.4360	10.5112
Standard Error	0.0185	0.0233	0.0202
Median	10.4400	10.4400	10.5000
Mode	10.3800	10.2500	10.4700
Standard Deviation	0.1406	0.1563	0.1562
Sample Variance	0.0198	0.0244	0.0244
Kurtosis	−0.4863	−0.8740	−1.1821
Skewness	0.3779	0.2921	0.0901
Range of Values	0.5700	0.5500	0.5200
Minimum	10.2000	10.2200	10.2600
Maximum	10.7700	10.7700	10.7800
Total	606.0300	469.6200	630.6700

mean, **median** and **mode** very close to each other and near the centre of the tolerance, i.e. around 10.5mm. This is about right for Supplier A and Supplier C. Data from Supplier B demonstrates a **mode** very close to the lower specification limit. This is unusual and needs to be checked.

Other indicators for the shape of the data are given in **kurtosis** and **skewness**. The chance for having data with normal distribution is high if both indicators are between –2 and +2. This seems to be given.

Having a **capable** process means producing with a defect rate considerably less than 0.27%, in other words the process must be able to deliver 99.73% good parts. Under normal distribution conditions – and we do not have any reason for deviation from the normality requirement – this can be achieved when the process is centred and performs with a **standard deviation** that can fit six times within the specifications.

The lowest standard deviation is delivered by Supplier A with 0.1406. When calculating 6 x 0.1406 = 0.8433, it becomes clear that with this process, we cannot expect a defect free flow of supplies because the process does not seem to be capable to do so. With this standard deviation, much more spacers will be produced out of specification. An expensive and never perfect final inspection needs to be installed to sort a lousy process result. Experience tells that this does not work. Supplier B and Supplier C seem to be worse.

Therefore, we calculate the yield Supplier A can achieve with the current process. We use Excel template ProcessCapability.xlsx (Task 3.2).

Figure 3.6 reveals the process of Supplier A will probably deliver a yield of 95.6%. Assuming an annual volume of 500,000 spacers, Supplier A will provide more than 22,000 spacers out of specification. Even if Supplier A

TASK 3.2   CALCULATE PROCESS PERFORMANCE FOR SUPPLIER A

1. Open ProcessCapability.xlsx.

2. Input mean, standard deviation, upper and lower specification limit.

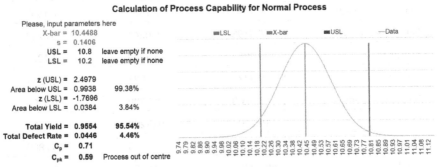

Figure 3.6 Analysis of Potential Process Capability using ProcessCapability.xlsx

would try to find all parts that do not meet the specification, it would be still risky to buy from them for at least two reasons:

- Firstly, no inspection can do a 100% check successfully over a longer period of time. We will receive parts that are out of specification. This means that we need to have an additional incoming inspection with a very high sampling rate.

- Secondly, both an incoming inspection on our side and a final inspection on supplier's side cost money. This is either money spent on an automatic inspection. Or – worst case – this is money spent on manual inspection. It is pretty obvious who has to pay for that.

It looks like no supplier can meet our requirements. This is a critical situation because we invited the suppliers whom we thought could do the job. If we need to look for others, we need to start the whole cycle of supplier qualification again. Before we start this process another time, we study the plots of the Spacer data of all suppliers.

Firstly, we generate a box and whisker plot using MS Excel. This plot offers the option to show the single data points by making use of Show Inner Points (Figure 3.7). It does not provide any surprise.

Yet, studying the plot, we recognise that the height of the boxes compared to whiskers at Supplier B and Supplier C do not seem to suggest a perfect bell shape. Supplier B data seems to assemble just above the lower

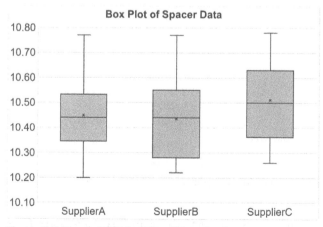

Figure 3.7 Box and Whisker Plot of Supplier Data

specification limit. This is the signal for a process that cannot perform without inspection. We assume, before sending the parts to us, Supplier B measured all data, recognised a series of spacers that were two narrow and took them out. They were obviously replaced with spacers that met the specification.

Such process is not only incapable to meet requirements. It is also evident that Supplier B tried to win the job by cheating. We all agree that we do not want to work with this supplier. A supplier–customer relationship must be based on trust. Without trust, any problem in future may not be handled in the right way.

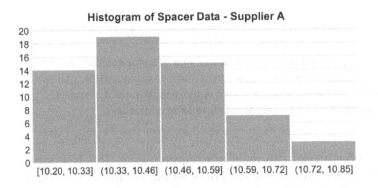

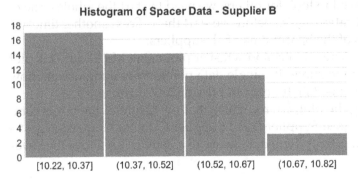

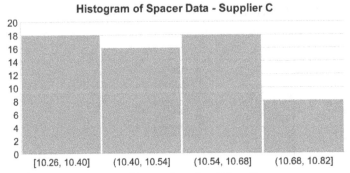

Figure 3.8 Histograms of Spacer Data for all Suppliers

Plotting histograms (Figure 3.8) with MS Excel and trying to learn from them is much easier when the number of data points is beyond 100. In our case, we plot only around 50 data points. Therefore, the histograms are not very telling. Still, the histogram confirms that Supplier B has delivered many spacers that are just above the lower specification limit. This is not a picture we expect from a process naturally. Our assumption of manual intervention is confirmed.

When we asked the supplier for parts for first article inspection, we asked for the respective data in production order. This is usually not given when a lot is received. But knowing the production sequence can help understanding what is going on in the process without even seeing the process. Since we have the data, plotting another key graph, the time series plot, is easily done.

The time series plot or run chart (Figure 3.9) shows Spacer data in production sequence. Supplier A data illustrates a process with a higher degree of variation, as Supplier B does. The apparent lump of datapoints at the lower specification limit of 10.20mm can be observed as well.

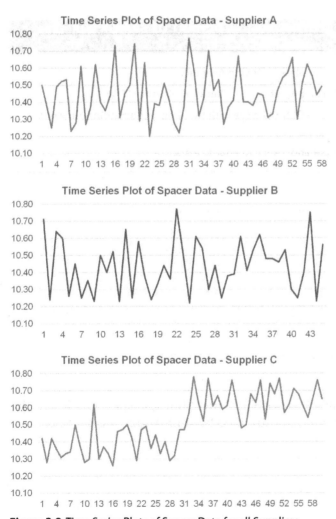

Figure 3.9 Time Series Plots of Spacer Data for all Suppliers

Supplier C offers a surprise for us. Even without consulting a control chart (Kaufmann, 2018) – the proper tool for identifying disturbances, signals, in processes – it becomes clear that Supplier C data consist of two batches. Batch one ends at around data point 31. It is a good assumption that something must have happened between batch one and batch two. The change in average is very apparent in the moving average plot in Figure 3.10.

After contacting Supplier C and their internal check, they willingly admitted that parts and data for this inspection were put together over two shifts. Shift one delivered the parts until number 31 whereas shift 2 made the rest of the spacers. We appreciate the honesty of Supplier C. Now we know that Supplier C could perform much better if there was no disturbance in the process. Since both shifts are able to deliver good parts even after adjusting the machine, we are quite confident that they have a capable process in place.

TASK 3.3   PLOT MOVING AVERAGE CHART OF SPACER FOR SUPPLIER C

1. Select Data – Data Analysis – Moving Average.

2. Select $D$1:$D$61 for Input Range. Check Labels in First Row.

3. Select Interval: 5 and Output Range with two empty columns in your worksheet.

4. Select Chart Output and Select Standard Errors.

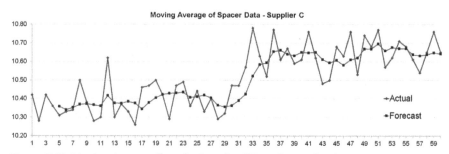

Figure 3.10 Moving Average Chart for Supplier C Data (interval = 5)

Since we know what makes Shift 1 and Shift 2, we perform descriptive statistics for Supplier C data stratified by shift (Figure 3.11).

SupplierC	Shift 1	Shift 2
Mean	10.3865	10.6445
Standard Error	0.0156	0.0163
Median	10.3700	10.6300
Mode	10.4700	10.6100
Standard Deviation	0.0869	0.0875
Sample Variance	0.0076	0.0077
Kurtosis	-0.0835	-0.9005
Skewness	0.5876	-0.0464
Range	0.3600	0.3000
Minimum	10.2600	10.4800
Maximum	10.6200	10.7800
Sum	321.9800	308.6900
Count	31	29
Confidence Level (95.0%)	0.0319	0.0333

Figure 3.11 Descriptive Statistics for Supplier C, Shift 1 and 2

 Plot the Data
Never make an important decision without plotting the data. Plotting data is usually not wasted time but adds some knowledge for making better decisions.

As a formality to verify the obvious, we run a t-test (Task 3.4) to confirm that both shifts really delivered significantly different results. Hence the standard deviation of 0.1562 (Figure 3.12) was not process immanent but caused by a process change.

TASK 3.4   CONDUCT 2 SAMPLE T-TEST TO CONFIRM DIFFERENCE BETWEEN SHIFT1 AND SHIFT2

1. Select Data – Data Analysis – t-Test: Two-Sample Assuming Equal Variances.

2. Select $K$1:$K$32 for Variable 1 Range.

3. Select $L$1:$L$30 for Variable 2 Range.

4. Set Hypothesised Mean Difference to 0 (Null Hypothesis).

5. Check Labels since we have included the column names.

6. Alpha does not change. It stays 0.05.

t-Test: Two-Sample Assuming Equal Variances		
SupplierC	Shift 1	Shift 2
Mean	10.3865	10.6445
Variance	0.0076	0.0077
Observations	31	29
Pooled Variance	0.007607361	
Hypothesized Mean Difference	0	
df	58.0000	
t Stat	-11.4514	
P(T<=t) one-tail	0.0000	
t Critical one-tail	1.6716	
P(T<=t) two-tail	**0.0000**	
t Critical two-tail	2.0017	

Figure 3.12 t-Test: Two-Sample Assuming Equal Variances

We confirm the significant difference between Shift 1 and Shift 2. There is no risk to assume, the process was run with two different settings since the p-value for the difference is 0.000 (P(T<=t) two-tail).

Our interest is immediately on the standard deviation, the variance. Standard deviation has fallen from 0.1562 (Table 3.3) to 0.0869 and 0.0875 for Shift 1 and Shift 2 (Figure 3.11), respectively. This is nearly down to 50% of what we saw before.

We know already that Supplier C can perform the way we need them to perform to ensure we get the spacers for high quality and reliable refrigerators.

If we assume Supplier C is able to run the Spacer process near to the centre of the tolerance, we could expect a process yield of 99.94% (Figure 3.13), provided normal distribution. Since Supplier C mentioned that they are upgrading their production equipment, we expect even better results in future.

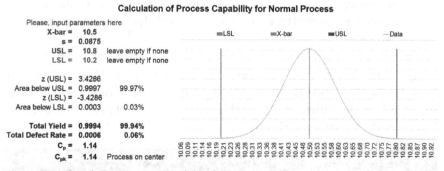

Figure 3.13 Simulating Process Capability for Supplier C using ProcessCapability.xlsx

After having all data analysed in different ways, using only MS Excel, we are confident that giving the order for making our critical refrigerator part to Supplier C will help us succeed in our production of high-quality fridges.

We agree with Supplier C to deliver the capability analysis including all plots whenever they supply us with Spacer parts.

Business Decision

Very often we draw conclusions and make decisions based on a limited perspective on data only. We look at means and evaluate yields and defects. However, that is usually not enough. Some simple yet powerful tools can help to make much more out of the data available.

The first three steps of any data analysis shall be: **Plot the Data, Plot the Data, Plot the Data.** In our case, these three steps have avoided making a wrong decision.

During the discussion with Supplier C, they admitted that the process was adjusted during the period when the sample of spacers for inspection were made. However, since all parts met the specification, the parts were sent as they were. No manipulation was made at all. This shows that this supplier has the superior process that is capable to deliver the critical Spacer parts reliably to FridgeMaker.

With this, now the procurement team can make the right decision, i.e. to buy from Supplier C. The key takeaway from this case is "Plot the Data".

Deploying Analytics Tools

The example shown in this case is rather typical for purchasing tasks in manufacturing organisations. The data is Spacer width with a dimension in mm, a continuous Y, whereas stratifying factors in X are discrete categories, namely Supplier and Shift.

Our objective was to show that all analysis can be performed with MS Excel and its Data Analysis ToolPak. All plots and statistics are done using this rather standard environment. We have added ProcessCapability.xlsx for simple prediction of the result of a close to normal distributed process.

One hypothesis test, a two-sample t-test (Table 3.4), has been applied to compare Shift 1 and Shift 2 data since the assumption of a much smaller variance (standard deviation) in Supplier C data was depending on the fact that the original variance was caused by a change in the settings of the process. If this shift would not be significant, we could not proceed with this assumption.

In order to compare the variance (standard deviation) of Pilot versus Shift 1 and Shift 2 of Supplier C, an F-test is needed (Table 3.5) (Chew, 2018).

Table 3.4 Two-sample t-test

TWO-SAMPLE T-TEST FOR COMPARING AVERAGES	
Data in X:	Discrete X – Groups (variable)
Data in Y:	Continuous Y, Discrete ordinal (value), normal
Null Hypothesis H_0:	$\mu_1 = \mu_2$
Alternative Hypothesis H_A:	$\mu_1 \neq \mu_2$
Decision:	If p-value is < 0.05 ($\alpha = 0.05$), reject H_0 and accept H_A.
Assumptions:	Samples must have normal data.
MS Excel:	**MS Excel Analysis ToolPak offers multiple Options**
	Data – Data Analysis –
	t-Test: Paired Two Sample for Mean
	t-Test: Two-Sample Assuming Equal Variances
	t-Test: Two-Sample Assuming Unequal Variances
	z-Test: Two-Sample for Means

Table 3.5 Two-sample F-test

TWO-SAMPLE F-TEST FOR COMPARING VARIANCES (STANDARD DEVIATIONS)	
Data in X:	Discrete X – Groups (variable)
Data in Y:	Continuous Y, Discrete ordinal (value), normal
Null Hypothesis H_0:	$\sigma_1 = \sigma_2$
Alternative Hypothesis H_A:	$\sigma_1 \neq \sigma_2$
Decision:	If p-value is < 0.05 ($\alpha = 0.05$), reject H_0 and accept H_A.
Assumptions:	Samples must have normal data.
MS Excel:	Data – Data Analysis – F-Test

Practice

- What are requirements on the data acquisition for operations analytics?
- How does one decide which tools for graphical and statistical analysis to apply?
- What are discrete data and continuous data? Name three examples for each.

Please, complete the following steps:

- Download the data for this case in FridgeMaker.xlsx from www.wiley.com.
- Supplier C has further improved their process. They promise to keep the price the same. Please study the Pilot data in column SupplierC – Pilot (column K).
- Calculate Descriptive Statistics for the Pilot Data.
- Plot box and whisker, histogram, time series plot, moving average chart for Pilot data.
- Conduct F-tests to find out whether the variation in Pilot is significantly better than Shift 1 and Shift 2.
- Perform potential yield analysis for Pilot. Use ProcessCapability.xlsx.
- Prepare a short presentation to report the result and your recommendation to the management about proceeding with Supplier C's new process.

Case 5: Why Does Finance Pay Our Vendors Late?

Whenever there is an opportunity for the Business Units at MyProperty-Developer, they remind Finance that the payment of invoices from their vendors is out of control. The vendors take the "lousy payment discipline" for their advantage. They have negotiation power for better terms, they do not start the next phase of large-scale projects because the previous phase has not been paid for, or they just spread the word about unsatisfactory payment processes at MyPropertyDeveloper.

Overall, these developments did not help the business. And, of course, the perception of the Business Units is, since this concerns payment matters, it is Finance's fault – very much to the disfavour of the CFO.

This case is based on more than 13,000 supplier invoices from four different departments at MyPropertyDeveloper. The data handling is completely done in MS Excel by using a series of rather simple graphical and arithmetic analysis tools supported by MS Excel's Analysis ToolPak. The analysis reveals that one major root cause for the problem, the late payment of supplier invoices, lies in business units who keep sending most invoices late to Finance. With this data, the CFO has a much better position when talking about process improvement with his counterparts in the business units.

Business Question

The business units at MyPropertyDeveloper are not happy with their Finance department, every now and then, they flag an email from one of their vendors who is complaining about his "very old" invoice that has not been paid yet. It is hard for Finance to react since these events are incidental and do not seem to show a consistent picture. The only clear message that can be read out of the email and the attached contract is that the invoice is overdue.

The CFO is unhappy with this situation and demands answers from his Finance team on some key questions:

1. How often does it happen that we pay late?

2. How late is late?

3. Is the overdue payment consistent across all units?

4. What are the root causes for that, and can we fix this situation?

So, the Finance team gets to work. They have some basic data analytics knowledge.

Data Acquisition

The data collection seems to be rather straight-forward since all invoices are tracked in the system. Downloading this data seems to be easy. More than thirteen thousand datasets have been taken from the system in February 2020 (Figure 3.15).

The accounts payable process includes four major steps. Measures have been created out of invoice date and system time stamps (Figure 3.14):

1. Checking of invoice by Business Unit (BU) and sending it to Finance. Measure for this step is called "**Days to Finance**".

2. Checking of invoice against attached papers by Accounts Payable (AP) Clerk and posting it into the system, with the measure "**Days to Check**".

3. Running AP proposal by AP clerk and sending it for approval, with measure "**Days to Proposal**".

4. Approving AP proposal and running payment including sending to bank, measured in "**Days to Pay**".

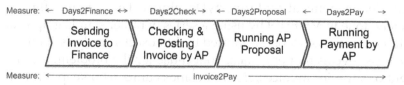

Figure 3.14 Payment Process Including KPI Following Time Stamps in Finance System

Data Preparation

Since all data have been downloaded from the Finance system, there is a general believe that the data can be trusted.

Wrong!

Looking at the data some cleaning was needed. First of all, some of the data were negative, i.e. some invoices seemed to be paid before invoicing date. After investigating the root causes for that, this obviously not useful data was taken out of the dataset before analysis.

ID	InvoiceDate	BU	Period	Terms	Status	Days2Finance	Days2Check	Days2Proposal	Days2Pay
1	9 Sep 2019	BusinessUnit1	Before	30	Paid	108	12	23	6
2	18 Dec 2019	BusinessUnit1	After	60	Paid	13	6	27	3
3	29 Dec 2019	BusinessUnit1	After	30	Paid	0	16	20	2
4	9 Nov 2019	BusinessUnit1	Before	30	Paid	73	1	6	8
5	3 Dec 2019	BusinessUnit1	After	30	Paid	25	7	24	8
6	11 Jan 2020	BusinessUnit1	After	30	Paid	7	1	9	8
7	24 Oct 2019	BusinessUnit1	Before	30	Paid	65	21	12	6
8	9 Jan 2020	BusinessUnit1	After	30	Paid	6	3	13	5
9	20 Dec 2019	BusinessUnit1	After	30	Paid	8	13	15	11
10	6 Jan 2020	BusinessUnit1	After	30	Paid	8	1	18	3

Figure 3.15 Raw Data as Downloaded from the Finance System
Source: Used with permission from Microsoft.

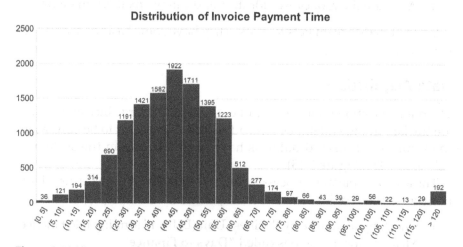

Figure 3.16 Histogram of Invoice Payment Time (MS Excel)

A second issue was discovered when going through the data in the system. Since the system was able to show the duration of certain steps in the payment process which could come in handy at a later stage, the integrity of this data was checked as well. Some datasets did show negative time for any of the four steps. The system data could not be true when comparing with the available paperwork. Hence, another task was to find out how certain data is logged into the system Figure 3.14.

Following common wisdom, if we fed garbage into the system, the system could only report garbage. In this kind of situation, it is usually better to have no data than to deal with misleading data resulting in wrong conclusions and decisions.

As part of the data preparation, three additional columns were created using Excel Figure 3.17.

Data Analysis

Firstly, we wish to get an overview about whether we really have a lot of overdue invoices.

TASK 3.5   LOAD DATA AND CREATE ADDITIONAL COLUMNS

1. Load data DaysToPay.xlsx.

2. Open worksheet Raw. Make sure the table is an Excel table. From anywhere in the table, Home – Format as Table, select format. Name the table Table Design – Table Name: "Raw".

3. Create a new column by writing Invoice2Pay in J1, since we want to add the variable for the total time from invoicing date to payment. A new column is added to the table.

4. Insert the following in J2: = D2 + E2+ F2+ G2.

5. Create a new column by writing Late in K1, since we want to add the variable for the indicator of late payments. A new column is added to the table.

6. Insert the following in K2: =IF([@Invoice2Pay]>[@Terms],"Late","On Time").

7. Create a new column by writing DaysCategory in L1, since we want to create categories for InvoiceToPay. A new column is added to the table.

8. Insert the following in L2: =IF(J2<=30,"1: 0..30 days", IF(J2<=60,"2: 30..60 days", IF(J2<=90,"3: 60..90 days", IF(J2<=120,"4: 90..120 days", IF(J2<=150,"5: 120..150 days", IF(J2<=180,"6: 150..180 days", IF(J2<=210,"7: 180..210 days","8: More than 210 days")))))))).

9. Open R Studio.

10. In the Files window, navigate to your directory and select DaysToPay.xlsx.

11. Select Import Dataset.

12. Select Sheet Raw.

13. Select Range A1:L13350.

ID	InvoiceDate	BU	Period	Terms	Status	Days2Finance	Days2Check
1	9 Sep 2019	BusinessUnit1	Before	30	Paid	108	12
2	18 Dec 2019	BusinessUnit1	After	60	Paid	13	6
3	29 Dec 2019	BusinessUnit1	After	30	Paid	0	16
4	9 Nov 2019	BusinessUnit1	Before	30	Paid	73	1
5	3 Dec 2019	BusinessUnit1	After	30	Paid	25	7
6	11 Jan 2020	BusinessUnit1	After	30	Paid	7	1
7	24 Oct 2019	BusinessUnit1	Before	30	Paid	65	21
8	9 Jan 2020	BusinessUnit1	After	30	Paid	6	3
9	20 Dec 2019	BusinessUnit1	After	30	Paid	8	13
10	6 Jan 2020	BusinessUnit1	After	30	Paid	8	1

Days2Proposal	Days2Pay	Invoice2Pay	Late	DaysCategory
23	6	149	Late	5: 120..150 days
27	3	49	On Time	2: 30..60 days
20	2	38	Late	2: 30..60 days
6	8	88	Late	3: 60..90 days
24	8	64	Late	3: 60..90 days
9	8	25	On Time	1: 0..30 days
12	6	104	Late	4: 90..120 days
13	5	27	On Time	1: 0..30 days
15	11	47	Late	2: 30..60 days
18	3	30	On Time	1: 0..30 days

Figure 3.17 Raw Data with Additional Columns

Source: Used with permission from Microsoft.

Getting an Overview

Figure 3.18 reveals that overall, nearly 80% of all invoices are paid late, i.e. not settled within terms promised. There is a drastic difference between business units. Whilst BU 3 has about 30% vendor invoices paid late, the other three BUs show more than 85% bills late.

From the comments Finance has been receiving, we learned that some of the invoices are overdue for a long time.

How long is long?

Descriptive statistics gives further details about the performance of our invoicing process (Table 3.6). In this case, the mean is not useful. The median tells us that 50% of all invoices are paid within 43 days. This seems to be the most common (Mode) payment turnaround time. Standard deviation and variance inform about a distribution with a very large variation.

Kurtosis and skewness indicate that the distribution of this dataset is far away from normality, since normality would have both indicators between –2 and +2. Minimum payment time is 0. This is thinkable since there might be invoices that are important enough to manually carry them through the process after receiving them. This usually happens when projects are put at risk to be delayed because the responsible vendor refuses to work until their invoices are paid. The maximum payment turnaround time lies at 1225 days.

Could it really be that some invoices from 2016 had not been cleared yet? This is unbelievable.

In order to get a better overview, the data were organised in 8 payment time categories as seen in column DaysCategory. The first category included all invoices that were paid within 30 days, the second showed all invoices

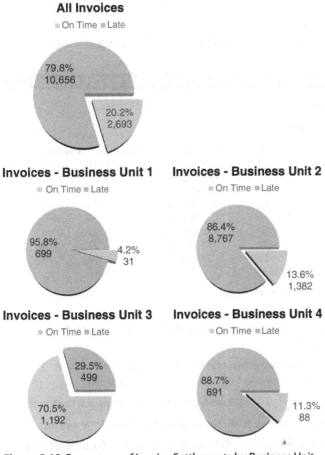

All Invoices

■ On Time ■ Late

79.8%
10,656

20.2%
2,693

Invoices - Business Unit 1

■ On Time ■ Late

95.8%
699

4.2%
31

Invoices - Business Unit 2

■ On Time ■ Late

86.4%
8,767

13.6%
1,382

Invoices - Business Unit 3

■ On Time ■ Late

29.5%
499

70.5%
1,192

Invoices - Business Unit 4

■ On Time ■ Late

88.7%
691

11.3%
88

Figure 3.18 Percentage of Invoice Settlements by Business Unit

Table 3.6 Descriptive Statistics for Invoice Payment Time (MS Excel)

PARAMETER	INVOICE2PAY
Mean	46.43
Standard Error	0.31
Median	43.00
Mode	43.00
Standard Deviation	36.23
Sample Variance	1312.88
Kurtosis	436.11
Skewness	16.46
Range	1225.00
Minimum	-
Maximum	1225.00
Total	619735.00
Count	13349.00

paid between 30 and 60 days, and so on. The last category counts the invoices paid after more than 210 days.

We create a PivotTable (Task 3.6 and Figure 3.19) using this column:

TASK 3.6   CREATE PIVOT TABLE AND CHART FOR DAYSCATEGORY

1. Position cursor in table Raw.

2. Insert – PivotTable – OK.

Row Labels	Count of ID		Category	Invoices	Cumulative
1: 0..30 days	2546		0..30 days	2546	19%
2: 30..60 days	9254		30..60 days	9254	88%
3: 60..90 days	1169		60..90 days	1169	97%
4: 90..120 days	188		90..120 days	188	99%
5: 120..150 days	70		120..150 days	70	99%
6: 150..180 days	37		150..180 days	37	99%
7: 180..210 days	27		180..210 days	27	100%
8: More than 210 days	58		> 210 days	58	100%
Grand Total	**13349**			**13349**	

Figure 3.19 PivotTable for Data Plot

Source: Used with permission from Microsoft.

3. Select DaysCategory in Rows. DaysCategory in Values. Make sure it shows Count of DaysCategory.

4. Create table next to PivotTable. Insert in headers Category, Number of Invoices, % of DaysCategory and Cumulative % of DaysCategory.

5. Insert in cells underneath =A4, = B4, =B4/B$12 and its cumulation next to it.

6. Copy it down until the last row. Keep the cells next to Grand Total empty.

7. Select D3:E11 and Insert – Charts – Column or Bar Charts – 2D Column Chart

8. Dress up the chart

9. With the cursor in the bar chart, select Chart Design – Select Data

10. Add – Series Name G3 – Series Values G4:G11

11. Select Chart Design – Change Chart Type – Combo Chart (Figure 3.20)

12. Set Cumulative % to Line and Secondary Axis

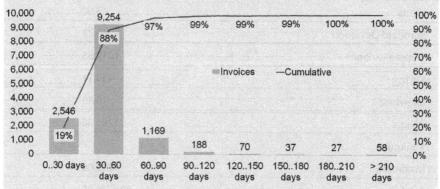

Figure 3.20 Column Chart with Number of Invoices and Percentage per Category

From the plot in Figure 3-20 it becomes apparent, that only 19.1% of all invoices have been paid within the 30-day window. Another 69.3% are paid between 30 to 60 days, i.e., more than 11% are paid after 60 days. 85 invoices are older than 180 days.

Hypothesis 1: Some Business Units are Better Than Others

This is a sobering picture for the CFO and his Finance staff.

Some colleagues declare that their business unit – Finance is organised by having business partners for certain business units – are not that bad. This leads to the next level of analysis.

As we know already, there is a difference between business units. Studying Figure 3-21 we find that Business Unit 1 seems to be worst case. Even Q1, the 25% line, is higher than 40 days. At BU 1, far more than 75% of invoices are overdue, assuming that most invoices are termed at 30 days. This confirms the pie chart. Only Business Unit 3 seems to be settling their accounts with higher discipline.

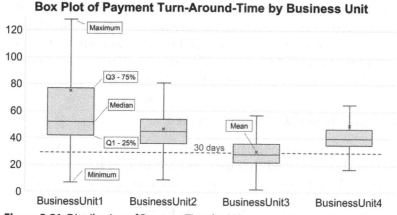

Figure 3.21 Distribution of Payment Time by BU

Hypothesis 2: Finance Receives Invoices after Payment Term

The other statement coming from Finance staff says, that they did not receive invoices early enough to be able to handle the payment. Hence, it is time to look into the payment process. Fortunately, the Finance IT system breaks down the process into four process steps

1. Step 1: Get Invoice to Finance (Days2Finance),
2. Step 2: Check and Post Invoice (Days2Check),
3. Step 3: Approve Payment (Days2Proposal),
4. Step 4: Transfer Payment to Vendor (Days2Pay).

Figure 3.22 Payment Steps by Business Unit

Figure 3.22 suggests, that at all business units, it takes a considerable amount of time to get invoices to Finance after receiving them from vendors with Business Unit 1 being the worst. There, for more than 25% of all invoices, the payment term of 30 days is eaten up by activities in the business unit before sending the invoice to Finance. This means, Finance has no chance to pay on time. Since not all business units show the same pattern, it might be wise to initiate best practice sharing amongst the business units and their Finance business partners.

Hypothesis 3: Business Unit 1 Has Improved

Finance business partners of Business Unit 1 claim that this was not the actual status. They reported that they had recognised the delay in getting invoices to Finance over the course of the year and had initiated an

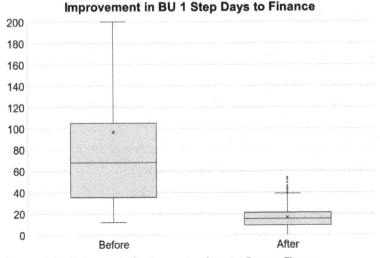

Figure 3.23 Before and After Improving Step 1 – Days to Finance

improvement in the process together with the business unit. They said from end November onwards, the process had improved.

Hence, the data for Step 1 at Business Unit 1 was stratified in two phases. Phase 1 was showing the data before improvement, Phase 2 marked the data after process improvement.

As demonstrated in Figure 3.23, the process improvement activities seem to have delivered results.

This is good news. There seems to be a significant difference between Before and After for Step 1, Days between Invoicing Date and Receiving of Invoice at Finance, for Business Unit 1. The question is still, is this improvement enough?

After working on the process to turn the vendor invoices to Finance faster, nearly 75% are sent to Finance within 20 days (boxplot at Figure 3.23). This means, the remaining 25% can spend up to 55 days in the Business Unit. This is still too long. Further improvement at the business unit is needed.

Business Decision

At the beginning of this data analytics task, questions were raised by the CFO and by the organisation. These questions need to be answered.

1. How often does it happen that we pay late?
   Well, if we assume that our vendors usually give a 30-day term for payment of invoices, about 80% of our invoices are paid late (Figure 3.18).

2. How late is late?
   More than 11% of all vendor invoices are paid only after 60 days. This includes more than 1500 during the period in focus. If we assume that some of these late payments could potentially lead to hesitations of these vendors in current and new contracts, this situation could seriously hurt our business. For 58 invoices, a payment delay of more than half a year was recognised. This could lead to remarkable damage of MyPropertyDeveloper's reputation (Figure 3.20).

3. Is the overdue payment consistent across all units?
   Data suggest that invoicing processes are handled in different business units differently. Business Unit 3 seems to have a slightly faster process for paying creditors. The breakdown of the payment process into four steps gives further insights into different handling per business unit (Figure 3.22).

4. What are the root causes for that, and can we fix this situation?
   There seems to be a series of different root causes driving late payment of vendor invoices. One obvious root cause for late payment is prolonging the time taken between invoicing date and invoice arriving at Finance, at least for Business Units 1, 2 and 4. In all Business Units, Step 3 needs to be investigated whereas Step 4 is a major issue only at Business Unit 2.

Working on root cause analysis for Step 1 needs the involvement and support of the Business Units, whereas Steps 2, 3 and 4 can be tackled by the Finance teams.

After listening to the presentation, the CFO decides to call for a review of the AP process. And, he suggests to his peers in the business units to invite them to fix their part of the process.

One more lesson we can learn from this case is *"Don't blame the people, blame the process".*

Deploying Analytics Tools

This case illustrates a rather straight forward dataset and how it appears in any organisation in many functions from time to time. We wanted to demonstrate how MS Excel in many situations does the job. The only toolsets required are the table function, Pivot Tables together with Pivot Charts, and compelling plots.

Choosing the right plot is an important skill that needs to be acquired by practice and trying. And amending the X- and Y- axes, chart elements, and the plot area make the plot useful. Excel plots without applying some "cosmetics" are often not attractive. This is not a fault of the software. It is our job to change this.

If you wish to do data plotting and some analysis, you will find many more variants of all kind of plots, far beyond MS Excel. MS Power BI allows the inclusion of R plots. This combination brings you the best of both worlds. Use it.

Here are some plots, R helps to generate.

Open R Studio.

```
# Loading necessary packages
install.packages("graphics")
library(graphics)
# Loading data file
DaysToPay <- read_excel("DaysToPay.xlsx")
attach(DaysToPay)
# Building continguency table for BU and Late
myTable <- table(BU, Late)
# Generating mosaicplot for BU and Late
mosaicplot(myTable, col = c("#ed9dae", "#b2edc4"), xlab = "",
    ylab = "", main = "Business Units and Their AP Performance",
    cex.axis = 1.1)
```

The Mosaic Plot displayed in Figure 3.24, has the power to move the focus from Business Unit 1 which has the highest percentage of late invoice payments, to Business Unit 2 which has by far the largest number of invoices paid late although the percentage might be less than in the former BU. After all, many more vendors wait for payments from BU 2 than from any other BU.

Business Units and Their AP Performance

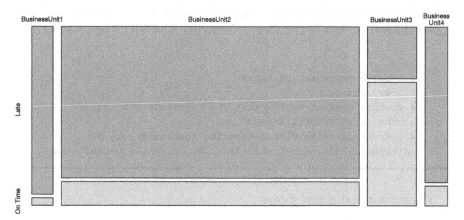

Figure 3.24 Mosaic Plot Showing Number of Invoices On Time and Late by Business Unit

The next tool is a violin plot (Figure 3.25) that shows a violin-like shape indicating the density of points around that measurement (Days).

```
# Loading necessary packages
library(ggplot2)
# Setting general font size
theme_set(theme_classic(base_size = 18))
# Stacking data for use in plots. Column 3 is fix, columns 7-10
get stacked
myData <- data.frame(DaysToPay[3], stack(DaysToPay[7:10]))
# Generating violin plot for BU and DaysToPay
ggplot(myData, aes(factor(BU), values, fill = BU)) + geom_violin()
   + ylim(0,120) + geom_boxplot(width = 0.1)
      + theme(legend.position = "none") + xlab("") + ylab("Days")
```

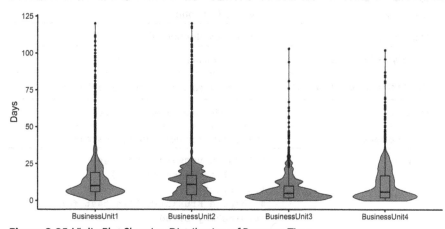

Figure 3.25 Violin Plot Showing Distribution of Payment Time

And, if there is a need to show that the payment turnaround time between BUs is significantly different, you may want to use the non-parametric Kruskal–Wallis test (Table 3.7). This tool performs like ANOVA for non-normal data.

```
# Loading necessary packages
library(stats)
# Compute Kruskal-Wallis test for Invoice2Pay by BU
kruskal.test(Invoice2Pay~BU)
# Compute pairwise Wilcox-test for Invoice2Pay by BU
pairwise.wilcox.test(Invoice2Pay, BU, p.adjust.method = "BH")
```

The output of this test shows:

```
Kruskal-Wallis rank sum test

data: Invoice2Pay by BU
Kruskal-Wallis chi-squared = 2042.3, df = 3, p-value < 2.2e-16


Pairwise comparisons using Wilcoxon rank sum test with
continuity correction
data: Invoice2Pay and BU
                BusinessUnit1   BusinessUnit2   BusinessUnit3
BusinessUnit2   < 2e-16 0 0
BusinessUnit3   < 2e-16         < 2e-16 0
BusinessUnit4   < 2e-16         3.8e-16         < 2e-16
P value adjustment method: BH (Benjamini & Hochberg, 1995)
```

The p-value of both tests is practically zero (see output). This means, there is no doubt that the BUs perform significantly different in settling the bills of their vendors.

Table 3.7 Kruskal–Wallis test

KRUSKAL–WALLIS TEST	
Data in X:	Discrete X – Groups
Data in Y:	Continuous. Not normal.
Null Hypothesis H_0:	$median_1 = median_2 = \ldots = median_n$
Alternative Hypothesis H_A:	t least one *median* is significantly different.
Decision:	If p-value is < 0.05, reject H_0 and accept H_A.
Assumptions:	Shape of distribution in groups is similar.

R code:	`# Loading necessary packages`
	`install.packages("stats")`
	`library(stats)`
	`# Compute Kruskal-Wallis test for`
	`Invoice2Pay by BU`
	`kruskal.test(Invoice2Pay~BU)`

Table 3.8 Two-Sample Wilcoxon test

TWO-SAMPLE WILCOXON TEST (KAUFMANN, 2020)	
Data in X:	Discrete X – Groups (Dept C, Dept D)
Data in Y:	Continuous Y, Discrete ordinal (values), non-normal
Null Hypothesis H_0:	$median_1 = median_2$
Alternative Hypothesis H_A:	$median_1 \neq median_2$
Decision:	If p-value is < 0.05 ($\alpha = 0.05$), reject H_0 and accept H_A.
Assumptions:	Sample sizes must be at least 6.
	Samples must have similar distribution.
R code:	``` # Loading necessary packages library(rstatix) # Compute pairwise Wilcox-test for Invoice2Pay by BU # Adjustment method BH by Benjamini & Hochberg, 1995 pairwise.wilcox.test(Invoice2Pay, BU, p.adjust.method = "BH") ```

Practice

- What are the requirements on the data acquisition for operations analytics?
- How does one decide which tools for graphical and statistical analysis to apply?
- What are discrete data and continuous data? Name three examples for each.

Please, complete the following steps:

- Download the data for this case from www.wiley.com.
- Perform data plots for each hypothesis.
- Perform statistical analysis for each hypothesis as described above.
- Prepare a short presentation to report the result and your recommendation to the management.

Case 6: Why Are We Wasting Blood?

Blood and blood products are used in hospitals across the world every day to save lives. The availability of blood and blood products is facilitated by the generosity of voluntary blood donors. In the process from blood collection to producing the final product for use in hospitals, a certain level of discards is both inevitable and appropriate to ensure that only high quality products are available where and when they are clinically necessary. However, if the proportion of discards of blood and blood products is too high, very expensive waste is the result. This could lead to a shortage of blood and, of course, waste of precious resources.

The group director of the blood bank is not happy with the level of wastage of platelets – the most precious blood component, after she had the chance to compare the blood bank indicators with those of other Asian countries during a meeting with the Heads of Asian blood banks. The Blood Bank reports higher wastage of platelet bags than many other Asian blood banks. She requested one of her department heads to investigate the matter.

For this case, data for about 2700 platelet bags are collected and analysed. The analysis follows a typical Six Sigma approach by defining and testing multiple potential root causes for the wastage problem and eliminating those that are non-significant. At the end, the detection of the relationship between a supposedly important driver, the type of centrifuge, and the underlying root cause, the operator, leads to the better decision and to the avoidance of a substantial investment. This case shows the importance of validating the data collection process by testing its repeatability and reproducibility, its Gage R&R.

Business Question

The obvious question was, why was the wastage of platelet units in our local blood bank relatively high compared to other Asian blood banks although our blood bank had the same or even better equipment available to support the blood donation and blood production process.

Since it was not exactly straight forward to conduct a detailed process benchmarking with other Asian blood banks, they decided to answer the question "Why are we wasting platelet units?" by looking into their own blood bank process.

During the respective meeting, nurses and scientists took the opportunity to request better equipment. The two most costly investments they suggested in order to get better quality of blood products were type of blood bags used for platelets and type of centrifuges used for platelet extraction. Whilst using the supposedly better blood bags would increase the running costs significantly, replacing centrifuges would ask for a rather large investment that was not budgeted for.

Apart from these two ideas, the team came up with other potential drivers for platelet wastage (Figure 3.26). In the team, they prioritised the variables X that could influence the Y (Bold item in Figure 3.26). This discussion led to the formulation of a series of assumptions brought up by blood process scientists, i.e. hypotheses that needed to be tested.

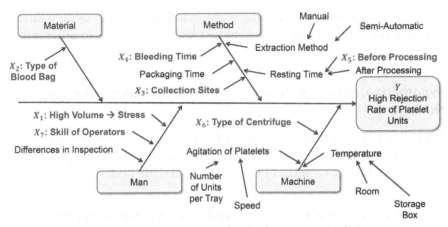

Figure 3.26 Building the Model of Variables for Platelet Wastage Analytics

Hypothesis 1: Work Stress Increases Wastage

There is an assumption that a higher volume of blood bags produced leads to higher work stress and fatigue which in turn contributes to higher amount of wastage, that means there is a correlation between percentage of wasted blood bags and number of blood bags processed.

Hypothesis 2: Different Material of Blood Bags Contributes to Higher Wastage

The blood bank buys blood bags from two suppliers in order to avoid single sourcing and dependency on only one supplier. Scientists stated concerns that the type of blood bag material drives the percentage of blood wastage. They raised an assumption that blood bag type C4 causes more platelet waste.

Hypothesis 3: Platelet Wastage Depends on Collection Site

Blood for platelet production can stem from the blood bank centre or from a mobile drive. Naturally, the treatment of the blood is slightly different, especially before it reaches the lab. If blood is collected in the blood bank centre, the temperature of the environment is quite stable at an ideal level. That cannot be guaranteed for the blood that is brought in from other collection sites such as blood mobiles. Although the transport is done using cooling boxes, some temperature fluctuations cannot be avoided. Therefore, the assumption is that blood received from mobile collection sites has a higher chance to turn into rejected platelet units.

Hypothesis 4: Time Taken for Bleeding Influences Platelet Wastage

Some blood donors have large veins, some have smaller ones. Larger veins allow blood to run faster, smaller ones need more time to fill the 450ml blood bag. Some scientists raised the concern that a longer bleeding time – due to small veins – could result in more platelet waste due to progressive blood coagulation.

Hypothesis 5: Resting Time Before Platelet Processing Influences Wastage

Since platelets – the most precious part of our blood – are very sensitive to time without activity, there is an assumption that delays before processing could cause higher wastage of the end product, the platelets.

Hypothesis 6: Type of Centrifuge Used Creates Different Amount of Wastage

The blood bank uses three different types, i.e. models, of centrifuge to perform platelet extraction. The models have a different age and slightly different characteristics. Naturally, this could influence the quality of the final product, the platelets.

Hypothesis 7: Some Operators Contribute to Higher Wastage

The assumption of the head of the blood bank is that nurses involved in blood collection, scientists conducting the platelet extraction, and inspectors who do the final assessment include veteran staff as well as new staff. All must have a certain minimum training and skills in order to be allowed to work on the process. However, their experience is certainly different. This could cause different results for the quality of blood bags with platelets.

The temporary model for Operations Analytics is:

$$Y = f\left(X_1, X_2, X_3, X_4, X_5, X_6, X_7\right)$$

It was decided to use scientific methods to test this model and to find the right answer on aforementioned assumptions before making any decision.

Data Acquisition

Data were downloaded in Excel format from different sources since the information to test the hypothesis was not available in one table together but in three (Figure 3.27).

The first table contained blood bag ID with test result, centrifuge used and blood bag type (Figure 3.27, top). The second table had the information about the blood collection process including the bleeding time (Figure 3.27, lower left). Additionally, this table had the actual processing time that could be used to determine the resting time before platelet extraction. The third table could be used to determine which

Blood Bag ID	Result	Date	DOW	Centrifuge Type	1st Spin Time - Start	Resting Time Before Pro	Resting Time - Start	Resting Time - End	Resting Time After Pro
64988	ok	14 Nov 2019	Thu	G9	14:35	264	16:30	18:00	90
64989	ok	14 Nov 2019	Thu	G9	14:35	256	16:30	18:00	90
64990	ok	14 Nov 2019	Thu	H10	14:40	218	16:30	18:00	90
64991	ok	14 Nov 2019	Thu	G9	14:35	204	16:30	18:00	90
64992	ok	14 Nov 2019	Thu	G9	14:35	201	16:30	18:00	90
64993									
64994									
64995									
64996									

Blood Bag ID	Date	Bag Type	Needle in	Needle Out	Bleeding Time	Bleeding Time in min	Collection Site	Extraction Method
64988	14 Nov 2019	F6	10:04	10:11	0:07	7	Mobile	M
64989	14 Nov 2019	F6	10:13	10:19	0:06	6	Mobile	M
64990	14 Nov 2019	F6	10:55	11:02	0:07	7	Mobile	M
64991	14 Nov 2019	F6	11:05	11:11	0:06	6	Mobile	M
64992	14 Nov 2019	F6	11:07	11:14	0:07	7	Mobile	M
64993	14 Nov 2019	F6	10:55	11:00	0:05	5	Mobile	M
64994	14 Nov 2019	F6	10:53	10:58	0:05	5	Mobile	M
64995	14 Nov 2019	F6	11:17	11:25	0:08	8	Mobile	M
64996	14 Nov 2019	F6	11:20	11:28	0:08	8	Mobile	M

Blood Bag ID	Labeller
64988	Wong
64989	Wong
64990	Wong
64991	Wong
64992	Wong
64993	Wong
64994	Wong
64995	Wong
64996	Wong

Figure 3.27 Data Collection Sheets for Platelet Wastage Analytics

Source: Used with permission from Microsoft.

members of staff were involved in the collection, in operating the centrifuge and in evaluating the quality of the blood bag with platelets (Figure 3.27, lower right).

Data Preparation

In order to analyse the acquired data with appropriate software, data need to be cleaned and transformed into a one-table format.

Since the data were manually entered, the data need to be checked for completeness, accuracy, and entry errors such as typos.

There are typical errors found, which compromise data integrity. Data was given in multiple tables with very different formats (Figure 3.27). Data collection was done in one table per day. Tables looked different from day to day, depending on the person doing the entry. The correct way to record the data is to organise them in variables and records (Figure 3.28). Variables in this case would be "Blood Bag ID", "Result", "Centrifuge Type", etc. These labels to be printed on the first row, with variables in columns. Records are all data that belong to the same data set, like all data that belong to "Blood Bag ID = 64988" make one row in the table. Each record is stored in one row. In order to avoid any confusion during data analysis, total rows or other aggregated data must be avoided. If data for the same record is stored in different tables, these tables must have at least one variable that identifies which records in the different tables belong together.

TASK 3.7   LOAD DATA AND TRANSFORM MULTIPLE TABLES INTO ONE TABLE

1. Load data PlateletWaste.xlsx.

2. Open worksheet Processing.

3. Create a new column by writing BagType in L1, since we want to add the variable Bag Type to this table. A new column is added to the table.

4. Insert the following in L2: =VLOOKUP([@[Blood Bag ID]],Collection[#All],3,0). Reference is Blood Bag ID which refers to worksheet Collection from which we use Column 3.

5. Do the same for BleedingTime and CollectionSite.

6. Create a new column by writing Inspector in O1 for adding the variable Inspector to this table. A new column is added to the table.

7. Insert the following in O2: =VLOOKUP([@[Blood Bag ID]],Scientist[#All],2,0). Reference is Blood Bag ID which refers to worksheet Inspector from which we use Column 2.

8. Save your work.

Variables

BloodBagID	Result	Date	DOW	CentrifugeType	Spin1Start
64988	ok	14 Nov 2019	Thu	G9	14:35
64989	ok	14 Nov 2019	Thu	G9	14:35
64990	ok	14 Nov 2019	Thu	H10	14:40
64991	ok	14 Nov 2019	Thu	G9	14:35
64992	ok	14 Nov 2019	Thu	G9	14:35
64993	ok	14 Nov 2019	Thu	H10	14:40
64994	ok	14 Nov 2019	Thu	H10	14:40
64995	ok	14 Nov 2019	Thu	H10	14:40
64996	ok	14 Nov 2019	Thu	H10	14:40
64997	ok	14 Nov 2019	Thu	G9	14:35

Records

RestingBeforePro	RestingStart	RestingEnd	RestingAfterPro
264	16:30	18:00	90
256	16:30	18:00	90
218	16:30	18:00	90
204	16:30	18:00	90
201	16:30	18:00	90
220	16:30	18:00	90
222	16:30	18:00	90
195	16:30	18:00	90
192	16:30	18:00	90
175	16:30	18:00	90

Figure 3.28 Structure of Data Table for Platelet Wastage Analytics
Source: Used with permission from Microsoft.

"Blood Bag ID" serves this purpose. Therefore, the identifier or matching indicator must be unique. If data is spread in different tables for different days, teams, shifts, locations etc. it must be copied in the same one table.

At the end of data preparation, there must be only one table with all variables X and Y in columns and all datasets (records) in rows with only one header row denominating the names of X and Y.

Date Format must be the same for each variable

Date and time are not always input in date/time format. For proper analysis of processing time, the input format of the underlying time stamps must be the same, in other words, it must be according to the settings of the computer so that it will be recognised as such.

Names must be input the same way per variable

Text has been entered in different ways. For example, bag type "C4" was recorded with multiple styles: "C4", "C 4" and "C-4". Type of Centrifuge "H10" was documented as "10", "H10" and "H 10". For proper data analysis, all bags and centrifuges of the same type must have exactly the same name. Any variation in the name will result in them being analysed as different bags or centrifuges respectively.

Records (rows) with missing inputs must be deleted or filled with data if possible

Some blood bag ID were missing in the Collection Table resulting in the dataset for this ID being incomplete. As a result, the other data of this record cannot be used by most analysis tools.

To carry out analysis, data must be raw. Aggregated data are much less useful for the analysis. More often than not, aggregated data hinders the analysis of the model. In our case, the unit of measure is one blood bag. This is the smallest unit possible. Therefore, the analysis has the highest possible power.

For illustration purpose, let's assume blood collection data is aggregated in daily pattern, i.e. the unit of measure would be date. For each date, number of blood bags and number of rejects are counted. This gives us the wastage percentage per day, a correct result. However, this option has critical disadvantages.

Firstly, let's assume there are multiple centrifuge types and multiple blood bag types deployed per day. We would have no way to find out which bag type or centrifuge type works better because we would not know which one produced the discarded bags. The same applies to many other variables. We cannot analyse them.

Secondly, aggregating the blood bags per day reduces the sample size. The 2,698 Blood Bag IDs (Figure 3.28) would shrink to 22 days of collection. The sample size would drop from 2,698 to 22. In data handling, this is the worst idea, since it reduces the analysis power of all tools drastically.

Thirdly, raw data can always be aggregated. This means, if the analysis requires aggregated data, it can be transformed. Unfortunately, aggregated data can never be disaggregated. This process is irreversible.

 For data analytics, it is imperative to acquire raw data. Aggregated data is of much less use. Aggregating data drastically reduces the analysis power.

Data Analysis

Any operations analytics needs to be done in two ways. Firstly, data plots are advisable. They will usually not answer the business question directly. Though, they may help to visualise the statistical result. The graphical displays are usually more powerful in presentations than statistics only.

In the following analysis steps, the data types for X and Y are considered first in order to select the right tool for graphical and statistical analysis (Table 1.4).

Hypothesis 1: Work Stress Increases Wastage

There is an assumption that higher volume of processed blood bags leads to higher wastage.

X is Number of platelets processed per day. Y is the percentage of waste. Unit of measure is day of processing. Therefore, the dataset is X with counts that can be treated like continuous data. Y is the percentage of waste that can be handled like continuous data.

For a continuous X–continuous Y-dataset, the appropriate data plot is a scatter plot (Table 1.4). The scatter plot in Figure 3.30 suggests that there is no relationship at all between X and Y.

The scatter plot (Figure 3.30) shows a slightly negative relationship between the number of platelet bags processed per day and the wastage. This relationship seems very weak since the R^2 is at 0.0972, i.e. 9.72%. Common sense should tell us that this does not seem right. Therefore, we perform a statistical analysis.

TASK 3.9   CREATE PIVOT TABLE AND SCATTER PLOT FOR % REJECTS (FIGURE 3.30)

1. Bring your cursor in the completed table Processing.

2. Select Insert – Pivot Table – OK. This will create the form of a Pivot Table on a new worksheet (Figure 3.29).

3. Since we wish to have the number of bags per day, we pull Date from Pivot Table Fields into Rows. Pull Month out of this field since we do not need any aggregation. Your cursor must be within the table for this to work.

4. Pull Blood Bag ID into Values so that Sum of Blood Bag ID appears in the Pivot Table. Double click this header and switch it to Count. Now we count the number of bags per day.

5. Pull Reject into Values. Now we sum up all rejected blood bags that show 1 in Reject.

6. Next to Sum of Reject, create a new column with Number of Platelet Bags and fill it with the contents of the second column using =B4. We have to do this because we cannot create a scatter plot with data from the Pivot Table. So, we need to copy both columns next to it.

7. Do the same for Number of Rejects using =C4.

8. Create a Column % Reject. Fill it with =E4/D4. Copy these three formulas down to 07 Dec.

9. Mark column Number of Platelet Bags and column % Rejects by using Ctrl and mouse.

10. Select Insert – Charts – Scatter Plot.

11. Beautify the chart by adding a proper header and amending the axes.

12. Select a data point in the plot, right click and select Add Trendline.

13. Select linear, check Display Equation on chart and Display R-squared value on chart. With this, we add some simple statistics to our chart.

Row Labels	Count of Blood Bag ID	Sum of Reject	Number of Platelet Bags	Number of Rejects	% Rejects
14 Nov	127	9	127	9	0.070866
15 Nov	136	23	136	23	0.169118
16 Nov	161	13	161	13	0.080745
17 Nov	147	26	147	26	0.176871
18 Nov	158	3	158	3	0.018987
19 Nov	109	9	109	9	0.082569
21 Nov	88	17	88	17	0.193182
22 Nov	95	2	95	2	0.021053
23 Nov	85	7	85	7	0.082353
24 Nov	85	20	85	20	0.235294
25 Nov	137	9	137	9	0.065693
26 Nov	128	9	128	9	0.070313
27 Nov	138	23	138	23	0.166667
28 Nov	164	13	164	13	0.079268
29 Nov	150	29	150	29	0.193333
30 Nov	161	3	161	3	0.018634
1 Dec	114	9	114	9	0.078947
3 Dec	93	19	93	19	0.204301
4 Dec	101	2	101	2	0.019802
5 Dec	91	9	91	9	0.098901
6 Dec	89	20	89	20	0.224719
7 Dec	141	9	141	9	0.06383
Grand Total	2698	283			

Figure 3.29 Adding Pivot Table and Calculation of % Rejects

Source: Used with permission from Microsoft.

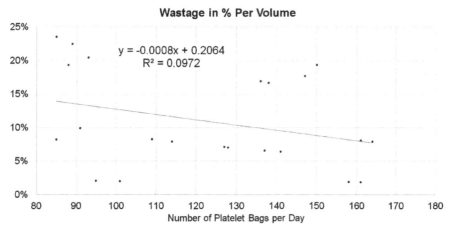

Figure 3.30 Scatter Plot for Hypothesis 1

For this situation, the right statistical tool is regression (Task 3.10).

As a result of the regression, a p-value of 0.1577 (Figure 3.22) for Volume is observed and a R-square of 0.0972 (Figure 3.30) is shown (Figure 3.32). The former one suggests that there is no relationship between X and Y. For a relationship between X and Y to be considered, the p-value for Volume must be below 0.05 or 5%. Only then, the relationship is significant, and the amount of Wastage is driven by processed Volume.

The latter means, the amount of variation in Y explained by X is only 9.72%, which is far too low. For a relationship that is of business value, R-square should be rather above 40%.

Significance F, the p-value for the model, shows 0.158 (Figure 3.32). This means, the model is not significant. It is not right to talk about a relationship between X and Y, between the number of Blood Bags Processed and the Wastage in % Reject. Furthermore, the coefficient for Volume is negative at -0.00079, i.e. the theoretical relationship detected by regression analysis is very small and negative. If the volume processed increases, the wastage goes down. This does not make any sense and is not more than a theoretical, a statistical value.

TASK 3.10   PERFORM REGRESSION ANALYSIS ON WASTAGE %

1. Select Data – Data Analysis – Regression (Figure 3.31).

2. Input range for %Reject for Input Y Range.

3. Input range for Number of Platelet Bags for Input X Range.

4. Do not forget to check Labels since our input ranges include these.

5. Select all Residuals Details and the Normal Probability Plot. They might be important to check if a relationship is likely.

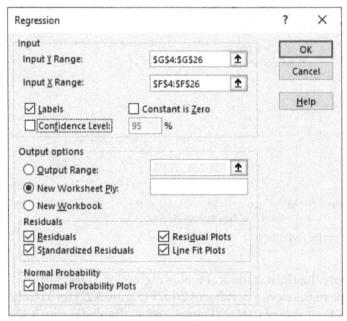

Figure 3.31 MS Excel Regression analysis for Hypothesis 1
Source: Used with permission from Microsoft.

Regression Statistics					
Multiple R	0.3118				
R Square	0.0972				
Adjusted R Square	0.0521				
Standard Error	0.0695				
Observations	22				

ANOVA					
	df	SS	MS	F	Significance F
Regression	1	0.0104	0.0104	2.1542	0.1577
Residual	20	0.0967	0.0048		
Total	21	0.1071			

	Coefficients	Standard Error	t Stat	P-value
Intercept	0.2064	0.0674	3.0597	0.0062
Volume	-0.0008	0.0005	-1.4677	0.1577

Figure 3.32 Regression Statistics for Hypothesis 1

Thus, this hypothesis is rejected.

☞ When applying statistics, do always keep your common sense switched on.

Hypothesis 2: Different Material of Blood Bags Contributes to Higher Wastage

The blood bank buys blood bags from two suppliers in order to avoid single sourcing and dependency on only one supplier. Is there a relationship between blood bag type and wastage?

In this situation, the X blood bag type is discrete whereas the result for each platelet unit is either rejected or ok, i.e., also discrete. Bar chart and two-proportion test should be applied.

The bar chart (Figure 3.33) shows that blood bag type C4 (Sample 1) and type F6 (Sample 2) show similar wastage with 11.3% versus 10.0%, respectively.

The two-proportion test (Figure 3.34) shows a p-value of 0.2647 (P(Sample1≠Sample2)) for both samples not to be equal, i.e. this relationship is non-significant. There is a 26.5% risk of being wrong with

---

TASK 3.11   PERFORM TWO-PROPORTION TEST (FIGURE 3.34)

1. Open file TwoProportionTest.xlsx.

2. Select worksheet Comparing 2 Disc Samples.

3. Insert 1005 (891+114) in Sample 1 and 1693 (1,524+169) in Sample 2.

4. Insert 114 in Number of Events 1 and 169 in Number of Events 2. Events can be either nok or ok for both samples. Both versions will give the same result.

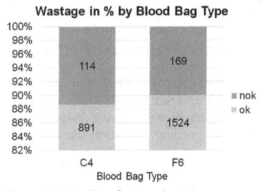

Figure 3.33 Bar Chart for Hypothesis 2

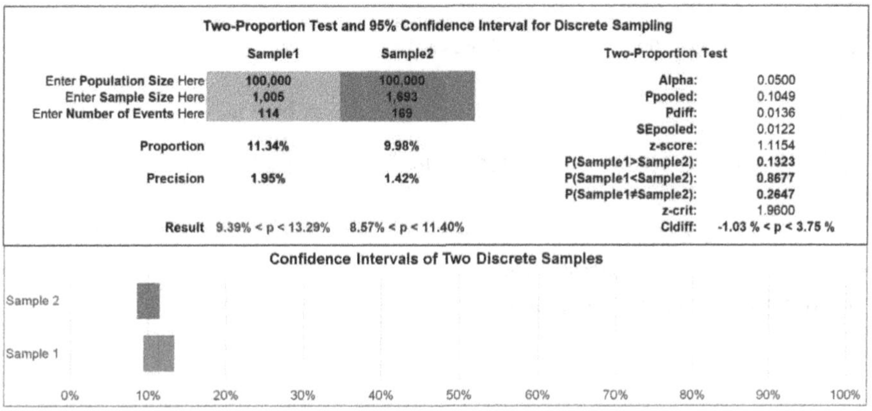

Figure 3.34 Two-proportion test Statistics for Hypothesis 2

the assumption that there is a difference. Since this analysis is based on sample data, the result comes with a confidence interval. This confidence interval means that the result shown might not be the "real" value, the value we would get if we would check a large number of blood bags with platelets.

For blood bag type C4, the waste percentage is expected to be between 9.39% and 13.29%. For blood bag type F6, the waste percentage is expected to be between 8.57% and 11.40%. Both confidence intervals assume 95% confidence level.

From this we may conclude that the waste percentage for C4 can be 10% and for F6 it can be 10% as well, for example. Therefore, there is a considerable chance that both blood bag types produce the same wastage.

As a result, this hypothesis is rejected.

Hypothesis 3: Platelet Wastage Depends on Collection Site

Blood for platelet production can stem from the blood bank centre or from a mobile drive. It is expected that the treatment of the blood is slightly different. Is there a relationship between collection site and wastage? Would it help, if we use only blood from the blood bank centre for platelet production as some scientists suggested? This would reduce the number of available blood bags for platelet production significantly.

Here, the X Collection Site is discrete whereas the result for each platelet unit is either rejected or ok, i.e. also discrete. Bar chart and two-proportion test should be applied.

The bar chart (Figure 3.35) shows that there is a rather small difference between wastage for Site M with 10.3% and Site Q with 10.6%.

The two-proportion test conducted using the same way as before reveals a p-value of 0.7682, i.e. the relationship between collection site and wastage cannot be confirmed.

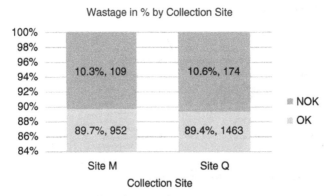

Figure 3.35 Bar Chart for Hypothesis 3

Additionally, the confidence intervals (95% confidence) reach from 8.46% to 12.09% and 9.15% to 12.11% respectively. That means, there is no evidence that both samples (Site M and Site Q) show a different waste percentage.

Therefore, this hypothesis is rejected.

Hypothesis 4: Time Taken for Bleeding Influences Platelet Wastage

The donation process, the bleeding, takes a different time depending on the physiology of the blood donors. Scientists argue that a longer bleeding process may influence the quality of the blood which influences the wastage of platelet bags.

During blood donation, much data is collected carefully, although manually. The time for "Needle in" and "Needle out" is tracked which allow the calculation of the Bleeding Time X. Bleeding Time is a continuous variable, whereas our Result (ok/nok) per blood bag is discrete. Following Table 1.4, this data set requires Logistic Regression. However, before we conduct Logistic Regression, we might want to make sure this is a promising option.

Plotting the data for a continuous-discrete dataset can be done in reverse. I.e. we pretend the continuous Bleeding Time is our Y and the discrete Result (ok/nok) is our X. This would enable one of the most powerful – and underused – graphical tools: the box plot (Figure 3.36).

The function of a Logistic Regression tries to find a probability of flipping of the Result from "ok" to "nok" with growing Bleeding Time. If this were true, our box plot would show a lower box of Bleeding Time for "ok" and a higher box of Bleeding time for "nok". The connecting line between both boxes includes both means.

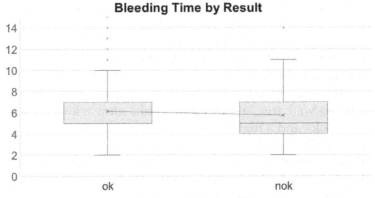

Figure 3.36 Reverse Box Plot for Hypothesis 4

Parameter	nok	ok
Mean	5.76	6.14
Standard Error	0.12	0.05
Median	5	5
Mode	4	4
Standard Deviation	2.02	2.21
Sample Variance	4.09	4.89
Kurtosis	1.98	6.28
Skewness	1.24	1.69
Range	12	24
Minimum	2	2
Maximum	14	26
Sum	1629	14823
Count	283	2415

Figure 3.37 Descriptive Statistics for Hypothesis 4

Descriptive statistics (Figure 3.37) reveal Bleeding Time for nok to be 5.76 and 6.14 for ok. The standard deviation (square root of variance) is very similar for both results. The maximum Time for nok is 14min, for ok it is 26min. Hence, there is no evidence whatsoever that a longer bleeding process would cause more waste. Hence, there is no need to conduct Logistic Regression.

This hypothesis is rejected.

Hypothesis 5: Resting Time Before Platelet Processing Influences Wastage

Resting time is the time between blood donation, i.e. bleeding, and blood production in the centrifuge. The assumption scientists brought up is that a longer rest of the blood before processing in the centrifuge causes a higher chance for rejection, in other words, more wastage.

The data situation is very similar to Hypothesis 4 with X being the continuous Resting Time and Y being the discrete Result (ok/nok).

As mentioned before, the function of a Logistic Regression tries to find a probability of flipping of the Result from "ok" to "nok" with growing Resting Time. If this were true, our box plot would show a lower box of Resting Time for "ok" and a higher box of Resting time for "nok". The mean for "ok" is 165.7min and for "nok" it is 146.8min.

From the box plot and the mean, we can conclude that there is no way that the Resting Time for "nok" results is higher. We can conclude that a longer Resting does not cause more wastage.

Consequently, this hypothesis is rejected.

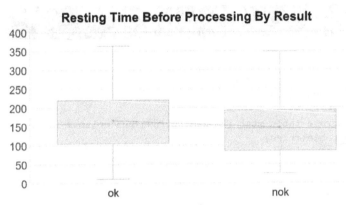

Figure 3.38 Reverse Box Plot for Hypothesis 5

Hypothesis 6: Type of Centrifuge Used Creates Different Amount of Wastage

The blood bank uses three different types, i.e. models, of centrifuges to perform the platelet extraction. The models have a different age and slightly different characteristics.

The data situation is different to the hypotheses before. The Y Waste percentage is discrete and X Centrifuge Type is discrete as well. Following Figure 3.39, bar or column chart and Chi^2 test are the appropriate tools.

The bar chart for Waste percentage over centrifuge type reveals that Centrifuge Type G9 shows higher wastage with 12.5% than centrifuge G7 with 8.8% and H10 with 9.5%. In this situation, it would be too fast to draw a conclusion. It is always a must to support the result of the graphical analysis with statistics.

In Excel, there is no Chi^2 test available. This can be done very easily with R.

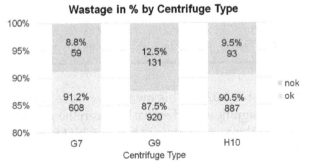

Figure 3.39 Bar Chart for Hypothesis 6

TASK 3.12   LOAD PACKAGE RSTATIX AND PERFORM CHI² TEST ON CENTRIFUGE:

Open R Studio.

```
# Loading necessary packages
install.packages("rstatix")
library(rstatix)
# Building cross table xtab and naming rows and columns
xtab <- as.table(rbind(
c(59, 131, 93),
c(608, 920, 887)))
dimnames(xtab) <- list(
Result = c("nok", "ok"),
Centri = c("G7", "G9", "H10"))
# Compute the Chi-square-test
Xsq <- chisq.test(xtab)
Xsq
Xsq$observed
Xsq$expected
Xsq$stdres
```

The output of this Chi² test:

n	statistic	p	df	method	p.signif
2698	7.33	0.0256	2	Chi-square test	*

```
Observed Values:
Result        G7              G9              H10
   nok        59              131             93
    ok        608             920             887

Expected Values:
Result        G7              G9              H10
   nok        69.96331        110.242         102.7947
    ok        597.03669       940.758         877.2053

Std.Residuals:
Result        G7              G9              H10
   nok        -1.596742       2.674532        -1.279605
    ok        1.596742        -2.674532       1.279605
```

The p-value for the Chi² test is 0.0256. This means, we have enough data to confirm that there is a significant difference between the groups.

The Chi² test result is shown above. As discussed before, Chi² test results are taken in three steps:

1. The p-value is less than 0.05. This means the test shows a significant difference. Hence, proceed with 2. and 3.

2. The highest absolute standardised residual (Std. Residual) is in cell centrifuge G9 with a result nok and ok.

3. The expected count for this combination is 110.24, whereas the real count is 131. This means, if centrifuge G9 would deliver a similar waste percentage as the other centrifuge types, then G9 would only have 110 rejected platelet units. But G9 produces 131. This is significantly higher than the other centrifuges.

With this, we have proven that centrifuge G9 delivers significantly more wastage than the other types. The risk for this assumption to be wrong is only 2.56%.

There was one interesting question asked: out of the 22 days when the test was performed, the higher wastage was only observed on eight days. How to explain this? Let us park this question for now.

Thus, this hypothesis is accepted.

Hypothesis 7: Some Operators Contribute to Higher Wastage

As some scientists and the head of the blood bank assume, personnel involved in the process steps include veteran staff as well as new staff. Is the difference in the experience driving a different waste percentage?

Since everyone has to undergo the same training, there is no variable related to training that can be used to check this hypothesis. Years of experience seems to be a better indicator for how well staff understands and masters the process in order to reduce waste. The easiest way of tackling this question is to check first whether there is any difference between different team members.

TASK 3.13   PERFORM CHI² TEST ON LABELLING OPERATOR:

```
# Loading necessary packages
install.packages("rstatix")
library(rstatix)
# Building cross table xtab and naming rows and columns
xtab <- as.table(rbind(
  c(21, 22, 85, 35, 32, 24, 64),
  c(260, 264, 284, 319, 520, 381, 387)))
dimnames(xtab) <- list(
  Result = c("nok", "ok"),
  Centri = c("Candy", "Cathy", "Max", "Sean", "Serene", "SP",
"Wong"))
# Compute the Chi-square test
Xsq <- chisq.test(xtab)
Xsq
Xsq$observed
Xsq$expected
Xsq$stdres
```

Figure 3.40 Bar Chart for Hypothesis 7

There are only seven team members who are involved in the blood production and platelet inspection process. These are Candy, Cathy, Max, Sean, Serene, Siew Ping, and Wong. Since it is imperative to have all operators who deal with blood products listed for each unit, it is not difficult to have reliable data for the X operator for each blood bag.

The "Wow!" after our data collection is seen in the plot at Figure 3.40. Whenever Max and Wong conduct the blood processing, the amount of waste in blood bags seems to go up.

The subsequently performed Chi^2 test confirms that there are significant differences at Max's nok-rate.

Hence, this hypothesis is accepted.

The output of this Chi^2 test:

```
X-squared = 95.61, df = 6, p-value < 2.2e-16
```

The Expensive Question

Whenever there are multiple X that potentially drive the Y, there is a possibility for these X to interact with each other or to confound each other. In our case, there is a chance to have the centrifuge confounding the influence of the operator, because operators tend to use only one centrifuge, the one that they are most familiar with. Checking the relationship between operator and centrifuge revealed an interesting insight: Max uses G9 most of the time whereas Wong is mostly registered on H10. G9 was found to produce higher waste percentage than G7 and H10.

If we take our findings to the Group Director, she will sure ask whether we need to buy a new centrifuge or is it only the operator who "makes the centrifuge look bad". Of course, the former is a rather large investment whereas the latter is a question of training on the job or amendment of standard operating precedures (SOPs) or both.

At the end of the process, inspectors decide whether the platelets are to be sent to hospitals or discarded. There is a quite simple way by using Gage R&R of finding out if there is a mismatch of the way the platelet bags are evaluated by the inspectors.

Saving the Money

Performing a Gage R&R means, testing different personnel on their repeatability and reproducibility when they perform a certain inspection. A Gage R&R can be formed on nearly any kind of inspection in nearly all industries. It is usually fast and inexpensive to do.

Repeatability means that the same inspector has to evaluate the same unit under the same circumstances – without knowing it is the unit he has checked before – and come to the same conclusion, which is "ok" or "nok".

Reproducibility means that different operators who check the same unit under the same circumstances come to the same conclusion.

Figure 3.41 shows the result of a Gage R&R conducted on all inspector staff. Repeatability has been tested and is 100% for all staff. This means, they make the same decision when given the same unit multiple times. Therefore, repeatability is not shown in Figure 3.41. Still, the reproducibility – the agreement between the Master and the staff is often less than 100% – the objective for both indicators, repeatability and reproducibility – with Max and Wong being far off. The column Master is showing the decision on these platelet bags made by a team of senior scientists and managers.

The good news is that all wrong evaluation results are wrong "nok", which means that inspectors rather stop "ok" platelet bags from going to

Unit	Master	Candy	Cathy	Max	Sean	Serene	Siew Ping	Wong
1	ok	nok	ok	nok	ok	nok	ok	nok
2	ok	ok	ok	nok	ok	ok	nok	nok
3	ok	ok	ok	ok	ok	ok	ok	ok
4	ok	ok	ok	nok	ok	ok	ok	ok
5	ok	ok	ok	ok	ok	ok	ok	ok
6	ok	ok	ok	nok	ok	ok	ok	nok
7	nok	nok	nok	nok	nok	nok	nok	nok
8	ok	ok	ok	ok	ok	ok	ok	ok
9	ok	ok	ok	nok	ok	ok	ok	ok
10	nok	nok	nok	nok	nok	nok	nok	nok
11	nok	nok	nok	nok	nok	nok	nok	nok
12	nok	nok	nok	nok	nok	nok	nok	nok
13	ok	ok	ok	nok	ok	ok	ok	nok
14	ok	ok	ok	ok	ok	ok	ok	ok
15	nok	nok	nok	nok	nok	nok	nok	nok
16	nok	nok	nok	nok	nok	nok	nok	nok
17	nok	nok	nok	nok	nok	nok	nok	nok
18	ok	ok	ok	ok	ok	ok	ok	ok
19	nok	nok	nok	nok	nok	nok	nok	nok
20	nok	nok	nok	nok	nok	nok	nok	nok
Reprod		95%	100%	70%	100%	95%	95%	80%

Figure 3.41 Result of Gage R&R for Inspectors

the hospital than sending "nok" units to the hospital. This is called over rejection and is expensive for the collecting organisation because good units are declared waste and get discarded. But it is safe for the hospitals.

Business Decision

The result of the analysis is summarised in Table 3.9.

Table 3.9 Analysis Results Overview

SN	HYPOTHESIS	STATISTICS	BUSINESS RESULT
H_1	Work stress leads to higher amount of wastage	Regression Not significant	Higher workload does not lead to more wastage.
H_2	Type of blood bag material used drives the percentage of blood wastage	Two-Proportion Test Not significant	There is no need to buy the more costly blood bag. It does not make any difference.
H_3	Collection site of whole blood influences percentage of blood wastage	Two-Proportion Test Not significant	Blood for platelet extraction can be used from all collection sites.
H_4	Donors bleeding time influences percentage of blood wastage	Logistic Regression Not significant	There is no need to select blood of certain bleeding time for platelet extraction.
H_5	Platelet resting time before processing of blood influences percentage of blood wastage	Logistic Regression Not significant	There is no need to reorganise the blood process.
H_6	Centrifuge used for blood production influences percentage of blood wastage	Chi^2 test Significant	Centrifuge C9 shows significantly higher wastage than all other centrifuges. However, this is caused by operator Max who creates more waste by his final inspection. C9 does not create more waste when other operators perform the routine on C9. Hence, there is no need to buy new equipment.
H_7	Operator influences percentage of blood wastage	Chi^2 test Significant	Seven different operators have been doing labelling, i.e. evaluating platelet bags with different understanding of the quality criteria. Two operators apply more stringent standards than others.

After the analysis and testing of the hypotheses, some myths turned out not to be true. There was no immediate need to invest in new centrifuges. Nor was there a reason for switching to the costlier blood bags for transporting and storing platelets.

By studying the data, it became apparent that the inspectors – operators who perform the final check on platelet blood bags (including labelling the bags) – had different standards. Out of the seven inspectors who were involved in the study, two were identified to have more stringent standards than the others. This resulted in a higher percentage of discarded units. In other words, the reproducibility of the blood bag evaluation process was not given. These two inspectors were the youngest in the team. They diligently tried to do their best in their job. However, this positive mindset may have caused an over rejection of blood bags.

The findings led to the review and redesign of the training process for operators. The organisation introduced concise description and pictures of a "good quality bag" and a "bad quality bag". Description and display were shared and discussed with some hospitals, the final customer of blood bags to ensure the internal inspection process was in line with customer requirements.

 Ensure repeatability and reproducibility of the data collection process before any analysis. Otherwise, analysis results might be misleading.

Deploying Analytics Tools

Analysing datasets with a discrete dependent variable Y (Result ok/nok) is quite common. Yet it is a challenge since it requires a larger amount of data to deliver useful results. A binary Y, i.e. a result variable with only two levels leaves only two-proportion test, X^2 test (Table 3.12), or binary logistic regression for analysis.

Two-proportion test and **X^2 test** are applied in the previous case to deal with discrete X variables (independent/predictor variable) when Y variable is discrete.

Regression has been used after aggregating the data to show the relationship between a quasi-continuous number of blood bags processed (X) and the number of rejected bags (Y). However, this aggregation has reduced the sample size of 2698 datasets with blood bag inspections to 22 data sets, i.e. 22 days of inspection. For the purpose of finding a relationship between workload and rejection rate, this seems to be enough data since there is no sign of the positive trend one would expect in this relationship.

Logistic Regression was not applied because the dataset did not show any indication of a relationship between Y (Result ok/nok) and the potential X, drivers bleeding time and resting time. We will use a more promising case later in the book to illustrate the use of Logistic Regression.

Table 3.10 Multiple Linear Regression

MULTIPLE LINEAR REGRESSION	
Data in X:	Continuous, no normality required.
	Can be applied for discrete ordinal data.
	Discrete X (groups) can be used as factors.
Data in Y:	Continuous, no normality required.
	Can be applied for discrete ordinal data.
Null Hypothesis H_0:	No significant relationship between any X and Y
Alternative Hypothesis H_A:	At least one X influences Y significantly
Decision:	1. All VIF must be < 5. Consider removing X with high VIF.
	2. If p-value of ANOVA is < 0.05, reject H_0 and accept H_A.
	3. X has significant influence if p-value of X < 0.05. Remove non-significant Xs and rerun model.
Assumptions:	■ Residuals are normally distributed.
	■ Residuals over all Xs do not show pattern.
	■ Residuals over time do not show pattern.
	■ Residuals over fits do not show pattern.
	■ No unusual observations (outliers). Consider removing.
	■ No points with influential observations (high leverage points). Consider removing.
R code:	```# Loading necessary packages
install.packages("tidyverse")
library(tidyverse)
install.packages("car")
library(car)
install.packages("olsrr")
library(olsrr)
# Building linear model
stepModel <- lm(Overall~Step1+Step2+Step3+Step4+Step5, data = ClinicSurveyData)
summary(stepModel)
# Determining VIF values (Must be less than 5)
VIF(stepModel)
# Plotting residuals
par(mfrow = c(2, 2))
plot(stepModel)
ols_plot_resid_stud_fit(stepModel)
ols_plot_resid_stand(stepModel)
# Listing outliers
outlierTest(stepModel)```

Table 3.11 Two-Proportion z-test

TWO-PROPORTION TEST	
Data in X:	Discrete X = Groups (1 and 2)
Data in Y:	Discrete Y – Counts
Null Hypothesis H_0:	$P_1 = P_2$
Alternative Hypothesis H_A:	$P_1 \neq P_2$
Decision:	If p-value is < 0.05, reject H_0 and accept H_A.
Assumptions:	Counts in all four cells must be at least 5, i.e. x_1, $n_1 - x_1$, x_2, $n_2 - x_2$ must be at least 5

R code:	```# Loading necessary packages```
	 ```install.packages("stats")```
	 ```library(stats)```
	 ```# Compute the two-proportion z-test```
	 ```result```
	 ```prop.test(x = c(x1, x2), n = c(n1, n2))```
	 ```# x1 … number of successes for group 1```
	 ```# n1 … number of trials for group 1```
	 ```# x2 … number of successes for group 2```
	 ```# n2 … number of trials for group 2```

Table 3.12 Chi^2 test

CHI^2 TEST	
Data in X:	Discrete X = Groups (1, 2 … n)
Data in Y:	Discrete Y – Counts
Null Hypothesis H_0:	$Proportion_1 = Proportion_2 = \ldots = Proportion_n$
Alternative Hypothesis H_A:	At least one proportion $Proportion$ is different.
Decision:	If p-value is < 0.05, reject H_0 and accept H_A.
Assumptions:	Counts in all cells of the cross table must be at least 5.

R code:	```# Loading necessary packages```
	 ```install.packages("rstatix")```
	 ```library(rstatix)```
	
	 ```# Building cross table xtab```
	 ```xtab <- as.table(rbind(```
	 ``` c(59, 131, 93),```
	 ``` c(608, 920, 887)))```
	 ```# Naming rows and columns```
	 ```dimnames(xtab) <- list(```
	 ``` Result = c("nok", "ok"),```
	 ``` Centri = c("G7", "G9", "H10"))```

CHI² TEST

```
# Computing Chi-square-test and saving
it in Xsq
Xsq <- chisq.test(xtab)
# Showing result in Xsq
Xsq
# Showing observed values
Xsq$observed
# Showing expected values
Xsq$expected
# Showing standardised residuals
Xsq$stdres
# Showing pairwise comparison for all
data
pairwise_prop_test(xtab)
# Plotting bar chart for xtab data frame
barplot(xtab, beside=T, legend=T)
```

Practice

- What are requirements on the data acquisition for operations analytics?
- How does one decide which tools for graphical and statistical analysis to apply?
- What are discrete data and continuous data? Name three examples for each.

Please, complete the following steps:

- After conducting a Gage R&R, we know that the data collection has been delivering erroneous results. Remove all data collected by Max and by Wong and reanalyse hypotheses 1 to 6.
- Complete the Chi² test in Hypothesis 7 of the previous case and generate all observed counts, expected counts, and standardised residuals. Please, comment.
- Download the data for this case from www.wiley.com.
- Perform data plots for each X-Y combination.
- Perform statistical analysis for each X-Y combination as described earlier.
- Prepare a short presentation to report the result and your recommendation to the management.

References

Aon. (2003). *Rath & Strong's Six Sigma Leadership Handbook*. Hoboken, NJ: John Wiley & Sons.

Box, G. E. (1976). Science and Statistics. *Journal of the American Statistical Association*, 791–799.

Capgemini. (2017). Operational Analytics: A Strategic Priority that Remains Unexploited. Retrieved from `https://www.capgemini.com/wp-content/uploads/2017/07/going_big-_why_companies_need_to_focus_on_operational_analytics.pdf`

Chew, J. C. (2018, Apr. 2). Making Sense of Test For Equal Variances. Retrieved from: `https://coe-partners.com/test-for-equal-variances/`

Gallo, A. (2018, Oct. 31). 4 Analytics Concepts Every Manager Should Understand. Retrieved from Harvard Business Review: `https://hbr.org/2018/10/4-analytics-concepts-every-manager-should-understand`

Kaufmann, U. H. (2018). *Lean Six Sigma Nuggets: A Fully Commented Project Documentation*. Singapore: Partridge.

Pierce, F. (2011, Sep. 27). Motorola's Six Sigma Journey: In pursuit of perfection. Retrieved from Supply Chain Digital: `https://www.supplychaindigital.com/procurement/motorolas-six-sigma-journey-pursuit-perfection`

Technet. (2014, May). Importance of Usage of Data The $371 Billion Opportunity for "Data Smart" Manufacturers. Retrieved from `https://www.capgemini.com/wp-content/uploads/2017/07/going_big-_why_companies_need_to_focus_on_operational_analytics.pdf`

Tesco saves millions with supply chain analytics. (2013, April 16). Retrieved from Information Age: `https://www.information-age.com/tesco-saves-millions-with-supply-chain-analytics-123456972/`

Woods, D. (2012, Jan. 25). What Is a Data Scientist?: Michael O'Connell of TIBCO Spotfire. *Forbes*. Retrieved from: `https://www.forbes.com/sites/danwoods/2012/01/25/what-is-a-data-scientist-michael-oconnell-of-tibco-spotfire/?sh=43b36099480a`

List of Figures and Tables

Workforce Domain – Workforce Analytics

"I am convinced that nothing we do is more important than hiring and developing people. At the end of the day, you bet on people not on strategies".

(Tichy and Charan, 1995)

Managers are constantly looking to HR to ensure the right people with the right skills, doing the right job at the right time, in the right place. Any data that will help managers make the right workforce decisions instead of fully depending on feelings and instincts are highly valued. In this chapter, we examine how the use of analytics is reshaping the role of HR in workforce decision-making processes. We will also focus on practical implementation and outline examples on unleashing the potential of workforce data in providing businesses the competitive advantage.

CONTENTS

CASE	CASE TITLE	TOOLS USED
7	Do We Have Enough People to Run Our Organisation?	Ex
8	What Makes Our Staff Innovate?	Ex, BI
9	What Does Our Engagement Survey Result Mean?	Ex, R
10	What Drives Our Staff Out?	Ex, R

Tools Used: Ex . . . MS Excel, BI . . . MS Power BI, R . . . R and R Studio

Highlights

After completing this chapter, you will be able to …

- Understand the importance of workforce analytics.
- Determine the dimensions of workforce analytics.
- Appreciate steps to workforce planning.
- Learn how to read, analyse, and present survey results.
- Apply Logistic Regression for decision making.
- Implement workforce analytics in your organisation.

Why Workforce Analytics?

The use of data has become more evident in nearly all functions of any organisation. With the acknowledgement that human talent leads to competitive advantage in a knowledge economy, any data that can help to attract, motivate, and retain the right people is bound to interest business leaders. More and more organisations are becoming involved in workforce analytics as a means for better managing their workforce as well as shaping future business strategies. These developments may not just have positive implications for the organisation, they also promise to elevate the standing of human resource (HR) as a function. HR's credibility increases once it starts using data to inform its decisions.

 Workforce analytics will help HR play a more strategic role in the business.

Workforce analytics uses statistical models and other techniques to analyse workforce-related data to enable leaders to improve the effectiveness of decisions concerning people matters and human resource strategies (Figure 4.1). It covers a larger scale, beyond HR analytics. When we talk about workforce analytics, we consider having data from different sources, whether it be company-specific measurements or data from the industry to address business challenges relating to the workforce. The scope of workforce analytics goes far beyond measuring the impact of HR activities such as recruitment, onboarding, training, performance management, etc.

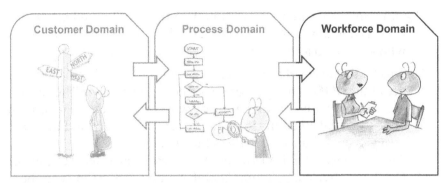

Figure 4.1 Workforce Analytics and its Focus on the Workforce Domain

Many Human Resource (HR) groups have been slow in expanding reporting and analytics capabilities for people-management purposes. The historical focus of reporting and analytical techniques has been in finance, marketing, and operations. Today, this has changed. HR has earned a seat at the boardroom table (Deloitte Touche Tohmatsu Limited, 2020). There are several drivers that make this change necessary and possible at the same time:

- A focus on the workforce is a priority.
- HR is striving to be a strategic function.
- The maturity of IT systems is enabling organisations to do more with their data.

Why has the topic "workforce analytics" developed into a priority?

The need for expanded workforce reporting and analytical capabilities has likely never been as urgent. Workforce-related challenges and issues are renowned on corporate agendas because the "war for talent" has never been so intense as it is now. We see these main reasons for that:

1. The workforce needed to bring the organisation into the future, the **digital-ready workforce is scarce.** In the past, this was a concern for organisations like Google or Amazon. Nowadays, this must be of growing interest for any organisation.

   New technology, like robotic process automation (RPA), for example, can be used to take over repetitive manual jobs like keying the contents of invoices or bills into a system. This RPA is available for a reasonable price. Even programming it is not rocket science. However, how many people are able to train our supervisors or staff to instruct and test RPA? The number of people with these kinds of skills is limited and we have to buy this specialised service externally without building our own competencies. Yet, some types of RPA are amongst the simplest tools under the new banner of AI.

How do we ensure we hire and retain the people needed? Do we have a company culture that attracts talent? Do we have managers who are able to lead this pool of specialised talent?

2. A factor that makes this war even more fierce is the reality that the **tenure of the staff** in an organisation has been **going down**. This means, even if we can find the digital-ready workforce for our organisation now, they will be on the lookout for new challenges and different business environments after less than two years.
    Are we prepared for them leaving after investing in their development? Or do we have a development path set up for them to keep them with the organisation?

3. Today employees are looking to have an experience with the companies they work for. Conventional ways of using employee satisfaction surveys or organisational climate surveys are no longer the only ways to assess the engagement of their new workforce. Many companies are now looking at employees' journeys, study the needs of their workforce, and score to **understand the employee experience**.

4. **Shift in leadership practice** – due to the speed and agility needed in the fourth industrial revolution, the organisational structure will become less dominant. There will be a shift from the command-and-control management style to empowering smaller teams for broader decision-making so that businesses can respond faster to the rapidly changing environment. Leaders will make more use of the power of small teams that can assemble and distribute capabilities and diverse perspectives to quickly make good decisions and produce quality work.

5. The environment, especially the IT and AI ecosystem and tools develop so fast that the **workforce needs to be developed continuously**. The digital-ready workforce of today is only partially ready for tomorrow and might be outdated the day after tomorrow. The main issue is that human capital strategies are not organised, managed, and developed to align people at work. In Thomas Friedman's (2017) book *Thank You for Being Late*, he refers to a graph created by Eric "Astro" Teller, CEO of Alphabet's Google X division, which suggests that technology is increasing in an ever-faster rate while human adaptability rises at a slower rate.
    While we partially agree with his conclusion, we believe individuals do and will adapt to technology very quickly. We think it is critical to understand the relationship between technology and people to effectively navigate the world of human capital. HR has a key role to play in helping leaders and employees to adapt and adopt technology, become accustomed to new models of work and careers.
    Are we planning our workforce and their development continuously? Do we have the right manpower and the right skills for today and tomorrow? Do we know our competency gaps, and do we have a way to assess and close them continuously?

6. AI, Robotics, sensors, and cognitive computing have gone mainstream, along with the war for talent. Companies can no longer consider employees to be the only workforce on their balance sheet but **must include freelancers and "gig economy" workers**. These "on" and "off" balance sheet workers are being augmented by machines and software.

Business leaders are not only looking into using data to understand their current situations but also turning to more evidence-based analysis to reach conclusions that can help HR alter approaches to a broad range of HR challenges, shape their business strategy, and confer their competitive advantage. Hence, we need a comprehensive set of indicators that help us navigate through these challenges in order to win and keep our share of talent to master current and future business challenges.

There are plenty of HR indicators, HR metrics, in practice. Some are generic and used in nearly all kinds of organisation such as turnover rate, staff engagement and satisfaction score, or time to fill and time to hire. Some are industry specific such as sales per employee, revenue per employee, labour cost per employee, or overtime expenses per employee. These rather traditional HR metrics help collect data about HR or HR-related activities.

There are also HR efficiency measures like absenteeism rate, average employee tenure, average turnover, percentage of employees trained per year, cycle time for key HR processes, response time per information request etc. (Becker et al., 2001).

These kinds of measures are no longer enough. We need HR metrics and their link, their data-proven relationship with important business indicators. HR metrics for the sake of HR metrics are obsolete. Workforce metrics in pursuance of the organisation's success is what we need. These metrics have to be used to serve the business. Hence, Business Questions need to be translated into Workforce Analytics that leads to Business Decisions (Figure 4.2).

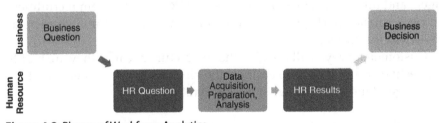

Figure 4.2 Phases of Workforce Analytics

"HR has to continue to deliver value to employees inside and customers, investors and communities outside. The outside-in logic leads HR to create internal organisation capabilities (like agility, customer-centricity, information, culture) that match external conditions. The outside-in logic also encourages HR to source and develop leaders and employees who have the competencies of anticipating and responding to change" wrote Dave Ulrich (Ulrich, 2013).

Let us look at an example.

Figure 4.3 Driver Tree Connecting Quality of Employees and Financial Impact as Result of a Customer Survey

Figure 4.3 highlights a driver tree that shows how business indicators are driven by workforce indicators for a bank. The relationship between retaining returning customer and their perception of value for money from this bank is quite strong with 43%. This means that 43% of variation in customer retention rating can be explained with the variation in rating for value for money. And, of course, each returning customer has some financial impact.

Furthermore, customers perceive *value for money* especially depending on *quality of staff*. This suggests that if these customers stay with this bank, it is highly likely due to the quality of the staff. Quality of staff seems to be even more important than the interest rate. Hence, having competent staff who work fast whilst answering customers' requests the first time with perfect service and support can compensate for higher interest rate. This itself is a particularly important message that can be brought to the management. It should lead to focus on staff training, development, and motivation because this most likely leads to returning customers.

Quality of staff is a survey feedback that is in the responsibility of managers and human resource. It includes all HR activities from recruitment to performance management and creates most value for customers as shown in this model.

Customer surveys will not give the full picture because they are highly subjective and will change easily if the circumstances change. Yet, they give a good indication of what is important and what is not.

 "Far better an approximate answer to the right question, which is often vague, than an exact answer to the wrong question, which can always be made precise"

(*Tukey, 1962*).

Dimensions of Workforce Analytics

Workforce analytics consists of a multitude of metrics that are used for multiple purposes. Some look into the past, some look into the future.

Most of the traditional metrics are used for **descriptive workforce analytics**, i.e., they describe workforce-related matters that have happened already. Descriptive workforce analytics give you the *hindsight* and *insight*, i.e., mining the historical data to look for reasons behind past success or failure. By knowing what was really happening with our workforce and what was driving it, we can optimise their performance through fact-based decision or control. Whilst it is always the objective to learn from metrics and improve the matter of interest, the related metrics are not designed for predicting the future. Turnover numbers collected on a monthly basis is one of these metrics.

Some of the metrics are used for **predictive workforce analytics**, i.e., they help to describe workforce-related matters that prepare future activities. Data from these indicators answer the questions on "What is going to happen?" and "What is likely to happen?". We learn from the past and current data to forecast or predict future actionable outcomes. Sometimes we refer to such analytics as *foresights*. For example, looking into the drivers for turnover may help organisations predict which units have a higher risk of key employees leaving. Predictive workforce analytics therefore enable HR managers to get ahead of the problem by acting wisely.

And there are metrics that collect unstructured text data, for example, interview transcripts, which need qualitative **text analysis** for "sense making" and understanding phenomena and patterns, rather than predicting or explaining.

Putting Workforce Analytics into Practice

Using Descriptive and Predictive Workforce Analytics in Workforce Planning

Workforce planning is the process of matching workforce demand and supply over a foreseeable time. It is a process of identifying the workforce capacity and capability the organisation needs to achieve its objectives now and into the future. Organisations conduct workforce planning that builds upon quantitative activities to ensure the right size workforce, with the right competencies, are placed at the right time and in the right place to deliver the desired organisational outcome.

Workforce planning is not just doing headcount planning. It should be an iterative process during which the workforce plan is reviewed and examined regularly to ensure alignment with organisational plans in order to respond to any changes in business direction. (Tan, 2016). By using business strategy to align shifts in demand with the existing and future supply of human capital, organisations optimise the workforce to meet business goals, increase market share, and improve employee engagement. No plan is totally accurate, the workforce plan needs regular review and update to ensure that approach and tactics are valid and cater for changes in demand and in supply.

 If you do not know the tasks you want to plan workforce for, your workforce planning is at the mercy of chance!

Workforce Planning for Transactional Processes

"Transactional process" refers to a sequence of activities that is executed in a way that guarantees transactional consistency of all activities or a subset of them. For example, industrial processes in manufacturing workshops or on assembly lines show these kinds of characteristics. Similarly, service processes such as loan approvals at banks or processing of payroll or conducting new employee inductions are transactional. For such processes with a fixed pattern and absence of drastic changes it is generally easier to predict workforce requirements. Typically, one would just extrapolate based on the change in demand to predict the workforce strength. However, this method does not mean that the increased number of staff tackle the demand in a more productive or smarter way. To the contrary, it means the new demand is handled the "old way" without any attempt of innovation and improvement. This is unacceptable in the current business environment.

Bending the straight line of correlation between demand and workforce is only possible by reducing the processing time, by working smarter. This means changing processes is at the heart of that (Figure 4.23). Methods like Business Process Reengineering as well as Lean Six Sigma, boosted by innovation tools, form the foundation for looking into processes – with remarkable success (Tan, 2015).

Workforce Planning for Less Transactional Processes

"But every day we handle different applications; no two applications are the same" is a common response when employees from less transactional environments are asked to describe what they do. It seems that planning the workforce for environments with a range of different tasks with apparently little repeatability is impossible.

But is it?

A good portion of obviously non-transactional processes with no repeatability show a certain degree of pattern, i.e., structure – just on a larger scale. For example, customer applications for approval of import of certain devices are totally different from Monday to Friday. Even from January to February there is little evidence that the cycle repeats. However, the percentage of simple, medium, and complex applications turns out to be repeatable and with it the amount of time needed to do the job.

It must be taken into account that the demand variation in this sort of environment is much higher and it has to be planned for it. At the same time, studies have shown that the working pattern on this kind of task is different to the pure transactional tasks driven partially by the environment and type of staff doing these non-transactional types of job.

Predicting the workforce for a less transactional activity such as policy writing, processing of complex applications, or managing employee engagement, etc. seems to be harder since the activities have much more variability in processing time needed. However, it pays off to collect information on the big picture, i.e., the demand variation over time, and on the sequence of work in order to understand what people actually do during their office hours.

And wouldn't it be better if we had more structure in the so-called unstructured processes anyway? *Go to Gemba* and study how the work gets done. You will certainly learn something new, that usually leads to better planning and forecasting. Refrain from conducting "data collection" in the meeting room.

GOING TO GEMBA IS KEY

During our interviews of the HR people in a public service organisation with nearly 7,000 staff, we met with many job holders, and Julia was one of them.

"Julia, tell me about your job. What do you do?"

"I handle leave application", and after a pause "Since the leave application process is fully automated, I am rather responsible for calculating all exceptions the system is not able to handle. Especially, when we have people resigning, it is not straight forward to calculate their rest leave or encashment. They call me because I am the specialist in this. They really trust me".

"What else do you do?"

"This is it. This has been my job for 15 years and I am really good in that. In case I am on leave myself, Joanna is backing me up. I have trained her, and we do this job together".

We learned that this organisation has two people only responsible for leave calculation.

And, they have two people dedicated to flexible benefit processing.

Additionally, they have the same setup for personal records entry and another one for medical benefits processing.

"Julia, I guess your job is rather seasonal. And the job of your colleagues is seasonal as well. Do you help them when you have a low demand?"

"No, I cannot. I am not trained for that, because that is not my job. I am the specialist for leave calculation!"

This organisation can afford to have eight full time staff specialised on four areas of work that are more or less satisfying seasonal demand.

Now the good news: When this project of business process reengineering and change management was approaching the finish line, we met Julia again for the wrap up. She was all smiles and told us proudly:

"I have started training to be able to handle other tasks in my department. This will make me more flexible and employable. Great!"

Benchmarking is a way of gathering data about best practices in workforce allocation. Even here, there is a need to support numbers with Gemba visits. Numbers can be grossly misleading if the underlying details are not considered, not studied, and hence not known. This may result in wrong assumptions about workforce utilisation, allocation, and competency.

Workforce Planning from the Workforce Perspective

In addition to the collection of process-related data, it could make sense to ask the question "What is my staff busy with?"

There are high chances that in addition to the transactions listed following the previous approaches, we will detect activities that are not listed yet. Some of them may never be listed since they are not core and sometimes not even known by managers.

However, when asking employees to list down the time spent per activity or task, they would take the opportunity to justify that they are "busy with" by recording the details. Such data collection can be part of the appraisal session when the job description (JD) is on the table showing the key result areas (KRA), i.e., key activities that are done by the employee. After going through the list discussing the performance for each KRA, the staff member will most likely add to the list "In addition, I do this and this and that".

We came to the conclusion that workforce planning based only on the listed activities for core and support processes may do our workforce a disservice. And, if our staff members smell that they are only measured on what is written in their JD, attempts to introduce a flexible workforce will most likely fail.

After asking all employees of a mid-sized service organisation what activities they are busy with over a year, a list of more than 20,000 steps was the result. Figure 4.4 shows a snippet of this given by personnel working at a recruitment function.

This includes the hierarchy of the activities from the **Department** down to the **Step**. Additionally, the number of **repetitions per year** is listed. For many functions this is not too hard to estimate since all steps are usually linked to an outcome like number of people interviewed and recruited. In column **Time**, the duration of this step is estimated in hours, whereas **VATime** determines how much of the Time is value-added.

Furthermore, the information pack incorporates the use of workforce per job grade (**JG1 to JG13**), shown in Figure 4.5. For instance, "Gathering job requirements from hiring manager" involves staff from four different

SN	Department	Section	MainActivity	SubActivity	PerYear	Step	Time	VATime
1	Dept A	Recruitment	Talent Acquisition	Recruitment Planning	122	Gather job requirements from hiring manager	02:30	02:00
2	Dept A	Recruitment	Talent Acquisition	Recruitment Planning	122	Prepare job description, with concurrence from hiring manager	00:30	00:20
3	Dept A	Recruitment	Talent Acquisition	Recruitment Planning	122	Prepare job posting materials	00:20	00:20
4	Dept A	Recruitment	Talent Acquisition	Searching	122	Upload job posting on various sourcing portals	01:00	01:00
5	Dept A	Recruitment	Talent Acquisition	Searching	122	Conduct pro-active search concurrently, i.e Database search, Linkedin Profile	01:30	01:30
6	Dept A	Recruitment	Talent Acquisition	Screening	122	Shortlist candidates based on job requirements	06:00	06:00
7	Dept A	Recruitment	Talent Acquisition	Screening	17	Conduct preliminary phone interview. Screening to review and shortlist potent	00:30	00:30
8	Dept A	Recruitment	Talent Acquisition	Screening	17	Form interview panel and map out interview schedules	02:00	02:00
9	Dept A	Recruitment	Talent Acquisition	Screening	17	Contact shortlisted candidates for interview	03:00	03:00
10	Dept A	Recruitment	Talent Acquisition	Screening	17	Receive candidate. Verify and ensure that required documents are submitted	00:45	00:45

Figure 4.4 Workforce Analysis Listing – Activities

Source: Used with permission from Microsoft.

SN	HCneeded	JG1	JG2	JG3	JG4	JG5	JG6	JG7	JG8	JG9	JG10	JG11	JG12	JG13	AutoAsIs	AutoToBe
1	1				0.35		0.35		0.15		0.15				1	1
2	1				0.35		0.35		0.15		0.15				3	3
3	1				0.35		0.35		0.15		0.15				1	2
4	1				0.35		0.35		0.15		0.15				1	4
5	1				0.15		0.15		0.35		0.35				2	4
6	1				0.35		0.35		0.15		0.15				2	2
7	1				0.30		0.50		0.10		0.10				3	3
8	1				1.00										1	1
9	1				1.00										1	1
10	1					1.00									2	2

Figure 4.5 Workforce Analysis Listing – Staff Allocation and Automation

Source: Used with permission from Microsoft.

job grades. Info about current (**AutoAsIs**) and potential automation (**Auto-ToBe**) for each process step is included as well.

Asking staff members to give this comprehensive data in a useful quality with as little as possible bias requires a training of all involved parties. For example, the definition of non-value-added steps is not easily understood without some explanation. Yet, this entry offers the staff the chance to state that there is a part of the work without an obvious benefit or need. This hints to improvement opportunities.

The indication of automation status and its potential follows a Likert scale from 1 for Completely Manual to 5 for Fully Automated. These indicators give staff another opportunity to highlight improvement potential. As you see from Figure 4.5, this recruitment team has emphasised that "Upload job posting on various sourcing portals" can be highly automated. Often enough, the potential solution for automation is given as comment by the staff. This helps identifying digitisation opportunities and solution ideas.

When prepared and conducted well, this kind of workforce analysis not only deliver an idea about activities that take most of the time but also show room for reengineering the organisation or function in scope.

When translating the listed time (Figure 4.6) into Full Time Equivalent (FTE) staff numbers, the weakness of this kind of data collection becomes obvious: most staff members show that they are really busy, i.e., they overstate the time they spend on activities. Nevertheless, the collected data is good enough for many purposes.

For instance, by searching text entries in steps, sub and main activities for related text, certain categories of activities can be identified and analysed. Figure 4.7 shows on the left such results for all activities that are associated with "Dealing with Issues". Even if the numbers might not be 100% correct,

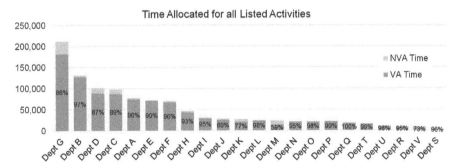

Figure 4.6 Time Allocation for All Activities

Figure 4.7 Analysis Result: Time Spent on Non-Core Activities at Department K

the steps that are tagged with this label deserve to be further analysed. No organisation should spend a significant amount of time on dealing with issues. The related activities and steps are all non-value-added although not always marked as such by the information provider.

When comparing all departments regarding their time spent on dealing with issues, the degree of improvement potential per department becomes obvious (Figure 4.8). One of these departments is IT, whose business is to deal with issues of hardware and software for all other units. In this case, a significant percentage of this indicator is justified. All other departments need to work on overcoming the root causes for such activities since they are most likely not their core activities nor value-added in any way.

Other results of text search deliver an indication for time spent on (Figure 4.7)

1. Review, verification, approval, check, and submission,
2. Meetings, of which some seem unnecessary and some cross-department meetings seem to be attended by multiple participants from the same department,
3. Procurement-related activities since this organisation seems to spend too much time on those.

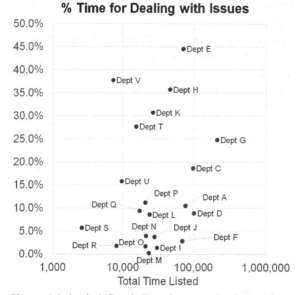

Figure 4.8 Analysis Result: Time Spent on Dealing with Issues Per Department

When analysing the data collected about automation status and potential (Figure 4.9), significant improvement and innovation opportunities are uncovered. Of course, not every implicit staff suggestion can be implemented. Yet, enough immediate, mid-term, and long-term actions can be derived based on automation potential (AutoPot) and major automation potential (Major AutoPot) stated by staff.

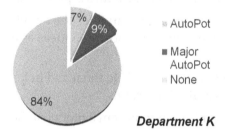

% of Time with Automation Potential

Department K

Figure 4.9 Analysis Result: Time with Automation Potential for Department K

Finally, data about the allocation of staff with certain job grades provides an overview like shown at Figure 4.10. Interesting enough, this analysis result does not match exactly the real staff working at this department.

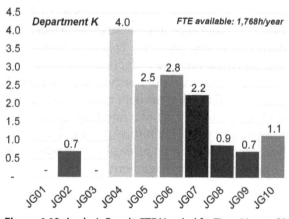

FTE Needed per Job Grade

Figure 4.10 Analysis Result: FTE Needed for Time Mapped by Job Grade for Department K

There are reasons for that. For instance, estimating the time spent per activity is not easy. As mentioned, most people may have the tendency to show that they are really busy resulting in the sum of time listed by them is much more than the 1768 hours we expect an employee to spend per year on the job. On the other hand, they might be very busy and "clock" much more than their office hours for the organisation.

This can be observed easily when they work in the office. Nowadays, working from home becomes more popular for nearly all working environments. Then there is no way for the supervisor to watch staff working overtime. This perceived disadvantage turns into an advantage when supervisors learn to lead by objectives instead of micro-managing.

This method of workforce analysis and the data gathered yield a list of advantages:

1. By collecting data from the perspective of the staff doing the work, a more comprehensive picture of organisational activities is produced.

2. Encouraging staff to highlight automation potential for the activities listed by them delivers improvement and innovation ideas as a side-product.

3. Urging staff to list non-value-added steps signals to them and helps the organisation focus on what is really important.

4. The sum of all activities in the organisation represent a model of the way the organisation works.

The result of this workforce analysis can be used during the appraisal discussion in many ways. Firstly, it might help to complete the list of KRAs in job descriptions. Secondly, it might also enable supervisors to better balance workload. Finally, the discussion could include their suggestions of innovative changes in their work processes supported by the necessary capability build-up.

With the information gathered that way, a rich foundation for organisation-wide workforce planning and capability development is available.

In this example, the underlying model was built completely in MS Excel with some visualisations done using MS Power BI. This way, there is no need to get familiar with new software for data collection.

Whilst MS Excel is not a database system, it often serves this purpose. A cloud-based solution with a relational database is better suited to support this workforce analysis. Building the model is not a one-time event since part of the data will be outdated very soon. Therefore, this model should be amended frequently. These amendments can be easily done when it is used for discussions during performance management.

Getting the Intent Right

Data alone do not have any meaning and will waste the time of staff collecting it and of managers looking at it. First, do a simple check by asking the following questions:

- Which of the data you collect every month have been looked at by non-HR people frequently? If no one is asking for it, there is a good chance that they are not considered of any value to the organisation.

- Which of the data you collect every month have been used for analytics, i.e., for analysing trends, relationships to other business indicators, forecasts for planning purpose?

- Which of the data you collect every month have been used for decision making, directly or indirectly, outside HR?

The list of data that make it through all three filters is usually quite short. Next, ask this question "What is the purpose of collecting this data?".

More often than not the sobering answer is "We collect a lot of data and we want to know what to do with it". This answer implies the same result as mentioned before: we have data and we do not use it.

To make workforce analytics work, i.e., make it a part of management decision making. Here are the basic steps needed to get started:

a) Connect HR Data and Business Outcomes

Do not look for a business problem that fits the data you have at hand. Begin with a business question the organisation wants or needs to answer (Figure 4.2). For example, "How can we increase employees' innovative job performance?" or "How can we grow our market share?" A specific question or problem will help determine what data or statistical models are needed.

The latter question does not really concern HR, right?

That is where we were often wrong. In most private and public organisations, the processes are heavily influenced by the workforce. It should be a basic assumption, that HR can do their share in any business situation.

Consider this:

All hardware and software in your organisation might be of a certain value. However, if hard- or software breaks down, gets stolen, or is not available for other reasons, you are able to replace it with little effect on the outcome. Hardware or software do not count as major differentiators in today's business environment. You do not win because of having the better systems.

However, can you say this about the workforce? Can you replace the workforce who was setting up and running this hardware or software easily? Can you effortlessly replace the team of leaders who keep the show running?

This is rather difficult. Therefore, everything in the organisation is driven by workforce and measured with related indicators. Many companies, especially in the retail and services sectors, need to have credible and comprehensive data to allocate their workforce in real time as a way of optimising work schedules and workflow. Retailers such as Amazon, Noel Gifts International, etc., use analytics to predict incoming orders as well as adjust their hourly employees' schedules to maximise efficiency and resource planning.

Even with the introduction of artificial intelligence (AI) we do not replace the workforce. We just bring them up in the value chain and redesign their jobs. For instance, the workforce who previously inputted incoming invoices and bills into the system is now programming RPA to do their rather boring jobs. Most workforce is able to do this . . . with our help and our consideration.

b) Determine Information Needed and Collect Data

What information is needed to tackle the business problem? Chances are that you need additional data. Often, collection of new data to describe previously unobserved behaviour has to be done in an iterative approach. Let us assume you want to help the business grow its market share, and the situation is similar to what is shown in Figure 4.3.

Step 1: Identify Potential Drivers for the Problem

Before you start collecting data, you need to develop some hypothesis, together with process stakeholders who are very familiar with the organisation and typical customer and staff behaviour. These hypotheses point to potential drivers or relationships and hence, to the data needed.

Hypotheses could be:

"The market share is driven by returning customers who perceive us delivering value for money".

"The extent of customer satisfaction and sales ratio is attributed by employee and management engagement".

"Older employees bring about higher business performance".

"Customers return, if they like the treatment by our staff".

"For customers, fast treatment is the most important criteria".

Step 2: Run Pilot Data Collection and Analyse

After having these hypotheses, the data collection can start. It is recommended to collect a pilot set of data to check whether there is a pattern visible. It might be necessary to change the approach, the questions, or the scope after learning from the pilot.

Especially data collection via newly developed surveys needs to be tested. After having some pilot data, this can be used to check validity and reliability of the survey instrument. Amendments of the survey questions might be necessary.

The pilot data may not show significant relationships between the factors involved due to a limited sample size. However, some trends should be visible.

The pilot data collected for the model shown in Figure 4.3 were used to run confirmatory factor analysis and Cronbach's Alpha and led to a change of the survey instrument.

Often, it is of an advantage to sketch out which analysis and visualisation tools are supposed to be used after data collection. Assuming the model used for data collection consists of a certain number of X-Y-relationships, the sample size for data collection can be decided. Tools used for analysis and plots need a certain number of datasets and a certain arrangement of the data. Beginning with the end in mind may save time and avoid frustration.

Step 3: Conduct Full-Scale Data Collection

After amending the instrument based on pilot data, the full-scale data collection can start.

In order to increase participation, data collection can be supported by cloud solutions and mobile phone apps.

For example, some simple AI can help to collect data from by-passing customers at the entrance of the bank. Some of them might enjoy talking to an Alexa-like device.

c) Analyse the Data

Analysing survey data is usually not complicated when the survey has been designed with the analysis in mind. There are plenty of tools at hand to get the data analysed.

If it is not a one-time event but a continuous data collection and analysis to detect changing customer behaviour and sentiments over time, data collection and analysis can be taught to a machine (machine learning) that automatically runs analysis whenever new data come in. This is an especially interesting concept since survey data are usually considered lagging data. By continuously collecting and analysing it, trends can be detected early.

d) Derive and Formulate a Business Answer – Tell a Story

Formulating a conclusion and recommendation out of the analysis results is the final step. As Figure 4.3 reveals, quality of staff is the strongest lever when it comes to customer satisfaction and retention and finally financial gain. If the survey is structured well, it delivers hints about the elements of quality of staff that are most important for customers. Now management and HR can do their job to work on these elements.

The sales people always said that our loan interest rate is too high. Our customers replied with their perspectives. It seems, spending money on staff development is smarter than reducing the interest rate.

☞ *You do not have to be the cheapest if you have the best people.*

Put your findings in a story. Do not overwhelm your colleagues with statistics. They trust you have done your job. Just give them the findings in a language they understand.

Workforce Analysts' Paradise is Employees' Nightmare – Managing the Change

The primary objective of developing capabilities in workforce analytics is to increase organisational effectiveness. Workforce analytics is a journey, not a destination. When trying to develop useful models for workforce analytics, you will sooner or later run into a prevalent problem: Workforce data are not easily available. Or better, the available data are often not the ones you want to have. The key is to get the staff supporting your data acquisition efforts. However, as soon as your employees know that you are going to collect data about them and how they do their work, they may become worried and we might end up with bias representation of information.

> Once, we were working with a client to identify future competencies and plan for the capability and capacity needed to achieve the organisational vision. HR communicated the initiative as "strategic workforce planning". We ended up spending hours in assuring the staff that the exercise of asking them to list down their current work and resources involved was not intended for downsizing.

Thus, it is important to first define the opportunities or problems that will associate with the organisational outcome when conducting workforce analytics. Start with a workforce problem or question that the organisation wants or needs to solve.

Secondly, the workforce analyst should expand reporting and analytics capabilities for people-management purpose and determine what information managers or executives would need in order to make a decision about the problem or question at hand. Simply producing a set of numbers from predictive workforce analytics holds little value to management because there is often no action to take. Data must be placed in context. For example, an organisation's "turnover for newly hired management trainees is 13%" is more meaningful when it can be placed in the context of the organisation's previous turnover history for this position. Is turnover raising or falling for this position, and if so, how quickly?

Thirdly, when packaging the analytics, the workforce analyst must understand the needs of the recipients and fit the data to the information needs of the decision maker. Analytics information can be reported in several ways. Generally, a combination of "push" and "pull" means of communication will work for most organisations.

Push communication channels such as email, actively promote **just-in-time information** and analyses to the attention of managers. These channels are used for information that is time critical or that the manager is unaware of. Push systems are excellent for getting information to decision makers. However, sending irrelevant information or poorly timed information through push systems can contribute to information over-load and may reduce managers' sensitivity to the messages. As a result, they may only skim the information sent through push systems, or even worst, not attend to it at all.

Pull channels, on the other hand, are ways of making **just-in-case** information available to managers so that they can access it at any point in time when it is most useful for their decision making. Examples include: (i) posting metrics and analytics reports on internal websites, (ii) offer access to searchable repositories, (iii) provide access to analytic tools such as Power BI, Tableau, etc. Such pull methods avoid cluttering email in-boxes, but it might be ineffective when not marketed well because managers may not know what information is available or when or where to look for it.

Fourthly, how frequently data is analysed and reported, and how narrowly data should be packaged are also important considerations. Creating reporting cycles that are too long produces lagging information and risks losing opportunities for making changes. Aggregating too much data from sub-units to higher-level units can result in the problem of causing difference between operating units, departments, or functions to be buried in the aggregated averages for the higher unit. This will, in turn, render information useless for lower-level managers.

Lastly, be willing to learn. Organisations that have an analytics function will develop an appetite for experimentation to try out new HR activities, programmes, or processes. One possible unintended consequence would be the on-going opportunity to recognise that there may be a better way to do things. To manage this, an organisation can consider setting up an *analytics laboratory* where HR professionals can experiment with new ways of analyses and test existing assumptions. This way, they can extract the full potential and insights from the available data, allow new analytics and metrics to be created as well as develop innovative thinking capabilities.

Summary

The central focus of this chapter was to define the domain of workforce analytics and discuss how it can contribute to improving organisational effectiveness. HR metrics are data elements that add to analysis by providing information to help make better decisions. Without meeting this objective, HR metrics and analytics activities provide no return on the organisation's investment.

Therefore, focusing on the development of HR metrics and workforce analytics around important organisational issues and opportunities is likely to increase the possibility of significant returns for the organisations. Hence, organisations can benefit greatly by employing powerful workforce analytics to back objective decisions that lead to saving cost and time.

As in all functions, HR will need to become better equipped to handle data analytics than is currently the case. This doesn't mean that HR practitioners need to become data scientists. But in a more data-centred world, they will certainly need to understand general statistical analysis and be able to translate findings in a way that the business leaders can relate to.

Do not forget: Human intervention and intuition are also mandatory for successful workforce analytics. Leaving workforce analytics to data scientists with a statistics mindset equipped with fancy software without business acumen and a hand for people will not work.

In the next section, we will illustrate workforce analytics on cases in practice.

Practice

- What makes workforce analytics more important than ever before?
- What is the difference between HR analytics and workforce analytics?
- What are different types of workforce planning?
- How is workforce analytics conducted?
- Why is it important to consider change management activities before workforce analytics is implemented?

Case 7: Do We Have Enough People to Run Our Organisation? – Workforce Planning Inside-Out

Staff members complain about having too much work. The proportion of people on short-term sick leave is consistently high. And the turnover rate is disturbingly elevated. Do these symptoms indicate that you need to increase your staffing (Tan, 2016)?

A polyclinic around the corner was facing this kind of problem. After presenting this issue to the board, the response was "Show your workforce planning before we approve additional headcount".

We analysed more than 51,000 entries of patients visiting the polyclinic and established patient demand patterns per time window as well as the characteristics of the duration of procedures performed by the doctors. Understanding demand characteristics and process parameters enables workforce planning. This case focuses on examining the variation in the two metrics to develop successful strategies for effective workforce optimisation. MS Excel and its Analysis ToolPak have been deployed for this purpose.

Data Acquisition and Data Wrangling

Predicting the workforce for the future is based on historical data that needs to be analysed. Fortunately, the full set of data from January to December 2019 is readily available for analysis. This data however only cover the details for patients and one of the steps of the patients' journey

ID	Procedure	Date	StartTime	EndTime
190000001	General	03 01 2019	09:05:00	09:15:00
190000002	Procedure1	03 01 2019	09:14:00	10:25:00
190000005	Procedure2	03 01 2019	09:20:00	10:20:00
190000009	Procedure2	03 01 2019	09:30:00	10:40:00
190000010	Procedure2	03 01 2019	09:32:00	11:44:00
190000014	Procedure2	03 01 2019	09:37:00	10:35:00
190000018	Procedure1	03 01 2019	09:45:00	10:30:00

Figure 4.11 Raw Data for Clinic Visits from 03 Jan to 31 Dec 2019

Source: Used with permission from Microsoft.

through the clinic. Out of the five steps – registration, screening, treatment, medicine dispensing, and payment/checkout – there is only timing data for the most important step, the treatment by the doctor. This treatment is categorised in General, a short consultation about small issues like flu or infection, and two procedures, that characterise more elaborate treatment cycles offered by this clinic.

So, firstly, we check what we have. Figure 4.11 shows the data downloaded from the system. Figure 4.12 gives an extended set of this data.

How do we know whether our data is of good "quality", i.e., is valid? There are some entries we cannot check. For example, the StartTime and EndTime stamps originate from the doctor or nurse receiving the patient (StartTime) and completing consultation (EndTime) of the patient who is referred to them physically and electronically by the registration desk.

TASK 4.1   GET AN OVERVIEW OF THE DATA

1. Open the clinic visit data in file ClinicVisit.xlsx in worksheet Visit.

2. Ensure table is formatted as Excel Table by pointing inside table Home – Format as Table – Select Format – Check My Table has Headers

3. Name the table by pointing inside table Table Design – Name Table "Visit". Ensure Header Row and Filter Button are checked.

4. Add column TimeStamp: =[@Date]+[@StartTime]

5. Add column Duration: =([@EndTime]-[@StartTime])*60*24

6. Add column TimeSlot: =IF([@StartTime]>18/24," 18-19",
   IF([@StartTime]>17/24," 17-18",IF([@StartTime]>16/24," 16-17",
   IF([@StartTime]>15/24," 15-16",IF([@StartTime]>14/24," 14-15",
   IF([@StartTime]>13/24," 13-14",IF([@StartTime]>12/24," 12-13",
   IF([@StartTime]>11/24," 11-12",IF([@StartTime]>10/24," 10-11"," 09-10")))))))))

7. Add column DOW: =WEEKDAY([@Date],2) & " " & TEXT([@Date],"ddd"). This ensures our weekday DOW is always sorted from Mon to Sun.

8. Add column Survey: =IF(ISERROR(VLOOKUP([@ID], ClinicSurvey.xlsx! Unstacked[#Data],8,FALSE)),"", VLOOKUP([@ID],ClinicSurvey.xlsx!Unstacked [#Data],8,FALSE)). This formula looks up the survey result for the respective patient if available.

TimeStamp	ID	Procedure	Date	StartTime	EndTime	TimeSlot	DOW	Duration	Survey
03 01 2019 09:05	190000001	Procedure2	03 01 2019	09:05:00	11:05:00	09-10	4 Thu	120	
03 01 2019 09:14	190000002	Procedure1	03 01 2019	09:14:00	10:25:00	09-10	4 Thu	71	
03 01 2019 09:15	190000003	General1	03 01 2019	09:15:00	09:22:00	09-10	4 Thu	7	
03 01 2019 09:19	190000004	General1	03 01 2019	09:19:00	09:28:00	09-10	4 Thu	9	
03 01 2019 09:20	190000005	Procedure2	03 01 2019	09:20:00	10:20:00	09-10	4 Thu	60	
03 01 2019 09:25	190000006	General1	03 01 2019	09:25:00	09:33:00	09-10	4 Thu	8	
03 01 2019 09:25	190000007	General1	03 01 2019	09:25:00	09:35:00	09-10	4 Thu	10	
03 01 2019 09:25	190000008	General1	03 01 2019	09:25:00	09:34:00	09-10	4 Thu	9	
03 01 2019 09:30	190000009	Procedure2	03 01 2019	09:30:00	10:40:00	09-10	4 Thu	70	
03 01 2019 09:32	190000010	Procedure2	03 01 2019	09:32:00	11:44:00	09-10	4 Thu	132	

Figure 4.12 Raw Data for Clinic Visits Extended

Source: Used with permission from Microsoft.

On the one hand, whether the doctor prompts the patient's StartTime and EndTime accurately, is rather questionable. On the other hand, if there is a next patient, the timing should be quite truthful because of some Poka Yoke in the process.

There are some tools available to help us check the data. It is always a good and easy start to get an overview of minimum and maximum of the data in each Excel table column. When selecting the filter button of a column, the list of entries appears (Figure 4.13). This reveals that StartTime starts with an entry at 06:54h. Since this is far earlier than the opening time of the clinic, this entry cannot be correct.

When scrolling down, the last StartTime entry is at 21:45h. This could be possible under some circumstances. Let us dig a bit deeper. After selecting only the patient entries with StartTime later than 21:15h (Figure 4.14), we recognise that all of them fall on the same day, 27 August 2019. Now

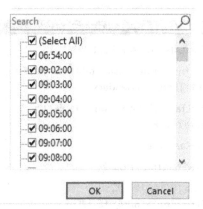

Figure 4.13 Filter for StartTime

Source: Used with permission from Microsoft.

TimeStamp	ID	Procedure	Date	StartTime	EndTime	TimeSlot	DOW	Duration	Survey
27 08 2019 21:45	190047065	General2	27 08 2019	21:45:00	21:51:00	18-19	2 Tue	6	
27 08 2019 21:42	190047064	General2	27 08 2019	21:42:00	21:51:00	18-19	2 Tue	9	
27 08 2019 21:36	190047063	General2	27 08 2019	21:36:00	21:46:00	18-19	2 Tue	10	
27 08 2019 21:35	190047062	General2	27 08 2019	21:35:00	21:44:00	18-19	2 Tue	9	
27 08 2019 21:30	190047061	General2	27 08 2019	21:30:00	21:36:00	18-19	2 Tue	6	
27 08 2019 21:25	190047059	General2	27 08 2019	21:25:00	21:37:00	18-19	2 Tue	12	
27 08 2019 21:25	190047060	General2	27 08 2019	21:25:00	21:32:00	18-19	2 Tue	7	
27 08 2019 21:17	190047058	General2	27 08 2019	21:17:00	21:27:00	18-19	2 Tue	10	
27 08 2019 21:16	190047057	General2	27 08 2019	21:16:00	21:25:00	18-19	2 Tue	9	

Figure 4.14 Patient Entries with StartTime later than 21:15h

Source: Used with permission from Microsoft.

business knowledge is important, which tells us that from time to time we have days when the clinic is full, and we exceed normal opening hours to serve everyone. This was one of those days.

Since Duration is calculated out of EndTime minus StartTime, Duration is another indicator for the potential correctness of StartTime and EndTime. Selecting the filter for duration discloses that there are entries that cannot make sense. Selecting these entries and filtering our dataset helps us to see the full picture of consultation & treatment durations that must be incorrect (Figure 4.15).

TimeStamp	ID	Procedure	Date	StartTime	EndTime	TimeSlot	DOW	Duration	Survey
13 04 2019 14:56	190027511	General2	13 04 2019	14:56:00	13:05:00	14-15	6 Sat	-111	
21 12 2019 14:56	190076361	General2	21 12 2019	14:56:00	13:05:00	14-15	6 Sat	-111	
03 08 2019 16:37	190044240	General2	03 08 2019	16:37:00	14:48:00	16-17	6 Sat	-109	
19 04 2019 15:56	190028360	General2	19 04 2019	15:56:00	14:07:00	15-16	5 Fri	-109	
27 12 2019 15:56	190077211	General2	27 12 2019	15:56:00	14:07:00	15-16	5 Fri	-109	
27 05 2019 14:49	190034659	General2	27 05 2019	14:49:00	13:05:00	14-15	1 Mon	-104	
03 08 2019 17:51	190044332	General2	03 08 2019	17:51:00	17:26:00	17-18	6 Sat	-25	
04 05 2019 13:57	190030789	General2	04 05 2019	13:57:00	13:48:00	13-14	6 Sat	-9	
28 06 2019 14:43	190038890	General2	28 06 2019	14:43:00	14:35:00	14-15	5 Fri	-8	
14 08 2019 16:48	190045418	General2	14 08 2019	16:48:00	16:47:00	16-17	3 Wed	-1	
15 02 2019 16:35	190012618	General1	15 02 2019	16:35:00	16:36:00	16-17	5 Fri	1	
28 02 2019 12:18	190017272	General2	28 02 2019	12:18:00	12:20:00	12-13	4 Thu	2	
13 02 2019 11:19	190011224	General2	13 02 2019	11:19:00	17:26:00	11-12	3 Wed	367	
23 10 2019 11:19	190060074	General2	23 10 2019	11:19:00	17:26:00	11-12	3 Wed	367	
04 06 2019 12:10	190035986	Procedure2	04 06 2019	12:10:00	18:30:00	12-13	2 Tue	380	
23 01 2019 06:54	190005582	General2	23 01 2019	06:54:00	17:00:00	09-10	3 Wed	606	
02 10 2019 06:54	190054432	General2	02 10 2019	06:54:00	17:00:00	09-10	3 Wed	606	

Figure 4.15 Patient Entries with Unexplainable Duration
Source: Used with permission from Microsoft.

Because some of these entries were obviously added manually, the correction should be quite easy. For example, on Saturday, 13 April 2019, the consultation with ID 190027511 started at 14:56h and most likely ended at 15:05h. With this approach, many typos can be corrected. If the correction is not possible, it is prudent to delete the entry. The impact of a handful of deleted entries out of more than 40,000 is negligible. Sometimes, deleting questionable entries (data sets) is a better solution than diving into old data files to find out what really happened.

Asking clerks or nurses to search, check, and correct old data for the sake of having a complete picture should be kept to critically important issues. This is not the case here. Requesting help from people who are "busy with their real work" should be explained properly.

Understanding the Demand Pattern

The workforce analysis is concentrated on understanding the demand pattern, i.e., the number of patients over time.

Everyone expects a certain pattern of demand over weekdays and anticipates peak demand on Fridays. And everyone would assume that most walk-in customers show up around lunch time – similar to many other service providers. This knowledge is used for the allocation of the workforce for different weekdays and for the opening hours over a day. And this is what the management of this service provider does very professionally. However, this did not result in higher customer satisfaction nor employee engagement. Why?

The real problem lies in the variation of the demand pattern (Figure 4.16).

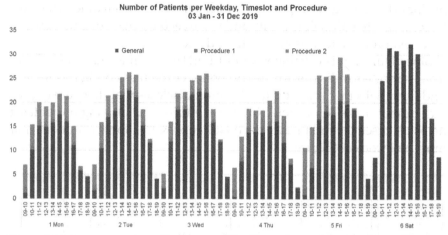

Figure 4.16 Average number of Patients per TimeSlot and Day of the Week for Different Treatment

The resulting column chart (Figure 4.16) shows the average number of patients per timeslot per day of the week.

For example, the average number of patients between 14:00h and 15:00h on a Friday is 29. Knowing this pattern would help with planning the doctors, nurses, pharmacists, and clerks. With these numbers, we could calculate a takt time for this time slot:

This takt time (Equation 4.1) means that, in average, every 2.07 minutes a new patient appears in the door. If we want to have no waiting time, we

---

TASK 4.2   PLOT A STACKED BAR CHART FOR PATIENTS PER TIMESLOT PER DOW

- Open the prepared and cleaned data out of Task 4.1.

- Position your cursor within table "Visit" and Insert – PivotTable.

- Pivot table rows are Date, DOW, TimeSlot. Pivot table column is Procedure. Pivot table value is Count of ID.

- Select Pivot table – right click Pivot Table Options – Totals & Filters – unselect all totals, Display – select classic Pivot Table Layout.

- Amend Field Settings for Date and DOW in Layout & Print, check Repeat Item Labels.

- Put a table next to the Pivot table and copy all contents. Name the new table "PatientsPerTimeSlot".

- In your table PatientsPerTimeSlot, Insert – PivotChart.

- Pivot chart rows are DOW, TimeSlot. Pivot table values are Average of General, Average of Procedure1, Average of Procedure2.

- Select Stacked Column Chart.

must have been done with the previous patient. Since this is hardly the case, we need to have multiple resources available.

Equation 4.1: Takt time for Fridays between 14:00h and 15:00h (all Treatments)

$$Takt = \frac{Available\ Time}{Demand} = \frac{60\,min}{29\,Patients} = 2.07\,min$$

The number of patients, the demand, for that Friday time slot is made out of 20 patients for General treatment, 1 for Procedure 1 and 8 for Procedure 2. If these three categories need different resources, i.e., different skills and experiences (competencies), the takt time is better calculated for each treatment:

Equation 4.2: Takt time for Fridays between 14:00h and 15:00h (by Treatment)

$$Takt_{General} = \frac{Available\ Time}{Demand_{General}} = \frac{60\,min}{20\,Patients} = 3\,min$$

$$Takt_{Procedure1} = \frac{Available\ Time}{Demand_{Procedure1}} = \frac{60\,min}{1\,Patient} = 60\,min$$

$$Takt_{Procedure2} = \frac{Available\ Time}{Demand_{Procedure2}} = \frac{60\,min}{8\,Patients} = 7.5\,min$$

☞ Takt time is an indicator specifying the available time per customer request. Namely, if you expect 200 customers (demand) per day and you are "open for business" for 10 hours (available time), takt time equals to three minutes per customer. All process steps involved need to be done within takt time. Consequently, process steps exceeding takt time require multiple resources. In other words, a process step that takes around 15 minutes requires at least five, better yet six resources.

Assuming a General consultation takes about 1 minute of registration time, 2 minutes of screening time and usually around 8.5 minutes for consultation, the workforce requirement (FTE) for this situation would be as follows:

Equation 4.3: Workforce Calculation for Fridays between 14:00h and 15:00h (by Treatment)

$$Workforce_{General,Registration} = \frac{Processing\ Time_{Registration}}{Takt\ Time_{General}} = \frac{1\,min}{3\,min} = 0.34\,FTE$$

$$Workforce_{General, Screening} = \frac{Processing\ Time_{Screening}}{Takt\ Time_{General}} = \frac{2\,min}{3\,min} = 0.67\,FTE$$

$$Workforce_{General, Consultation} = \frac{Processing\ Time_{Consultation}}{Takt\ Time_{General}} = \frac{8.5\,min}{3\,min} = 2.8\,FTE$$

This looks complicated, right? However, this is just the simplified version because of two facts.

- Firstly, patients have the tendency to ignore our calculations and show up whenever they can make it. Whilst the prediction to have 29 patients between 14:00h and 15:00h on a typical Friday is surely not bad in average because it is based on a year of observations, in reality we have to be prepared for different numbers and different arrival times of patients.

- Secondly, as everyone knows the consultation time at the doctor is not fixed to exactly 8.5 minutes. It varies (Figure 4.20).

The good news is we can do an even better workforce demand calculation after understanding the variation in both, the number of patients and the time typical routines take.

For understanding variation, box and whisker charts (box plots) are preferred over column or bar charts. Whilst column (Figure 4.16) and bar charts just show the average of number of patients per timeslot, box plots contain much more information.

The box plot at Figure 4.17 reveals, that between 14:00h and 15:00h on Fridays in 2019, never less than six patients and at most 67 patients arrived. In only 25% (Q1) of all cases, less than 19 patients arrived in that timeframe, whereas in 50% of all cases (Q2), more than 25 patients registered at the clinic. In 25% (Q3) of all Fridays, 44 patients or more registered at the clinic.

In other words, there is a chance of around 25% that the clinic must handle 44 patients or more.

If we would have taken the average of 29 shown by the column chart (Figure 4.16), we would not be prepared for many situations.

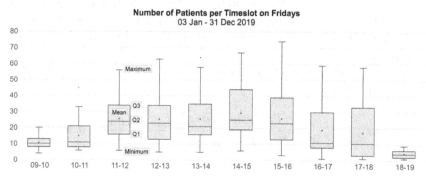

Figure 4.17 Box Plot of Patient Numbers per TimeSlot for All Treatments

☞ *Average numbers are not suitable for workforce planning.* Understanding the variation in data is key.

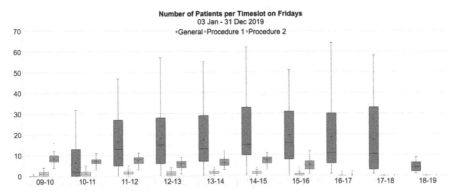

Figure 4.18 Box Plot of Patient Numbers per TimeSlot by Treatment

Figure 4.18 displays, how these numbers look like if the data is plotted by treatment type. General treatment shows a large variation in terms of patient numbers, whereas number of patients for Procedures 1 and 2 are rather predictable. All these patterns show the variation on a micro scale.

Additionally, there might be variation on a macro level. Every finance department knows about the month end and year end periods when the workload goes up manifold. This kind of pattern could be present in our clinic case as well.

The presence of an explainable pattern could be very helpful for planning workforce. Since finance staff know about their higher demand at year end, for example, they ensure that less leave is planned for that period and temporary staff is on alert.

The presence of patterns over time that are not easy to explain does not offer support for forecasting and planning. Figure 4.19 shows the plot of number of patients per day over time. Even if we know that February and May strained our workforce in year 2019 since the demand was very high, it might not help to get prepared for that peak for the next years if we do not understand the root causes for the demand surge.

Predicting a Potential Future Problem

When examining the plot in Figure 4.19, an indication for an overall trend downward over the year is visible. Therefore, we use Excel to add a trendline for the General graph. Combining the trendline with equation and R^2 with the Excel function in the line graph discloses a rather small trend down. Every month, the number of patients goes down by 1.4 per day. This sounds small. But it means that for General treatment, the daily number of patients drops in average by 17 from January to December. This implies that 388 less patients were treated in December.

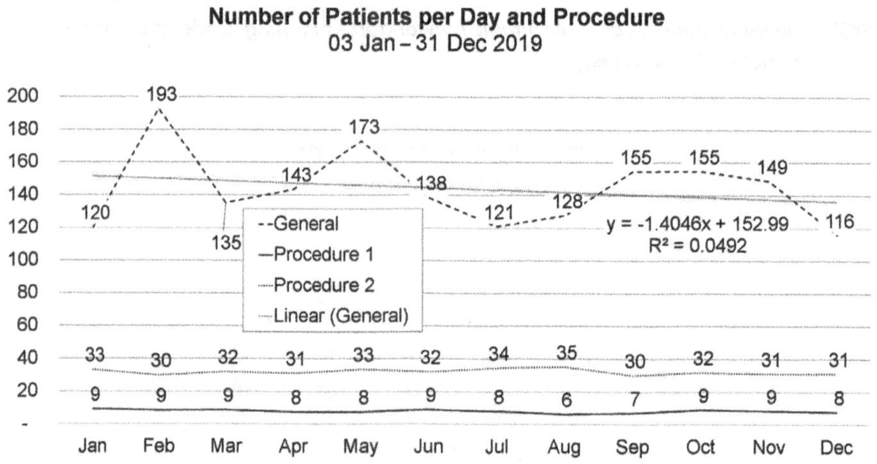

Number of Patients per Day and Procedure
03 Jan – 31 Dec 2019

Figure 4.19 with data series plotted monthly Jan–Dec:
General values: 193, 173, 143, 138, 121, 128, 155, 155, 149, 116 (with 120, 135 on left)
Procedure 1 values: 33, 30, 32, 31, 33, 32, 34, 35, 30, 32, 31, 31
Procedure 2 values: 9, 9, 9, 8, 8, 9, 8, 6, 7, 9, 9, 8

Legend:
--General
—Procedure 1
······Procedure 2
—Linear (General)

$y = -1.4046x + 152.99$
$R^2 = 0.0492$

Figure 4.19 Time Series Plot for Patient Numbers by Treatment with Trendline for General

Although, statistically this trend is insignificant with an R^2 of only 4.92% and a p-value of 0.488 (subsequent regression performed), a data analyst might consider highlighting this to the management. The good news for workload is certainly bad news for the revenue stream of the clinic. A root cause analysis, starting with the patient satisfaction survey, would be a necessary next step to avoid losing even more business.

> *Waiting for an apparent adverse change to turn significant could be the wrong strategy. Carefully evaluating even a non-significant change could help the business.*

Figure 4.19 also discloses that planning workforce for Procedure1 and Procedure2 should be rather straight forward due to less variation.

Understanding the Activity Pattern

In order to plan workforce for these activities, it is necessary to comprehend the duration of process steps. As mentioned earlier, the whole patient experience consists of five steps: registration, screening, consultation, dispense of medicine, and payment/checkout.

Whilst registration and payment/checkout are process steps that are short with about one minute and do not show queues, screening and medicine dispensation take some two minutes and could build a queue. Most patients who spend time in a clinic wait for the doctors for their consultation (treatment). Hence, planning the workforce should start with this process step.

When analysing the time needed for consultation, the three different treatment types show a distinctly different picture (Figure 4.20).

The General treatment was performed more than 32,000 times in 2019 with 75% of all cases done in less than ten minutes (Q3 = 75%) and the rest take

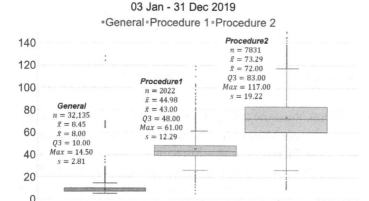

Figure 4.20 Box Plots and Descriptive Statistics for Treatment Types

less than 14.5 minutes all together. We ignore the outliers that make a dozen patients out of 32,000, i.e., 0.03% only.

Procedure1 and Procedure2 take considerably longer due to their nature. For Procedure1, 50% of all treatments are between 39 and 48 minutes (within the box of the box plot), whereas the same number for Procedure2 lies between 60 and 83 minutes. Whilst General consultation usually needs 100% of time with the doctor, Procedure1 and Procedure2 are only partially done face-to-face with the doctor. The rest of the time, the patient undergoes a certain standardised cycle of treatment that is fully automated.

For these procedures, the doctor face-to-face time is estimated to be even shorter than for the General treatment, because in contrast to that the diagnose phase is not needed. Both procedures are planned treatments that do not need any diagnosis. This means at the same time, workforce planning for these procedures is very easy because there is no element of surprise. All variation in the arrival pattern of patients is controlled by the booking system.

Not so for General consultation. Patients appear after they fall sick. Most of the time, these patients are not scheduled. A flu outbreak in the neighbourhood will most likely be seen as a surge of patients in the clinic. And this cannot be planned.

Planning the Workforce

As an example, planning the workforce will be shown for General treatment only. If we assume, we want to plan the workforce for 75% of the situations expected. This means, we need to consider a doctor being busy for around ten minutes with most of the patients for General consultation. Another 25% could take up to 14.5 minutes. We do not consider outliers due to their very small chance of happening.

As Figure 4.21 highlights, if we want to be prepared for 75% of all demand eventualities on Fridays, we need to be able to deal with around 30 patients

Clinic Hours	09-10	10-11	11-12	12-13	13-14	14-15	15-16	16-17	17-18	18-19
Minimum	-	-	-	-	-	-	-	1.0	1.0	1.0
25% of Days	-	-	5.0	6.0	7.0	10.0	8.0	6.0	3.0	2.0
50% of Days	-	2.0	13.0	15.0	13.0	15.0	16.0	11.0	10.5	4.0
75 % of Days	-	13.0	27.0	28.0	29.0	33.0	31.0	30.0	33.0	6.3
Maximum	10.0	32.0	47.0	57.0	55.0	62.0	66.0	64.0	58.0	9.0
Takt for Q3	-	4.8	2.2	2.1	2.1	1.8	1.9	2.0	1.8	9.6
No of Doctors for Q3 and 10 min Treatment		2.2	4.5	4.7	4.8	5.5	5.2	5.0	5.5	1.0

Figure 4.21 Patient Number Distribution for General Treatment on Fridays

from 11:00h until 18:00h. From 09:00h to 11:00h, we have a slow start and from 18:00h to 19:00h we would have to deal with a much smaller number of patients as well. These 30 patients would require about six doctors for a processing time (PT) of ten minutes (75% process duration covered).

The assumptions for these calculations are based on the experience of one year. Therefore, the conclusions should be quite good.

However, in only 25% of all General treatments is the processing time that long. Additionally, there is only a 25% chance that we have around 30 patients or more. Statistically speaking, in only 6.25% (0.25 x 0.25) of all treatments, slightly longer processing time and large patient arrival come together (0.25 x 0.25 = 0.0625). From a business perspective, it is not very prudent to have the workforce on the payroll that you need only in less than 10% of all situations.

Moreover, the above-mentioned calculation is based on the assumption that the probability of having a certain patient number is totally independent of the processing time. In reality, this will not be the case. If the doctors would know that a long queue was building up, they would most likely be able to speed up the consultation, hence, to shorten the chat with the patient and reduce the processing time.

Smart workforce planning would hold up two to three doctors for General treatment and additional staff for Procedure1 and Procedure2. Hopefully, doctors, nurses and other clinic staff are cross trained so that they can cover workforce gaps in any kind of situation.

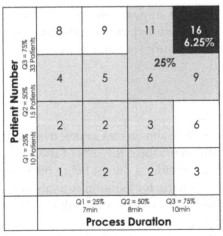

Figure 4.22 Doctors Needed for Processing Time and Takt Time Quartiles

"Fighting Variation"

No workforce planning can accommodate this kind of situation entirely (Tan, 2016). The approach to deal with this sort of issue involves:

1. reducing variation in demand, namely patient volume,
2. decreasing variation in processing time, that is treatment time, and
3. developing a flexible approach to resource (workforce) allocation.

"Teach" Your Customers

In service organisations, customer demand variation is hard to completely overcome. But it is almost somewhat controllable. Offering an appointment system is one way to help reducing variation in customer arrival numbers, or, at least, make the variation more predictable. As always, not everyone will make use of the appointment system. But some will. With some incentives as motivator, this will reduce the variation.

By offering a mobile app that takes appointments and, at the same time, publishes patient queues, customers can be channelled to non-peak hours. For some customers, this will work.

Flexible Work Arrangements for Staff

Analysing the waiting time by going to Gemba, that is, visiting the clinic at multiple times, we recognised that after 15:00h, the queues grew. This can only partially be explained by growing patient numbers. In reality, the first shift of staff, mostly nurses and clerks, end their working hours. This is exactly the people who were not busy at all until 11:00h, because there was very low patient influx. On top of increased waiting time for patients, the remaining staff is never looking forward to fight through the last busy hours with a smaller workforce.

In order to overcome workforce shortages in service organisations, inflexible working hours are not helpful at all. Our customers do not follow our working hours. We need to make our working hours follow our customers.

Cover Peak Periods with Temporary Staff

As mentioned earlier, it is not viable for any organisation to adjust the staff strength to the highest possible customer number. However, there are usually ways of having additional staff when there is a short-term shortage. This must not and will not mean decreased service level if the temp staff is not new but knows the environment and is tested. This polyclinic works with visiting doctors, who cover or support the permanent doctors when there is a need.

Employees on Payroll do not Translate into Employees Available

If your opening hours are from 09:00h to 18:00h from Mondays to Saturdays, this translates into 54 hours per week. However, there is some preparation that needs to be done before the clinic can open. And, there is some work like cleaning and disinfecting of equipment, that has to be done after the clinic is closed. In addition to that, closing the registration at 18:00h does not mean all patients are out. As 2019 data confirm, treatment is performed much later than 18:00h. This needs to be covered by workforce as well.

Of course, if we put our workforce on a 20h, 30h, or 40h shift pattern, we need to ensure that this shift pattern is able to cater for the real treatment hours plus the necessary preparation and housekeeping work that can only be done when the patients are not around.

To make matters worse, workforce hired for a full-time job, will not be available full-time. Study has shown that we need to take into account a certain number of vacation days, sick-days, training and development hours or days.

Overall, it is a good assumption that staff is only available between 75% and 90% of the time they are hired for. Hence, there is a need to plan for more people than actually required in the process because of their unavailable time. Or, there needs to be another way of dealing with this kind of situation. Temporary workforce is one consideration.

Rethinking and Innovating the Process

Whenever an organisation introduces strategic workforce planning, it is usually not so much for establishing the workforce needed in the current business environment. Much more is it about planning for the future.

An important input for strategic workforce planning is the estimation of future demand. This future demand leads to conclusions about future processes and finally to the staff strength and competencies needed.

If the future demand is known, the workforce prediction could be derived from the straight line displayed for processing time ten minutes (Figure 4.23, referring to General treatment).

However, this will be a grave mistake. Strategic workforce planning is about understanding how the work gets done. Hence, it is a great way of learning about your own processes and developing opportunities for improvement.

Every organisation needs to consider investing in up-to-date technology, necessary staff development, and modern procedures to get the work done. As a result, the organisation will be able to bend down the curve between demand and workforce, to work smarter.

Conclusion

This case was written with the intention to show how descriptive analytics and predictive analytics are used for workforce planning. This case

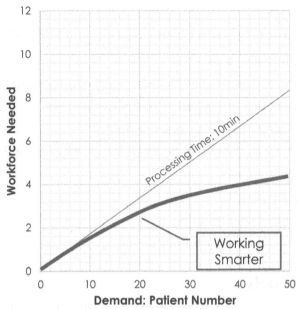

Figure 4.23 Flattening the Curve by Working Smarter

has all the ingredients that make workforce planning complicated. And, it highlights some important learnings:

- Workforce planning is first about understanding the process. Going to Gemba (Tan, 2017) will help.

- Before planning the workforce, make sure your process and organisation are ready for the future. There is no point in planning workforce for an outdated process.

- Understanding variation in the customer demand is key for planning resources to serve the customers.

- There is no way to predict the variation completely. Reducing variation will ease stress on the workforce.

- Flexible workforce, i.e., staff with a wide range of competencies and the mindset to apply them to serve the organisation will reduce the need for workforce adjustments and further decrease stress on our workforce.

Practice

- What are some simple checks of data correctness?
- What are potential strategies for fighting variation?
- What is the rational for assuming your workforce hired is not available full time?
- What does takt mean and how can you use it for workforce planning?

- How is takt calculated?
- What is the takt time for Nurses in General treatment on Fridays?

Please, complete the following steps:

1. Download the data for this case in ClinicVisit.xlsx from www.wiley.com.
2. Perform all steps described in Task 4.1 to complete the table.
3. Select only those patients that have done the survey.
4. Analyse whether there is a relationship between the survey result and
   a. the duration of the treatment,
   b. the nature of the treatment,
   c. the number of patients per timeslot.
5. Prepare a short report about your findings.

Deploying Analytics Tools

This workforce planning case exhibits the utilisation of Excel with its built-in Analysis ToolPak.

Case 8: What Makes Our Staff Innovate?

Innovative work behaviour of their employees is on top of the wish list of almost all managers nowadays (Drucker, 2015). However, just sending employees for creativity and innovation workshops is hardly enough to accomplish their innovative job behaviour.

There have been many studies about drivers for innovative work behaviour of employees. However, these studies came to the conclusion that there is always an influence of environment and leadership style on staff's work behaviour. The importance of these factors depends on the organisation and even the organisational unit. Hence, there is no generic answer. It needs to be studied for each case.

For this case, ratings of 160 survey participants of an "Innovation Readiness Survey" have been analysed. As a result, we have a dynamic model that helps in identifying weaknesses and strengths as well as drivers for innovative work behaviour using MS Power BI. Deploying MS Power BI for building a dynamic dashboard has the advantage that drilling down into any detail is a breeze. And connecting to any data source dynamically and including new data can be done by nearly anyone.

Business Question

So, what exactly drives our staff to:

1. Explore opportunities for innovation, i.e., see the need for an innovative change and generate ideas for satisfying this need,

2. Champion these ideas, i.e., "sell" them to colleagues and to managers and

3. Implement these ideas, i.e., turn them into solutions and help realizing them, either directly or as member of a team.

The answer will be sought through a comprehensive survey. In order to structure the survey, we start with a model of potential influencing factors on Innovative Work Behaviour. Figure 4.24 illustrates these with the name of the variable in raw data.

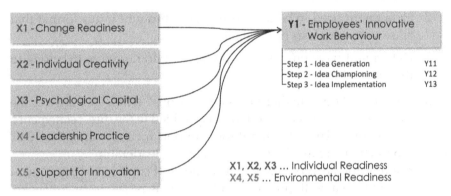

Figure 4.24 Potential Influencing Factors on Innovative Work Behaviour of Employees

Data Acquisition

A study with about 700 participants from private (49%) and government (51%) organisations was performed to identify drivers for employees' innovative work behaviour. Data were collected using a survey comprising proven questionnaires. All questions and statements were answered on a 7-point Likert scale, ranging from either never (1) to always (7) or strongly disagree (1) to strongly agree (7).

Innovative Work Behaviour consists of nine Janssen (2000) items (Cronbach's alpha = 0.93). **Individual Creativity** is based on Farmer (2010) and consists of 13 statements (Cronbach's alpha = 0.92). **Individual Innovation Readiness** is measured using a composition of the Holt et al. (2007) change efficacy and the Rafferty et al. (2013) readiness for change questionnaires. (Cronbach's alpha = 0.80). **Psychological Capital** is assessed using a questionnaire by Luthans et al. (2007) with a Cronbach's alpha of 0.86. **Transformational Leadership** is determined by a Multifactor Leadership Questionnaire (Bass, 1997) with a Cronbach's alpha of 0.97. **Support for Innovation** includes eleven statements based on Scott and Bruce (1994) with a Cronbach's alpha of 0.90. Related research is available (Tan Bee Choo et al., 2018).

Cronbach's alpha is a measure for the consistency of a questionnaire. For researchers, this indicator is critical, whereas practitioners just need to check whether their market research company can ensure that this indicator is above 0.70. If this is the case, the questionnaire is reliable. Since the reliability of a questionnaire may change from application to application, from culture to culture, it is necessary that your researcher can show pilot results for the actual application before rolling out the questionnaire.

Data Preparation

Since the data have been collected using a survey, the survey input needs some checking for at least the following reasons:

1. Data might be invalid, i.e., especially subjective data could be a result of careless input.

2. Data might need to be transformed, i.e., brought into a format that allows easy analysis of the data.

3. Data might have outliers, i.e., points that do not seem to belong to that data table.

In order to find out whether raters are "serious" when they answer the questionnaire, reverse statements have been added to the direct statements. An example for a **direct statement** for "Support for Innovation" is "Our ability to function creatively is respected by the leadership".

An example for a **reverse statement** would be "People in my department are expected to deal with problems in the same way".

This means, ratings for reverse questions need to be converted in order to be comparable with ratings for direct questions. Reverse statements are flagged with a correlation of –1 whereas direct statements are shown with correlation of 1. Reverse items need to be converted using formula CoRating = (7 + 1) – Rating with 7 being the length of the scale.

By using a PivotTable, the long format (stacked format, Figure 4.25 has been transformed into a short format (unstacked format) that is needed for some analysis functions. For cleaning purpose, the column Blank and StdDev have been added with formulas to identify **empty fields** and **fields that have no standard deviation.** Both show inputs that should not be used. Using the pivot table, the respective PaxID have been deactivated. After that, the pivot table has been copied into a new worksheet since some functions cannot be performed out of a PivotTable.

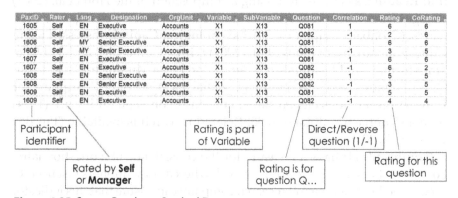

PaxID	Rater	Lang	Designation	OrgUnit	Variable	SubVariable	Question	Correlation	Rating	CoRating
1605	Self	EN	Executive	Accounts	X1	X13	Q081	1	6	6
1605	Self	EN	Executive	Accounts	X1	X13	Q082	-1	2	6
1606	Self	MY	Senior Executive	Accounts	X1	X13	Q081	1	6	6
1606	Self	MY	Senior Executive	Accounts	X1	X13	Q082	-1	3	5
1607	Self	EN	Executive	Accounts	X1	X13	Q081	1	6	6
1607	Self	EN	Executive	Accounts	X1	X13	Q082	-1	6	2
1608	Self	EN	Senior Executive	Accounts	X1	X13	Q081	1	5	5
1608	Self	EN	Senior Executive	Accounts	X1	X13	Q082	-1	3	5
1609	Self	EN	Executive	Accounts	X1	X13	Q081	1	5	5
1609	Self	EN	Executive	Accounts	X1	X13	Q082	-1	4	4

Participant identifier — Rated by **Self** or **Manager** — Rating is part of Variable — Rating is for question Q... — Direct/Reverse question (1/-1) — Rating for this question

Figure 4.25 Survey Results as Stacked Dataset

Source: Used with permission from Microsoft.

Additionally, SubVariables X11, X12, X13 have been aggregated to Variables X1 and X21, X22, X23 to X2 etc. Out of the average of X1, X2, and X3, Individual Readiness and out of the average of X4 and X5, Environmental Readiness have been calculated.

All operations can be followed through in file InnoReady.xlsx. The final stacked dataset is available in Sheet ByVariableFinal in the table "Unstacked Data" (Figure 4.26).

Data Analysis

The data analysis will be made using Power BI supported by some Excel functions. The analysis needs to answer at least two questions:

- Which variables (X1 = Individual Creativity, X2 = Change Readiness, X3 = Psychological Capital, X4 = Leadership Practice, X5 = Support for Innovation) drive Y1 (= Innovative Work Behaviour) in our organisation?

- Of the driving categories, which one is low and needs the first attention?

Now, stacked and unstacked data are available in PowerBI visible under Fields on the right (Task 4.4 and 4.5).

Our variables are only called X1, X2 etc. This is practical for survey data because it reduces the amount of data to be transported over the internet. However, for reporting purpose, it would be good to have the real names of the variables. These variable names are decoded on our website URL https://coe-partners.com/?p=3537. Excel and PowerBI offer the option to link to any website – be it Wikipedia, Facebook, LinkedIn, or any other site – and download data from there. The link can be dynamic, i.e., after the website gets updated the excel data get updated as well when reloading the Excel file. Therefore, we link our PowerBI to the table presented on the mentioned website.

PaxID	OrgUnit	D1	D2	D3	D4	D5	D6	X1	X2	X3	X4	X5	Y1	E-Readyness	I-Readiness
1605	Accounts	2.0000	0.5000	Female	24.0000	4.0000	2.0000	5.6444	5.5278	6.4375	6.0625	4.6000	6.7778	5.3313	5.8699
1606	Accounts	2.0000	11.0000	Female	45.0000	4.0000	11.0000	6.1667	6.1528	6.2917	6.0893	5.2750	7.0000	5.6821	6.2037
1607	Accounts	2.0000	5.0000	Female	48.0000	2.0000	1.0000	5.0222	5.2222	6.0000	5.5714	4.4875	6.0000	5.0295	5.4148
1608	Accounts	2.0000	3.2500	Female	32.0000	5.0000	3.2500	4.7111	3.7083	4.9375	5.8229	4.0917	4.9444	4.9573	4.4523
1609	Accounts	2.0000	3.1100	Female	29.0000	2.0000	3.1100	4.7222	4.4583	5.7083	4.5223	4.9876	4.2222	4.7549	4.9630
1617	Accounts	1.0000	0.5000	Female	29.0000	5.0000	0.5000	5.5333	5.3194	6.0208	6.6830	5.0125	5.3333	5.3478	5.6245
1619	Accounts	1.0000	0.5000	Female	28.0000	5.0000	0.5000	6.2333	5.5000	6.0000	5.5893	5.2000	6.0000	5.3946	5.9111
1625	Accounts	2.0000	1.0000	Male	24.0000	5.0000	1.0000	5.6000	4.3472	5.2917	5.2321	4.5625	5.0000	4.8973	5.0796
1647	Accounts	3.0000		Female	45.0000	4.0000		6.4333	6.6250	6.6250	1.7455	1.6125	6.8889	1.6790	6.5611

Figure 4.26 Unstacked Dataset after Cleaning and Transforming
Source: Used with permission from Microsoft.

> **TASK 4.4   LOAD POWERBI AND LOAD DATA**
>
> 1. Open Power BI.
> 2. Get Data – Excel – Connect – InnoReady.xlsx – Open.
> 3. Select tables StackedData and UnstackedData – Open.

TASK 4.5   LOAD DATA TABLE FROM WEBSITE WITH NAMES OF VARIABLES

1. Get Data – Other – Web – Connect – https://coe-partners.com/?p=3537 – OK.

2. Select Table 1 – Load.

3. On the right-hand side under Fields, right click on Table 1 – Edit Query.

4. If the top row shows Column1, Column2, Column3, on top in the Transform Menu – select Use First Row as Header – Close and Apply.

5. In Menu Modeling select Manage relationships – New.

6. Select Stacked Data and Table 1 and ensure, Variable is selected in both.

7. OK.

With this, we have the variable names X1, X2 etc. decoded with their full name. The table for decoding is used from the web.

In PowerBI, under Visualisations, Get more Visuals – search for Box and Whisker Plot and Violin Plot and add both.

Firstly, we generate an overview of ratings by organisational unit and category.

TASK 4.6   BUILD OVERVIEW PAGE FOR INNOVATION RATING RESULTS (FIGURE 4.27)

1. Select Stacked Bar Chart from Visualisations, position and size it.

2. Choose OrgUnit for Axis, and Average of CoRating for Values. Dress it up using Format. Use filter and allow X1 to X5. This bar chart is showing potential drivers for innovation per organisational unit.

3. Select Violin Plot or Box and Whisker Chart, position it and size it.

4. Choose PaxID for Sampling, Average of CoRating for Measure Data and Category for Category. Dress it up using Format.

5. Select Slicer or Table from Visualisations, position it and size it.

6. Choose Category for Field. Set Category Filter on Change Readiness, Individual Creativity, Leadership Practice, Psychological Capital, Support for Innovation. If you have selected Table, add Variable in Values. Dress it up using Format.

7. Select Card from Visualisations. Add PaxID in Fields. Rename it to Survey Raters. Set Count (Distinct) for this Field. Position it, size it and dress it up.

8. Select Insert – Image InnoReadyScale.jpg and put the image representing the rating scale on the report page.

9. Select Table from Visualisations. Add Variable and Category from Table 1. Position it, size it and dress it up.

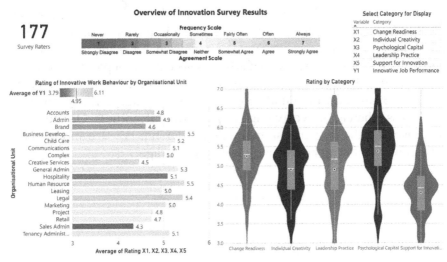

Figure 4.27 Overview of Innovation Readiness Survey Rating

With this page, it will be easy to compare contributors for innovative work behaviour per department with each other. Selections can be made by organisational unit and by category. As usual in PowerBI, the visuals are connected, i.e., filtering in one visual will impact the other visuals.

Secondly, we build a visualisation for the X–Y relationship of the data, the driver model (Task 4.7).

TASK 4.7   BUILD INFLUENCER PAGE FOR DRIVERS OF INNOVATIVE WORK BEHAVIOUR (FIGURE 4.28)

1. Press on + at bottom of page to create a new Page. Rename it if you like.

2. Select Stacked Bar Chart from Visualisations, position and size it.

3. Choose Category for Axis, and Average of CoRating for Values. Dress it up using Format.

4. Select Table or Slicer, position it and size it.

5. Choose Unit, Staff, E-Readiness and I-Readiness for Table Values.

6. Select Key Influencer, position it and size it.

7. Choose Y11 (Generating Ideas) for Analyse and X1, . . . X5, D1, . . . D6 for Explain by.

8. Select second Key Influencer, position it and size it.

9. Choose Y11 (Generating Ideas) for Analyse and X41, X42, X43, X44 for Explain by.

10. Right Click the Page name and Duplicate Page.

11. Repeat Steps 6 to 9 and choose Y12 (Championing Ideas) for Analyse.

12. Right Click the Page name and Duplicate Page.

13. Repeat Steps 6 to 9 and choose Y13 (Implementing Ideas) for Analyse.

Figure 4.28 shows how this Power BI visual can be used to illustrate the Key Influencer for Innovative Work Behaviour, Step 3: Implementing Ideas. Tapping on the organisational unit table on the lower left-hand side, department Project with 32 staff has been selected. For department Project, the columns E-Readiness (average of X4 and X5) and I-Readiness (average of X1 to X3) are indicating that Project is below average in Environmental Readiness whereas above average in Individual Readiness. On the right, the reason for the former is shown with Leadership Practice and Support for Innovation faring below organisational average.

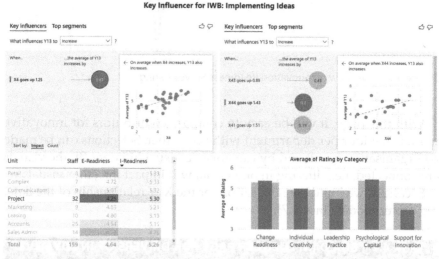

Figure 4.28 Analysing Key Influencers for Y13 (Implementing Ideas) for Department Projects

Source: Used with permission from Microsoft.

For analysing the drivers for Y13, Implementing Ideas, two steps are shown. Firstly, the variables X1 to X5 are checked to find a model that explains the variation in Y13. Power BI is running linear regression and shows that for department Project, only X4, Leadership Practice, is a significant driver, a Key Influencer for Y13, Implementing Ideas. The regression result illustrates a positive relationship by statement "When X4 goes up by 1.25, Y13 would increase by 0.47". Since X4 is an aggregated value for Leadership Practice with four factors from the Transformational Leadership model, we would like to find out which of these factors is the most important driver for department Project. The factors representing X4, Transformational Leadership are

- X41: Idealised Influence,
- X42: Individualised Consideration,

- X43: Inspirational Motivation and
- X44: Intellectual Stimulation.

Therefore, we deploy the Power BI visual Key Influencer a second time (upper right-hand side in Figure 4.28) and include X41 to X44 as potential drivers for Y13. Three Key Influencers are identified by the statistics running in the background resulting in these three statements:

"When X43 goes up by 0.89, the average of Y13 would increase by 0.43".

"When X44 goes up by 1.43, the average of Y13 would increase by 0.20".

"When X41 goes up by 1.51, the average of Y13 would increase by 0.19".

This kind of analysis could be done for all departments with a large enough number of survey participants involved. We do not need to know the statistics but trust that Power BI applies proven tools before developing statements like the above.

Business Decision and Storytelling

MS Power BI offers the presentation that we need to give our management the full picture and drill through all details if necessary, since Power BI is dynamic and allows very user-friendly interaction between audience and report.

Firstly, we present the overall picture using the report page at Figure 4.27. This one informs about the style of the survey, number of participants per organisational unit, scales used, and high-level results.

In order to compare Environmental Readiness and Individual Readiness for all business units, Figure 4.29 comes in handy.

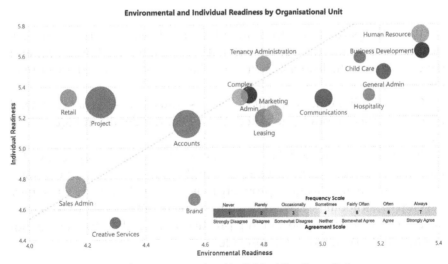

Figure 4.29 Overview of Environmental and Individual Readiness Rating

There are some remarkable findings. Retail, for example shows an individual readiness for innovation above average but one of the lowest averages in environmental readiness. This certainly needs some attention.

Additionally, Creative Services although small but important for a property developer reveals a low rating in both environmental and individual readiness. Is this good for a property developer? The management decides to work on that.

After Director Retail is concerned about his overall result that seems to be lower than most other departments, we just select Retail in the bar chart and the whole report informs about Retail (Figure 4.30).

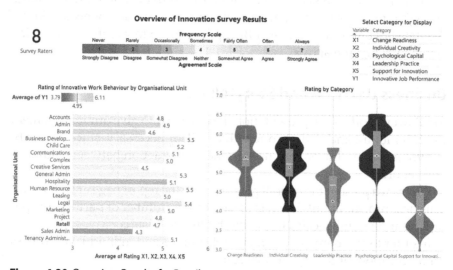

Figure 4.30 Overview Results for Retail

"We had 8 participants from Retail taking the survey. They fed back that the support for innovation in Retail is comparatively low. This might have to do with the leadership Practice that seems to be rated lower than other categories".

"Can you tell me more about our lowest rated areas? What do I need to be concerned about?", he asked. We reveal the details in Figure 4.31. And we explain:

"It seems that your staff is worried about the support they receive for innovation. X54 is lowest and means that the tolerance for staff diversity is quite low. Their colleagues probably look at those differently when they develop ideas about new ways of doing things. X52 talks about resources not being given. X43 is a leadership practice and signifies that staff do not feel inspired to come up with new ideas.

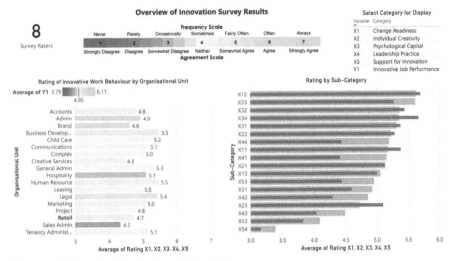

Figure 4.31 Detailed Rating Results for Retail

To the contrary, staff have rated X23 higher than the rest of the organisation. With this they say that they have a high confidence that they can innovate when needed. They feel ready".

After answering some more departments' questions about their rating, we remind them that all Directors have access to the Power BI report and can perform further analysis on their own.

We make the point that the rating itself is only important for indicators that seem to drive Innovative Work Behaviour Y1. This means, it is critical to look at the key influencers for all stages of the innovative process from Idea Generation after detecting an opportunity (Y11) over Idea Championing (Y12) to finally Idea Implementation (Y13).

We explain to the Deputy Director Business Development, that he is obviously doing well with a rating consistently above the average (column chart at Figure 4.32). If we wish to know what makes our staff generate ideas, we get some hints from the Key Influencer visuals. On the left it demonstrates that Individual Creativity (X2) strongly drives the idea Generation (Y11). If X2 increases by only 0.58. it could result in Y11 going up by 0.92. The mark in the table of Business Units shows that Y1 is highly rated by Business Development. On the right, Creative Role Identity (X21) and Self-Expectations for Creativity (X23) are rated highest on their influence on the Idea Generation outcome.

The Deputy Director concludes that this has probably to do with their innovation and productivity workshops they had recently. Good news.

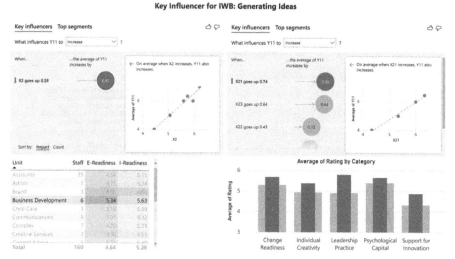

Figure 4.32 Key Influencers for Idea Generation at Business Development

The presentation and information discovery goes on with many questions and hypothesis raised by almost all participants. Since the report is shared online, everyone is very interested to do more digging into the details.

The findings result in a package of action items concluded based on data. Action items have been selected based on two criteria. Firstly, key influencers have been identified for each department. Then, key influencers have been prioritised by rating received. Hence, actions should target X2 and X4 first with X5 following (Figure 4.33).

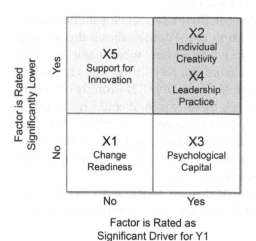

Figure 4.33 Action Planning Based on Low Rating and Significant Influence

Deploying Analytics Tools

Using Power BI, the focus of the presentation has moved from statistical details to business insights. Since all reports are dynamic, time has been saved for creating the report. Instead of producing 18 analysis packages for 18 business units and its cut and paste on PowerPoint or Word, only one report has been prepared that shows overall rating and rating details for each department just by applying filters.

Amending this report and adding more pages is very straightforward and comfortable in a well-known and proven user interface.

Background

This innovation readiness survey has been developed as part of a research project with the University of Twente in the Netherlands. More information about the survey can be found here: https://coe-partners.com/?p=3537 (Tan Bee Choo et al., 2018).

Case 9: What Does Our Engagement Survey Result Mean?

An organisation has completed their employee engagement survey. More than 70 statements have been rated by more than 400 employees, using a 5-point Likert Agreement Scale (1 . . . Strongly Disagree, 2 . . . Disagree, 3 . . . Neither, 4 . . . Agree, 5 . . . Strongly Agree). The survey result has been reported in percentage of favourable answers, i.e., percentage rating 4 or 5 (Figure 4.34).

In Figure 4.34, differences have been marked to highlight the "good news" and the "bad news". The change from the previous year (EES2018) to the actual year (EES2019) has been shown with arrows next to the percentage in EES2019, whereas the comparison of each department's survey results to the whole organisation has been marked with shading.

In EES2018, the lowest rating was received by statement "My manager does a good job in establishing performance targets." Hence, this item is in the focus of attention.

Good news! The rating for this statement by all employees has increased. Is this increase significant? Applying a two-proportion test comparing the two proportions 50% (215 out of 427 employees rated 4 or 5) and 60% (248 out of 416 employees rated 4 or 5) shows that the percentages are significantly different with p-value = 0.0069 (P(Sample1 ≠ Sample2) in

Statement	EES 2018 (427)	EES 2019 (417)	Dept A (35)	Dept B (88)	Dept C (25)	Dept D (40)	Dept E (129)	Dept F (42)	Dept G (58)
1. Senior management of my organisation does a good job in confronting issues before they become major problems.	63	72↑	79	78	58	67	91	58	76
2. My manager gives me regular, informal feedback on my performance.	59	74↑	69	77	54	75	84	63	71
3. My manager does a good job in establishing performance targets.	50	60↑	60	60	60	60	60	60	60
4. I believe that I have the opportunity for growth and development in my organisation.	51	49↓	42	26	35	48	57	46	61
5. I have enough flexibility in my job to do what is necessary to provide good service to my customers.	80	73↓	52	92	56	64	86	61	59
6. In my organisation, employees are able to maintain a healthy balance between their work and personal lives.	59	54↓	51	57	48	57	76	54	47
7. I see activities beyond my core job responsibilities as contributing to my personal development.	58	67↑	58	70	55	63	83	47	67
8. I feel adequately informed about the essentials (e.g. targets, developments, results) regarding my area of work.	66	62↓	56	56	72	57	70	52	70
9. The people I work with cooperate to get the job done.	72	65↓	62	78	70	63	77	55	69
10. My organisation provides good opportunities for me to improve my employability.	67	70↑	54	86	57	69	86	63	68
Rated higher than EES2019				Rated lower than EES2019					

Figure 4.34 Extract of Employee Engagement Survey Results 2019 (partially simulated)

Figure 4.35, using TwoProportionTest.xlsx). Which is to say, the risk for being wrong with the assumption that there is an improvement is only 0.69%. This sounds quite safe, right?

In most cases, this would be the final conclusion.

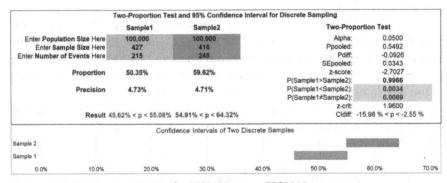

Figure 4.35 Two-proportion test for EES2018 versus EES2019

Why We Should not Trust this Data Easily

The organisation had invested a significant amount of money and time into training all managers and supervisors in the setting of performance targets. Of course, they want to know whether this investment has paid off. This is a question that should be asked to the market research company conducting and analysing the survey data.

In our special situation, we have access to the raw data that have been collected from the survey participants. Data have been acquired through a website in order to avoid manual data transfer and inherent typos from the start. Participants had to answer all statements of the survey. This could usually lead to random rating where participants don't have an opinion. However, random rating has been avoided as much as possible by providing "NA" as a rating option.

Survey responses "NA" have been taken out of the rating. And, survey responses without variation – all ratings are 4, for example – have also been eliminated so that the remaining rating should be of good quality.

For demonstration purposes, the data have been amended slightly.

Performing a Proper Data Analysis

Since the statement "My manager does a good job in establishing performance targets" (statement 3) is of special interest, the analysis of data is shown for this statement.

The sobering truth: We have not improved

Figure 4.36 illustrates the rating for this statement in 2018 and 2019. It indicates for EES2018, that 28 raters have given a rating of 1, 23 a rating of 2, 161 a rating of 3, 159 a rating of 4 and 56 a rating of 5. And, it does so for EES2019 similarly.

On the one hand, this confirms that 50% (50.35%) have given a rating of 4 or 5 in 2018, whilst 60% (59.62%) did so in 2019. On the other hand, this reveals that the average rating for EES2018 and 2019 is nearly the similar with 3.45 and 3.43, respectively. Contrary to what we learned from the percentages; this implies there was no improvement at all.

	EES2018	EES2019
Rating1	28	54
Rating2	23	31
Rating3	161	82
Rating4	159	181
Rating5	56	69
Count	427	417
%4/5	50%	60%
Mean	3.45	3.43
StdDev	1.01	1.23

Figure 4.36 Rating for EES2018 and EES2019 for Statement 3
Source: Used with permission from Microsoft.

TASK 4.9   CALCULATE STATISTICS FOR EES2018, EES2019 AND FOR ALL DEPARTMENTS A TO G

1. Open the engagement survey data file EES.xlsx in worksheet EES.

2. Calculate %4/5: =SUM(C5:C6)/SUM(C2:C6), i.e., the number of rating 4 and 5 over the total number of ratings for EES2018. Repeat this step for EES2019 and for all Departments A to G.

3. Calculate Mean: =AVERAGE(C13:C439), i.e., the average of all ratings for EES2018. Repeat this step for EES2019 and for all Departments A to G.

4. Calculate StdDev: =STDEV.S(C13:C439), i.e., the standard deviation of all ratings for EES2018. Repeat this step for EES2019 and for all Departments A to G.

Which data should we trust? Of course, we trust the mean more than the percentage. The mean takes every single rating into account. If one rating changes, the mean will change. To the contrary, percentages only calculate the number of 4 or 5 ratings over the total number of ratings. A change of ratings will only affect the percentage if a rating moves from the 1-2-3 category to 4-5 category or vice versa.

 Do not trust percentages when you compare survey results. Compare averages instead.

We are both doing well. Aren't we?

The heads of departments A and B see their satisfaction rates for statement 3 both being at 60% and conclude that their way of setting performance targets looks very much the same. Still, they have just learned that trusting only the percentage might not be enough. They ask the market research company for calculating the mean for both departments. To their surprise, the mean, the average for department A is 3.11 and for department B is 3.89 (Figure 4.37).

The question is never whether these means are different. The real question always is "Is there a significant difference between both means? Can we trust the difference?"

	Dept A	Dept B
Rating1	8	2
Rating2	4	6
Rating3	2	27
Rating4	18	18
Rating5	3	35
Count	35	88
%4/5	60%	60%
Mean	3.11	3.89
StdDev	1.39	1.09

Figure 4.37 Rating for Departments A and B for Statement 3

Source: Used with permission from Microsoft.

In the following, we compare two sets of non-normal data with each other.

TASK 4.9   LOAD THE DATA FROM EES.XLSX INTO R STUDIO AND PERFORM WILCOXON TEST:

1. Open R Studio.

2. In the Files window, navigate to your directory and select EES.xlsx.

3. Select Import Dataset.

4. Select Sheet Raw.

5. Select Range A1:F428.

```
# Loading library for inserting Excel file loads automati-
cally, test in rstatix
library(readxl)
library(rstatix)
# Uploading Excel file EES.xlsx is loaded into data frame
EES
EES <- read_excel("EES.xlsx", sheet = "Raw", range =
"A1:I428")
# Performing non-parametric Wilcox test
attach(EES)
wilcox.test(DeptA,DeptB)
```

Test output:

```
data: DeptA and DeptB
W = 1074.5, p-value = 0.006915
alternative hypothesis: true location shift is not equal to 0
```

The Wilcoxon test (Table 4.2) is a substitute for the two-sample t-test for non-normal data. Line 1 shows a p-value of 0.006915. As the p-value for assuming a difference confirms, the chance that both departments have received a similar rating (not statistically different) is only 0.69%. Hence, we assume there is a difference in the rating, although both departments show the same 60% agreement score.

Because this question is answered in the affirmative, we are allowed to look into potential reasons for that different rating both managers have received, different methods they use etc.

Departments A and B receive significantly different rating!

But, we do equally well, don't we?

The heads of departments C and D follow what they just learned. They do not trust the percentage and compare the means for their rating results for statement 3.

	Dept C	Dept D
Rating1	0	7
Rating2	2	9
Rating3	8	0
Rating4	15	4
Rating5	0	20
Count	25	40
%4/5	60%	60%
Mean	3.52	3.53
StdDev	0.65	1.68

Figure 4.38 Rating for Departments C and D for Statement 3

Source: Used with permission from Microsoft.

The rating mean for Dept C amounts to 3.52 whereas Dept D averages at 3.53 (Figure 4.38). This should be enough to conclude that managers in both departments are appreciated similarly for their objective setting performance, right?

TASK 4.10   PERFORM WILCOXON TEST ON DEPT C AND DEPT D:

```
# Performing non-parametric Wilcox-test
wilcox.test(DeptC, DeptD)
```

Test output:

```
data: Dept C and Dept D
W = 421, p-value = 0.2745
alternative hypothesis: true location shift is not equal to 0
```

Since we do not have normal data, we use the Wilcoxon test again. It seems a formality.

This output says that Department C and D are not different in their rating since the p-value is > 0.05.

So, they are really doing the same job, right?

Even this could be a wrong conclusion. Looking at the standard deviation of 0.65 for Dept C and 1.68 for Dept D (StdDev in Figure 4.38), there should be some doubts about similar ratings at both departments.

After plotting the data for the rating at both departments (Figure 4.39), it becomes obvious that the rating at Dept C is homogeneous, i.e., only ratings of 2, 3 and 4 have been used by all 25 raters. The rating at Dept D seems to show two groups of raters, those 16 who are rather dissatisfied – expressed with rating 1 or 2 – and those 24 who are rather satisfied – expressed with rating 4 or 5.

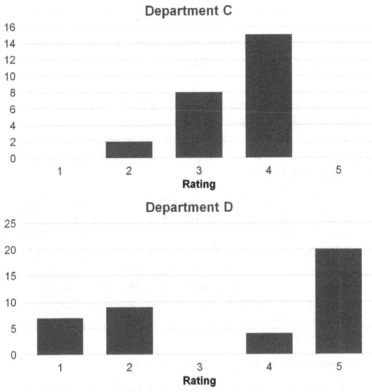

Figure 4.39 Rating Details for Departments C and D for Statement 3

In order to check whether there is a significant difference between rating variances of Dept C and Dept D, a Levene test is deployed (Table 4.3).

TASK 4.11   PERFORM LEVENE TEST ON DEPT C AND DEPT D:

```
# Stack data for Dept C and Dept D
EESstacked <- stack(EES, select=c(DeptC, DeptD))
# Performing non-parametric Levene-test for equal variance
levene_test(data=EESstacked, values ~ ind)
```

Test output:

df1	df2	statistic	p-value
1	63	13.5	0.000500

This output says that Departments C and D are different in variation of their rating since the p-value is less than 0.05. As mentioned, Department C shows a homogeneous rating whereas Department D displays two teams with a significantly different rating. This means there might be another factor, a lurking variable that makes the difference between these two teams. A likely explanation might be that within department D, two teams with two different team leaders have created this heterogeneous rating resulting in a large standard deviation and in a plot with two obvious clusters.

Departments C and D receive significantly different ratings shown in their variation, i.e., their standard deviation.

 Do not trust averages alone. Means are lies. Analyse the Variation, the Standard Deviation, too. And never forget: Plot the Data.

Making a Better Decision

The investment in educating managers on performance target setting did not make a difference in the overall rating for the organisation. EES2018 and EES2019 show a change in rating measured in percentage (EES2018: 50%, EES2019: 60%) but the mean is the same for both years with 3.45.

However, there are certainly further findings. Department A receives a significantly lower rating than Department B. Within Department D, there seem to be two teams generating an inhomogeneous rating pattern.

Therefore, some rules might help avoid drawing wrong conclusions when evaluating survey results:

1. Don't look only at percentages. They can be lies.

2. Looking at averages in addition to percentages improves the information content. To stay focused and avoid getting lost in too many details, pay attention to significant differences only. Use statistics to determine them.

3. Understanding the patterns in data would be best. However, it is not advisable and most likely not even possible for you to analyse the raw data. Therefore, develop a list of potential stratifying factors and have them applied to your data by your market researcher hoping that by doing so you discover most patterns in your data.

After applying some statistics to the survey data, the presentation of the data looks different and allows management to focus on what is really important, i.e., significantly different (Figure 4.40).

There is only statement 9 "The people I work with cooperate to get the job done", in which the overall rating has dropped from EES2018 to EES2019. This decrease in cooperation and teamwork within departments might be a reason for some action.

Department E seems to show mostly better rating in EES2019 than the rest of the organisation. Why is this? What can we learn from them?

Apart from Departments B and E, other departments rate statement 5 "I have enough flexibility in my job to do what is necessary to provide good service to my customers" significantly lower. This should be reason for concern and trigger some action.

Statement	EES 2018 (427)	EES 2019 (417)	Dept A (35)	Dept B (88)	Dept C (25)	Dept D (40)	Dept E (129)	Dept F (42)	Dept G (58)
1. Senior management of my organisation does a good job in confronting issues before they become major problems.	63	72	79	78	58	67	91	58	76
2. My manager gives me regular, informal feedback on my performance.	59	74↑	69	77	54	75	84	63	71
3. My manager does a good job in establishing performance targets.	50	60	60	60	60	60	60	60	60
4. I believe that I have the opportunity for growth and development in my organisation.	51	49	42	26	35	48	57	46	61
5. I have enough flexibility in my job to do what is necessary to provide good service to my customers.	80	73	52	92	56	64	86	61	59
6. In my organisation, employees are able to maintain a healthy balance between their work and personal lives.	59	54	51	57	48	57	76	54	47
7. I see activities beyond my core job responsibilities as contributing to my personal development.	58	67↑	58	70	55	63	83	47	67
8. I feel adequately informed about the essentials (e.g. targets, developments, results) regarding my area of work.	66	62	56	56	72	57	70	52	70
9. The people I work with cooperate to get the job done.	72	65↓	62	78	70	63	77	55	69
10. My organisation provides good opportunities for me to improve my employability.	67	70	54	86	57	69	86	63	68

Rated significantly higher than EES2019	Rated significantly lower than EES2019

Figure 4.40 Extract of Employee Engagement Survey Results 2019 (partially simulated, showing only significant differences)

All white cells indicate that there is no significant difference between department rating and EES2019 rating. And, this is the only way to look at the result.

As shown earlier, everyone who wanted to explain differences between ratings in non-coloured fields would make a mistake – and would probably spend money and effort on areas that do neither need an investment nor warrant any celebration.

 Only significant differences are variations we should focus on. Trying to explain non-significant differences is usually a waste of time and resources.

Practice

■ Why is it not good enough to trust the percentage of rating results in any kind of survey?

■ What indicators must be examined when analysing survey results?

■ Why is it mostly beneficial to plot the data?

Please, complete the following steps:

- Download the data for this case in EES.xlsx from www.wiley.com.
- Study the ratings for Departments E, F, and G.
- Prepare a short report about your findings.

Deploying Analytics Tools

This case illustrates how employee engagement scores are often reported. Since the rating data usually comes in Likert scales, it would statistically be perfect to be treated as discrete ordinal. Analysing discrete ordinal data offers a limited set of tools that are generally less powerful than tools that deal with continuous data.

The first analysis was done with a two-proportion test comparing the proportion of ratings 4 or 5 for 2018 and 2019.

Treating survey results as percentages has some considerable disadvantages. On a 5-point scale on which we consider rating 4 or 5 desirable, all ratings of 1, 2 and 3 are treated as undesirable, when calculating the percentage. There is no difference between rating 1, 2 and 3. And, there is no difference between rating 4 or 5. In case 1, we have illustrated the impact of this every-day-reality. Hence, we use tools that deal with Likert scale results as continuous data.

Likert scale output is usually not normally distributed. Therefore, we consider using non-parametric (non-normal) tests. These tests do not compare means but medians, i.e., the sequence and counts of the data in the samples.

If there is a need for comparing variances, i.e., standard deviations, there are a family of tests available. For normally distributed data, the F test (available in Excel) or Bartlett test will be applicable. Our survey data, coming from a Likert scale is rarely normal. Therefore, we have to apply Levene's test for equal variances.

Case 10: What Drives Our Staff Out? – Logistic Regression for Prediction and Decision Making

MySupplyChain is part of a logistics MNC with about 650 staff locally. They are quite successful in all their business units: air and sea freight, land transport, and supply chain management.

Table 4.1 Two-Proportion z test

TWO-PROPORTION TEST	
Data in *X*:	Discrete X – Groups (1 and 2)
Data in *Y*:	Discrete Y – Counts
Null Hypothesis H_0:	*Proportion$_1$ = Proportion$_2$*
Alternative Hypothesis H_A:	*Proportion$_1$ ≠ Proportion$_2$*
Decision:	If p-value is < 0.05, reject H_0 and accept H_A.
Assumptions:	Counts in all four cells must be at least 5, i.e., x_1, n_1-x_1, x_2, n_2-x_2 must be at least 5

R code:	```
	# Loading necessary packages
	install.packages("stats")
	library(stats)
	# Compute the two-proportion z-test result
	prop.test(x = c(x1, x2), n = c(n1, n2))
	# x1 … number of successes for group 1
	# n1 … number of trials for group 1
	# x2 … number of successes for group 2
	# n2 … number of trials for group 2
	``

Table 4.2 Two-Sample Wilcoxon test

TWO-SAMPLE WILCOXON TEST (KAUFMANN, 2020)	
Data in *X*:	Discrete X – Groups (Dept C, Dept D)
Data in *Y*:	Continuous Y, Discrete ordinal (values), non-normal
Null Hypothesis H_0:	*median$_1$ = median$_2$*
Alternative Hypothesis H_A:	*median$_1$ ≠ median$_2$*
Decision:	If p-value is < 0.05 ($\alpha = 0.05$), reject H_0 and accept H_A.
Assumptions:	Sample sizes must be at least 6.
	Samples must have similar distribution.

R code:	```
	# Loading necessary packages
	library(rstatix)
	# Performing non-parametric Wilcox test
	wilcox.test(DeptC, DeptD)
	``

Table 4.3 Two-Sample Levene test

TWO-SAMPLE LEVENE TEST (CHEW, 2018)	
Data in X:	Discrete X – Groups (ind)
Data in Y:	Continuous Y, Discrete ordinal (values), non-normal
Null Hypothesis H_0:	$variance_1 = variance_2$
Alternative Hypothesis H_A:	$variance_1 \neq variance_2$.
Decision:	If p-value is < 0.05 ($\alpha = 0.05$), reject H_0 and accept H_A.
Assumptions:	No assumptions.

R code:	```
	# Loading necessary packages
	library(rstatix)
	# Performing non-parametric Levene test
	levene_test(data=EESstacked, values ~ ind)```

During the monthly management meeting, the new Sales Director, let's call him Donald, is trying to learn more about his new employer and asks many questions. As it is HR's turn, his question is about the annual staff turnover.

"About 29% annually" answered the HR Director, Susan. Donald did not comment since he did not want to put his new colleague in an awkward position. After the meeting, he took Susan aside and asked her:

"As far as I know this is a bit on the high side, right?"

Susan knew her stuff too and nodded to his comment. She replied "We have just started a project to look into this. Turnover has always been around 12%. But the last couple of years it has gone up. We are concerned because every exit means a certain disruption to the business operations. It requires our clients and subcontractors to get familiar with new faces. And, of course, we need to train the new staff, and this costs money and time. We are worried about our branding as an employer, too. We have asked a consulting firm to help us with the analytics".

Very often, Susan and her team are pressured by line departments due to the high turnover and the associated negative effects on the departments. The suggestions – and sometimes demands – towards HR include the amendments of salary and benefits. However, Susan does not easily give in for two reasons. Firstly, such amendments would change the cost base drastically. Secondly, Susan is quite sure that salary and benefits are not the most important drivers for people leaving. Therefore, this analysis was triggered by HR to prove with data what Susan assumes and, of course, to identify the real drivers for the attrition.

Using logistic regression, we discovered that the remuneration package is not amongst the most important drivers. The analysis not only provides this evidence but also enables building a model, that helps to guesstimate the risk of staff leaving. We conclude our findings with some suggestions for increasing employee retention.

Most importantly, the myth that people leave the organisation because of their remuneration package is busted.

Business Question

The consulting firm dealing with workforce analytics together with the management of MySupplyChain has charged the analytics project with the following objectives:

1. Identify the main drivers for employee attrition at MySupplyChain.

2. Develop a model to predict attrition of employees at MySupplyChain and train HR in using this model.

3. Recommend actions to curb the attrition at MySupplyChain with the target of less than 15% by end of next year.

Identifying the potential drivers that make this model work is key. However, this task is not too easy. On the one hand, there are always some people in the organisation who "know exactly" why their colleagues left. That might even be true from time to time. But then, getting this information out and making it part of the model is impossible, because this kind of information is often rumour-based and anecdotal and not useful as data. On the other hand, if the drivers were obvious to everyone, there would not be the need for any project to find out.

Data Acquisition

When trying to develop a useful model for workforce analytics, you will sooner or later run into a prevalent problem: A large variety of workforce data is easily available. However, the available data is often not the data you need for the specific analysis you want to perform. Is this different for our staff attrition analysis?

Scanning through exit interviews and brainstorming potential drivers for staff attrition brings a long list of items in the categories: organisation, compensation and opportunities, job nature, personal factors, and leadership-related factors (Table 4.4).

Table 4.4 Potential Causes for Staff Attrition

ID	POTENTIAL CAUSE	CATEGORY	M
1	No childcare benefits	Compensation & Benefits	B
2	My benefits are not comparable with the market	Compensation & Benefits	B
3	Dental benefits are poor	Compensation & Benefits	B
4	Salary is not comparable with the industry	Compensation & Benefits	B
5	I am not paid fairly compared to others outside the organisation	Compensation & Benefits	B
6	I am not paid fairly compared to others who are doing the same job as me	Compensation & Benefits	D
7	The job I am given is not challenging	Job Motivation	P
8	I do not have autonomy to do my job effectively	Job Motivation	P
9	I do not feel the sense of belonging	Job Motivation	P
10	I do not feel the sense of accomplishment	Job Motivation	P
11	I cannot make use of my skills and knowledge to perform my job	Job Motivation	P
12	Distance from Home – travelling time and inconvenience	Travelling	D
13	Too much overseas travelling assignment	Travelling	D
14	No opportunity to work from home	Work–life balance	D
15	I do not have work–life balance	Work–life balance	P
16	Workload is too high for me	Work–life balance	P
17	Working hours are too long	Work–life balance	B
18	Unfair workload distribution in my department	Work–life balance	P
19	Too much overtime	Work–life balance	D
20	I do not know my career path	Career Development	P
21	Progression is too slow	Career Development	P
22	No career development opportunities	Career Development	P
23	I do not know my future	Career Development	P

(Continued)

Table 4.4 (Continued)

ID	POTENTIAL CAUSE	CATEGORY	M
24	I do not have opportunities to grow with the company	Career Development	P
25	I am doing the same thing every day and every year	Career Development	P
26	I go through the same training every year. I am not sure if I have improved my employability within my company	Career Development	P
27	I do not receive training to improve my skills in order to do my job well	Career Development	P
28	I do not have opportunity to take up training courses	Career Development	P
29	The customers are not happy with our company	Customer Relationship	P
30	Too many complaints from customers	Customer Relationship	P
31	The leaders do not lead by example	Leadership	P
32	The leaders do not communicate vision and plans for the organisation	Leadership	P
33	The leaders do not care about the employees' wellbeing	Leadership	P
34	The performance management system is not fair	Performance Management	P
35	Promotion rules are not visible	Performance Management	P
36	My supervisor does not have the flexibility to reward and recognise good performance	Performance Management	P
37	I do not understand how my performance is evaluated	Performance Management	P
38	I am not paid fairly considering my performance and contributions in the company	Performance Management	P
39	Unfair treatment by my supervisor	Supervisory Practice	P
40	Unfair performance grading	Supervisory Practice	P
41	Supervisor shows favouritism	Supervisory Practice	P
42	Supervisor does not give me feedback about my performance	Supervisory Practice	P

(Continued)

Table 4.4 (Continued)

ID	POTENTIAL CAUSE	CATEGORY	M
43	My supervisor uses sarcastic remarks all the time	Supervisory Practice	P
44	My supervisor raises his voice at me	Supervisory Practice	P
45	My supervisor is not competent to do his job	Supervisory Practice	P
46	My supervisor is not available for me when I need him	Supervisory Practice	P
47	My supervisor does not set work objectives for me	Supervisory Practice	P
48	My supervisor does not have open communication with me	Supervisory Practice	P
49	My supervisor does not coach me to improve my performance	Supervisory Practice	P
50	My supervisor does not appreciate my work	Supervisory Practice	P
51	My supervisor belittles my experience and knowledge	Supervisory Practice	P
52	My boss is jealous about my achievement	Supervisory Practice	-
53	My boss criticises my work	Supervisory Practice	P
54	There is no support from my colleagues to get the work done even for the common goals	Teamwork	P
55	My department does not work as a team	Teamwork	P
56	My colleagues criticise my work	Teamwork	P
57	I am not treated with respect by my colleagues in my department	Teamwork	P

Column M (Metrics): B . . . Benchmarking D . . . Direct Metrics P . . . Proxy Metrics

It becomes obvious that not all drivers, all potential causes for attrition, can be verified directly. For some, it is quite hard to get any data. For some, data from outside the organisation is needed in order to perform an analysis because within the organisation, there is no difference. Namely, everyone in the organisation receives the same package of dental benefits (ID 3). It can well be that people leave because of that item "Dental benefits are poor". However, if having only data from internal staff who all receive the same dental package, we cannot check whether people who left had a worse package than people who have been staying. Again, this is because this item does not show any variation, no difference whatsoever.

Comparing with Benchmarks

Therefore, most items in category Compensation & Benefits (ID 1 to 5), for example, cannot be analysed with only internal data regarding their influence on the decision for people to leave the organisation. There is a need to compare our benefits and salary with benchmarks in the industry. Usually, the Ministry of Labour, the International Labour Organisation, and some Associations offer this kind of information for a variety of industries.

In contrast, item "I am not paid fairly compared to others who are doing the same job as me" (ID 6) can be analysed regarding its influence on the decision to leave, because it is very likely that there is some variation in the salary even for staff with a similar job in our organisation.

Using Proxy Measurements

Some items cannot be measured directly. "My department does not work as a team" (ID 55) is a voice raised a few times during the exit interviews. But it is not a statement with available data. Nor is it possible to run a survey including this question for the leavers.

Nevertheless, our organisation runs an Employee Engagement Survey (EES) every other year with a Pulse Survey in between. Although, the above-mentioned statements are not part of either survey directly. Proxy statements that would cover **Teamwork** within Department and Cross-department **Collaboration** are

- There is good teamwork across departments in our organisation.
- There is good teamwork within my department.
- I can rely on my colleagues when I need support.

Proxy statements for category **Job Motivation** are

- My responsibilities suit my personal skills and expertise.
- In my job I am given the right amount of freedom to make decisions.
- I am proud to work for my company.
- I enjoy my work.

The **Supervisory Practice** statements are represented, amongst others, by

- My direct supervisor provides me with clear and helpful feedback regarding my performance
- My direct supervisor shows me that my work is meaningful and important.
- My direct supervisor takes into account my personal concerns as an employee.

Similarly, other categories are covered with EES statements.

There is a caveat: These proxy statements cannot be linked to a stayer or leaver directly because the engagement survey is done with the promise of anonymity. Individual data is not communicated to HR by the market researcher. Even if you conduct the Employee Engagement Survey in-house, the promise of anonymity is an important prerequisite for getting honest, i.e., less biased, and less beautified input. (This can be achieved by running the survey on a public platform like SurveyMonkey or Google Forms, which makes it virtually impossible to track back the entry to the device or IP address.)

This caveat means, that our EES or Pulse survey results can only be linked to the person via organisational units, namely, by using the aggregated data for departments and sections. Section averages are only available for sections of a certain size. This is not perfect, but this could help. After all, organisational, teamwork or supervisory drivers are likely similar for the same department and might be different from department to department, this means from supervisor to supervisor.

For leavers, data of the last EES they have participated in have been taken into the datasets.

Employing Direct Measurements

Some statements can be covered with data from direct measurements. For example, "I am not paid fairly compared to others who are doing the same job as me" means that this person has a way of comparing his salary with his colleagues in our organisation. Salary can be compared directly. The same applies for the overtime our staff clocks and for business travel and distance from home. All these data can be downloaded from the system and are not a secret to HR.

The category Career Development cannot be covered entirely. However, number of training hours received during the last year in service has been included into the dataset since this is personal data that can be retrieved from the learning and development system easily. During exit interviews, lack of training options was raised as important for staff. Information about satisfaction with career development could be retrieved from the EES as well. However, as we know already, this would only be available as department and section average.

Including a Control Group

After going through the list of potential root causes with her team and with the consultants, Susan offers her full support "I see the list of potential drivers. I will make sure you get all the data we have for the people who left us over the last five years".

Stop! Bad idea!

For Analysing Variation, we Need to Have Variation
In order to analyse the influence of a potential root cause X on the output Y, root cause X and output Y must show some variation. If there is no variation in either of them, there is no way of analysing the relationship between X and Y.

Analysing only the staff who have left us will not work. It is essential to compare the characteristics of leavers with those of the stayers. A rule of thumb is to have at least the same sample size for a control group, the stayers compared to the leavers. To make our life easier, we just download the data for all people who are still with the organisation and all data we can get for those who have left over a certain timeframe by choice.

In order to increase the sample size, that is, rise the analysis power of our tools, we download the data of staff for the last three years. Actual staff data form the control group, and people who have left the organisation in 2019, 2018, and 2017 are taken into the dataset for analysis.

Including Demographics

Demographics like gender, age, marital status, tenure, distance between home and office cannot be considered as drivers for people leaving the organisation. However, there could be a difference between different groups of staff such as older staff and younger staff, on the attrition. Since this data is easily available from the system, it will be included in the analysis.

Data Preparation

The data are collected in an Excel file Retention.xlsx. Each row carries the information, the dataset, for one employee, where column ID marks the employee identifier. When collecting data, especially whilst involving non-HR staff, elimination of personal data like name and email address is a must. The outcome variable Y is shown in column Left and has only two levels, Left or Stayed. Column LeftWhen carries the year of resignation. Columns Department and Section display organisational unit and BusinessTravel can be 1_none, 2_some, 3_frequent. Age, Gender and MaritalStatus (1_single, 2_married, 3_divorced) stand for basic demographics. The numbering forces a certain sequence.

Column Tenure shows years with the company, DistanceToHome presents kilometres between workplace and home. In Education, the level of education is marked from 1 to 5 (1 = secondary school and below, 5 = degree and above). JobMotiv, Super, and Teamwork show the rating of the organisational unit in the categories Job Motivation, Supervisory Practice, and Teamwork & Collaboration in the last EES the staff has participated in. This rating is using the mean instead of the percentage since this usually gives a better resolution. Hence, we have insisted that your market researcher gives a mean in addition to the percentage when collating EES

ID	Left	LeftWhen	Department	Section	Business Travel	JobLevel	Age	Gender	Marital Status
19921660	Left	2018	Land	Transport	3_frequent	1	38	Male	2_married
19921705	Stayed		Air and Sea	Air	2_some	1	45	Male	1_single
19922048	Left	2018	Air and Sea	Air	3_frequent	1	26	Male	2_married
19922483	Stayed		Land	Transport	2_some	2	34	Male	1_single
19922552	Left	2018	SCM	Logistics	2_some	1	20	Male	1_single
19922933	Stayed		SCM	Logistics	2_some	1	60	Male	2_married
19923071	Stayed		Air and Sea	Air	2_some	2	38	Female	2_married

ID	Tenure	Distance ToHome	Education	JobMotiv	Super	Teamwork	Salary	Training Hours
19921660	16	13	3	4	3.2	3.5	$ 1,758	0
19921705	8	10	4	3.7	3.4	3.9	$ 1,921	14
19922048	6	5	3	3.2	2.9	3.1	$ 3,043	7
19922483	6	6	2	4	3.7	4.2	$ 4,156	7
19922552	0.5	6	5	3.9	2.9	3.1	$ 1,942	0
19922933	37	11	4	3.9	3.6	4.1	$ 2,313	14
19923071	9	27	3	3.7	3.4	3.9	$ 4,757	28

Figure 4.41 Extract of Dataset Retention.xlsx

Source: Used with permission from Microsoft.

results. Salary indicates the staff salary and TrainingHours reveals the investment of training in the staff during the last year with the organisation.

Our outcome variable, i.e., result variable, is Left. Left is discrete with only the two levels Left and Stayed. As shown in an earlier chapter, analysing the influence of one or multiple factors on a discrete Y can be done with Logistic Regression.

Since it is not easy to run Logistic Regression in Excel with only the Analysis ToolPak installed, we switch to R where there are analysis tools available for all possible data situations. Before starting the analysis, we upload, check, clean and transform our dataset.

TASK 4.12   LOAD THE DATA FROM RETENTION.XLSX INTO R STUDIO AND TEST FOR COMPLETENESS:

1. Open R Studio.

2. In the Files window, navigate to your directory and select Retention.xlsx.

3. Select Import Dataset.

4. Select Sheet Raw.

5. Select Range A1: R1389.

```
# Loading library for inserting Excel file loads automat-
ically
library(readxl)
# Uploading Excel file Retention.xlsx is loaded into data
frame Retention
Retention <- read_excel("Retention.xlsx", sheet = "Reten-
tion", range = "A1:R1389")
attach(Retention)
# Performing test for empty cells (NA) in table
(dataframe) Retention
colSums(is.na(Retention))
```

```
ID Left LeftWhen BusinessTravel Department Section JobLevel Age
 0  0     737        0             0          0        0      0
Gender MaritalStatus Tenure DistanceToHome Education JobMotiv Super
  0         0           1        0             0         0       0
Teamwork Salary TrainingHours
   0       0         0
```

As the output indicates, column LeftWhen has 737 empty cells. On the one hand, this is not surprising because these empty cells are in rows of employees who have not left. On the other hand, since we are not planning any analysis including this column, we can just ignore these empty cells for now.

Additionally, there must be an empty cell in column Tenure. This cannot be accepted since Tenure is intended to be part of the Logistic Regression. There are different ways of dealing with empty entries:

1. This empty cell can be filled by inputting the correct value. This would be an approach to take when the input requires a category like Department or Section etc.

2. This empty cell can be filled with the average of the column if it is numerical and it is hard to retrieve the real input.

3. This empty cell can be deleted by removing the whole row, the entire data set. This approach is advisable if the above-mentioned steps cannot be taken and/or the sample size is large enough.

We have decided to replace the empty cell in Tenure by the average of the column.

TASK 4.13   REPLACE EMPTY CELL IN TENURE WITH AVERAGE OF COLUMN:

```
# Checking if Tenure is NA then replacing it with mean(Tenure)
Retention$Tenure <- ifelse(is.na(Tenure), mean(Tenure,
na.rm=TRUE), Tenure)
# Performing test for empty cells (NA) in table (dataframe)
Retention
colSums(is.na(Retention))
```

The output shows that Tenure has no NA any longer. Great!

If we wish to perform a Logistic Regression on Retention with Left as a Y, we will experience an error since the Y must be numeric. This means, we need to transform our Y in Left into a numeric Y LeftNum.

TASK 4.14   CREATE NEW NUMERIC COLUMN LEFTNUM BASED ON LEFT:

```
# Creating column LeftNum to 1 where Left is Left and other rows
to 0
Retention$LeftNum <- ifelse(Left == "Left", 1, 0)
# Displaying new data frame Retention including column LeftNum
View(Retention)
```

By scrolling to the right, the newly created column LeftNum is visible. With this step, our data should be prepared for analysis.

Data Analysis

Analysing this complex R data frame Retention will start with an overview of the data.

TASK 4.15   GENERATE OVERVIEW OF ALL DATA IN RETENTION:

```
# Showing number of rows and columns
dim(Retention)
# Showing the structure of the data frame
str(Retention)
# Showing the names of columns in the data frame
colnames(Retention)
# Showing the descriptive statistics on the data frame
summary(Retention)
# Showing the data frame in a window in R Studio
View(Retention)
```

Output:

```
# dim(Retention)
[1] 1388 19
# str(Retention)
tibble [1,388 x 19] (S3: tbl_df/tbl/data.frame)
$ ID            : num [1:1388] 19921660 19921705 19922048  ...
$ Left          : chr [1:1388] "Left" "Stayed" "Left" "Stayed" ...
$ LeftWhen      : num [1:1388] 2018 NA 2018 NA 2018 ...
$ BusinessTravel: chr [1:1388] "3_frequent" "2_some" ...
$ Department    : chr [1:1388] "Land" "Air and Sea" ...
$ Section       : chr [1:1388] "Transport" "Air" "Transport" ...
$ JobLevel      : num [1:1388] 1 1 1 2 1 1 2 1 2 1 3 1 ...
$ Age           : num [1:1388] 38 45 26 34 20 60 38 26 40 26 ...
$ Gender        : chr [1:1388] "Male" "Male" "Male" "Male" ...
$ MaritalStatus : chr [1:1388] "2_married" "1_single" ...
$ Tenure        : num [1:1388] 16 8 6 6 0.5 37 9 1 1 1 ...
$ DistanceToHome: num [1:1388] 13 10 5 6 6 11 27 9 9 9 ...
$ Education     : num [1:1388] 3 4 3 2 5 4 3 2 4 2 ...
$ JobMotiv      : num [1:1388] 4 3.7 3.2 4 3.9 3.9 3.7 3.6 3.9 ...
$ Super         : num [1:1388] 3.2 3.4 2.9 3.7 2.9 3.6 3.4 ...
$ Teamwork      : num [1:1388] 3.5 3.9 3.1 4.2 3.1 4.1 3.9 4.2 ...
$ Salary        : num [1:1388] 1758 1921 3043 4156 1942 ...
$ TrainingHours : num [1:1388] 0 14 7 7 0 14 28 14 0 7 ...
$ LeftNum       : num [1:1388] 1 0 1 0 1 0 0 1 1 1 ...#
```

```
colnames(Retention)
 [1] "ID" "Left" "LeftWhen" "BusinessTravel" "Department"
     "Section"
 [7] "JobLevel" "Age" "Gender" "MaritalStatus" "Tenure" "Distanc-
     eToHome"
[13] "Education" "JobMotiv" "Super" "Teamwork" "Salary" "Train-
     ingHours"
[19] "LeftNum"


# summary(Retention)

      ID                 Left             LeftWhen       Department          Section
Min.   :19921660   Length:1388       Min.   :2017   Length:1388       Length:1388
1st Qu.:19991011   Class :character  1st Qu.:2017   Class :character  Class :character
Median :20059818   Mode  :character  Median :2018   Mode  :character  Mode  :character
Mean   :20059196                     Mean   :2018
3rd Qu.:20124584                     3rd Qu.:2019
Max.   :20199886                     Max.   :2019
                                     NA's   :737


BusinessTravel        JobLevel           Age             Gender        MaritalStatus
Length:1388       Min.   :1.00      Min.   :20.00   Length:1388       Length:1388
Class :character  1st Qu.:1.00      1st Qu.:31.00   Class :character  Class :character
Mode  :character  Median :2.00      Median :36.00   Mode  :character  Mode  :character
                  Mean   :1.89      Mean   :37.59
                  3rd Qu.:2.00      3rd Qu.:44.00
                  Max.   :5.00      Max.   :62.00


    Tenure         DistanceToHome     Education         JobMotiv          Super             Teamwork
Min.   : 0.500    Min.   : 4.00     Min.   :1.000   Min.   :2.800   Min.   :2.400     Min.   :2.600
1st Qu.: 2.000    1st Qu.: 5.00     1st Qu.:2.000   1st Qu.:3.300   1st Qu.:3.000     1st Qu.:3.400
Median : 5.000    Median :10.00     Median :3.000   Median :3.700   Median :3.400     Median :3.900
Mean   : 6.272    Mean   :12.16     Mean   :2.882   Mean   :3.665   Mean   :3.374     Mean   :3.813
3rd Qu.: 8.000    3rd Qu.:17.00     3rd Qu.:4.000   3rd Qu.:4.000   3rd Qu.:3.700     3rd Qu.:4.200
Max.   :40.000    Max.   :32.00     Max.   :5.000   Max.   :4.100   Max.   :3.900     Max.   :4.400


    Salary        TrainingHours       LeftNum
Min.   :   794    Min.   : 0.00     Min.   :0.000
1st Qu.: 2234     1st Qu.: 7.00     1st Qu.:0.000
Median : 3808     Median :14.00     Median :0.000
Mean   : 4902     Mean   :12.53     Mean   :0.469
3rd Qu.: 5927     3rd Qu.:21.00     3rd Qu.:1.000
Max.   :15313     Max.   :56.00     Max.   :1.000
```

The overview of the data shows that our data frame has 1388 lines with 19 columns (**dim** function). The structure (**str** function) indicates the datatypes per column, the length of each column and sample data from each column. As the name suggests, function **colnames** gives a very simple list of the names of the columns in the data frame. The **summary** function provides minimum, Q1 (25% quartile), median (50% quartile), mean, Q3 (75% quartile) and maximum per column if the column is numeric. Function **view** displays the complete data frame (if the size permits) in a window above the console in R Studio. This window comes with scrollbars for exploring all rows and all columns of the data frame, similar to MS Excel.

As mentioned before, this data frame shows the Y in column Left with either the value Left or Stayed. Additionally, we have created column LeftNum that carries the code 1 for Left and 0 for Stayed. Apart from column ID, the identifier for staff, all other columns from BusinessTravel to TrainingHours, columns 4 to 18, contain potential drivers for the Y, potential Xs. Before we can develop a model to calculate the probability for staff to leave the organisation, we will check all discrete Xs one by one on their impact on Y.

Translating these potential Xs, the columns in our table, into hypotheses will yield in the following:

Hypothesis 1: Business Travel Has a Significant Influence on Staff Intention to Leave the Organisation

Business Travel is a discrete variable with three levels, and Left is discrete with two levels. This constellation asks for a PivotTable (Figure 4.42) and a PivotGraph (Figure 4.43) in MS Excel. Opening a PivotTable

Neither PivotTable nor column chart indicate that there is a clear difference between the degree of business travel and people who resign from the organisation. To the contrary, 55% of the frequent travellers stayed with the organisation whereas 45% of frequent travellers left.

As always, plots are necessary to get an overview of the data, but they are hardly enough to draw conclusions. For a safe decision, a hypothesis test is needed. For discrete X and discrete Y, a Chi^2 test needs to be applied. Excel does not help here easily. Therefore, we apply the R Chi^2 test.

TASK 4.16   CREATE PIVOT TABLE FOR COLUMN LEFT OVER BUSINESSTRAVEL:

1. Open data in Retention.xlsx.

2. Position your cursor within table "Retention" and Insert – PivotTable.

3. Pivot table row is Left. Pivot table column is BusinessTravel. Pivot table value is Count of ID.

4. In the PivotTable, Insert – PivotChart.

5. Select 100% Stacked Column Chart.

6. Columns for %Left and %Stayed are manually added applied to columns by Add DataLabels on columns.

7. Beautify your chart.

Count of ID	Column Labels				
Row Labels	Left	Stayed	Grand Total	%Left	%Stayed
1_none	49	57	106	46%	54%
2_some	452	497	949	48%	52%
3_frequent	150	183	333	45%	55%
Grand Total	651	737	1388		

Figure 4.42 PivotTable of Business Travel versus Stayed/Left

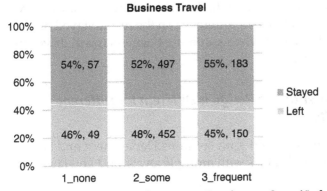

Figure 4.43 Column Chart for Business Travel versus Stayed/Left

---

TASK 4.17   LOAD PACKAGE RSTATIX AND PERFORM CHI² TEST ON BUSINESSTRAVEL:

Open R Studio.

```
# Loading necessary packages
install.packages("rstatix")
library(rstatix)
# Building cross table xtab and naming rows and columns
xtab <- as.table(rbind(c(49, 452, 150), c(57, 497, 183)))
dimnames(xtab) <- list(Result = c("Left", "Stayed"),
  BusinessTravel = c("1_none", "2_some", "3_frequent"))
# Computing the Chi-square-test
Xsq <- chisq.test(xtab)
Xsq$observed
Xsq$expected
Xsq$stdres
```

The output of this Chi² test:

```
Pearson's Chi-squared test
data: xtab
X-squared = 0.68196, df = 2, p-value = 0.7111

Observed Values:
Result     1_none        2_some        3_frequent
  Left        49           452            150
  Stayed      57           497            183

Expected Values:
Result     1_none        2_some        3_frequent
  Left      49.71614      445.1001      156.1837
  Stayed    56.28386      503.8999      176.8163

Std.Residuals:
Result     1_none        2_some        3_frequent
  Left     -0.1450307     0.7980583     -0.7788633
  Stayed    0.1450307    -0.7980583      0.7788633
```

The p-value for the Chi^2 test shows 0.7111. This means, we have no evidence that BusinessTravel makes a difference on the result Stayed or Left. The risk of being in the wrong when assuming business travel drives the decision of staff to leave is 71%.

Hypothesis 2: The Intention to Resign is Different for Different Organisational Units

The organisational unit is coded with columns Department and Section with both being discrete variables with multiple levels, and Left is discrete with two levels.

Here, PivotTable and PivotGraph (Rows: Department and Section) are applied. Following the method shown for Hypothesis 1, the PivotGraph is seen in Figure 4.44.

Obviously, the turnover is quite different from department to department, from section to section. We expect the Chi^2 test to show a significant difference for some departments.

Since Chi^2 test needs a minimum sample size in expected values which cannot be achieved for small sections like all management units and some HR and Admin units, we perform it only on department level. If there is a difference found, further study needs to be done anyway.

TASK 4.18   PERFORM CHI^2 TEST ON DEPARTMENT:

Open R Studio.

```
# Loading necessary packages, if not done before
install.packages("rstatix")
library(rstatix)
# Building cross table xtab using table function
xtab <- xtab <- table(Retention$Left,Retention$Department)
# Computing the Chi-square-test
Xsq <- chisq.test(xtab)
Xsq            # Print Chi-squared test
Xsq$observed   # Print observed values
Xsq$expected   # Print expected values
Xsq$stdres     # Print standardised residuals
# Showing balloon plot of components
library("gplots")
balloonplot(t(xtab), main ="Departments Turnover", xlab
="Departments", ylab="Decision", label = FALSE, show.margins =
FALSE)
# Showing plot of standardised residuals of stayed/left by
department
library("corrplot")
corrplot(Xsq$stdres, is.cor = FALSE)
# Showing plot of contributions to stayed/left by department
contrib <- 100*Xsq$residuals^2/Xsq$statistic
corrplot(contrib, is.cor = FALSE)
```

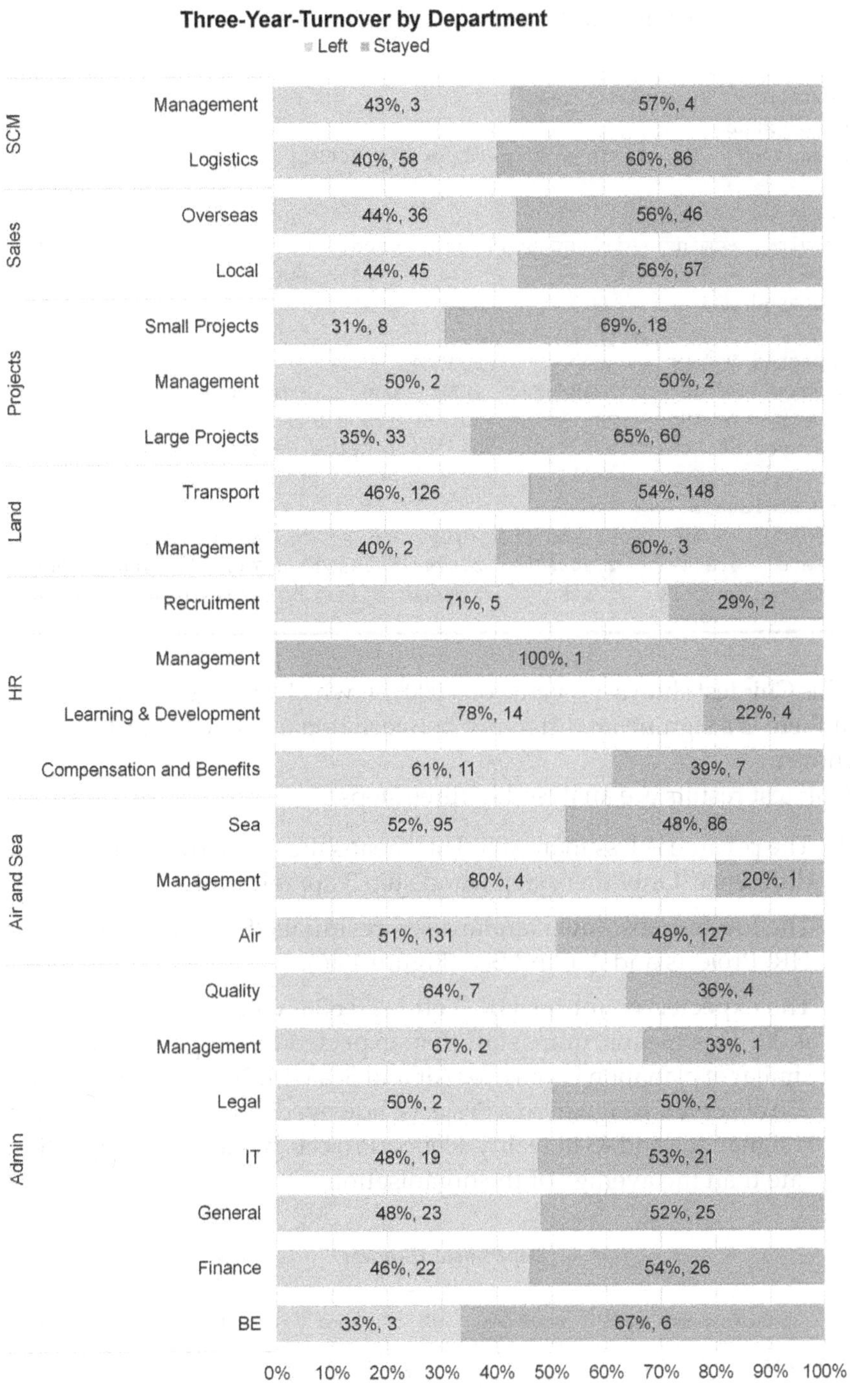

Three-Year-Turnover by Department
▨ Left ▪ Stayed

		Left	Stayed
SCM	Management	43%, 3	57%, 4
	Logistics	40%, 58	60%, 86
Sales	Overseas	44%, 36	56%, 46
	Local	44%, 45	56%, 57
Projects	Small Projects	31%, 8	69%, 18
	Management	50%, 2	50%, 2
	Large Projects	35%, 33	65%, 60
Land	Transport	46%, 126	54%, 148
	Management	40%, 2	60%, 3
HR	Recruitment	71%, 5	29%, 2
	Management	100%, 1	
	Learning & Development	78%, 14	22%, 4
	Compensation and Benefits	61%, 11	39%, 7
Air and Sea	Sea	52%, 95	48%, 86
	Management	80%, 4	20%, 1
	Air	51%, 131	49%, 127
Admin	Quality	64%, 7	36%, 4
	Management	67%, 2	33%, 1
	Legal	50%, 2	50%, 2
	IT	48%, 19	53%, 21
	General	48%, 23	52%, 25
	Finance	46%, 22	54%, 26
	BE	33%, 3	67%, 6

0%   10%   20%   30%   40%   50%   60%   70%   80%   90%   100%

Figure 4.44 Departments and Sections over Stayed/Left

The output of this Chi^2 test:

```
Pearson's Chi-squared test
data: xtab
X-squared = 22.68, df = 6, p-value = 0.000911

Observed Values:
Result    Admin    Air and Sea    HR    Land    Projects    Sales    SCM
  Left     78        230          30    128      43          81       61
  Stayed   85        214          14    151      80         103       90

Expected Values:
Result    Admin    Air and Sea     HR     Land     Projects    Sales    SCM
  Left    76.4509   208.245      20.636  130.856   57.689     86.299   70.822
  Stayed  86.5491   235.755      23.363  148.143   65.310     97.700   80.177

Std.Residuals:
Result    Admin    Air and Sea     HR      Land     Projects    Sales    SCM
  Left    0.2589    2.5086        2.8744  -0.3833  -2.7801   -0.8406   1.6966
  Stayed -0.2589   -2.5086       -2.8744   0.3833   2.78015   0.8406   1.6966
```

This Chi^2 test shows a p-value of 0.000911, which leads to the conclusion that there is a significant difference between departments regarding their turnover.

Chi^2 test results are analysed in three steps:

1. The p-value is less than 0.05. This means the test shows a significant difference. Only then, step 2 and step 3 are relevant.

2. The highest absolute standardised residuals (Std. Residual) are at HR, Projects and Air and Sea (Figure 4.46).

3. The expected count for HR/Left is 20.636, whereas the real count is 30. This means, more staff than expected left department HR. A similar explanation is valid for Air and Sea with 208.245 expected and 230 observed resignations. Projects, however shows 57.689 expected resignations and 43 in reality. Hence, Projects has a lower resignation rate than the average of the organisation.

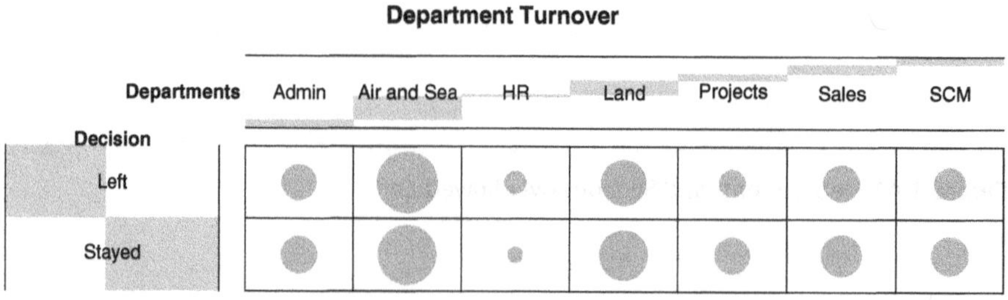

Department Turnover

Figure 4.45 Balloon Plot of Observed Values of Turnover by Department

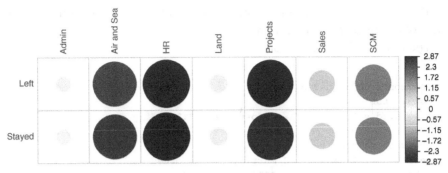

Figure 4.46 Contribution to Stayed/Left by Department

Further analysis is due to identify the root causes for these differences. Departments or sections are not root causes but rather hints for root causes.

Hypothesis 3: The Decision of Staff to Resign Depends on their Marital Status

Although there was no mention during the exit interviews that the marital status could influence people's decision to leave the company, marital status was suggested by one of the HR colleagues. Therefore, the dataset contains information about the marital status for all existing staff and for those who have left in the last three years.

This hypothesis seems to receive confirmation by the data plot in Figure 4.47.

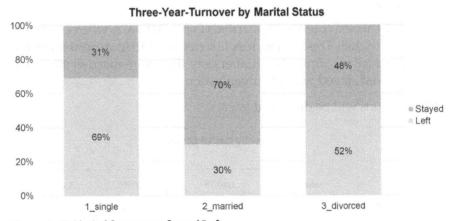

Figure 4.47 Marital Status over Stayed/Left

The Chi^2 test has been conducted similar to the previous examples. The output of this test is shown here:

The output of this Chi^2 test:

```
Pearson's Chi-squared test
data: xtab
X-squared = 175.97, df = 2, p-value < 2.2e-16

Observed Values:
Result      1_single   2_married   3_divorced
  Left         330        205         116
  Stayed       148        481         108

Expected Values:
Result      1_single   2_married   3_divorced
  Left      224.1916    321.7478    105.0605
  Stayed    253.8084    364.2522    118.9395

Std.Residuals:
Result      1_single   2_married   3_divorced
  Left       11.9769    -12.5596     1.5993
  Stayed    -11.9769     12.5596    -1.5993
```

This Chi^2 test shows a p-value of 0.000, which means that there is a significant difference between staff's marital status regarding their turnover. Chi^2 test results are analysed in three steps:

1. The p-value is less than 0.05. This means the test shows a significant difference.

2. The highest absolute standardised residuals (Std. Residual) are at 2_married.

3. The expected count for 2_married/Left is 321.7478, whereas the real count is 205. This means, less married staff than expected left the organisation. Similarly, numbers say that more married staff than expected stayed with the organisation.

Conclusions will be discussed later.

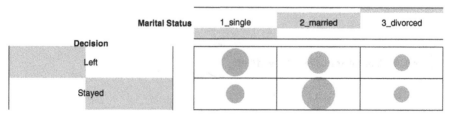

Figure 4.48 Balloon Plot of Observed Values of Turnover by Marital Status

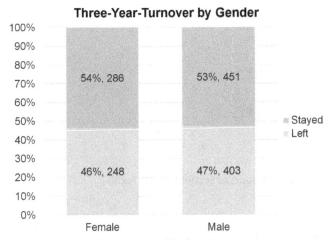

Figure 4.49 Gender over Stayed/Left

Hypothesis 4: The Decision of Staff to Resign Depends on their Gender

In order to complete the picture, gender has been analysed regarding its influence on the decision to leave the company.

This hypothesis does not seem true when comparing the bars for Female and Male staff in Figure 4.49.

The Chi^2 test was conducted as well. The shortened output of this test is shown here:

```
Pearson's Chi-squared test
X-squared = 0.046795, df = 1, p-value = 0.8287
```

From this p-value we may conclude that this hypothesis is rejected. There is a risk of 82.87% for assuming that there is a difference between male and female staff regarding their turnover.

Hypothesis 5: The Decision of Staff to Resign Depends on Training Opportunities Given

The above-stated factor shows continuous data or quasi-continuous data (ordinal discrete data that behaves like continuous data, under some circumstances). This means X TrainingHours is continuous that supposedly drives a discrete binary Y, Left or Stayed in variable Left.

This combination of X and Y needs a special set of tools. For plotting this data, scatter plots are not useful because it is hard to distinguish whether there is a relationship between X and Y by inspecting this plot (Figure 4.50).

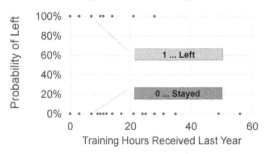

Left or Stayed over Training Hours

Figure 4.50 Left/Stayed over Training Hours as Scatter Plot (MS Excel)

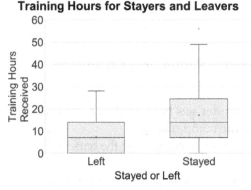

Training Hours for Stayers and Leavers

Figure 4.51 Left/Stayed over Training Hours as Box Plot

Still, there are other ways to show this relationship. Highly informative plots for the combination discrete data versus continuous data are dot plots and box plots (Figure 4.51).

Having the box plot in Figure 4.51 makes it much easier to judge whether there is a relationship between both variables or not. It seems that people who left had received less training than people who have been staying. In order to ensure we "compare apples with apples", we must assume that the training information was collected for the whole year before the resignees left.

The trick is to swap X and Y, i.e., X is presented on the Y axis and Y is shown on the X axis (Figure 4.51).

In reality, there is mostly no switch from Left to Stayed at a certain number of training hours provided. Some people might feel more appreciated with two training days given and stay with the company. For others, this might not be something they value a lot and still leave. Hence, a certain number of training hours provided does not guarantee someone staying with the organisation. But there might be a higher probability for staying

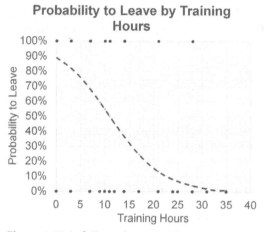

Figure 4.52 Left/Stayed over Training Hours as Scatter Plot and Probability Curve

than leaving if the number of training hours goes up (bonded employees are not included in this consideration).

The probability to leave depending on the number of training hours provided is shown in Figure 4.52. Using the chart produced in R, the probability to leave can be estimated with about 35% if the staff receives two days of training.

The statistics that model this relationship is called the Logit model. The Logit function models the relationship between a categorical output variable Y – in our case the decision to leave or stay – and one or multiple continuous input variables X – in our case the number of training hours provided to the staff. The probability to leave p, the odds ratio, can be expressed with

Equation 4.4: Logit Model for Probability to Leave as Function of Training Hours Provided

$$Ln\,odds = ln\,\frac{p_{leave}}{1-p_{leave}} = b_0 + b_1 TrainingHours$$

TASK 4.19   PERFORM LOGISTIC REGRESSION ON TRAINING HOURS:

Open R Studio.

```
# Loading necessary packages, if not done before
library(stats)
# Building general linear model using logit function
model <- glm(LeftNum ~ TrainingHours,
family=binomial(link='logit'), data=Retention)
# Inspecting the general linear model
summary(model)
# Calculating the ANOVA for deviance, i.e., indicator for
quality of model
anova(model, test="Chisq")
```

This model is used by a statistical tool: Logistic Regression (Chew, 2017). Performing logistic regression analysis is easier done in R than in MS Excel.

The output of this logistic regression:

```
Deviance Residuals:
Deviance Residuals:
Min           1Q      Median        3Q       Max
 -2.0889   -0.9502   -0.2849    0.8794    2.5396

Coefficients:
                 Estimate    Std. Error    z value     Pr(>|z|)
(Intercept)       2.06207      0.13266      15.54      <2e-16 ***
TrainingHours    -0.18736      0.01057     -17.72      <2e-16 ***
Signif. codes:   0 '***' 0.001 '**' 0.01 '*' 0.05 '.' 0.1 ' ' 1

Null deviance: 1918.8   on 1387 degrees of freedom
Residual deviance: 1387.1   on 1386 degrees of freedomCRAIC: 1391.1
```

This output means that TrainingHours serves as a predictor for staff's decision to leave because of the p-value of zero. $Pr(>|z|) = < 2 \times 10^{-16}$ is extremely small, in other words practically zero. How good is this prediction?

The output of the ANOVA will help:

```
Analysis of Deviance Table
Model: binomial, link: logit
Response: LeftNum

Terms added sequentially (first to last)
                Df Deviance   Resid. Df   Resid. Dev   Pr(>Chi)
NULL                            1387        1918.8
Training-Hours  1 531.71        1386        1387.1     < 2.2e-16 ***
```

Logistic regression results are evaluated with a series of indicators:

1. Check out **AIC** (Akaike Information Criteria) that has a similar function as adjusted R^2 in multiple regression. The difference is that AIC is the better the smaller it is. There is no ideal AIC. Only having multiple models with their AIC gives a hint for the best model, the one with the smallest AIC (Date, 2019).

2. **Null and Residual Deviance** are comparable to total sum of squares and residual sum of squares in multiple linear regression,

respectively. Residual Deviance should be comparatively small to Null Deviance in order to have a good model. In our case, they are 1918.8 versus 1363.2. This means, the difference is explained by X TrainingHours.

3. As known from the multiple linear regression, R^2 serves as an indicator for the quality of the regression. R^2 indicates, how much variation in output Y is explained by the Xs included in the regression model. For logistic regression, **McFadden's R^2** has a similar meaning. The higher McFadden's R^2, the better the model is.

4. The **Prediction Accuracy** can be calculated by applying the model to all values in the data frame and comparing the outcome with the observed value in Y Figure 4.52.

Next, we calculate McFadden's R^2.

TASK 4.20   CALCULATE MCFADDEN'S PSEUDO-R^2 FOR LOGISTIC REGRESSION:

Open R Studio.

```
# Loading necessary packages, if not done before
library(pscl)
# Generating McFadden R² similar to linear regression
pR2(model)
```

The output of this McFadden R^2 looks like this:

```
Fitting null model for pseudo-r2
   llh          llhNull        G2         McFadden    r2ML       r2CU
-693.5665572 -959.4223142 531.7115139  0.2770998  0.3182399  0.4248650
```

McFadden's R^2 shows a low level of coverage of variation in the decision to leave by the amount of training provided. This means, TrainingHours seems to be a significant predictor. However, there could be other predictors for the resignation of staff.

Furthermore, it would be good to know how well our first predictor works. Therefore, we generate a new column in our data frame carrying the model fit (Retention$LeftFit), that is the value for each row that is the result of applying the model. Another column is generated that shows the decision based on the modelled values. The decision is made using the 50% threshold (Retention$LeftFit10).

TASK 4.21   CALCULATE THE PREDICTION ACCURACY FOR LOGISTIC REGRESSION:

Open R Studio.

```
# Adding column to Retention data frame for calculated Y
following model
Retention$LeftFit <- predict(model, type='response')
# Adding column to Retention data frame for decision following
model 50/50
Retention$LeftFit10 <- ifelse(Retention$LeftFit > 0.5,1,0)
Retention$LeftFitDec <- ifelse(Retention$LeftFit > 0.5,
"Leave","Stay")
# Calculating prediction accuracy for model
PredictAccuracy <- 1-mean(Retention$LeftFit10 !=
Retention$LeftNum)
PredictAccuracy # Prints the prediction accuracy
# Generating cross table of Prediction versus Decision
xtab <- table(Retention$Left, Retention$LeftFitDec)
# Generating a balloon plot to show ratio of prediction and
decision
balloonplot(t(xtab), main ="Prediction Accuracy 70.7%", xlab
="Prediction", ylab="Decision", label=TRUE, show.margins=TRUE)
```

Calculating the model fit follows the formula generated out of the model:
Equation 4.5: Prediction Formula for Logistic Regression

$$P_Y = \frac{1}{1 + e^{-(b0 + b1\,X)}}$$

Hence, for $b_0 = 2.062$ and $b_1 = -0.187$, the probability for someone leaving the organisation is calculated depending on variable TrainingHours following this equation:

Equation 4.6: Prediction Formula for Probability of Resignation Depending on Training Hours Provided

$$P_{Left} = \frac{1}{1 + e^{-(2.062 + (-0.187)*\,TrainingHours)}}$$

For example, the likelihood for someone resigning who has received 14 training hours is about 36.45%, for 28 training hours only 4.02%.

As a result of this, column LeftFit in Retention shows the modelled probability for resigning based on training hours, whereas LeftFit10 contains the decision Left (1) or Stayed (0) based on the threshold of 50%.

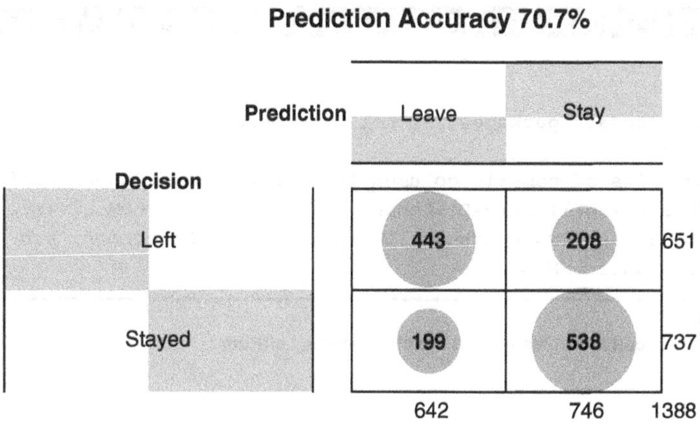

Prediction Accuracy 70.7%

Figure 4.53 Confusion Matrix of Prediction Accuracy for the Model

Figure 4.53 shows the confusion matrix that indicates the relationship of predictions to real decisions.

The correct predictions are:

- 538 (38.8%) staff predicted to stay who stayed. and
- 443 (31.9%) staff predicted to leave who left.

Wrong predictions are:

- 199 (14.3%) staff predicted to leave who stayed. and
- 208 (15.0%) staff predicted to stay who left.

This means 538 + 443 out of 1388 predictions are correct. Hence, the prediction accuracy of our model is about 70.7%.

Since McFadden's R^2 shows a low 27.71% only, we try to improve our model by adding more variables into the logistic regression equation.

Hypotheses 6.14: The Decision of Staff to Resign Depends on the Factors Job Level, Age, Tenure, Distance to Home, Education Level, Job Motivation, Supervisory Practice, Teamwork, and Salary

The right-hand side of the logistic regression equation behaves pretty much like that of a multiple linear regression. This means, we can add more factors, more X, that could be continuous and even discrete ordinal or discrete categories. First, we add the continuous factors, we have not analysed yet. And we keep TrainingHours in the model since this has proven to be a significant predictor.

At first, we plot the scatter plot matrix for all possible combinations of numeric factors and the numeric version of the result variable Left in LeftNum.

The scatter plot matrix is seen in Figure 4.54. Here are some of the discoveries, from left to right:

1. JobLevel seems to strongly correlate with Salary. This is not surprising and will most likely lead to high VIF for both. One of them might need to be omitted.

TASK 4.22 PERFORM SCATTER PLOT ON MULTIPLE FACTORS:

Open R Studio.

```
# Loading necessary packages, if not done before
library(graphics)
# Plotting pairs of numeric columns in matrix without upper half
pairs(~JobLevel+Age+Tenure+DistanceToHome+Education+JobMotiv+Sup
er+Teamwork+Salary+TrainingHours+LeftNum, data = Retention, pch
= 19, upper.panel = NULL)
```

Scatter Plot Matrix of All Factors versus LeftNum

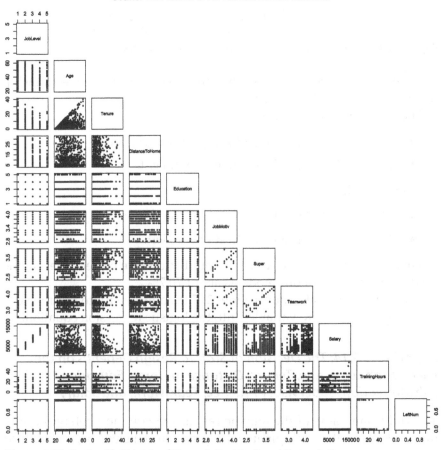

Figure 4.54 Scatter Plot Matrix of Numeric Factors X and Numeric Y

2. Age and Tenure seem to have some weak correlation. Tenure might not be needed in the model since it could be represented by Age.

3. JobMotiv, Super and Teamwork seem to have some correlation. It might be necessary to omit one or two of these items from the model.

4. The last item in the command for plot is LeftNum. This brings Left-Num, the Y, in the last row and enables the comparison with all X in one row of plots. Unfortunately, due to the binary nature of LeftNum, it is almost impossible to draw any conclusion. Only TrainingHours seems to be correlated to LeftNum. It shows that TrainingHours above 20 only happen with LeftNum = 0 (Stayed).

TASK 4.23   PERFORM LOGISTIC REGRESSION ON MULTIPLE FACTORS:

Open R Studio.

```
# Loading necessary packages, if not done before
library(stats)
# Building general linear model using logit function including
TrainingHours
model1 <- glm(LeftNum ~ JobLevel +Age +Tenure +DistanceToHome
+Education +JobMotiv +Super +Teamwork +Salary +TrainingHours,
family=binomial(link='logit'), data=Retention)
# Inspecting the general linear model
summary(model1)
```

The output of this logistic regression on model1:

```
Deviance Residuals:
    Min        1Q      Median        3Q        Max
 -2.4270    -0.4996    -0.1090     0.5587     2.7061


Coefficients:
                 Estimate    Std. Error   z value    Pr(>|z|)
(Intercept)      1.351e+01    1.041e+00    12.969    < 2e-16  ***
JobLevel         4.858e-01    2.869e-01     1.693    0.09036  .
Age             -9.567e-02    9.590e-03    -9.976    < 2e-16  ***
Tenure          -3.715e-02    1.510e-02    -2.460    0.01389  *
DistanceToHome  -7.814e-05    1.009e-02    -0.008    0.99382
Education       -3.818e-02    7.550e-02    -0.506    0.61306
JobMotiv         9.517e-01    3.588e-01     2.652    0.00799  **
Super           -3.075e+00    7.446e-01    -4.130    3.63e-05 ***
Teamwork        -1.654e-01    5.213e-01    -0.317    0.75096
Salary          -1.389e-04    8.591e-05    -1.617    0.10593
TrainingHours   -2.111e-01    1.352e-02   -15.612    < 2e-16  ***
Signif. codes:   0 '***' 0.001 '**' 0.01 '*' 0.05 '.' 0.1 ' ' 1


    Null deviance: 1918.8   on 1387   degrees of freedom
Residual deviance: 1040.1   on 1377   degrees of freedomCRAIC: 1062.8
```

AIC has dropped from 1391.1 to 1062.8 and so has residual deviance from 1387.1 to 1040.1. This indicates an improved model1. Checking out the p-values ($Pr(>|z|)$) for all factors reveals that only six out of ten show significance with less than 0.05. Still, as we have learned in previous analysis projects, there is a risk that the numbers we see now, especially the p-values, are not true because there is a possibility of multi-collinearity. This means that X variables, potential drivers, interact with each other. If they did, they would spoil the model.

Figure 4.55 Scatter Plot of Salary over JobLevel (MS Excel)

Simply put, if variables JobLevel and Salary are both in the model, it is very likely that they have a strong correlation since people are most likely paid according to job level. If this is correct, JobLevel is represented by Salary and vice versa. This would mean an over-representation of these variables, for example. Consequently, the model could be invalid.

The relationship between Salary and JobLevel is confirmed by the scatter plot shown in Figure 4.55.

A commonly used method of identifying multicollinearity between X variables is the calculation of VIF (variance inflation factors) for the model. Multicollinearity is when there is correlation between predictors, i.e., X variables, in a model. Its presence can adversely affect your regression results. The VIF estimates how much the variance of a regression coefficient is inflated due to multicollinearity in the model.

A rule of thumb for interpreting VIF:

- About 1 = not correlated,
- Between 1 and 5 = moderately correlated,
- Greater than 5 = highly correlated.

TASK 4.24A   CALCULATE VARIANCE INFLATION FACTORS FOR LATEST MODEL AND IMPROVE MODEL:

Open R Studio.

```
# Loading necessary packages, if not done before
library(car)
# Calculating variance inflation factors (Objective: VIF < 5)
vif(model1)
```

The list of VIF of this logistic regression (truncated decimals):

```
JobLevel  Age     Tenure  DistanceToHome  Education  JobMotiv
15.09     1.19    1.10    1.02            1.02       2.78
Super     TeamWork
11.64     9.03
Salary    TrainingHours
15.05     1.14
```

All VIF must be less than 5 for having a model without variance inflation (inter-correlation). It is safest to remove one factor at a time, run the
model again and check VIF.

How do we decide which factor to remove? It is not about the highest
VIF but about factors that are harder to measure or to control. In our case,
we know JobLevel is correlated to Salary. Both can be retrieved easily. Yet,
Salary shows more variation than JobLevel because staff with the same
job level might be receiving different salary. This could be exactly the
issue people raise during the exit interview. Hence, we keep Salary and
remove JobLevel.

**TASK 4.24B   REDUCE MODEL AND RE-CALCULATE VARIANCE
INFLATION FACTORS:**

```
# Reducing general linear model by JobLevel
model2 <- glm(LeftNum ~ Age +Tenure +DistanceToHome
+Education +JobMotiv +Super +Teamwork +Salary +TrainingHours,
family=binomial(link='logit'), data=Retention)
# Calculating variance inflation factors (Objective: VIF < 5)
vif(model2)
```

The VIF now looks like this (truncated decimals):

```
Age   Tenure DistanceToHome Education JobMotiv Super Teamwork Salary
1.20  1.10   1.01           1.01      2.78     11.54 8.95     1.00
TrainingHours
1.14
```

**TASK 4.24C   FURTHER REDUCE MODEL AND RE-CALCULATE
VARIANCE INFLATION FACTORS:**

```
# Further reducing general linear model by TeamWork
model3 <- glm(LeftNum ~ Age +Tenure +DistanceToHome
+Education +JobMotiv +Super +Salary +TrainingHours,
family=binomial(link='logit'), data=Retention)
# Calculating variance inflation factors (Objective: VIF < 5)
vif(model3)
```

The list of VIF after removing TeamWork is like this (truncated decimals):

```
Age    Tenure  DistanceToHome  Education  JobMotiv   Super   Salary
1.20   1.10            1.01        1.00      2.74     2.79     1.00
TrainingHours
1.13
```

Variable TeamWork has been removed because Super (supervisory practice) could be a mediator for teamwork, assuming that working on supervisory skills could probably improve teamwork as well. Now, our model3 does not show any multi-collinearity.

The reduced model3 needs to be inspected regarding p-values for variables and finally AIC, Deviance, and McFadden's R^2.

TASK 4.25A   PERFORM LOGISTIC REGRESSION ON REMAINING FACTORS:

Open R Studio.

```
# Inspecting the general linear model
summary(model3)
```

The output of this logistic regression on model3 displays:

```
Coefficients:
                    Estimate    Std. Error    z value    Pr(>|z|)
(Intercept)        1.367e+01     1.038e+00     13.176    < 2e-16 ***
Age               -9.574e-02     9.559e-03    -10.015    < 2e-16 ***
Tenure            -3.727e-02     1.506e-02     -2.474    0.01334 *
DistanceToHome    -1.253e-03     1.004e-02     -0.125    0.90065
Education         -2.616e-02     7.508e-02     -0.348    0.72751
JobMotiv           9.814e-01     3.549e-01      2.766    0.00568 **
Super             -3.281e+00     3.634e-01     -9.030    < 2e-16 ***
Salary             1.714e-06     2.215e-05      0.077    0.93832
Signif. codes:  0 '***' 0.001 '**' 0.01 '*' 0.05 '.' 0.1 ' ' 1

(Dispersion parameter for binomial family taken to be 1)

    Null deviance: 1918.8   on 1387   degrees of freedom
Residual deviance: 1043.9   on 1379   degrees of freedomCRAIC: 1061.9
```

There are still three factors with p-value above 0.05 in the model that are removed and the model is rerun.

TASK 4.25B   REDUCE MODEL AND PERFORM LOGISTIC REGRESSION ON REMAINING FACTORS:

```
# Further reducing general linear model by DistanceToHome,
Education, Salary
model4 <- glm(LeftNum ~ Age +Tenure +JobMotiv +Super
+TrainingHours, family=binomial(link='logit'), data=Retention)
# Inspecting the general linear model
summary(model4)
```

The output of this logistic regression on model4 looks like this:

```
Coefficients:
                 Estimate   Std. Error   z value   Pr(>|z|)
(Intercept)     13.576873    0.999802    13.580    <2e-16 ***
Age             -0.095592    0.009549   -10.011    <2e-16 ***
Tenure          -0.037561    0.015024    -2.500    0.0124 *
JobMotiv         0.981902    0.353720     2.776    0.0055 **
Super           -3.278653    0.362171    -9.053    <2e-16 ***
TrainingHours   -0.211132    0.013498   -15.642    <2e-16 ***
Signif. codes:   0 '***' 0.001 '**' 0.01 '*' 0.05 '.' 0.1 ' ' 1

    Null deviance: 1918.8   on 1387   degrees of freedom
Residual deviance: 1044.0   on 1382   degrees of freedomCRAIC: 1056
```

All factors in the model are significant. Now, the question is whether the model has improved compared to the previous model. Firstly, AIC has dropped. That is always Good News! Residual deviance is about the same.

TASK 4.26   CALCULATE MCFADDEN'S PSEUDO-R^2 FOR NEW MODEL:

Open R Studio.

```
# Loading necessary packages, if not done before
library(pscl)
# Generating McFadden R² similar to linear regression
pR2(model4)
```

The output of this new McFadden R^2 is like this:

```
Fitting null model for pseudo-R2
  llh           llhNull          G2           McFadden      r2ML
-522.0120575  -959.4223142  874.8205133    0.4559100    0.4675542
r2CU
0.6242064
```

McFadden's R^2 has improved from 27.7% to 45.6% now. In Hypotheses 2 and 3 we have established that Department and Marital Status are significant drivers for the output Left (decision to resign). Therefore, we include both drivers in the model.

TASK 4.27   ADD MARITAL STATUS AND DEPARTMENT TO LOGISTIC REGRESSION:

Open R Studio.

```
# Adding Department and MaritalStatus to general linear model
model5 <- glm(LeftNum ~ Department +Age +MaritalStatus +Tenure
+JobMotiv +Super +TrainingHours, family=binomial(link='logit'),d
ata=Retention)
# Inspecting the general linear model
summary(model5)
```

The output of this regression on model5 including Department and MaritalStatus:

```
Coefficients:
                        Estimate  Std. Error  z value   Pr(>|z|)
(Intercept)             22.62131    1.74720    12.947   < 2e-16  ***
DepartmentAir and Sea    0.62374    0.28977     2.153    0.0314  *
DepartmentHR            -1.47551    0.61497    -2.399    0.0164  *
DepartmentLand           0.76825    0.35521     2.163    0.0306  *
DepartmentProjects      -2.63232    0.43624    -6.034  1.60e-09  ***
DepartmentSales          2.32310    0.40346     5.758  8.51e-09  ***
DepartmentSCM           -1.19408    0.41257    -2.894    0.0038  **
Age                     -0.10273    0.01118    -9.187   < 2e-16  ***
MaritalStatus2_married  -1.26801    0.19952    -6.355  2.08e-10  ***
MaritalStatus3_divorced -0.12639    0.25613    -0.493    0.6217
Tenure                  -0.03218    0.01669    -1.928    0.0539  .
JobMotiv                 1.27493    0.56169     2.270    0.0232  *
Super                   -6.06263    0.56914   -10.652   < 2e-16  ***
TrainingHours           -0.21444    0.01529   -14.021   < 2e-16  ***
Signif. codes:   0 '***' 0.001 '**' 0.01 '*' 0.05 '.' 0.1 ' ' 1

    Null deviance: 1918.84  on 1387   degrees of freedom
Residual deviance: 846.31  on 1374   degrees of freedomCRAIC: 874.31
```

Analysing the output of the summary of the model tells us the following:

1. We may remove tenure from the model since it turned insignificant (Pr(>|z| = 0.0539).

2. Different settings for the variable Department create different outcomes. The base is the first in alphabetical order "Admin" which is not shown in the list. Department "Air and Sea" has a positive coefficient, hence staff in this department have a higher probability to leave.

3. Predictor Age is negative. Since the output is Left = 1 and Stayed = 0, increase in age reduces the probability for leaving of staff. This is explainable.

4. The basis for MaritalStatus is Single with the name "1_single" which is not mentioned. Both married and divorced staff have a lower risk of leaving than single staff. This makes sense.

5. Predictor JobMotiv (job motivation) has a small positive coefficient, which means higher job motivation increases the probability for leaving. This is against common sense. Since job motivation is a group indicator coming from department or section, we decide to remove it. After removing it McFadden does not change. It means, it is significant but not important.

6. Supervisory practice seems to be an important predictor.

7. The importance of TrainingHours was established earlier.

TASK 4.28   REDUCE MODEL AND RECALCULATE MCFADDEN R²:

```
# Removing Tenure and JobMotiv
model6 <- glm(LeftNum ~ Department +Age +MaritalStatus +Super
+TrainingHours, family=binomial(link='logit'),data=Retention)
# Generating McFadden R² after removing Tenure and JobMotiv
pR2(model6)
```

The output of this new McFadden R² on model6 is like this:

```
Fitting null model for pseudo-R²
   llh              llhNull          G2           McFadden       r2ML
 -427.8473559    -959.4223142   1063.1499166     0.5540573     0.5351117
r2CU
 0.7143988
```

The latest model including above-mentioned factors without Tenure and JobMotiv seems to be the best predictor for the probability of someone resigning. AIC and residual deviance are lowest whereas McFadden's R² is highest with 55.4%.

Calculating Prediction Accuracy

In order to use our model for prediction, it is important to know how good the model is.

TASK 4.29   CALCULATE PREDICTION ACCURACY FOR FINAL MODEL:

Open R Studio.

```
# Recalculating column to Retention data frame for estimated Y
following model6
Retention$LeftFit <- predict(model6, type='response')
# Recalculating column for decision following model6 with cut-
off 0.5
Retention$LeftFit10 <- ifelse(Retention$LeftFit > 0.5,1,0)
# Recalculating prediction accuracy for model6
PredictAccuracy <- 1-mean(Retention$LeftFit10 !=
Retention$LeftNum)
# Prints prediction accuracy
PredictAccuracy
# Generating cross table of Prediction versus Decision
Retention$LeftDecision <- ifelse(Retention$LeftFit >
0.5,"Leave","Stay")
xtab <- table(Retention$Left,Retention$LeftDecision)
# Generating a balloon plot to show ratio of prediction and
decision
balloonplot(t(xtab), main ="Prediction Accuracy 85.2%", xlab
="Decision", ylab="Prediction", label=TRUE, show.margins=TRUE)
```

As before, the fit values (Retention$LeftFit) have been calculated using the final model6. They have been used to save the decision in Retention$LeftFit10. By comparing LeftNum with LeftFit10, the prediction accuracy has been calculated.

As a result of this, column LeftFit in Retention shows the modelled probability, the fit, for resigning, whereas LeftFit10 contains the decision Left (1) or Stayed (0) based on the threshold of 50%.

Figure 4.56 shows the confusion matrix that indicates the relationship of predictions to real decisions. Left is coded with 1, whereas Stayed is coded with 0.

Correct predictions are:

- 638 (46.0%) staff predicted to stay who stayed and
- 544 (39.2%) staff predicted to leave who left.

Wrong predictions are:

- 99 (7.1%) staff predicted to leave who stayed and
- 107 (7.7%) staff predicted to stay who left.

This means 638 + 544 out of 1,388 predictions are correct. Hence, the prediction accuracy of our model6 is about 85.16%.

This means as well, that the misclassification rate (error rate) is 99 + 107 out of 1388. Hence, the error rate is 14.84%.

There is one final question an analyst might have: which of the predictors are more important, which are less important?

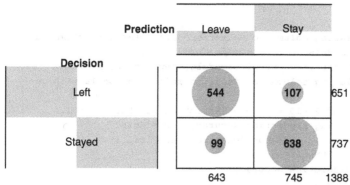

Figure 4.56 Confusion Matrix of Prediction Accuracy for the latest Model

Prioritising Predictors

Dominance analysis will help to prioritise predictors regarding their relative importance for the outcome of the prediction model (Azen, 2009). Dominance analysis determines the change of McFadden's R^2 when a certain factor is added to the model. With the following R functions, we check exactly this and show it graphically.

TASK 4.30   PERFORM DOMINANCE ANALYSIS:

```
# Loading necessary packages, if not done before
install.packages("dominanceanalysis")
library(dominanceanalysis)
library(ggplot2)
# Performing dominance analysis of logistic regression model5
domAn <-dominanceAnalysis(model6)
# Calculating average contribution using McFadden
averageContribution(domAn,fit.functions = "r2.m")
# Plotting General dominance plot
plot(domAn, fit.function = "r2.m") + theme(legend.position =
"none", plot.title = element_text(hjust = 0.5)) + labs(title =
"List of Contributors to Regression Result", y = "", x = "")
```

The output of this dominance analysis reads like this:

```
Average Contribution by predictor
          Department   Age   MaritalStatus   Super   TrainingHours
   r2.m     0.052     0.079      0.059        0.129      0.236
```

With Figure 4.57, there is a clear indication for priorities to focus on managing staff retention.

Most importantly, staff want to have the feeling that they are being appreciated, i.e., developed.

Secondly, they value a boss who knows what it takes to support and lead them.

Age makes an understandable difference. Younger staff are more eager to change and find a better spot if they are not treated well.

This is in line with marital status. Single people are mostly the younger people who are more flexible to change their jobs. The department itself does not make a difference but, so it seems, the working climate and the supervisory practice they find in the department. This is an analysis result, that we should be able to "sell" to the management.

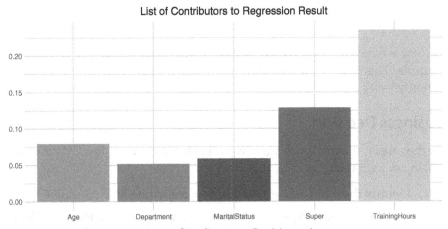

Figure 4.57 Relative Importance of Predictors on Decision to Leave

Calculate Risk for Staff to Leave			
Coefficient	Predictor	Enter Values:	Risk for Staff to Leave
- 0.10847	Age	35	5.05%
- 5.25370	Super	2.8	
- 0.21489	TrainingHours	28	
- 1.28232	MaritalStatus_2_married	1	
- 0.15737	MaritalStatus_3_divorced	0	
0.61624	Department_Air and Sea	0	
- 1.69826	Department_HR	1	
1.04631	Department_Land	0	
- 2.98778	Department_Projects	0	
2.09895	Department_Sales	0	
- 0.88775	Department_SCM	0	
24.57075	Intercept		

Figure 4.58 Excel template for calculating the probability for staff resignation

Source: Used with permission from Microsoft.

Out of the final coefficients, we can build a formula to calculate the probability for a staff member to leave similar to Equation 4.5. A sample calculation for a certain set of input variables is given in Figure 4.58.

A 35-year-old married employee working in HR who received four days of training during the last 12 months and who has an average supervisor, runs a risk for leaving of about 5%.

TASK 4.31   PERFORM A PREDICTION USING MODEL6:

```
# Loading input for prediction in data frame
toPredict <- data.frame(Age=35, Super=2.8, TrainingHours=28,
MaritalStatus="2_married", Department = "HR")
# Performing prediction using data frame
ProbabilityToLeave <- predict(model6, newdata = toPredict,
type="response")
# Printing output
ProbabilityToLeave
```

The output of this prediction using model6 is:

```
0.05052015
```

Now we have at least two very easy ways for applying the prediction formula. This helps us in calculating the risk for staff leaving before they actually leave.

Business Decision

At the outset, the analytics team was chartered to work towards the following deliverables:

1. Identify the main drivers for employee attrition at MySupplyChain.

2. Develop a model to predict attrition of employees at MySupplyChain and train HR in using this model.

3. Recommend actions to curb the attrition at MySupplyChain with the target of less than 15% by end of next year.

Here are the deliverables the management has asked for.

Main Drivers for Staff Leaving Our Organisation

The main drivers identified for staff leaving our organisation are

1. Lack of development options, especially training, provided to them. If we were able to provide a career plan and attractive development options to staff, we would have a very high chance to keeping them longer (Tan, 2014). There is a caveat. It could also be, that supervisors do not invest development options in staff who seems to be on the lookout for other jobs. Statistics will not be able to inform about the direction of the correlation between variables Training-Hours and Left.

2. Inadequate supervisory practices (Tan, 2020).

3. Younger staff are more likely to leave than older staff.

4. Singles are more likely to leave the organisation than married or divorced staff.

5. There is a difference in turnover from department to department. Drivers are probably to be found in employee engagement survey results.

Model for Predicting Staff Leaving the Organisation

An easy-to-use model has been developed by the analytics team. This model has been implemented in Excel and is available for use.

Recommend Actions to Curb Turnover

Once you have determined which general groups are expecting high rates of turnover, you need to ask: What is the population that has a high impact on business outcome and is at highest risk of leaving?

Now that you know what you need to focus your efforts, you can start crafting a programme based on an understanding of both what drives away and what retains key people at your organisation.

In MySupplyChain, HR recognised that a demanding workload may leave little room for an employee to spend time on learning, which may hold them back from advancing their careers. Instead of justifying a learning budget increase, HR recommended time to be allocated for learning. They started by creating fortnightly brownbag sessions to enable employees to learn during their lunch time. This way, they build up the habit for learning, and at the same time, protect time for employees to participate in training. Besides the brownbag sessions, they have also introduced an annual learning festival, which runs over a period of a month, with varieties of topics and learning options for employees to take part at their own convenience.

Summary

Collecting and analysing data beats anecdotes and rumours.

For example, based on the anecdotes collected by the supervisors, distance to home was said to affect employees' retention. Despite introducing transport allowance to retain the staff, it did not achieve much for some staff. By performing in-depth workforce data analytics, HR discovered that the issue lies with the recruitment process. Interviews were conducted at the headquarter, whereas the actual working place was at the other end of the island. So, when employees reported to work on their first day, they were often unpleasantly surprised.

With this insight, HR made adjustments to the recruitment process. They now indicate the location of work on the job post and conduct interviews at the worksite. What seemed to be a disadvantage turned into an advantage for some new hires.

Another anecdote was on convincing the staff to perform night shift. The supervisor thought it was going to be a difficult conversation to "sell night shift". It turned out that some employees even welcome permanent night shift arrangements. To our surprise, they had no issue finding persons for night shifts at all. So, they did not hide the fact that night shift was required but used it in their advertisement. Some people are in a stage in their life when night shift works perfectly for them.

Lastly, the myth about the company not paying enough to keep people has been busted with facts. Outstanding packages are always ways for enticing people. However, there are other, less expensive, ways of attracting and retaining staff. They must be explored before draining the budget.

Practice

- What data types in X and Y require logistic regression to be deployed?
- What is the Null-Hypothesis for logistic regression?
- What are assumptions for a logistic regression model to be valid?
- How do we evaluate logistic regression results?

- What is a confusion matrix when evaluating the prediction accuracy?
- What does dominance analysis of a logistic regression model study?
- How can the coefficients of the logistic regression model be used to calculate the probability of an output for certain settings of Xs?

Please, complete the following steps:

- Download the data for this case in Retention.xlsx from www.wiley.com.
- Build a model for only X_1: TrainingHours, X_2: Super and X_3: Age.
- Evaluate the model with all necessary indicators.
- Perform scatter matrix plot and prediction matrix (confusion matrix).
- Compare the model to model6 in the case.
- Predict the risk of a 42-year-old employee leaving after having only 10 training hours in a department that received a supervisory practice rating of 3.2.
- Prepare a short report about your findings.

Deploying Analytics Tools

In the previous case, a series of analytics tools have been put to work. This case's special feature is the discrete, binary Y Left that distinguishes stayers ("Stayed") from resignees ("Left"). This Y Left is categorical. In order to apply some of the tools, this Y Left has been transformed into a numerical binomial Y, LeftNum that shows 1 for "Left" and 0 for "Stayed". The information is the same, but it suits some tools that require numerical data and do not accept categorical data.

Many tasks have been performed using Microsoft Excel and its powerful Pivot Table. Microsoft Excel offers a wide range of plots that have been applied.

Data preparation such as checking for empty cells and filling them with the column average for numerical contents has been done in R.

Since this case features a discrete, binary Y, the resignation of staff in Left (Stayed/Left), the tools applied are two-proportion test, Chi^2 test, and logistic regression. The former tool has been explained earlier, logistic regression and the Chi^2 test are described in Table 4.5 and Table 4.6:

Additionally, we show the application of the Chi^2 test again since this one shows some additional features that could be useful for our readers.

Table 4.5 Logistic Regression

LOGISTIC REGRESSION	
Data in X:	Continuous, no normality required.
	Can be applied for discrete ordinal data.
	Discrete X (groups) can be used as factors.
Data in Y:	Discrete Y – Categories or Counts, binary or ordinal
Null Hypothesis H_0:	No significant relationship between any X and Y
Alternative Hypothesis H_A:	At least one X influences Y significantly
Decision:	1. If multiple X, all VIF must be < 5. Consider removing X with high VIF.
	2. X has significant influence if p-value of X < 0.05. Remove non-significant Xs and rerun model.
	3. Check out AIC (Akaike Information Criteria) that is similar to adjusted R^2 in multiple regression. AIC is to be minimised.
	4. Null and Residual Deviance are comparable to total sum of squares and residual sum of squares in multiple linear regression. Residual Deviance is to be minimised.
	5. McFadden's R^2 has a similar meaning as R^2 in multiple linear regression. The higher McFadden's R^2, the better the model is.
	6. Prediction Accuracy can be calculated by comparing the model output to the observed values.
Assumptions:	■ Dependent variable to be binary.
	■ For a binary regression, the factor level 1 of the dependent variable Y should stand for the desired outcome.
	■ Model should have little or no multi-collinearity (VIF < 5).

R code:
 	
(more code and explanation in the chapter)
	``
	# Loading necessary packages, if not done before
	library(graphics)
	
	# Plotting pairs of numeric columns in matrix
	without upper half
	pairs(~JobLevel+Age+Tenure+DistanceToHome+Educati
	on+JobMotiv+Super+Teamwork+Salary+TrainingHours+
	LeftNum, data = Retention, pch = 19, upper.panel
	= NULL)
	
	# Loading necessary packages, if not done before
	library(stats)
	# Building general linear model using logit
	function
	model <- glm(LeftNum ~ JobLevel +Age +Tenure
	+DistanceToHome +Education +JobMotiv +Super
	+Teamwork +Salary +TrainingHours,
	family=binomial(link='logit'), data=Retention)
	# Inspecting the general linear model
	summary(model)
	``

LOGISTIC REGRESSION

```r
# Loading necessary packages, if not done before
library(car)
# Calculating VIF (Objective: VIF < 5)
vif(model)


# Loading necessary packages, if not done before
library(pscl)
# Generating McFadden R² similar to linear
regression
pR2(model)


# Recalculating column to Retention data frame
for estimated Y following model
Retention$LeftFit <- predict(model, type=
'response')
# Recalculating column for decision following
model with cut-off 0.5
Retention$LeftFit10 <- ifelse(Retention$LeftFit >
0.5,1,0)

# Recalculating prediction accuracy for model
PredictAccuracy <- 1-mean(Retention$LeftFit10 !=
Retention$LeftNum)
# Prints prediction accuracy
PredictAccuracy


# Generating cross table of prediction versus
decision
Retention$LeftDecision <- ifelse(Retention
$LeftFit > 0.5,"Leave","Stay")
xtab <- table(Retention$Left,Retention$LeftDecision)
# Generating a balloon plot to show ratio of
prediction and decision
balloonplot(t(xtab), main = "Prediction Accuracy",
xlab = "Decision", ylab = "Prediction",
label = TRUE, show.margins=TRUE)


# Loading necessary packages, if not done before
install.packages("dominanceanalysis")
library(dominanceanalysis)
# Performing dominance analysis of logistic
regression model
domAn <-dominanceAnalysis(model)
# Calculating average contribution using McFadden
averageContribution(domAn,fit.functions = "r2.m")
# Plotting General dominance plot
plot(domAn, fit.function = "r2.m")


# Loading input for prediction in data frame
toPredict <- data.frame(Age=35, Super=2.8,
TrainingHours=28, MaritalStatus="2_married",
Department = "HR")
# Performing prediction using data frame
ProbabilityToLeave <- predict(model, newdata =
toPredict, type="response")
# Printing output
ProbabilityToLeave
```

Table 4.6 Chi² Test

CHI² TEST	
Data in X:	Discrete X – Groups (1, 2 ... n)
Data in Y:	Discrete Y – Counts
Null Hypothesis H_0:	Proportion$_1$ = Proportion$_2$ = ... = Proportion$_n$
Alternative Hypothesis H_A:	At least one proportion Proportion is different.
Decision:	If p-value is < 0.05, reject H_0 and accept H_A.
Assumptions:	Counts in all cells of the cross table must be at least 5.
R code:	(see code below)

```
# Loading necessary packages, if not done
before
install.packages("rstatix")
library(rstatix)

# Building cross table xtab using table
function
xtab <- xtab <- table(Retention$Left,
Retention$Department)

# Computing the Chi-square-test
Xsq <- chisq.test(xtab)
Xsq             # Print Chi-squared test
Xsq$observed  # Print observed values
Xsq$expected  # Print expected values
Xsq$stdres    # Print standardised
residuals

# Showing balloon plot of components
library("gplots")
balloonplot(t(xtab), main ="Departments
Turnover", xlab ="Departments",
ylab="Decision", label = FALSE, show.
margins = FALSE)

# Showing plot of standardised residuals
of stayed/left
library("corrplot")
corrplot(Xsq$stdres, is.cor = FALSE)

# Showing plot of contributions to
stayed/left
contribution <- 100*Xsq$residuals^2/
Xsq$statistic
corrplot(contribution, is.cor = FALSE)
```

References

Amy Tan Bee Choo, van Dun, D. H., & Wilderom, C.P. (2018). *Perceived support for innovation and individual innovation readiness as mediators between transformational leadership and innovative work behaviour. 19th International CINet Conference,* (p. 11). Dublin, Ireland.

Azen, R. T. (2009). Using Dominance Analysis to Determine Predictor Importance in Logistic Regression. *Journal of Educational and Behavioural Statistics,* 319–347.

Bass, B. M. (1997). *Full Range Leadership Development: Manual for the Multifactor Leadership Questionnaire. Palo Alto, CA; Mind Garden.*

Becker, B. E., Huselid, M. A., and Ulrich, D. (2001). *The HR Scorecard: Linking People, Strategy, and Performance.* Harvard Business Press.

Bonn, J. (1994). *Beschwerdemanagement in Kreditinstituten. In J. Süchting (ed.) Semesterbericht Nr. 40 des Vereins zur Förderung des Instituts für Kredit- und Finanzwirtschaft e.V. in der Gesellschaft der Freunde der Ruhruniversität Bochum e.V. (S. 26).* Bochum.

Chew, J. (2017, Dec. 2). Making Sense of Binary Logistic Regression. Retrieved from COE Partners: `https://coe-partners.com/making-sense-of-the-binary-logistic-regression-tool/`

Chew, J. C. (2018, Apr. 2). Making Sense of Test for Equal Variances. Retrieved from COE: `https://coe-partners.com/test-for-equal-variances/`

Date, S. (2019, Nov. 09). The Akaike Information Criterion. Retrieved from towards data science: `https://towardsdatascience.com/the-akaike-information-criterion-c20c8fd832f2`

Deloitte Touche Tohmatsu Limited. (2020). Global Business Driven HR Transformation The Journey Continues. Retrieved from Global Business Driven HR Transformation: `https://www2.deloitte.com/global/en/pages/human-capital/articles/global-business-driven-hr-transformation.html`

Drucker, P. F. (2015). *Innovation and entrepreneurship: Practice and Principles.* London: Routledge.

Farmer, T. a.-M. (2010). Creative Self-Efficacy Development and Creative Performance Over Time. *Journal of Applied Psychology,* 277–293.

Friedman, T.L. (2017, *Thank You For Being Late: An Optimist's Guide to Thriving in the Age of Accelerations.* London: Penguin Books.

Holt, D. T., Armenakis, A. A., Feild, H. S., et al. (2007). Readiness for Organizational Change: The Systematic Development of a Scale. *The Journal of Applied Behavioral Science,* 43(2): 232–255.

Janssen, O. (2000). Job demands, perceptions of effort: Reward fairness and innovative work behaviour. *Journal of Occupational and Organizational Psychology*, 73(3): 287–302.

Kaufmann, U. H. (2020, Jun. 13). *Making Sense of the Wilcoxon Test*. Retrieved from COE: https://coe-partners.com/making-sense-of-the-wilcoxon-test/

Luthans, F. Y., Youssef, C. M., and Avolio, B. J. (2007). *Psychological Capital: Developing the Human Competitive Edge*. Oxford: Oxford University Press.

Russom, P. (2011, Q4). Big Data Analytics. *TDWI* Best Practices Report, pp. 04-10.

Scott, S. G., & Bruce, R. A. (1994). Determinants of innovative behavior: A path model of individual innovation in the workplace. *Academy of Management Journal. 37(3)*, 580–607.

Tan, A. (2014, Aug. 15). Navigating Your Career Aspirations. Retrieved from: https://coe-partners.com/navigating-career-aspirations/

Tan, A. (2015, Aug. 18). Excuse Me, Why Should HR Know About Six Sigma? Retrieved from COE: https://coe-partners.com/hr-know-six-sigma/

Tan, A. (2016, Apr. 18). Strategic Workforce Planning. Retrieved from COE: https://coe-partners.com/services/strategic-workforce-planning/

Tan Bee Choo A., van Dun, D. H., & Wilderom, C.P. (2018). *Perceived support for innovation and individual innovation readiness as mediators between transformational leadership and innovative work behaviour*. 19th International CINet Conference, (p. 11). Dublin, Ireland.

Tan, A. (2020, Jan. 2). Do You Have Quality Conversations with Your Staff? Retrieved from: https://coe-partners.com/do-you-have-quality-conversations-with-your-staff/

Tan, E. (2017, Apr. 24). Gemba? I was there. Retrieved from COE Partners: https://coe-partners.com/gemba-i-was-there/

Tichy, N. M. and Charan, R. (1995. Mar.–Apr.). The CEO as Coach: An Interview with AlliedSignal's Lawrence A. Bossidy. *Harvard Business Review*. Retrieved from: https://hbr.org/1995/03/the-ceo-as-coach-an-interview-with-alliedsignals-lawrence-a-bossidy

Tukey, J. W. (1962). The Future of Data Analysis. *The Annals of Mathematical Statistics*, 1–67.

Ulrich, D. (2013, Mar. 13). *Dave Ulrich On The Outside In View Of HR*. Retrieved from Think:Act Magazine: https://www.roland-berger.com/en/Point-of-View/Dave-Ulrich-on-the-outside-in-view-of-HR.html

Table of Equations, Figures, Tables

Implementing Data Analytics for Organisational Development

"Every company has big data in its future, and every company will eventually be in the data business."

(Davenport, 2012)

Today, most organisations have realised that developing their analytical capabilities is essential for their future. And they know that the responsibility for data analytics cannot be delegated to IT and statisticians. Data analytics must be adopted by managers and staff so that it becomes part of normal business life.

This chapter sketches out a roadmap for building a successful data analytics environment.

CONTENTS

Highlights

After completing this chapter, you will be able to . . .

- Explain and calculate the risk of decision making.
- Appreciate the factors for a successful application of data analytics in an organisation.
- Understand the steps necessary for building a body of knowledge for data analytics deployment.
- Describe the necessary steps for building a data analytics environment.
- Establish a model for open and closed feedback loop for data analytics.
- Implement data analytics in your organisation.

Making Better Decisions – Knowing the Risk of Being Wrong

Data analytics supports better decisions (Gallo, 2018). In previous chapters, we have mentioned that many times. Yet, what does this actually mean? What kind of decision would have been worse without data analytics? After all, decisions have been made long before the focus was on data. And, who says those decisions were bad?

Let us have a look at one of these decisions we made in the case "Why are We Wasting Blood?". Working on this case, scientists mentioned that the type of blood bag material influenced the amount of platelet wastage. They hinted that blood bag type C4 delivered sub-par quality.

If we had followed their advice, we would have made the decision to invest a substantial amount of money in blood bags of type F6.

Often, we do not know the reality. This is the reason for collecting data and trying to conclude what our data suggests. All statistical tests as well as regression models work in a similar way. The unknown reality and our decision result in four different combinations, two of which lead to correct decisions and two to erroneous ones (Figure 5.1).

There is No Difference, and We Decide There Is None

This is a correct decision.

We suppose all blood bag types deliver a similar result in terms of wastage of platelets. In reality, there is no evidence for blood bag types making a difference in the amount of platelet wastage.

There is No Difference, and We Decide There Is One – Type I Error

This is a wrong decision.

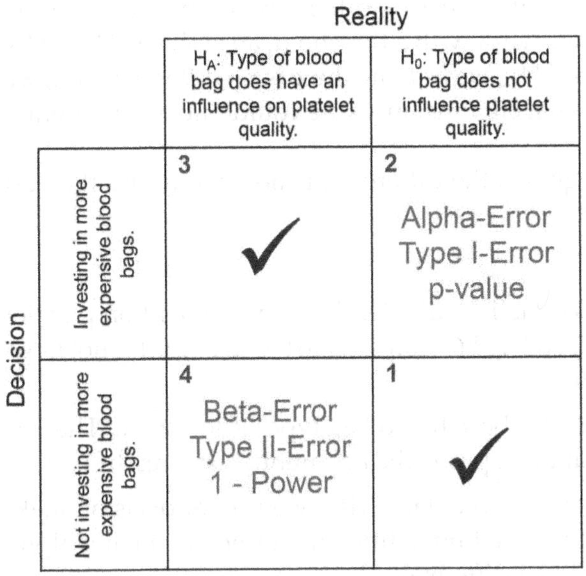

Reality

	H_A: Type of blood bag does have an influence on platelet quality.	H_0: Type of blood bag does not influence platelet quality.
Investing in more expensive blood bags.	3 ✓	2 Alpha-Error Type I-Error p-value
Not investing in more expensive blood bags.	4 Beta-Error Type II-Error 1 - Power	1 ✓

Decision

Figure 5.1 Potential Errors when Making Decisions

We suppose the use of blood bag type F6 would result in less wastage of platelets. But in reality, the type of blood bag makes no difference in the amount of wastage.

The risk for this situation is always given in the p-value. The p-value is the risk of being wrong when assuming a difference. In this case, a p-value of 0.2647 means that investing in the supposedly better blood bags and not getting a lower wastage has a likelihood of 26.47%. Who would make an investment if the risk of squandering it is 26.47%?

 The p-value is the risk of being wrong when assuming a difference.

There Is a Difference, and We Decide There Is One

This is a correct decision.

We suppose the use of blood bag type F6 would result in less wastage of platelets. And in reality, the type of blood bag makes a difference in the amount of wastage.

There Is a Difference, but We Decide There Is None – Type II Error

This would be a wrong decision.

We suppose all blood bag types deliver a similar result in terms of wastage of platelets. However, in reality blood bag types make a difference on the amount of wastage created.

If we make the decision that there is no difference, we decide based on the p-value. In this book we work with a threshold, an alpha of 0.05 = 5%. If the p-value is higher than 5%, we assume there is no difference. Yet, we can still calculate under what circumstances we could find an apparently existing difference.

If the p-value is too high, i.e. the difference is not significant, it could be due to various reasons:

1. There is no difference.

2. The difference is too small. The potential improvement on platelet wastage by using blood bag F6 compared to blood bag C4 is not large enough to be significant.

3. The sample size used for both blood bag types is too small. There is not enough information to prove the apparently existing difference.

4. Obviously, the alpha, the acceptable risk, we use for decision making, influences whether we find a difference or not. A smaller alpha makes it harder to find a difference.

Here is how to calculate the sample size needed to find a difference in this case, if it does exist. We use R for this task:

TASK 5.1   LOAD PACKAGE PWR AND CALCULATE SAMPLE SIZE NEEDED:

Open R Studio.

```
# Loading necessary package pwr for power analysis
install.packages("pwr")
library(pwr)
# Calculating sample size for p1 = 10% and p2 = 11.3%
pwr.2p.test(h = ES.h(p1 = 0.100, p2 = 0.113),
    power = 0.8,
    sig.level = 0.05,
    alternative = "two.sided")
```

The output of this Power Analysis:

```
Difference of proportion power calculation for binomial
distribution (arcsine transformation)
  h = 0.04216097     # Effect size: < 0.2 is considered small
  n = 8831.114       # Sample size needed
  sig.level = 0.05
  power = 0.8
  alternative = two.sided
NOTE: same sample sizes
```

We have used the conditions explained in our case: wastage proportion of C4 = 11.3% and F6 = 10.0%. We keep our alpha at 5% (sig.level) and set the power to 80%, a commonly used test power.

In order to have this difference showing up as significant, we need at least 8,831 tests with each blood bag.

Now the question is: Is this improvement by 1.3% less wastage good enough? If yes, it would probably pay off running more tests to justify the investment. However, it can well be that after collecting more than 8831 platelet units with each blood bag, the difference is still non-significant. This just means, there is no real, no significant difference.

Making Better Decisions – Do not Trust Statistics Blindly

When checking the influence of the centrifuge on the amount of wastage of platelet bags, we conducted a Chi^2 test and received a p-value of 2.56%. Since this is less than our acceptable alpha risk of 5%, we conclude that the centrifuge used for platelet extraction does have an influence on the amount of waste produced. Centrifuge C9 seems worse than the other ones.

This is correct, isn't it?

It always pays off to plot the data. When displaying the data in a time series plot, it became obvious that centrifuge C9 did not always produce higher waste. There was a clear pattern with "bad days" and "normal days" for the same device. When checking further, it was discovered that only certain operators, who preferred using C9, delivered increased wastage. These operators were on shift on those "bad days".

At the end, a considerable investment for a new centrifuge was avoided by getting the full picture and applying business sense.

 When employing statistics have your business knowledge and your common sense on high alert.

Significant Difference Does Not Mean Important Difference

After collecting data for the relationship between type of blood bag and amount of waste, the calculation delivered a difference of 1.3% wastage for two different types. The hypothesis test could not prove the difference to be significant. It might be that the difference could be found significant by increasing the sample size.

The real question is, does a significant difference of 1.3% make business sense? Is the amount of money invested in more expensive and supposedly better blood bags paid back by the additional blood bags that could be sold to the hospitals? This calculation is rather straight forward and should be done in this kind of situation, before making a decision based on data and following statistics.

A significant difference is not necessarily a business-relevant difference.

A Non-Significant Difference Could Be Important for The Organisation

When analysing the data for case "Do We Have Enough People to Run Our Organisation? – Workforce Planning for Transactional Processes", the patient numbers for General treatment were showing a small decline from January to December 2019. This decline was in no way significant with a p-value for the regression of 0.488 and a R^2 of only 4.92%.

This insignificant, that means not proven trend would mean a drop of patients of 388 in December compared to January 2019.

Now we could wait until this trend turns into a significant one. Or we could sensibly start thinking about root causes for the decline before it got worse, always having in mind that there might be nothing.

 A non-significant difference might be a weak signal for a significant and business-relevant signal to come. Consider getting prepared.

Data Analytics Does Not Take Over Decision Making

 "Analytics was never intended to replace intuition, but to supplement it instead."

(Farrand, 2014)

All cases in this book are intended to show how gathering, preparing, and analysing data in the right way may enable managers to make better decisions.

It is important to keep in mind that the decision is still the manager's responsibility. There is little sense in blaming software or machine for a wrong decision. Even if the data analytics has gone wrong resulting in a less favourable decision, the responsibility for that still stays with the manager – who has put too much trust in algorithms without understanding them first.

Ensuring the Success of Your Data Analytics Journey

Using data and analytics to improve decision-making, raise productivity, and gain a competitive advantage in the market is an opportunity for every organisation. When consulting various sources about how to implement data analytics into an organisation, the impression is created that data analytics is first and foremost about implementing a new IT environment and fancy analytics software.

We think, this impression is partially wrong.

Implementing data analytics needs to be highly customised. The degree of automation depends on factors like the nature of the business, volume of transactions, and size of the organisation.

There are certain organisations, that have implemented a **fully automated system** that collects data from internal and external sources, processes and analyses the data, and executes some actions in a very short time. The result of these systems land in our inboxes daily, some are helpful, some are not really.

Some systems are semi-automatic. They do part of the tasks automatically and then present the information to the decision maker. A search engine could be considered as such a system. We never worry about all the data sources a search engine taps on to get us the information after we asked a question. We just get the result. This result needs to be screened by ourselves before it is used for a purpose, i.e. sent as a link via a WhatsApp chat or made the decision to buy.

The process of buying a watch for a relative, our son in law, is still **semi-automatic or hybrid** because there is a lot of human intervention involved. Before we buy the watch, we probably consider different sources to get the best technical parameters that suit our son-in-law. We consult search engines to compare specifications and prices. Since cheapest is a lousy decision criterion in this case, we apply other criteria like country of origin and brand. And do not underestimate personal taste. If you are a watchmaker and you want to help us by automating this process – good luck.

If you are this watchmaker and you wish to automate your supply chain following the behaviour of online shoppers or online searchers, you can get much luckier.

As a result of someone's data analytics, we are quite sure to receive an advertisement for exactly the type of watch we have bought online. You can conclude that their data analytics is only half-done from the fact that this advertisement will go on for months without a chance for us to stop it – after we have purchased the watch long ago. We would call this, data analytics gone wrong.

The robots doing this job are developed by humans. These data analysts creating routines for this kind of robot follow a very similar data analytics cycle. However, the thresholds put into the program for starting or stopping sending out these ads seems to be not very thought through.

Other service providers do much smarter analytics and come up with helpful routines. For example, we have the habit to send flowers, surprises, or gifts to certain people. I am very thankful to selected service providers when they remind me that certain birthdays or anniversaries come up again. My wife values me not forgetting our wedding day. So, in turn I do value this kind of service. These are fully automated robots doing this job after some data analysts have come up with a quite straightforward routine for that. A simplified version of that would be a macro put into your own Outlook that sends an email – if a reminder does not do the job. This would be for the people who usually ignore the alarm clock.

SMART HOME IS A REALITY

We have been quite successful with implementing smart switches and cameras with timer and app control for nearly everything in the house. Theoretically, we could control our living room blind from a Cruise Liner in the South Pacific – if we had to. Most of these systems are hybrids, some are fully automated.

Now, we want to advance further. One of my dreams is to have a fridge that orders milk and beer whenever there is a minimum stock. This works for fridges with special switches to detect certain containers. However, these systems assume that the milk is always in the door on the right and the beer is on the left. They do not consider my wife's creativity. The system needs to be smarter than that.

Whenever all goods carry RFID code – as they usually do in the shop anyway – this automation is a breeze.

Even this system of the fridge follows our data analytics cycle:

- Data Acquisition: Every day, the system detects how many milk or beer bottles are in the fridge.

- Data Analysis: This information is analysed just by comparing it against a threshold.

- Decision and Action: Before an order goes out, the fridge checks whether we have vacation in the calendar or other order stops. If ok, order goes out.

All this is not complicated and will probably be reality very soon. It just needs a small RFID reader that connects to the smart home system. The rest is a child's play.

We acknowledge that there are business activities that are not so easy to automate. And, before automating anything, the business as well as its automation opportunities need to be completely understood. Otherwise, we will be more victims of automated analytics gone wrong.

So, what does it take to implement data analytics into an organisation that is not far away from the starting line?

Steps for Implementing Data Analytics

Data analytics does not start with buying software that enables the plot of wonderful new graphs. And it does not start with sending some people to some data analytics workshops hoping they change the organisation when they come back.

They won't.

It needs more than that to ensure data analytics becomes part of the culture – in any kind of organisation (Figure 5.2).

Here is a recommendation for potential steps to implement a data analytics culture:

- Ensure the management walks and talks analytics. Inform them in a **management workshop** what this is about and have them decide about organisational needs for analytics.

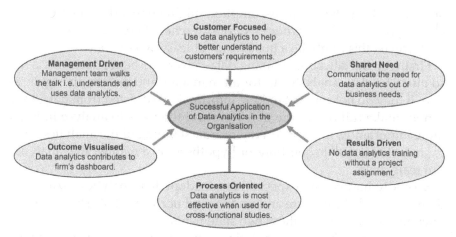

Figure 5.2 Success Factors for Data Analytics to Become Part of the Culture

- Offer **data analytics workshops** to the staff who are supposed to run projects. Themes for the projects stem from the management workshop.

- Make sure management keeps monitoring data analytics activities and makes use of newly built capabilities. Results of **data analytics projects** must be used and communicated.

- Avoid data analytics to be limited to certain departments. Build cross-functional teams to solve **cross-functional problems**.

- After enough knowledge and experience has been acquired, consider **extending hard- and software bases** to enhance the scope of data analytics.

- **Sustain the gains** by making data analytics an integral part of daily work, of planning, and reporting.

Ensuring the Management Walks and Talks Analytics

Whenever someone talks about the objectives of data analytics and data science, making data-based decisions is on top of the list. Who makes these decisions after data is collected, transformed and analysed? As Amy Gallo (*2018*) mentioned, **management needs to upgrade their skillset before asking others to do so.**

"The data-analytics revolution now under way has the potential to transform how companies organise, operate, manage talent, and create value. That's starting to happen in a few companies – typically ones that are reaping major rewards from their data – but it's far from the norm." (Mayhew et al., 2016)

This is because business leaders do not always see the benefits of deploying data science in their organisations. They deem data science as complex and challenging. Therefore, they leave it to the data analytics department or to the data analysts. The assumption might be that data analytics is a field of specialty like IT whom we consult when there is a need.

However, this might be a mistake for at least two reasons.

Firstly, all the talk about making data-driven, i.e. better decisions is not so much for data analysts but for all managers and staff in an organisation. If they do not understand the information extracted from data, they cannot make full use of the new data and the tools to analyse it. Even more importantly, it needs a certain understanding of the analytics environment to formulate questions or hypotheses in a manner that analytics can really help.

Secondly, how can we expect others to adopt data analytics if managers do not show that they care and understand nor want that. There is a distinct difference between these two statements:

"Go and learn about data analytics. You never know when we need it."

"We experience too much platelet loss in our donation process costing us x dollars per month. Go and learn about data analytics and use it to answer why we waste precious blood. I want our organisation to be able to analyse and solve this kind of problem internally. Suggest to me how I can learn about this."

If the second statement comes from a manager, it drives things in the right direction. It hints that managers have to learn, too. Data analytics is not something that can be delegated completely. Managers have to understand the key concepts in order to be able to make full use of them.

Start with a short introduction of data analytics for the management team. It would be best to have the presenter being prepared with data from the organisation and using that for some analytics together with the participants.

This knowledge enables the management team to decide about the next steps. In our experience, only a fraction of leaders and staff are familiar with the nuts and bolts of data analytics.

 "Understanding Variation is the Key to Success in Business."
                    W. Edwards Deming (Maleyeff, 2020)

The major reason why managers must know about data analytics is the need for them to be capable of generating the right questions for data analytics as well as the necessity to be able to understand the answers.

During their management workshop, they can practice the former capability to develop the business-relevant questions that their data analytics teams need to answer when they go through their own workshop.

One University in Singapore set up a Data Analytics Steering Committee, that comprises of Chief Human Resource Officer, Chief Finance Officer, and some other functional heads. Their job is to decide about steps on the implementation of data science, to select the staff who get training beyond the introduction to data science and to choose and monitor data science projects from business question to business decision or implementation.

Sitting in another presentation to our headquarter in Stamford/CT, Anne was well prepared with an impressive PowerPoint pitch to be delivered via video link. These quarterly project review presentations had just been implemented as part of our project work. At the start, after completing the analysis and near project closure, projects had to be presented to our SVP.

Anne was tasked to start a new project to investigate the efficiency of the call centre. After elaborating the project charter, our boss interrupted her.

"How did you derive this objective? Do you have data to show that your efficiency is below par? What does your project have to do with customer satisfaction?"

Anne could not show any data, nor could she link her task to customer satisfaction.

"Please, go back and examine the baseline for the call centre efficiency. I want to see that we work on something important. Alternatively, change your project objective."

After this incident, we were always prepared to support project selection, improvement proposals, and project closure with data.

When General Electric implemented their famous Six Sigma some twenty years ago, they made very sure that management walked the talk. And they did.

Creating Excitement for Data Analytics and its Benefits

Data analytics is not naturally the sexiest subject for an introduction workshop because it smells like data, statistics, and programming. Albeit this impression is not completely wrong, there are ways to make even this workshop fun.

First of all, it must be obvious that data analytics adds value to the participants. Knowing about Mr Gauss and his bell shape does not really strike anyone as key for the survival of the organisation. We must do better than that.

As mentioned earlier, any training about data analytics or data science should only start after analysing trainees needs. This requires looking into their daily work processes and determining situations where existing data could be analysed in a better way to generate value-added information. This could also result in the need for collecting additional data. All this should help the participants in their daily job.

For example, analysing the reason for wasting expensive bags with platelets instead of selling them to hospitals is a very practical application of data analytics. And it is in no way full of statistics, but rather a smart use of existing data put into MS Excel (Case: Why are We Wasting Blood?).

Or understanding the drivers for staff leaving the organisation helps busting many rumours and myth about that topic. And it gives a data-driven justification for some organisational development activities – such as introducing a mentoring programme or training of mangers in coaching skills – that are hard to "sell" otherwise (Case: What Drives Our Staff Out?).

It is important to shift the focus from learning data analytics tools to acquiring some methods that are fairly easy to use and certainly beneficial for staff and organisation. Don't forget: most employees want to do their best in their job, and they want to gain new competencies. Nowadays, data analytics is a valuable addition to anyone's CV. It should not be too hard to motivate staff to participate in this kind of development activities.

> "But I hate statistics", was John's statement when we met him the first time. He said this on the first day of his Lean Six Sigma training after being nominated by his boss to lead a project. Then he apologised and explained that his data skills were very limited, and he saw a real possibility that he would not be able to follow the program when this kind of topic came up.
>
> Fortunately, John was open-minded and smart. He "survived" the challenging workshops and was very diligent in applying the learnings to his project. Tools he was really appreciating and using were box plots and ANOVA. And this was not because these tools were very attractive or John suddenly developing a liking for the stats.
>
> The reason for John having some fun using especially these tools was the application. He recognised that the box plot was the best tool to tell his story. And the ANOVA was just a way of supporting the picture, the story, with some statistics.
>
> At the end, John proudly gave an outstanding project presentation showing off his newly acquired skills to the president of his university.
>
> This was not the end. He has been using such tools whenever needed. And, as Deputy Director, he makes sure that everyone in his reach gets equipped with basic data analytics skills.

Apart from the content, make your output appealing to the eyes of your audience. Even basic tools like MS Excel and especially MS Power BI offer ways to beautify the output.

Using a bar chart to show that the average delivery time of Company 2 is the lowest is not an option to choose (Figure 5.3). Your audience deserves to know more than that.

Box plots as part of MS Excel and MS Power BI offer much more information to the audience (Figure 5.3). Apart from the mean displayed in the bar chart, minimum, q1, median, q3 and maximum are shown, and potential outliers are highlighted.

A combination of box plot and violin plot has even more to offer (Figure 5.3). In addition to the rich information content of the box plot, the violin shapes illustrate the distribution of the data points between minimum and maximum (or outlier).

It would be surprising if the audience would not be interested in the meaning of this kind of plot. And there is a good chance that your colleagues want to learn how to do that.

Then, any of these plots can be customised to emphasise what is important. Even the simplest tools present many options to "let your plots talk" (Figure 5.3). Just make sure they talk what you intend to bring across.

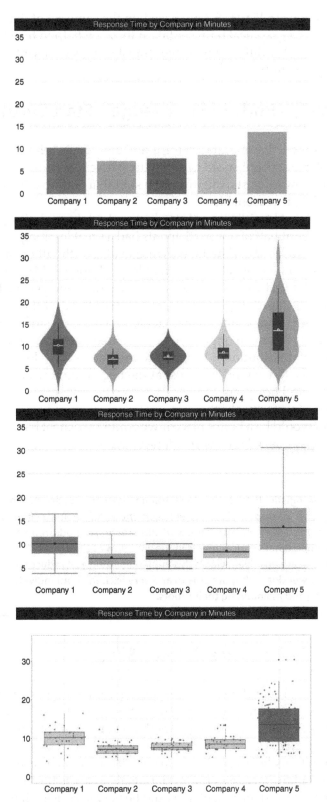

Figure 5.3 Four Ways to Plot the Same Dataset

All illustrations in Figure 5.3 are based on the same set of data. Due to the differences in graphical representation they can help to turn the same data into remarkably different messages transferring various intelligences. Use these opportunities.

Developing a Body of Knowledge – Start Small

The body of knowledge for data scientists and data analysts is very comprehensive. Not many people need to attain the whole spectrum. Developing the body of knowledge starting from the skill that is time-critical for the exact workplace is reasonable.

When we started training on "Introduction to data analytics", we recognised that about half of our participants had a great learning experience when they got exposed and had the chance to play with rather basic tools.

Two best-sellers: Pivot Table and Box Plots, all done in MS Excel!

On the one hand, I would not call someone a data analyst just because they can master these simple tools. On the other hand, if it is so easy to interest people in data analytics and create little success stories, then we should certainly seize the opportunity. Of course, they touched applications of normal distribution, t-test, and regression as well. But if I had to bet, which tools they would use most at the beginning, I would put a lot on pivot table and box plots.

And – this is perfectly alright.

The world would be a better place if we could turn most bar or column charts into box plots, whenever the dataset allows that.

A client in the logistics industry has been training staff and supervisors in basic RPA skills. This is in support of their new document workflow automation. The bots assist staff to carry out mundane work like creating periodic reports and checking completeness of documents in the workflow of the process.

Employees were positive towards this implementation as it reduces their manual entry workload. They are able to and very excited about individually programming and maintaining their robots.

Using Analytics to Breakdown Silos

It is quite normal that the start for building data analytics capabilities and with it working on projects begins within departments. It is a safer working environment for piloting something new and for failing and trying again if needed.

However, data analytics can rarely run the full cycle from business question via data acquisition, data preparation, data analysis, up to business decision within the silo of the department. It would be very surprising if not at least one of these steps, most likely data acquisition, requires bridging to another department to get additional data for completing the picture.

In our experience, this is a very good development for the organisation. Departments are just vehicles built to get organised. Departments usually do not reflect the flow of value creation, not for customer nor staff. Value creation usually needs cross-functional processes and so does data analytics – if it is supposed to add value.

Nearly all cases mentioned in this book require cross-functional perspectives in order to get the best out of data analytics. In the case "Why does Finance pay out vendors late?", Finance alone cannot answer and certainly not solve the problem about late payments to vendors without involving the business units who – as we know after some data collection and analysis – sit on their invoices for too long. In case "Why are We Wasting Blood?" it would even be of advantage to clarify the delicate requirements for platelet bags with the hospital in order to save precious blood products from being discarded.

And don't forget, building cross-functional teams for data analytics avoids finger-pointing, which could be the result of collecting data about processes that are run by people.

 Do not Allow the Use of Data for Blaming People. Blame the Process instead.

Closing the Analytics Loop – Sustaining the Gains

As we keep talking about data analytics projects, it suggests that we undergo the phases from business question to business decision only once. This would assume that there is no change in whatever we made the business decision for. It is quite obvious that this assumption does not hold. We live at a time of continuous change, some gradual some disruptive.

What does this mean for our data analytics environment? It needs to stay buoyant, i.e. there is a need to continuously monitor those critical indicators that led to the business question in the first place. The simplest way of monitoring, an **open feedback loop**, uses the means of a **dashboard** that is the result of a data analytics project. This dashboard is presented regularly to the management where new developments are discussed that may lead to a new business question and a new analytics cycle.

The more advanced version of monitoring is a **closed feedback loop**, an automatic adjustment in the process that is driven by automated data acquisition, cleaning, and analysis. These automated adjustments have been part of manufacturing processes for a long time. The advantage of these mechanisms is that human intervention is reduced to an absolute minimum. In service organisations, human interventions are necessary and cannot be reduced the way, manufacturing does this.

Let us take the example of the case "Why does Finance pay our vendors late?" We can all agree that paying vendors on time is important., since new

Figure 5.4 Running the Analytics Feedback Loop

projects with the respective vendor are delayed if we do not. The solutions for this case are most likely policy changes, changes policy, in the SOP, system reminders, etc. All these changes are not foolproof like a Poka Yoke would be. Business units and the Finance department can still unintentionally delay the process if settling the supplier invoice gets out of focus. Even a system - generated reminder is just an email amongst many other emails. Most of them are considered more important than a reminder to pay supplier.

Therefore, putting the data highlighting the payment discipline by business unit on the monthly dashboard for the management team will have the power to change behaviour. No owner of a business unit wants to be singled out for the wrong reason.

Dashboards have at least two functions. Firstly, they encourage the right behaviour. Secondly, they highlight when it is time to start the analytics cycle again.

 "We combine human expertise with accurate statistical models – delivering timely, dependable information to support our decision-making processes."
André Birrenbach, CIO, Rotkäppchen-Mumm Sektkellereien GmbH
(IBM, 2016)

Calibrating Your Data Analytics Implementation

How do you know that you have successfully established data analytics in your organisation? The following checklist can help to assess the status of your data analytics implementation (Table 5.1).

The table contains 18 statements in four categories:

- Get the basics right.
- Build advanced capabilities.
- Internalise capabilities.
- Develop Analysts.

Consider creating your data analytics culture by starting with the basics. After all items in category "Get the basics right" have received a "yes", it makes sense to build up and internalise capabilities.

Table 5.1 Scorecard for Status of Data Analytics Implementation

	NO	STATEMENT	YES/NO
Get the basics right	01	Management team has been trained in data analytics tools and methods.	
	02	Each organisational unit has basic to advanced data analytics capabilities.	
	03	Business-relevant indicators have been established in all business units and processes. Leading indicators have priority over lagging ones.	
	04	Data are acquired frequently from these indicators. Depending on the indicator, daily, weekly, or monthly.	
	05	Data are analysed after acquisition using proven graphical and statistical methods. Business-relevant information is extracted.	
	06	Business-relevant information is aggregated in multi-level dashboards and presented to the respective audience.	
	07	Business decisions are based on data analytics information.	
Build advanced capabilities	08	Data are used to build predictive models for customer lead scoring.	
	09	Data are used to build predictive models for operations performance modelling.	
	10	Data are used to build predictive models for staff behaviour and staff performance.	
	11	Predictive data analytics models are part of management dashboards.	
	12	Business decisions consider predictive model information.	
Internalise capabilities	13	Organisational units keep themselves informed about AI solutions for their processes.	
	14	Organisational units educate staff about AI solutions to support their processes (RPA, Expert Systems, etc.).	
	15	Organisational units develop and apply AI solutions to support their processes (RPA, Expert Systems, etc.).	
Develop Analysts	16	Organisation offers career tracks for data analyst/ scientist roles.	
	17	Organisation offers structured training (in-house or external) for data analyst/scientist roles.	
	18	Organisation uses "Contributions to adoption of data analytics" as part of performance management and recognition.	

You know that data analytics is part of the blood stream when your staff reports to you with some remarkable charts that they have successfully collected and analysed data for one of their key processes and therefore suggest a change that would result in reduced cycle time and increased customer satisfaction score.

 The best would be when they finish their explanation with the statement "I did this myself!"

Outlook

Throughout this book, we have stressed the importance of understanding the mechanisms of data analytics. Using analytics correctly is not as easy as it appears. Organisations must proceed carefully to reap the full benefits of data analytics. While some organisations may be more advanced than others, the trend is clear: data analytics is here to stay, and its growth is inevitable. And this is just the beginning of the data science journey.

Feeding this understanding into semi-automated or fully automated processes is one of the next steps. Machine Learning is another topic that should not be left to a few specialists. Machine Learning (ML), Robotic Process Automation (RPA) and other Artificial Intelligence (AI) solutions gain traction amazingly fast. Every interested staff member can learn the basics of RPA to help reinventing their own work processes in the same way many of us do this with Home Automation Systems such as Amazon's Alexa and Google Home. There are no limits for transferring these solutions into our professional life, too.

Practice Questions

- Under what circumstances do wrong decisions occur?
- Explain Type I (Alpha) error and Type II (Beta) error.
- Which risk in decision making is usually represented by the p-value?
- What could be reasons for an assumed difference between groups not to be found by the statistical test?
- What are differences between semi-automated and fully automated data analytics systems?
- What are steps for building a data analytics culture?
- What does the management need to be role model in use of data analytics?
- Why do all departments need to be involved for an effective data analytics culture?

- What is the difference between open and closed feedback loops for data analytics?
- What are success factors for a data analytics deployment?

References

Davenport, T. H. (2012, Jun. 12). What's So Big About Big Data? *Raconteur*, Retrieved from: `https://www.raconteur.net/whats-so-big-about-big-data/`

Farrand, S. (2014, Nov. 18). Organizational Development: Balancing Analytics and Intuition. *Gotham Culture*. Retrieved from: `https://gothamculture.com/2014/11/18/organizational-development-analytics-intuition/`

Gallo, A. (2018, Oct. 31). 4 Analytics Concepts Every Manager Should Understand. Retrieved from Harvard Business Review: `https://hbr.org/2018/10/4-analytics-concepts-every-manager-should-understand`

IBM (2016). Rotkäppchen-Mumm. IBM Case Studies. Retrieved from: `https://www.ibm.com/case-studies/rotkappchen-mumm`

Maleyeff, J. (2020). *Service Science: Analysis and Improvement of Business Processes*. New York: Routledge.

Mayhew, H., Saleh, T., and Williams, S. (2016, Oct. 7). Making Data Analytics Work for You – Instead of the Other Way Around. Retrieved from McKinsey Quarterly: `https://www.mckinsey.com/business-functions/mckinsey-digital/our-insights/making-data-analytics-work-for-you-instead-of-the-other-way-around`

List of Figures and Tables

Materials for Download

With this book you receive the data files used for all cases elaborated in this book. Additionally, MS Excel analyses, MS Power BI dashboards and R markdown notebooks are shared with you.

To download the files, please visit www.wiley.com and enter "9781119758334" in the search box at the top of the homepage to locate the webpage for this book. Click on "downloads" on the left side of the book's webpage or scroll all the way down to the bottom of the page to see the list of downloadable materials.

The following table shows an overview of files provided for download.

Chapter	Filename
Introduction	Norm.xlsx
	Norm.pbix
	DataAnalysis.xlsx
Chapter 1	PlateletDonation.xlsx
Phases of Data Analytics	ClinicSurveyStacked.xlsx
	DeliveryTime.xlsx
	Chapter01.zip

Chapter	Filename
Chapter 2	TwoProportionTest.xlsx
Case 1: Great, We Have Improved . . . or Not?	Great.xlsx
	Great.zip
Chapter 2	ClinicSurvey.xlsx
Case 2: What Drives Our Patient Satisfaction?	ClinicSurveyStacked.xlsx
	ClinicSurvey.zip
Chapter 2	ClinicSurvey.xlsx
Case 3: How to Create a Patient Satisfaction Dashboard?	ClinicSurvey.pbix
Chapter 3	FridgeMaker.xlsx
Case 4: Which Supplier has the Better Product Quality?	ProcessCapability.xlsx
Chapter 3	DaysToPay.xlsx
Case 5: Why Does Finance Pay Our Vendors Late?	DaysToPay.zip
Chapter 3	TwoProportionTest.xlsx
Case 6: Why are we Wasting Blood?	PlateletWaste.xlsx
	PlateletWaste.zip
Chapter 4	ClinicVisit.xlsx
Case 7: Do We Have Enough People to Run Our Organisation?	
Chapter 4	InnoReady.xlsx
Case 8: What Makes our Staff Innovate?	InnoReady.pbix
Chapter 4	TwoProportionTest.xlsx
Case 9: What Does Our Engagement Survey Result Mean?	EES.xlsx
	EES.zip
Chapter 4	Retention.xlsx
Case 10: What Drives our Staff Out?	Retention.zip
Chapter 5	Power.zip
Making Better Decisions - Knowing the Risk of Being Wrong	

Note: All R files are packed in respective zip archives.

Index